FREE MONEY®

FOR GRADUATE SCHOOL

Third Edition

by Laurie Blum

Facts On File, Inc.

Free Money® for Graduate School: Third Edition

Copyright © 1990, 1993, 1996 by Laurie Blum

Facts On File, Inc.
11 Penn Plaza
New York NY 10001

Library of Congress Cataloging-in-Publication Data
Blum, Laurie.
    Free money for graduate school / Laurie Blum. — 2nd rev. ed.
      p. cm.
    Includes bibliographical references (p.   ) and index.
    ISBN 0-8160-3562-8 (hc : alk. paper). —ISBN 0-8160-3563-6 (pb :
alk. paper)
     1. Scholarships—United States—Directories. 2. Graduate
students—Scholarships, fellowships, etc.—United States—
Directories. I. Title.
LB2337.2.B58   1996
378.3′025′73—dc20   96-35426

Facts On File books are available at special discounts when purchased in bulk quantities for businesses, associations, institutions, or sales promotions. Please call our Special Sales Department in New York at 212/967-8800 or 800/322-8755.

You can find Facts On File on the World Wide Web at http://www.factsonfile.com

Cover design by Ellie Nigretto

Printed in the United States of America

MP FOF 10 9 8 7 6 5 4 3 2 1
    (pbk) 10 9 8 7 6 5 4 3 2

This book is printed on acid-free paper.

Contents

Introduction

Graduate education is a long, rigorous, expensive undertaking. The academic demands are enough of a challenge without having to worry about how to pay for it.

Fortunately, there is an enormous amount of money available in both low-cost loans and direct grants to fund advanced degrees. In many fields, graduate funding is more plentiful and accessible than undergraduate funding.

The hardest part has always been finding the sources of money, which is why I wrote this book. Sure there are many books that explain *how* students can attempt to locate sources to fund their education. There are a few extremely expensive and largely unavailable reference books one can try to find in the public library. And there are other books that have some student scholarship information, but they're combined with things like contests, awards, and prizes. This book provides you, the reader, with the actual sources of monies available.

Wherever possible, I have included the total amount of money awarded to students, the number of grants given, the average size of an award, and the range of monies given.

HOW TO APPLY

Applying for grants and scholarships is similar to applying for graduate school: it takes work, some thought, and organization—but at this stage in your life, you know what you have to do.

First comes the sorting-out process. Go through this book and mark off all of the listings that could give you money. Pay close attention to the restrictions, and eliminate the least likely foundations. Although very few of the foundations in this book require an application fee, the effort you will have to put in will probably limit you to no more than eight applications (if you are ambitious and want to apply to more than eight foundations, bravo, go right ahead.) Write or call the most likely foundations for a copy of their guidelines. (In cases where the contact's name is not listed, begin your letter: "To Whom It May Concern.") If you call, simply request the guidelines; do not interrogate the person who answers the phone.

Grant applications take time to fill out. Often you will be required to write one or more essays. Proposals should be neatly typed and double-spaced. Be *sure* to make a copy for your records. Many applications require undergraduate transcripts. Often the tax returns of both the applicant (if you filed a return the previous year) and the applicant's parents are needed. You may be asked to include personal references (to avoid embarrassment, be sure to get permission from the people you are planning to use). Sometimes an interview is required. Remember, you have to sell yourself and persuade the grantors to give the money to you and not to someone else.

FEDERAL MONEY

Federal aid has long been a funding mainstay for the graduate student. It remains one of the first sources of money to pursue. The process is not complicated, but you must fill out the applications to be considered. It is well worth your time and effort. In 1994-1995, approximately $4.4 billion was available in this type of student aid. The U.S. Department of Education offers four graduate student aid programs; some are grants that do not have to be paid back, others are loans that must be paid back with interest. These programs include College Work Study (CWS), Perkins Loans (GSL) and Plus Loans/Supplemental Loans for

Students (SLS). Check with your financial aid office for further information about these programs or call the Federal Student Aid Information Center at 1-800-433-3243.

OTHER SOURCES OF MONEY

Although you have probably been told this many times, you ought to check with the various organizations you have belonged to (professional organizations, fraternities, etc.), places of worship you attend, and employers you or your parents have worked for. Thousands of corporations have programs that will pay for all or part of their employees' or employees' children's university expenses. There is an enormous amount of unused employee tuition benefits. Your hobbies or talents may qualify you for prizes or awards. If you are a veteran or the child of a veteran, you probably qualify for another source of grant money.

As a graduate student, you will have opportunities to work within your department. Possibilities include reading assistantships, in which you grade examinations and papers for professors; teaching assistantships, in which you actually teach students on a limited basis; and research assistantships. Almost every department has a number of the latter available. Check with your department and with individual professors in your department.

Finally, be sure to request information on scholarships and other forms of aid from the financial aid office at each school to which you have applied.

Paying for graduate school isn't a one-year, one-shot deal. You must plan ahead to consider the costs of the entire program.

I divided this book into broad areas of study. The index lists more specific subject categories or academic disciplines (e.g., architecture, women's studies). Check all listings that pertain to your subject. Regardless of your field of study, you should qualify for at least some of the grants covered in this book.

ONE FINAL NOTE

No reference book can be as up-to-date as the reader (or the author) would like. By the time this book is published, some of the information will have changed. Names, addresses, dollar amounts, telephone numbers, and other data are always in flux. Most of the information, however, will still be accurate.

Good Luck!

Humanities and Social Sciences

Alpha Delta Kappa Foundation
Alpha Delta Kappa Fine Arts Grants
1615 West 92nd Street
Kansas City, MO 64114
(816) 363-5525

Description: Grants for the fine and performing arts; available at any academic level; recipients chosen on the basis of artistic skills and professional or advanced study plans.
Restrictions: Applicants may not have received grants from ADK within the past five years.
$ Given: Two grants per category; $5,000 for first place, $3,000 for second place.
Application Information: Grants available every two years; categories change each two-year period.
Deadline: June 1 of even-numbered years.
Contact: Scholarship and Grants Secretary.

American Academy in Rome
Samuel H. Kress Foundation
Predoctoral Fellowships
7 East 60th Street
New York, NY 10022-1001
(212) 751-7200

Description: Two two-year fellowships for independent study and research; one fellowship in classical art history, one fellowship in Italian art history; tenable at the American Academy in Rome; awarded to doctoral candidates who have completed coursework and are beginning the second year of dissertation work; recipients chosen on the basis of proposed research.
Restrictions: United States citizenship required.
$ Given: Two fellowships awarded annually; amount varies; travel allowance included.
Application Information: Write for details.
Deadline: November 15.
Contact: Fellowship Coordinator.

American Academy in Rome
National Endowment for the Arts/AAR Advanced Fellowships in Design Arts
7 East 60th Street
New York, NY 10022-1001
(212) 751-7200

Description: Three six-month fellowships in architecture, design arts and landscape architecture; tenable at the American Academy in Rome.
Restrictions: Applicants must be B.A./B.S. holders with at least seven years professional experience in the relevant fields; United States citizenship required.
$ Given: Three fellowships awarded annually; $5,000 stipend plus $800 travel allowance each.
Application Information: Write for details.
Deadline: November 15.
Contact: Fellowship Coordinator.

American Academy in Rome
National Gallery of Art
Predoctoral Fellowship in Art
History
7 East 60th Street
New York, NY 10022-1001
(212) 751-7200

Description: One-year fellowship for doctoral candidates in art history to conduct independent study/research at the American Academy in Rome; award made by National Gallery of Art jury with Academy representation.
Restrictions: Applicants must be sponsored by their schools; United States citizenship required.
$ Given: One fellowship awarded annually, cash award for travel, expenses, study, room & board.
Application Information: Application must be submitted by chairperson of graduate art history department at United States university; for details, contact Professor Henry Millon, National Gallery of Art, 6th and Constitution Avenues, N.W., Washington, DC 20565.
Deadline: November 15.
Contact: Fellowship Coordinator.

American Academy in Rome
Rome Prize Creative
Disciplines Fellowships
7 East 60th Street
New York, NY 10022-1001
(212) 751-7200

Description: Six- to twelve-month fellowships for independent creative work or researching architecture, landscape design, musical composition, fine arts, classical studies, archaeology, and art history; tenable at the American Academy in Rome.
Restrictions: Applicants must hold bachelor's or master's degree; United States citizenship required.
$ Given: Thirty fellowships awarded annually; each with stipend of $7,500–$17,000 plus housing and studio.
Application Information: Write for details.
Deadline: November 15.
Contact: Fellowship Coordinator.

American Academy in Rome
Rome Prize Fellowships
School of Classical Studies
7 East 60th Street
New York, NY 10022-1001
(212) 751-7200

Description: One-year residential fellowships for doctoral candidates in classical studies, archaeology, classical art, history of art, postclassical humanistic studies, and Medieval and Renaissance studies; tenable at the American Academy in Rome.
Restrictions: Applicants must have completed all doctoral coursework and one year of dissertation work; recipients may not hold job or travel extensively during fellowship year.
$ Given: An unspecified number of fellowships awarded annually; each with $7,500 stipend plus $800 travel allowance.
Application Information: Write for details.
Deadline: November 15.
Contact: Fellowships Coordinator.

American Academy in Rome
Rome Prize Fellowships
School of Fine Arts
7 East 60th Street
New York, NY 10022-1001
(212) 751-7200

Description: Several one-year fellowships in architecture, landscape architecture, design art, painting, sculpture, visual arts, and musical compositions; tenable at the American Academy in Rome.
Restrictions: Painting, sculpture, and visual arts candidates need not hold a degree but must have three years professional commitment, clear ability, and current studio work; architecture and landscape architecture candidates need appropriate degree; other applicants need B.A. degree; recipients may not hold job or travel extensively during fellowship year.
$ Given: Ten fellowships awarded annually; each with $7,500 stipend plus $800 travel allowance and $600 allowance for supplies for painters, sculptors, and visual artists.
Application Information: Write for details.
Deadline: November 15.
Contact: Fellowships Coordinator.

American Antiquarian Society
Stephen Botein
Short-Term Visiting Research
Fellowships
185 Salisbury Street
Worcester, MA 01609-1634
(508) 752-5813

Description: One- to two-month fellowships for scholars engaged in research into the history of the book in American culture; tenable at the American Antiquarian Society library.
Restrictions: N/A.
$ Given: An unspecified number of fellowships awarded annually; maximum $1,700 stipend each.
Application Information: Write for details.
Deadline: January 15.
Contact: Mr. John B. Hench, Director of Research and Publication.

American Antiquarian Society
Kate B. and Hall J. Peterson
Short-Term Visiting Research
Fellowships
185 Salisbury Street
Worcester, MA 01609-1634
(508) 752-5813

Description: Fellowships for doctoral candidates in American history (through 1876); for research at the American Antiquarian Society library.
Restrictions: One- to three-month period of study at the AAS library required.
$ Given: An unspecified number of fellowships awarded annually; $850/month stipend each.
Application Information: Write for details.
Deadline: January 15.
Contact: Mr. John B. Hench, Director of Research and Publication.

American Association for the Advancement of Science Mass Media Science and Engineering Fellows Program
1333 H Street, N.W.
Washington, DC 20005
(202) 326-6760

Description: Ten-week summer fellowships for science graduate students to work as journalists (print, radio, or television) to increase their understanding of the news media; available to students at any graduate level of study in the natural and social sciences, as well as engineering; recipients chosen on the basis of academic achievement and demonstrated commitment of conveying to the public a better understanding and appreciation of science and technology.
Restrictions: No funding to non-technical applicants; United States citizenship required; no concurrent funding allowed.
$ Given: Twenty fellowships awarded annually; weekly living stipend for 10 weeks plus travel costs.
Application Information: Write for details and application form; minorities and individuals with disabilities encouraged to apply.
Deadline: January 15.
Contact: Amie Hubbard, Program Manager.

American Association of University Women Educational Foundation AAUW Selected Professions Fellowships
P.O. Box 4030
Iowa City, IA 52243-4030
(319) 337-1716

Description: Fellowships for graduate students entering their final year of study in fields with traditionally low female representation, including architecture, business administration, computer science, dentistry, engineering, law, mathematics/statistics, medicine, and veterinary medicine; recipients chosen on the basis of academic achievement; tenable for full-time study at accredited United States institutions.
Restrictions: Limited to women who are members of minority groups; United States citizenship or permanent resident status required.
$ Given: An unspecified number of fellowships of $5,000–$9,500 each are awarded annually.
Application Information: Application forms available August 1 through November 1.
Deadline: December 15, February 1 for M.B.A.

American Catholic Historical Association The Peter Guilday Prize
Catholic University of America
Washington, DC 20064
(202) 653-5079

Description: Prize for article on the history of the Catholic Church.
Restrictions: Must be written by previously unpublished author; sections or doctoral dissertation accepted; United States or Canadian citizenship or permanent resident status required.
$ Given: One annual prize of $100.
Application Information: Write for details.
Deadline: October 1.
Contact: The Rev. Robert Trisco, Secretary-Treasurer.

American Council of Learned Societies
Eastern European Advanced Graduate Training Fellowships
Office of Fellowships and Grants
228 East 45th Street
New York, NY 10017-3398
(212) 697-1505

Description: Fellowships for graduate students to study the humanities and social sciences as related to Eastern Europe (Albania, Bulgaria, Czech Republic, Germany, Hungary, Poland, Romania, Slovakia, and (former) Yugoslavia); recipients chosen on the basis of academic achievement, financial need, and quality of proposed research.
Restrictions: United States citizenship or legal residency required; must have completed two years of graduate study by June 30 following deadline.
$ Given: An unspecified number of fellowships awarded annually; the predoctoral fellowship has a maximum of $12,000.
Application Information: Write for details.
Deadline: December 1.

American Council of Learned Societies
Eastern European Dissertation Fellowships
Office of Fellowships and Grants
228 East 45th Street
New York, NY 10017-3398
(212) 697-1505

Description: Fellowships for doctoral dissertation research related to Eastern Europe (Albania, Bulgaria, Czech Republic, Germany, Hungary, Poland, Romania, Slovakia, and (former) Yugoslavia); for research-related study at a university abroad, but not within Eastern Europe; for doctoral candidates in the humanities and social sciences; recipients chosen on the basis of academic achievement, financial need, and quality of proposed research.
Restrictions: United States citizenship or legal residency required.
$ Given: An unspecified number of fellowships awarded annually; each carries an annual stipend of up to $15,000; renewable for second year.
Application Information: Write for details.
Deadline: December 1.

American Council of Learned Societies
Fellowships for Dissertation Research Abroad Related to China
Office of Fellowships and Grants
228 East 45th Street
New York, NY 10017-3398
(212) 697-1505

Description: Fellowships for doctoral dissertation research related to China; for research-related travel abroad, but not within the People's Republic of China or within the United States; for doctoral candidates in the humanities and social sciences; recipients chosen on the basis of academic achievement, financial need, and quality of proposed research.
Restrictions: Foreign national applicants must be enrolled as full-time Ph.D. candidates at United States universities.
$ Given: An unspecified number of fellowships awarded annually; each carries an annual stipend of up to $15,000.
Application Information: Write for details.
Deadline: December 1.

**American Defense Institute
Fellowship in National
Security Studies**
1055 N. Fairfax Street, 2nd
Floor
Alexandria, VA 22314
(202) 519-7000

Description: One-year fellowships funding work in security policy, public policy, political science,
international relations, history, international law, or economics; for master's and doctoral candidates in national
security studies.
Restrictions: United States citizenship required;
applicants must be near degree completion.
$ Given: An unspecified number of fellowships are
offered for $18,000 to $20,000.
Application Information: Write for details.
Deadline: January 15.

**American Foundation for the
Blind
Karen D. Carsel Memorial
Scholarship**
15 West 16th Street
New York, NY 10011
(212) 620-2064

Description: Funding to support full-time graduate
studies; recipients chosen on the basis of financial need.
Restrictions: Limited to legally blind applicants only;
United States citizenship required.
$ Given: One grant for $500 is awarded annually.
Application Information: Applications must include
proof of legal blindness, proof of graduate school accep-
tance, evidence of financial need, personal statement,
and letters of recommendation.
Deadline: April 1.
Contact: Leslye S. Piqueras, National Consultant in
Low Vision.

**American Geophysical Union
Horton Research
Grant in Hydrology and
Water Resources**
2000 Florida Avenue, N.W.
Washington, DC 20009
(202) 462-6900

Description: Grants for doctoral candidates, to support
research projects in hydrology and water resources; relevant disciplines include physical/chemical/biological
aspects of hydrology, as well as water resources policy
sciences (economy, sociology, and law).
Restrictions: Membership in American Geophysical
Union required.
$ Given: One or more grants awarded annually;
approximately $9,000 plus travel allowance to ensure at-
tendance at awards luncheon.
Application Information: Proposal must be signed by
faculty advisor; application forms required.
Deadline: March 1.

**American Home Economics
Association Foundation
Carley-Canoyer-Cutler
Fellowships**
1555 King Street
Alexandria, VA 22314
(703) 704-4600

Description: Fellowships for graduate students in con-
sumer studies.
Restrictions: Minority group members or non-United
States citizens only.
$ Given: One $3,000 fellowship awarded annually.
Application Information: $15 application fee for
AHEA members; $30 for non-members.
Deadline: January 15.
Contact: Fellowships and Awards Committee.

American Home Economics Association Foundation Frieda A. DeKnight Memorial Fellowship
1555 King Street
Alexandria, VA 22314
(703) 704-4600

Description: Fellowship for master's and doctoral candidates in home economics, communication, and cooperative extension; recipients chosen on the basis of academic achievement.
Restrictions: African-American applicants only; United States citizenship or legal residency required.
$ Given: One fellowship of $3,000 awarded annually.
Application Information: $15 application fee for AHEA members, $30 for non-members.
Deadline: January 15.
Contact: Fellowships and Awards Committee.

American Home Economics Association Foundation Marie Dye Memorial Fellowship
1555 King Street
Alexandria, VA 22314
(703) 704-4600

Description: One-year fellowship for graduate studies in home economics; tenable at United States institutions.
Restrictions: Membership in AHEA required; one year of professional home economics experience required; United States citizenship required.
$ Given: One fellowship of $3,000 awarded annually.
Application Information: $15 application fee for AHEA members, $30 for non-members.
Deadline: January 15.
Contact: Fellowships and Awards Committee.

American Home Economics Association Foundation Fellowships in Home Economics
1555 King Street
Alexandria, VA 22314
(703) 704-4600

Description: Fellowship for graduate students in home economics and related fields.
Restrictions: United States citizenship or legal residency required.
$ Given: Seven to ten fellowships of $3,000 awarded annually.
Application Information: $15 application fee for AHEA members, $30 for non-members.
Deadline: January 15.
Contact: Fellowships and Awards Committee.

American Home Economics Association Foundation Marion K. Piper International Fellowship
1555 King Street
Alexandria, VA 22314
(703) 704-4600

Description: Fellowship for foreign graduate students to study home economics in the United States; recipients chosen on the basis of academic achievements, quality of proposed research/study.
Restrictions: Limited to non-United States citizens/legal residents.
$ Given: One fellowship of $3,000 awarded annually
Application Information: $15 application fee for AHEA members, $30 for non-members.
Deadline: January 15.
Contact: Fellowships and Awards Committee.

American Home Economics Association Foundation Flemmie P. Kittrell Minorities Fellowship in Home Economics
1555 King Street
Alexandria, VA 22314
(703) 704-4600

Description: Fellowship for graduate students in home economics; recipients chosen on the basis of academic achievement and quality of proposed research/study; tenable at United States institutions.
Restrictions: Limited to members of United States minority groups and citizens of developing countries.
$ Given: One fellowship of $3,000 awarded annually.
Application Information: $15 application fee for AHEA members, $30 for non-members.
Deadline: January 15.
Contact: Fellowships and Awards Committee.

American Home Economics Association Foundation National Fellowships
1555 King Street
Alexandria, VA 22314
(703) 704-4600

Description: Fellowship for graduate students in home economics; priority topics include nutrition, aging, administration, and communications; recipients chosen on the basis of academic achievement, quality of proposed research/study, and personal/professional/educational characteristics.
Restrictions: Minimum of one year professional home economics experience required; United States citizenship or legal residency required.
$ Given: Several fellowships of $1,000–$3,000 each awarded annually.
Application Information: $15 application fee for AHEA members, $30 for non-members.
Deadline: January 15.
Contact: Fellowships and Awards Committee.

American Home Economics Association Foundation Ethel L. Parker Fellowship
1555 King Street
Alexandria, VA 22314
(703) 704-4600

Description: Fellowship for foreign graduate students in home economics; recipients chosen on the basis of academic achievement, quality of proposed research/study, and home countries' needs.
Restrictions: Eligibility limited to non-United States citizens/legal residents.
$ Given: One fellowship of $3,000 awarded annually.
Application Information: Write for details.
Deadline: January 15.
Contact: Fellowships and Awards Committee.

American Home Economics Association Foundation Ellen H. Richards Fellowship
1555 King Street
Alexandria, VA 22314
(703) 704-4600

Description: Fellowship for advanced graduate students in home economics with an emphasis on administration; recipients chosen on the basis of academic achievement and quality of proposed research/study; tenable at United States institutions.
Restrictions: Minimum of one year professional experience in home economics administration required; AHEA membership required; United States citizenship or legal residency required.

$ Given: One fellowship of $3,000 is awarded as available.
Application Information: $15 application fee.
Deadline: January 15.
Contact: Fellowships and Awards Committee.

American Home Economics Association Foundation D. Elizabeth Williams Fellowship
1555 King Street
Alexandria, VA 22314
(703) 704-4600

Description: Fellowship for graduate students in home economics; recipients chosen on the basis of academic achievement and quality of proposed research/study; tenable at United States institutions.
Restrictions: Open to non-United States citizens only.
$ Given: One fellowship of $3,000 awarded annually.
Application Information: Write for details.
Deadline: January 15.
Contact: Fellowships and Awards Committee.

American Institute for Economic Research Summer Fellowship Program; In-Absentia Awards
P. O. Box 1000
Great Barrington, MA 01230
(413) 528-1217

Description: Two-month summer fellowships for college seniors, graduate students, and professionals in economics; successful summer fellows eligible for In-Absentia Awards of partial to total tuition for the following academic year; recipients chosen on the basis of academic achievement.
Restrictions: United States citizens preferred.
$ Given: Ten to twelve two-month summer fellowships are awarded annually with a $500/month stipend plus room and board.
Application Information: Write for details.
Deadline: March 31.
Contact: Pamela P. Allard, Assistant to the Director.

American Institute of Architects AIA/AIAF Scholarships for First Professional Degree Candidates
1735 New York Avenue, N.W.
Washington, DC 20006
(202) 626-7511

Description: Scholarships for master's candidates and undergraduates in the final two years of degree programs in architecture; recipients chosen on the basis of academic achievement and financial need; tenable at accredited United States and Canadian institutions.
Restrictions: For full-year study only.
$ Given: An unspecified number of grants of $500–$2,500 are awarded annually.
Application Information: Applications must be made through students' schools.
Deadline: February 1.
Contact: Mary Felber, Director, Scholarship Programs.

**American Institute of
Architects AIA/AIAF
Scholarships for Advanced
Degree/Research Candidates**
735 New York Avenue, N.W.
Washington, DC 20006
(202) 626-7511

Description: Scholarships for bachelor's and master's
candidates in the final year of degree programs in architecture and related fields; recipients chosen on the
basis of merits of proposed research/study; tenable for
full academic year.
Restrictions: Limited to students enrolled in United
States or Canadian universities.
$ Given: An unspecified number of grants of
$500–$2,500 are awarded annually.
Application Information: Write for details.
Deadline: February 15.
Contact: Mary Felber, Director, Scholarship Programs.

**American Institute of
Certified Public Accountants
John L. Carey Scholarships in
Accounting**
1211 Avenue of the Americas
New York, NY 10036-8775
(212) 575-5504

Description: Scholarships for college liberal arts majors
to study accounting on the graduate level; tenable at
United States graduate schools.
Restrictions: Applicants must be college seniors who are
liberal arts majors at Yale, University of Georgia, or University of Illinois; recipients must plan careers in
accounting.
$ Given: An unspecified number of scholarships
awarded annually; each for $4,000/year; renewable for
second year.
Application Information: Write for details.
Deadline: April 1.

**American Institute of
Pakistan Studies
American Institute of
Pakistan Studies Fellowships**
P.O. Box 7568
Wake Forest University
Winston-Salem, NC 27109
(919) 759-5453

Description: Fellowships for doctoral candidates,
postdoctoral scholars, and professional researchers to
undertake study/research in Pakistan; for students of
humanities and social sciences, especially rural development, agriculture, local government, economics,
demography, history, and culture; recipients chosen
on the basis of proposed research.
Restrictions: Doctoral candidates must have completed
all preliminary Ph.D. requirements; United States citizenship required.
$ Given: An unspecified number of fellowships
awarded annually; each to cover air travel, maintenance,
rental allowance, research allowance, internal travel, and
excess baggage allowance.
Application Information: Write for details.
Deadline: January 1.
Contact: Dr. Charles H. Kennedy, Director.

**American Jewish Archives
Lowenstein-Wiener Summer
Fellowship Awards in
American Jewish Studies**
3101 Clifton Avenue
Cincinnati, OH 45220-2488
(513) 221-1875

Description: Summer fellowships for ABDs and post-doctoral scholars studying American Jewish aspects of folklore, history, languages, literatures and linguistics, liberal studies, philosophy, religion, political science, public policy, sociology, anthropology, archaeology, women's studies, and interdisciplinary topics in the humanities and social sciences, education, and international affairs, recipients chosen on the basis or proposed research; tenable for one month of research and writing at the American Jewish Archives.
Restrictions: N/A.
$ Given: Five to eight grants are awarded annually; ABDs receive a $1,000 stipend; postdoctoral scholars receive a $2,000 stipend.
Application Information: Write for details.
Deadline: April 1.
Contact: Dr. Abraham J. Peck, Associate Director.

**American Library Association
David H. Clift Scholarship
Program**
50 East Huron Street
Chicago, IL 60611-2795
(312) 944-6780

Description: Scholarships for master's candidates in library sciences; recipients chosen on the basis of academic achievement, leadership characteristics, and commitment to library career.
Restrictions: United States or Canadian citizenship required; tenable only for graduate program accredited by ALA.
$ Given: One or more grants of $3,000 are awarded annually.
Application Information: Write for details.
Deadline: January 5.
Contact: Margaret Myers, Staff Liaison.

**American Library Association
Louise Giles Minority
Scholarship**
50 East Huron Street
Chicago, IL 60611-2795
(312) 944-6780

Description: Scholarships for master's candidates in library sciences; recipients chosen on the basis of academic achievement, leadership characteristics, and commitment to library career.
Restrictions: Limited to African-American, Alaskan Native, Native American, Asian-American, and Pacific Islander applicants; United States or Canadian citizenship required; tenable only for graduate program accredited by ALA.
$ Given: One grant of $3,000 awarded annually; paid in two installments.
Application Information: Write for details.
Deadline: January 5.
Contact: Margaret Myers, Staff Liaison.

American Library Association
Frederick G. Melcher
Scholarships
50 East Huron Street
Chicago, IL 60611-2795
(312) 944-6780

Description: Scholarships for master's candidates specializing in children's library sciences; recipients chosen on the basis of academic achievement and career commitment/desire to work with children.
Restrictions: Tenable only for graduate program accredited by ALA.
$ Given: Two grants of $5,000 each are awarded annually.
Application Information: Write for details.
Deadline: March 1.
Contact: Executive Director, ALSC c/o ALA.

American Numismatic Society
Dissertation Fellowships
Broadway at 155th Street
New York, NY 10032-7598
(212) 234-3130

Description: Fellowships for dissertation research on the significance of numismatics in the humanities and social sciences; recipients chosen on the basis of quality of proposed research.
Restrictions: Limited to doctoral candidates enrolled in United States or Canadian programs who have completed general examinations; previous attendance at one ANS summer seminar required.
$ Given: One grant of $3,500 awarded annually.
Application Information: Write for details.
Deadline: March 1.
Contact: Chief Curator.

American Numismatic Society
Frances M. Schwartz
Fellowship
Broadway at 155th Street
New York, NY 10032-7598
(212) 234-3130

Description: Fellowship for graduate students in numanistics and museum practices; recipients chosen on the basis of academic achievement; fellowship includes employment at the American Numanistic Society.
Restrictions: N/A.
$ Given: A variable number of grants up to $2,000 awarded annually.
Application Information: Write for details.
Deadline: March 1.
Contact: Chief Curator.

American Numismatic Society
Summer Seminar Grants
Broadway at 155th Street
New York, NY 10032-7598
(212) 234-3130

Description: Grants to graduate students in archaeology; recipients chosen on the basis of academic achievement; tenable for attendance/participation in 9-week summer seminar (June-August).
Restrictions: Applicants must have completed at least one year of graduate study in the classics, archaeology, history, art history, or related fields in a program in the United States or Canada.
$ Given: Approximately 10 grants for $2,000 are awarded annually.
Application Information: Write for details.
Deadline: March 1.
Contact: Chief Curator.

American Philosophical Society
John Clarke Slater Fellowships
104 South Fifth Street
Philadelphia, PA 19106-3386
(215) 440-3403

Description: Fellowships for doctoral candidates writing dissertations on the history of physical sciences in the twentieth century; recipients chosen on the basis of academic achievement and quality of proposed dissertation research.
Restrictions: Applicants must have completed all Ph.D. degree requirements except dissertation.
$ Given: An unspecified number of fellowships of $12,000 are awarded annually.
Application Information: Write for details.
Deadline: December 1.

American Philosophical Society Library
Mellon Resident Research Fellowships
104 South Fifth Street
Philadelphia, PA 19106-3386
(215) 440-3400

Description: One- to three-month residential fellowships for doctoral candidates at dissertation level and postdoctoral scholars studying the history of American science and technology, its European roots, and its relation to American history and culture; tenable at the Society Library for short-term research using the library's collections.
Restrictions: United States citizenship required.
$ Given: An unspecified number of fellowships awarded annually; each for $1,800/month; tenable at Society for one to three months.
Application Information: Write for details.
Deadline: March 1.

American Philosophical Society Library
Phillips Fund Grants in North American Indian Linguistics and Ethnohistory
104 South Fifth Street
Philadelphia, PA 19106-3386
(215) 440-3400

Description: Grants for graduate students, as well as postdoctoral scholars, studying North American Indian linguistics and ethnohistory; recipients chosen on the basis of proposed research.
Restrictions: N/A.
$ Given: A few grants for up to $1,600 each are awarded annually to cover expenses, not personal maintenance.
Application Information: Write for details.
Deadline: March 1.

American Planning Association
Charles Abrams Scholarship Program
1776 Massachusetts Avenue, N.W.
Washington, DC 20036
(202) 872-0611

Description: Scholarships for master's candidates in urban planning; recipients chosen on the basis of financial need.
Restrictions: Applicants must attend and be nominated by one of these participating schools: Columbia University, Harvard University, MIT, New School for Social Research, or the University of Pennsylvania; United States citizenship required.
$ Given: One fellowship of $2,000 awarded annually.
Application Information: Application by school nomination only.
Deadline: April 30.
Contact: Assistant for Division of Student Services.

**American Planning
Association
Minority Fellowships Program**
1776 Massachusetts
Avenue, N.W.
Washington, DC 20036
(202) 872-0611

Description: Scholarships for master's candidates in urban planning; tenable for first year of graduate study (renewable for second year) at PAB-accredited institutions; recipients chosen on the basis of financial need.
Restrictions: Limited to African-American, Hispanic, and Native American applicants only; United States or Canadian citizenship required.
$ Given: An unspecified number of fellowships of $1,000–$4,000 per year are awarded annually.
Application Information: Write for details.
Deadline: May 15.
Contact: Assistant for Division of Student Services.

**American Political Science
Association
Doctoral Dissertation Awards**
1527 New Hampshire
Avenue, N.W.
Washington, DC 20036
(202) 483-2512

Description: Awards for outstanding dissertations written by doctoral candidates in various fields of political science; Almond Award for comparative politics, Anderson Award for general state and local politics, Corwin Award for public law and judicial process, Lasswell Award for policy studies, Reid Award for international relations/law/politics, Schattschneider Award for American government and politics, Strauss Award for political philosophy, and White Award for public administration.
Restrictions: Dissertation must have been completed within the last two calendar years.
$ Given: Eight named prizes of $250 each are awarded annually.
Application Information: A copy of the dissertation and a letter of nomination from the department chair must be sent to each member of the award committee.
Deadline: January 15.
Contact: Rob Hauck.

**American Psychological
Association
APA Minority Fellowship
Program in Psychology**
750 First Street, N.E.
Washington, DC 20002-4242
(202) 336-6027

Description: Fellowships for doctoral candidates in psychology; one program to support the training of clinicians, another program to support the training of researchers; recipients chosen on the basis of academic achievement and financial need.
Restrictions: African-American, Hispanic, Native American, Alaskan Native, Asian-American, and Pacific Islander applicants preferred; United States citizenship or legal residency required; applicants must be planning career in psychology.
$ Given: An unspecified number of fellowships awarded annually; $10,008 for 10 months; renewable for up to three years.
Application Information: Write for details.
Deadline: January 15.
Contact: Dr. James M. Jones, Director; or Ernesto Guerra, Minorities Fellowship Program.

**American Research
Center in Egypt
Fellowships for Research in
Egypt**
New York University
50 Washington Square South
NYU Kevorkian Center
New York, NY 10012
(212) 998-8890

Description: Fellowships for doctoral candidates and postdoctoral scholars in archaeology, art, humanities, and social sciences in Egypt; recipients chosen on the basis of quality of proposed research; intended as maintenance support for research conducted in Egypt for three- to twelve-month period.
Restrictions: Proficiency in Arabic required; recipients may not hold outside employment during fellowship period; United States and Egyptian citizens only.
$ Given: Up to 20 fellowships awarded annually; each with stipend of $1,000/month plus round-trip airfare and dependents' stipends, if needed.
Application Information: Write for details.
Deadline: November 1.
Contact: Dr. Terence Walz, United States Director.

**American Research Institute
in Turkey
ARIT Fellowships**
University Museum
33rd and Spruce Streets
Philadelphia, PA 19104
(215) 898-3474

Description: Fellowships for doctoral candidates to conduct research concerning Turkey in ancient, medieval, and modern times in any field of the humanities or social sciences; recipients chosen on the basis of quality of proposed research; intended as maintenance support for dissertation research in Turkey over one- to twelve-month fellowship period.
Restrictions: Applicants must have satisfied all doctoral requirements except dissertation; recipients must obtain research permission from the Turkish government; applicants must be affiliated with United States or Canadian institutions.
$ Given: Six to 10 fellowships for $1,000–$4,000 per year are awarded annually.
Application Information: Write for details.
Deadline: November 15.
Contact: Nancy Leinwand.

**American Research Institute
in Turkey
Bosphorus University
Summer Turkish Language
Program**
University Museum
33rd and Spruce Streets
Philadelphia, PA 19104
(215) 898-3474

Description: Fellowships for college graduates through doctoral candidates; for the study of Turkish language in an eight-week summer program at Bosphorus University in Istanbul; recipients chosen on the basis of academic achievement (minimum 3.0 GPA).
Restrictions: Preference for individuals planning career in Turkish studies; two years of college-level Turkish language courses or equivalent required (written and oral exam required); United States citizenship or permanent resident status required.
$ Given: Ten to fifteen grants are awarded annually; grant covers tuition, maintenance stipend, and round-trip travel; nonrenewable.

Application Information: Write for details.
Deadline: February 15.
Contact: Nancy Leinwand.

American School of Classical Studies at Athens Fellowships
993 Lenox Drive, Suite 101
Lawrenceville, NJ 08648
(609) 844-7577

Description: Fellowships for graduate students to engage in study/research in Greece for one academic year; intended for students of archaeology, classical studies, classical art history, and ancient Greece; named fellowships include Thomas Day Seymour Fellowship, John Williams White Fellowship, Samuel H. Kress Fellowship, and James Rignall Wheeler Fellowship.
Restrictions: Applicants must be affiliated with United States or Canadian institution; United States or Canadian citizenship required; B.A. major in classics or classical archaeology required.
$ Given: Four fellowships awarded annually; each for $5,650 plus fees, room & partial board.
Application Information: Write for details.
Deadline: January 5.
Contact: Committee on Admissions and Fellowships.

American School of Classical Studies at Athens Gennadeion Fellowship
993 Lenox Drive, Suite 101
Lawrenceville, NJ 08648
(609) 844-7577

Description: Fellowship for doctoral candidates at dissertation level to engage in study/research at the Gennadius Library in Athens for one academic year; intended for students of Byzantine and Greek studies; recipients chosen on the basis of academic achievement and quality of proposed research.
Restrictions: Applicants must be affiliated with a United States or Canadian institution; United States or Canadian citizenship required.
$ Given: One fellowship awarded annually for $5,650 plus fees, room, and partial board.
Application Information: Write for details.
Deadline: January 31.
Contact Committee on Admissions and Fellowships.

American School of Classical Studies at Athens Jacob Hirsch Fellowship
993 Lenox Drive, Suite 101
Lawrenceville, NJ 08648
(609) 844-7577

Description: Fellowship for doctoral candidates at dissertation level to engage in study/research in Greece; intended for students of archaeology; recipients chosen on the basis of academic achievement and quality of proposed research.
Restrictions: United States or Israeli citizenship required.
$ Given: One fellowship awarded annually for $5,650 plus room and partial board; non-renewable.
Application Information: Write for details.
Deadline: January 31.
Contact: Committee on Admissions and Fellowships.

American School of Classical Studies at Athens
Summer Study in Archaeology
993 Lenox Drive, Suite 101
Lawrenceville, NJ 08648
(609) 844-7577

Description: Scholarships for graduate students to support summer study in archaeology with an emphasis on topography and antiquities of Greece; tenable at the School in Athens.
Restrictions: Applicants must be affiliated with a United States institution; United States or Canadian citizenship required.
$ Given: Five scholarships to cover tuition, room and partial board.
Application Information: Write for details.
Deadline: February 1.
Contacts Committee on Admissions and Fellowships.

American Schools of Oriental Research
George A. Barton Fellowship at the Albright Institute for Archaeological Research, Jerusalem
3301 North Charles Street
Baltimore, MD 21218
(401) 516-3498

Description: Residential fellowships for doctoral study in humanistic disciplines of the Middle East; for one to five months of study/research at the Albright Institute in Jerusalem; recipients chosen on the basis of proposed research.
Restrictions: Fellowship may not be used for summer study.
$ Given: An unspecified number of fellowships are awarded annually; each with a $2,000 stipend plus room and half-board.
Application Information: Write for details.
Deadlines: September 15, October 15.
Contact: Dr. Rudolph H. Dornemann, Administrative Director.

Schools of Oriental Research
Endowment for Biblical Research
Summer Research Grants & Travel Scholarships
3301 North Charles Street
Baltimore, MD 21218
(401) 516-3498

Description: Grants and scholarships for graduate and seminary students; for study of archaeology, linguistics, natural sciences, and anthropology in the Holy Land; recipients chosen on the basis of proposed study/research.
Restrictions: Membership in ASOR required; citizenship in any country outside the Middle East required.
$ Given: Two one- to three-month research grants of $1,500 each are awarded annually; 16 summer travel scholarships of $1,000 each are awarded annually.
Application Information: Write for details.
Deadline: February 1.
Contact: Dr. Rudolph H. Dornemann, Administrative Director.

American Schools of Oriental Research
Samuel H. Kress Foundation Fellowship at the Albright Institute for Archaeological Research, Jerusalem
3301 North Charles Street
Baltimore, MD 21218
(401) 516-3498

Description: Residential fellowships for doctoral candidates at dissertation level in art history, archaeology, and architecture; for nine to ten months of dissertation research at the Albright Institute in Jerusalem; recipients chosen on the basis of proposed research.
Restrictions: N/A.
$ Given: An unspecified number of fellowships awarded annually; each with $4,500 stipend plus room and half-board.
Application Information: Write for details.
Deadline: October 15.
Contact: Dr. Rudolph H. Dornemann, Administrative Director.

American Schools of Oriental Research
Mesopotamian Fellowship
3301 North Charles Street
Baltimore, MD 21218
(401) 516-3498

Description: Fellowship for doctoral candidates and postdoctoral scholars studying ancient Mesopotamian civilization and culture; recipients chosen on the basis of proposed research.
Restrictions: Membership in ASOR required; preference to projects affiliated with ASOR.
$ Given: One fellowship with $5,000 stipend is awarded annually.
Application Information: Write for details.
Deadline: February 1.
Contact: Dr. Rudolph H. Dornemann, Administrative Director.

American Society for Eighteenth Century Studies Predoctoral Fellowships
William Andrews Clark
Memorial Library
UCLA
2520 Cimarron Street
Los Angeles, CA 90018
(213) 735-7605
FAX (213) 731-8617

Description: Fellowships to support advanced doctoral students in study/research in any area represented in the Clark's collections or linked to programs supported by these or other collections at UCLA.
Restrictions: Open to advanced doctoral students.
$ Given: A variable number of fellowships offered annually; each for $4,500.
Application Information: Write for details.
Deadline: March 15.
Contact: Beverly Onley, Fellowship Coordinator.

American Statistical Association ASA/NSF Census Research Fellow and Associate Program
1429 Duke Street
Alexandria, VA 22314-3402
(703) 684-1221

Description: Fellowships/associateships for doctoral candidates and recent Ph.D.s in demography and population studies; for participation in research at the United States Bureau of Census; recipients chosen on the basis of academic achievement and quality of proposed research.
Restrictions: Significant computer experience required.
$ Given: An unspecified number of associateships are awarded annually; stipend is commensurate with qualifications and experience; fringe benefits and travel allowance also included.

Application Information: Write for details.
Deadline: January 14.
Contact: Carolee Bush, Fellowship Program Director.

American Statistical Association ASA/NSF/BLS Senior Research Fellow and Associate Program
1429 Duke Street
Alexandria, VA 22314-3402
(703) 684-1221

Description: Fellowships/associateships for doctoral candidates and recent Ph.D.s in economics, business, and labor studies; for participation in research at the Bureau of Labor Statistics; recipients chosen on the basis of academic achievement and quality of proposed research.
Restrictions: Significant computer experience required.
$ Given: An unspecified number of associateships are awarded annually; stipend is commensurate with qualifications and experience; fringe benefits and travel allowance also included.
Application Information: Write for details.
Deadline: January 14.
Contact: Carolee Bush, Fellowship Program Director.

Archaeological Institute of America Anna C. and Oliver C. Colburn Fellowship
675 Commonwealth Avenue
Boston, MA 02215
(617) 353-9361

Description: One-year fellowship for doctoral candidates and postdoctoral scholars, for study/research in classical studies; tenable at the American School of Classical Studies in Athens.
Restrictions: United States or Canadian citizenship or legal residency required.
$ Given: One fellowship of $5,500–$6,000 is awarded annually.
Application Information: Write for details.
Deadline: February 1.
Contact: Colburn Fellowship.

Archaeological Institute of America Olivia James Traveling Fellowships
675 Commonwealth Avenue
Boston, MA 02215
(617) 353-9361

Description: Fellowships for doctoral candidates at dissertation level in architecture; for travel to Greece, the Aegean islands, Sicily, southern Italy, Asia Minor, and/or Mesopotamia; recipients chosen on the basis of proposed research/study.
Restrictions: Preference to project of at least six months duration; no funding for field excavation; United States citizenship or legal residency required .
$ Given: One fellowship of up to $15,000 is awarded annually.
Application Information: Write for details.
Deadline: November 15.
Contact: Olivia James Traveling Fellowship.

Archaeological Institute of America
Harriet Pomerance Fellowship
675 Commonwealth Avenue
Boston, MA 02215
(617) 353-9361

Description: Fellowship for doctoral candidates studying Aegean Bronze Age archaeology; for travel to the Mediterranean; recipients chosen on the basis of proposed research/study.
Restrictions: United States or Canadian citizenship required.
$ Given: One fellowship of $3,000 is awarded annually; non-renewable.
Application Information: Write for details.
Deadline: November 15.
Contact: Harriet Pomerance Fellowship.

Arctic Institute of North America
Grant-in-Aid Program
University of Calgary
2500 University Drive, N.W.
Calgary, Alberta T2N 1N4
Canada
(403) 220-7515

Description: Grants for graduate students for natural/social sciences field work in the northern regions; recipients chosen on the basis of academic achievement and quality of proposed research.
Restrictions: N/A.
$ Given: An unspecified number of grants of up to $5,000 Canadian are awarded annually.
Application Information: Write for details.
Deadline: January 15.
Contact: Mike Robinson, Executive Director.

Armenian General Benevolent Union
Excellence Grant
585 Saddle River Road
Saddle Brook, NJ 07662
(201) 797-7600

Description: Grant for graduate students in Armenian studies, international affairs, education, public administration, and journalism; recipients chosen on the basis of outstanding academic achievement and competence in subject area.
Restrictions: Limited to individuals of Armenian descent who are enrolled at Columbia University, Harvard University, University of Michigan, or UCLA.
$ Given: One grant of $5,000 is awarded annually.
Application Information: Write for details.
Deadline: April 30.

Armenian General Benevolent Union
Graduate Scholarship Program
585 Saddle River Road
Saddle Brook, NJ 07662
(201) 797-7600

Description: Scholarships for graduate students in law, medicine, international relations, and Armenian studies; recipients chosen on the basis of academic achievement, financial need, and involvement in the Armenian community.
Restrictions: Limited to individuals of Armenian descent who are enrolled in accredited United States institutions.
$ Given: Seventy grants of $1,000 are awarded annually; renewable.
Application Information: Write for details.
Deadline: April 30.

Asian Cultural Council Fellowship Grants
1290 Avenue of the Americas
Suite 3450
New York, NY 10104
(212) 373-4300

Description: Grants for doctoral candidates and post-doctoral scholars in the visual and performing arts, archaeology, printmaking, architecture, art history, conservation, crafts, dance, design, film, musicology, music, painting, photography, sculpture, and theater; funding primarily for Asian scholars to visit the United States (and some support for United States citizens to visit Asia) for three- to twelve-month fellowship periods.
Restrictions: N/A.
$ Given: An unspecified number of grants are awarded annually; each grant covers airfare, per diem, maintenance stipend, health insurance, and expenses.
Application Information: Write for details.
Deadline: February 1.

Association for Library and Information Science Education Doctoral Students' Dissertation Competition Awards
4101 Lake Boone Trail
Suite 201
Raleigh, NC 27607
(919) 787-5181

Description: Awards for outstanding doctoral dissertations in library and information sciences; recipients chosen on the basis of academic achievement and quality of doctoral dissertation.
Restrictions: Applicants must present summary of dissertation to ALISE annual conference and complete dissertation within the current calendar year.
$ Given: Two awards of $400 each are awarded annually; conference registration and one-year membership in ALISE also included.
Application Information: Write for details.
Deadline: October 1.
Contact: Penny DePas, CAE, Executive Director.

Association for Library and Information Science Education Jane Anne Hannigan Research Award
4101 Lake Boone Trail
Suite 201
Raleigh, NC 27607
(919) 787-5181

Description: Awards for doctoral candidates in library and information sciences; to support research.
Restrictions: ALISE membership required.
$ Given: One award of $500 is made annually.
Application Information: Write for details.
Deadline: October 1.
Contact: Penny DePas, CAE, Executive Director

Association fr Library and Information Science Education Research Grants
4101 Lake Boone Trail
Suite 201
Raleigh, NC 27607
(919) 787-5181

Description: Research grants for students in library and information sciences; recipients chosen on the basis of previous work and quality of proposed research.
Restrictions: membership in ALISE required; no funding for doctoral dissertation work.
$ Given: An unspecified number of grants totaling $2,500 are awarded annually.
Application Information: Write for details.
Deadline: October 1.
Contact: Research Committee.

Association for Library and Information Science Education Research Paper Competition Awards
4101 Lake Boone Trail
Suite 201
Raleigh, NC 27607
(919) 787-5181

Description: Awards for outstanding research papers on library and information sciences.
Restrictions: Although master's and doctoral candidates are eligible to submit original research papers, any papers submitted for degree requirements cannot be considered for awards; membership in ALISE required.
$ Given: A maximum of two awards of $500 each are awarded annually.
Application Information: Write for details.
Deadline: October 1.
Contact: Penny DePas, CAE, Executive Director.

Association for Women in Science Educational Foundation
AWIS Predoctoral Award
1522 K Street, N.W., Suite 820
Washington, DC 20005
(202) 408-0742

Description: Awards for doctoral candidates in life sciences, physical sciences, social sciences, engineering, mathematics, and behavioral sciences; recipients chosen on the basis of academic achievement and quality of proposed research.
Restrictions: Limited to women only; United States citizenship and enrollment in United States institution required.
$ Given: An unspecified number of grants of $500 each are awarded annually.
Application Information: Write for details.
Deadline: January 15.

Association of American Geographers
The Robert D. Hodgson Fund Dissertation Research Grant
1710 Sixteenth Street, N.W.
Washington, DC 20009-3198
(202) 234-1450

Description: Research grants for doctoral candidates at dissertation level in the field of geography, especially as related to international cooperation; recipients chosen on the basis of proposed research.
Restrictions: Applicants must complete all doctoral requirements except dissertation by the term following the date of the award; minimum one-year membership in AAG required; funding for direct research expenses only.
$ Given: An unspecified number of grants of up to $500 each are awarded annually.
Application Information: Write for application forms.
Deadline: December 31.
Contact: Elizabeth Beetschen.

Association of American Geographers
The Otis Paul Starkey Fund Dissertation Research Grant
1710 Sixteenth Street, N.W.
Washington, DC 20009-3198
(202) 234-1450

Description: Research grants for doctoral candidates at dissertation level in the field of regional geography, especially as related to a specific problem area in the United States or its possessions; recipients chosen on the basis of proposed research.
Restrictions: Applicants must complete all doctoral requirements except dissertation by the term following the date of the award; minimum one-year membership

in AAG required; funding for direct research expenses only.
$ Given: An unspecified number of grants of up to $500 each are awarded annually.
Application Information: Write for application forms.
Deadline: December 31.
Contact: Elizabeth Beetschen.

Association of American Geographers
The Paul P. Vouras Fund Dissertation Research Grant
1710 Sixteenth Street, N.W.
Washington, DC 20009-3198
(202) 234-1450

Description: Research grants for doctoral candidates at dissertation level in the field of geography; recipients chosen on the basis of proposed research.
Restrictions: Preference for applicants who are members of minority groups; applicants must complete all doctoral requirements except dissertation by the term following the date of the award; minimum one-year membership in AAG required; funding for direct research expenses only.
$ Given: An unspecified number of grants of up to $500 each are awarded annually.
Application Information: Write for application forms.
Deadline: December 31.
Contact: Elizabeth Beetschen.

Association of College and Research Libraries
Doctoral Dissertation Fellowship
50 East Huron Street
Chicago, IL 60611
(312) 280-2510
(800) 545-2433

Description: Research fellowship for doctoral candidates at dissertation level in library science; recipients chosen on the basis of proposed research.
Restrictions: N/A.
$ Given: One grant of $1,000 is awarded annually; nonrenewable.
Application Information: Write for details.
Deadline: December 1.
Contact: Carolyn Bernero.

Association of College and Research Libraries
Martinus Nijhoff International West European Specialist Study Grant
50 East Huron Street
Chicago, IL 60611
(312) 280-2510
(800) 545-2433

Description: Grant for scholars in library science to travel for 10 days to study West European professional librarianship; recipients chosen on the basis of proposed research.
Restrictions: Personal membership in ALA required.
$ Given: An unspecified number of grants are awarded annually; award covers air travel, surface travel, expenses, room, and board.
Application Information: Write for details.
Deadline: December 1.
Contact: Mary Taylor.

Association of Former Agents of the U.S. Secret Service J. Clifford Dietrich & Julie Y. Cross Scholarships
P.O. Box 11681
Alexandria, VA 22312

Description: Scholarships for undergraduate and graduate students (college sophomores through master's candidates) studying law enforcement/police administration and planning careers in criminal justice; recipients chosen on the basis of academic achievement and financial need.
Restrictions: United States citizenship required.
$ Given: An unspecified number of scholarships for $1,000 each are awarded annually.
Application Information: Write for details.
Deadline: May 1.
Contact: Executive Secretary.

Charles Babbage Institute, University of Minnesota Adelle and Erwin Tomash Fellowship in the History of Information Processing
103 Walter Library
117 Pleasant Street, S.E.
Minneapolis, MN 55455
(612) 624-5050

Description: Research fellowship for doctoral candidates at dissertation level studying the history of information processing; recipients chosen on the basis of academic achievement and quality of proposed research; tenable at any appropriate research institution.
Restrictions: All nationalities eligible.
$ Given: One fellowship awarded annually for $10,000 plus up to $2,000 toward tuition, fees, travel and research expenses; renewable.
Application Information: Write for details.
Deadline: January 15.
Contact: Arthur L. Norberg, Director.

Leo Baeck Institute David Baumgardt Memorial Fellowships
129 East 73rd Street
New York, NY 10021
(212) 744-6400

Description: Research fellowships for doctoral candidates studying the writings of Professor Baumgardt or the intellectual history of German-speaking Jewry; recipients chosen on the basis of proposed research.
Restrictions: N/A.
$ Given: One fellowship awarded annually; amount based on project requirements; usually not more than $3,000.
Application Information: Write for details.
Deadline: November 1.
Contact:: Robert A. Jacobs, Executive Director.

Leo Baeck Institute/ DAAD German-Jewish History and Culture Fellowships
129 East 73rd Street
New York, NY 10021
(212) 744-6400

Description: Research fellowships for doctoral candidates and recent Ph.D.s studying the social, communal, and intellectual history of German-speaking Jewry; recipients chosen on the basis of academic achievement and quality of proposed research; use of the Leo Baeck Institute resources in New York City offered.
Restrictions: United States citizenship required; maximum age range of 32-35.
$ Given: One fellowship of $2,000 is awarded annually; paid in two installments.

Application Information: Write for details.
Deadline: November 1.
Contact: Robert A. Jacobs, Executive Director.

**Leo Baeck Institute
Fritz Halbers Fellowships**
129 East 73rd Street
New York, NY 10021
(212) 744-6400

Description: Research fellowships for doctoral candidates studying the history and culture of German-speaking Jewry; recipients chosen on the basis of proposed research.
Restrictions: N/A.
$ Given: One fellowship awarded annually; amount based on project requirements; $3,000 maximum.
Application Information: Write for details.
Deadline: November 1.
Contact: Robert A. Jacobs, Executive Director.

**Beta Phi Mu International
Library and Information
Science Honor Society
Harold Lancour Scholarship
for Foreign Study**
School of Library and
Information Science
University of Pittsburgh
Pittsburgh, PA 15260
(412) 624-9435

Description: Scholarship for professional librarians and graduate students in library science (in ALA-accredited graduate programs), for foreign study and research; recipients chosen on the basis of proposed research.
Restrictions: N/A.
$ Given: An unspecified number of scholarships of $1,000 are awarded annually.
Application Information: Write for details.
Deadline: March 1.
Contact: Executive Secretary.

**Beta Phi Mu International
Library and Information
Science Honor Society
Sarah Rebecca Reed
Scholarship**
School of Library and
Information Science
University of Pittsburgh
Pittsburgh, PA 15260
(412) 624-9435

Description: Scholarship for master's candidates in library science; recipients chosen on the basis of academic achievement.
Restrictions: Applicants must be accepted into or currently enrolled in ALA-accredited library science graduate program.
$ Given: One scholarship of $1,500 is awarded annually.
Application Information: Application form, transcripts, and references required.
Deadline: March 1.
Contact: Executive Secretary.

**Beta Phi Mu International
Library and Information
Science Honor Society
Frank B. Sessa Scholarship for
Continuing Education**
School of Library and
Information Science
University of Pittsburgh
Pittsburgh, PA 15260
(412) 624-9435

Description: Scholarship for scholars of library science, recipients chosen on the basis of proposed study/research plan.
Restrictions: Membership in Beta Phi Mu required.
$ Given: One scholarship of $750 is awarded annually.
Application Information: Applicants must submit specific plans for course of continuing education (graduate study or professional development).
Deadline: March 1.
Contact: Executive Secretary.

Bibliographical Society of America
Bibliographical Fellowships
P.O. Box 397
Grand Central Station
New York, NY 10163
(212) 647-9171

Description: Short-term fellowships (one to two months) for graduate students studying bibliography; recipients chosen on the basis of proposed research; preference for research projects focusing on physical materials (books, manuscripts, documents).
Restrictions: N/A.
$ Given: Eight to ten fellowships awarded annually; each for up to $1,000 per month.
Application Information: Write for details.
Deadline: January 31.
Contact: Marjory Zaik, Executive Secretary.

Brookings Institution
Predoctoral Research
Fellowships in Economic
Studies
1775 Massachusetts Avenue, N.W.
Washington, DC 20036
(202) 797-6000

Description: One-year residential fellowships for doctoral candidates conducting policy-oriented dissertation research in economics as related to public policy; emphasis on economic growth, international economics, industrial organization, regulation, human resources, public finance, and economic stabilization; recipients chosen on the basis of academic achievement, quality of proposed research, and relevance of research topic to Brookings Institution interests; fellowship includes access to Brookings Institution data and staff; women and minorities encouraged to apply.
Restrictions: Applicants must have completed all preliminary doctoral exams.
$ Given: A few fellowships three to five awarded annually; each with $15,000 stipend, up to $600 for expenses, and up to $500 for research related travel.
Application Information: Applicants must be nominated by their university graduate departments.
Deadline: December 15 for departmental nomination; February 15 for individual application.

Brookings Institution
Predoctoral Research
Fellowships in Foreign Policy
Studies
1775 Massachusetts Avenue, N.W.
Washington, DC 20036
(202) 797-6000

Description: One-year residential fellowships for doctoral candidates conducting policy-oriented dissertation research in United States foreign policy and international relations; emphasis on security policy and economic issues; recipients chosen on the basis of academic achievement, quality of proposed research, and relevance of research topic to United States foreign policy; fellowship includes access to Brookings Institution data and staff; women and minorities encouraged to apply.
Restrictions: N/A.
$ Given: A few fellowships awarded annually; each with $15,000 stipend, up to $600 for research expenses, and up to $500 for research related travel.

Application Information: Applicants must be nominated by their university graduate departments.
Deadline: December 15 for departmental nomination; February 15 for individual application.

Brookings Institution Predoctoral Research Fellowships in Governmental Studies
1775 Massachusetts Avenue, N.W.
Washington, DC 20036
(202) 797-6000

Description: One-year residential fellowships for doctoral candidates conducting policy-oriented dissertation research in governmental studies; emphasis on American political institutions, politics, economic and social policy, and government regulation; recipients chosen on the basis of academic achievement, quality of proposed research, and relevance of research topic to Brookings Institution interests; fellowship includes access to Brookings Institution data and staff; women and minorities encouraged to apply.
Restrictions: N/A.
$ Given: A few fellowships awarded annually; each with $15,000 stipend, up to $600 for expenses, and up to $500 for research related travel.
Application Information: Applicants must be nominated by their university graduate departments.
Deadline: December 15 for departmental nomination; February 15 for individual application.

Business and Professional Women's Clubs–New York State
Grace LeGendre Fellowships and Endowment Fund
239 Genesee Street
Mayro Building
Suite 212
Utica, NY 13501
(518) 585-7087

Description: Fellowships and grants for graduate students in all fields of study; tenable at accredited New York State institutions.
Restrictions: Limited to women applicants who are residents of New York State; United States citizenship or legal residency required.
$ Given: An unspecified number of $1,000 grants are awarded annually.
Application Information: Write for details.
Deadline: February 28.

Business and Professional Women's Foundation
BPW Career Advancement Scholarships
2012 Massachusetts Avenue, N.W.
Washington, DC 20036
(202) 296-9118

Description: One-year scholarships for undergraduate and graduate study in all disciplines, with emphasis on computer science, education, science, and paralegal training; scholarships are awarded within 24 months of the applicant's completing an undergraduate or graduate program in the United States; recipients chosen on the basis of financial need; funding designed to improve recipients' chances for career advancement/success.
Restrictions: Limited to women only; applicants must be at least 30 years old; no funding for Ph.D. studies, study abroad, or correspondence courses; United States citizenship and affiliation with United States institution required.

$ Given: Approximately 150 scholarships of up to $1,000 each are awarded annually.
Application Information: Request application materials between October 1 and April 1.
Deadline: April 15.
Contact: Assistant Director, Education and Training.

Canadian Embassy
Canadian Studies Graduate
Student Fellowships
501 Pennsylvania Avenue, N.W.
Washington, DC 20001
(202) 682-1740

Description: Fellowships for doctoral candidates in the humanities, social sciences, fine arts, business, law, or environmental studies who are working on dissertation topics related in substantial part to Canada; funding for dissertation research in Canada over a three- to nine-month fellowship period.
Restrictions: Applicants must be doctoral students at accredited institutions in Canada or the United States; applicants must have completed all degree requirements other than the dissertation; United States citizenship or permanent resident status required.
$ Given: An unspecified number of fellowships with $850/month stipends are awarded annually; nonrenewable.
Application Information: Write for details.
Deadline: October 30.
Contact: Dr. Norman T. London, Academic Relations Officer.

Canadian Federation of
University Women
Georgette LeMoyne Award
55 Parkdale Avenue
Ottawa, Ontario K1Y 1E5
Canada
(613) 722-8732

Description: Award for graduate studies in any field; intended for women taking refresher studies at universities where instruction is in French.
Restrictions: Limited to women only; applicant must hold B.S./B.A. degree and have been accepted to proposed program of graduate study; Canadian citizenship or minimum landed immigrant status required.
$ Given: One award for $1,000 Canadian made annually.
Application Information: Write for details.
Deadline: November 30.
Contact: Chair, Fellowships Committee.

Canadian Federation of
University Women
CFUW Polytechnique
Commemorative Awards
55 Parkdale Avenue
Ottawa, Ontario K1Y 1E5
Canada
(613) 722-8732

Description: Awards for graduate studies in any field, with preference for studies related to women's issues.
Restrictions: Applicant must hold B.S./B.A. degree and have been accepted to proposed program of graduate study; Canadian citizenship or minimum one-year landed immigrant status required.
$ Given: One grant of $1,400 Canadian awarded annually.

Application Information: Write for details.
Deadline: November 30.
Contact: Fellowships Committee.

Canadian Federation of University Women Margaret Dale Philip Award
55 Parkdale Avenue
Ottawa, Ontario K1Y 1E5
Canada
(613) 722-8732

Description: Award to graduate students in the humanities and social sciences, with preference to applicants studying Canadian history; recipients chosen on the basis of academic achievement in college, personal qualities, and potential.
Restrictions: Limited to women only; applicants must hold B.A./B.A. degree and have been accepted to proposed program of graduate study; Canadian citizenship or minimum one-year landed immigrant status required.
$ Given: One grant of $1,000 Canadian is awarded annually.
Application Information: Write for details.
Deadline: November 30.
Contact: Fellowships Committee.

Canadian Institute of Ukrainian Studies Doctoral Thesis Fellowships
352 Athabasca Hall
University of Alberta
Edmonton, Alberta T6G 2E8
Canada
(403) 492-2972

Description: Fellowships for doctoral candidates at dissertation level studying education, law, history, humanities, social sciences, or library sciences as related to Ukrainian or Ukrainian-Canadian topics; recipients chosen on the basis of academic achievement and dissertation topic; tenable in Canada or elsewhere.
Restrictions: Canadian citizenship or landed immigrant status required.
$ Given: An unspecified number of grants, each for $8,000 Canadian, are awarded annually; renewable.
Application Information: Write for details.
Deadline: May 1.

Canadian Institute of Ukrainian Studies Thesis Fellowships
352 Athabasca Hall
University of Alberta
Edmonton, Alberta T6G 2E8
Canada
(403) 492-2972

Description: Fellowships for master's candidates studying education, law, history, humanities, social sciences, or library sciences as related to Ukrainian or Ukrainian-Canadian topics; recipients chosen on the basis or academic achievement and thesis topic; tenable in Canada or elsewhere.
Restrictions: Canadian citizenship or landed immigrant status required.
$ Given: An unspecified number of one-year grants, each for $4,500 Canadian, are awarded annually.
Application Information: Write for details.
Deadline: May 1.

**Canadian Library Association
CLA Graduate Scholarship**
200 Elgin Street
Suite 602
Ottawa, Ontario K2P 1L5
Canada
(613) 232-9625

Description: Scholarship for B.L.S. and M.L.S. degree holders in library science, for further study; recipients chosen on the basis or academic achievement and financial need.
Restrictions: Canadian citizenship or one-year landed immigrant status required.
$ Given: One grant of up to $2,500 Canadian is awarded annually.
Application Information: Write for details.
Deadline: March 1.
Contact: Scholarships and Awards Committee.

**CDS International Robert
Bosch Foundation Fellowships**
330 Seventh Avenue
19th Floor
New York, NY 10001
(212) 760-1400
FAX (212) 268-1288

Description: Nine-month internships at German government and business institutions (September–May) for master's degree holders and professionals in communications, journalism, economics, political science, public affairs, business administration, law, and German studies; German internships provided in a framework of government and commerce; recipients chosen on the basis of academic achievement, evidence of leadership, and community participation.
Restrictions: Recipients must be proficient in German by the start of the internship (fees for language courses reimbursed); United States citizenship required.
$ Given: Fifteen fellowships awarded annually; each with DM3,500/month stipend plus travel expenses and possible spouse stipend.
Application Information: Write for details.
Deadline: October 15.
Contact: Rick Blanckmeister, Program Officer.

**Center for Defense
Information Internship**
1500 Massachusetts Avenue,
N.W.
Washington, DC 20005
(202) 826-0700

Description: Internships for undergraduate and graduate students interested in political science and public policy as related to military issues; for a minimum four month period of full-time work as research and outreach assistants at CDI; recipients chosen on the basis of academic achievement and interest in United States military policy and related public policy.
Restrictions: Writing skills essential.
$ Given: An unspecified number of internships paying $700/month are awarded annually.
Application Information: Write for details.
Deadlines: April 1, July 15, November 1.
Contact: Glenn Baker, Intern Program Coordinator.

Committee on Scholarly Communication with the People's Republic of China National Program for Advanced Study and Research in China—Graduate Program
1055 Thomas Jefferson Street, N.W.
Suite 2013
Washington, DC 20007
(202) 337-1250

Description: Funding for one academic year of advanced study/research in China; for master's and doctoral candidates in the humanities and social sciences; recipients chosen on the basis of academic achievement and proposed research; tenable at university or research institute in China.
Restrictions: Three years of Chinese language training; United States citizenship required.
$ Given: N/A.
Application Information: Write for details.
Deadline: October 16.
Contact: Program Officer.

Council for Advancement and Support of Education John Grenzebach Outstanding Doctoral Dissertation Award
11 Dupont Circle
Suite 400
Washington, DC 20036
(202) 328-5985

Description: Award for outstanding doctoral dissertation addressing philanthropy for education.
Restrictions: N/A.
$ Given: One award of $2,000 for the author, plus travel and lodging expenses for the author and a faculty member to attend the CASE annual assembly.
Application Information: Write for details.
Deadline: February 28.
Contact: Judy Grace, Grenzebach Research Awards.

Council for the Advancement of Science Writing Nate Haseltine Memorial Fellowships in Science Writing
P.O. Box 404
Greenlawn, NY 11740

Description: Fellowships for the study of science writing, available to B.S./B.A. holders in science of journalism, as well as to professional reporters and graduate students; recipients chosen on the basis of academic achievement, quality of writing, and commitment to writing career.
Restrictions: Preference to journalists with two years professional experience who want to specialize in science writing.
$ Given: An unspecified number of grants of up to $2,000 each are awarded annually.
Application Information: Write for details.
Deadline: June 1.
Contact: Executive Director.

Council for European Studies Pre-Dissertation Fellowship Program
Box 44
Schermerhorn Hall
Columbia University
New York, NY 10027
(212) 854-4172

Description: Two- to three-month research fellowships in European Union countries for doctoral candidates in European history, sociology, political science, anthropology, and economics.
Restrictions: Applicants must have completed at least two years of graduate study; language proficiency required; United States citizenship or permanent resident status required.

$ **Given:** Three grants of $3,000 each are awarded annually.
Application Information: Write for details.
Deadline: February 1.

Council on Social Work Education
CSWE Doctoral Fellowships in Social Work Minority Fellowship Program
1600 Duke Street
Alexandria, VA 22314-3421
(703) 683-8080

Description: One-year fellowships for doctoral candidates to conduct mental health research relevant to ethnic minorities; recipients chosen on the basis of academic achievement, financial need, and quality of proposed research; preference for applicants planning careers in social work specializing in ethnic minority issues of mental health.
Restrictions: Preference for African-American, Hispanic, Native American, and Asian-American applicants, as well as applicants of other ethnic minority groups; M.S.W. degree required; applicants must be full-time doctoral students; United States citizenship or permanent resident status required.
$ **Given:** An unspecified number of one-year fellowships are awarded annually; each carries a $708/month stipend plus tuition support, as negotiated with recipient's university; renewable.
Application Information: Write for details.
Deadline: February 28.
Contact: Dr. E. Aracelis Francis, Director.

Dirksen Center Congressional Research Grants Program
301 South 4th Street, Suite A
Pekin, IL 61554-4219
(309) 347-7113

Description: Research grants for individuals studying Congress, especially its historical and contemporary leadership; recipients chosen on the basis of proposed research.
Restrictions: N/A.
$ **Given:** An unspecified number of grants of up to $3,000 each are awarded annually.
Application Information: Write for details.
Deadline: March 31.
Contact: James Komacki, Executive Director.

Dumbarton Oaks Bliss Prize Fellowships in Byzantine Studies
1703 32nd Street, N.W.
Washington, DC 20007
(202) 342-3200

Description: Two-year fellowships for college seniors and B.A. holders entering graduate school in Byzantine Studies; participation includes summer travel for improved understanding of Byzantine civilization and culture.
Restrictions: Enrollment in United States or Canadian university required; minimum one-year of Greek required.
$ **Given:** An unspecified number of fellowships awarded annually; each for graduate school tuition and living expenses (up to $25,000 per year) for two years, plus summer travel (up to $5,000).

Application Information: By advisor nomination only; application must include transcripts, recommendations, study plans, and writing sample.
Deadline: November 1.
Contact: Assistant Director.

Dumbarton Oaks
Dumbarton Oaks Junior
Fellowships
1703 32nd Street, N.W.
Washington, DC 20007
(202) 342-3200

Description: Travel fellowships for doctoral candidates at dissertation level in Byzantine studies; for independent research; recipients chosen on the basis of academic achievement and quality of proposed research.
Restrictions: Open to all nationalities; working knowledge of relevant languages required; applicants must have completed all coursework and passed preliminary exams.
$ Given: An unspecified number of fellowships are awarded annually; each for $11,000 plus $800 research allowance, $1,300 maximum travel expense allowance, and $1,500 dependents' allowance (if needed).
Application Information: Write for details.
Deadline: November 1.
Contact: Assistant Director.

Dumbarton Oaks
Dumbarton Oaks Summer
Fellowship
1703 32nd Street, N.W.
Washington, DC 20007
(202) 342-3200

Description: Four- to nine-week summer fellowships for students of Byzantine studies; for June-August fellowship period; recipients chosen on the basis of academic achievement and quality of proposed research.
Restrictions: N/A.
$ Given: Ten fellowships awarded annually; each for $125/week plus housing, weekday lunches, and up to $1,300 travel allowance.
Application Information: Write for details.
Deadline: November 1.
Contact: Assistant Director.

Early American Industrial
Association
Grants-in-Aid
1324 Shalleross Avenue
Wilmington, DE 19806

Description: Research grants for graduate and doctoral scholars/researchers who are either sponsored by institutions or doing self-directed work related to early American industries in homes and shops, on farms, and at sea, as well as the discovery, identification, classification and preservation of obsolete tools, implements, and mechanical devices; recipients chosen on the basis of financial need and proposed research.
Restrictions: United States citizenship or permanent resident status required.
$ Given: Three to five grants for up to $1,000 each are awarded annually.
Application Information: Write for details.
Deadline: March 15.
Contact: Justine Mataleno, Coordinator.

**Friedrich Ebert Foundation
Doctoral Research
Fellowships**
950 Third Avenue
27th Floor
New York, NY 10022-2705
(212) 688-8770
or (212) 688-8775

Description: Five- to twelve-month residential study/research fellowships in Germany for doctoral candidates at dissertation level in political science, sociology, history, or economics as related to German/European affairs or German-American relations.
Restrictions: Applicants must have completed all degree requirements except dissertation; affiliation with American university required; knowledge of German adequate for research required; United States citizenship required .
$ Given: An unspecified number of fellowships awarded annually; each with DM1,150/month stipend plus airfare, domestic travel allowance, tuition and fees, luggage/books allowance, and dependents' allowance (if needed).
Application Information: Write for details.
Deadline: February 28
Additional Addresses: 806 Fifteenth Street, N.W., Suite 230, Washington, DC 20005, (202) 347-5570; and Godesberger Allee 149, Bonn 2, D-5300, Germany

**Friedrich Ebert
Foundation
Pre-Dissertation/Advanced
Graduate Fellowships**
950 Third Avenue
27th Floor
New York, NY 10022-2705
(212) 688-8770
or (212) 688-8775

Description: Five- to twelve-month independent study/research fellowships in Germany for doctoral candidates in political science, sociology, history, or economics as related to German/European affairs or German-American relations.
Restrictions: Applicants must have completed as least two years of graduate study at an American university; knowledge of German adequate for research required; United States citizenship required.
$ Given: An unspecified number of fellowships awarded annually; each with DM1,010/month stipend plus airfare, domestic travel allowance, tuition and fees, luggage/books allowance, and dependents' allowance (if needed).
Application Information: Write for details.
Deadline: February 28.
Additional Addresses: 806 Fifteenth Street, N.W., Suite 230, Washington, DC 20005, (202) 347-5570; and Godesberger Allee 149, Bonn 2, D-5300, Germany.

**Educational Testing Service
Second/Foreign Language
Dissertation RResearch
Grants**
P.O. Box 6155
Princeton, NJ 08541
(609) 921-9000

Description: Annual awards for research on second/foreign language testing conducted as part of dissertation work for doctoral degree.
Restrictions: Dissertation level students only.
$ Given: An unspecified number of grants of $2,500 each are awarded annually.

Application Information: Write for details.
Deadline: N/A.
Contact: Dr. Carol Taylor, Director, TOEFL Research Program.

Electrical Women's Round Table, Inc.
Julia Kiene Fellowship/Lyle Mamer Fellowship
P.O. Box 292793
Nashville, TN 37229-2793
(615) 890-1272

Description: One-year research fellowship for graduate students in communications, education, research, advertising, home economics, electrical and power engineering, and business administration; recipients chosen on the basis of academic achievement, financial need, and quality of proposed research.
Restrictions: Limited to women only; United States citizenship or legal residency required.
$ Given: One Julia Kiene Fellowship for $2,000 and one Lyle Mamer Fellowship for $1,000 are awarded annually; renewable.
Application Information: Write for details.
Deadline: March 1.
Contact: Fellowships Administrator.

Epilepsy Foundation of America
EFA Behavioral Sciences Student Research Fellowships
4351 Garden City Drive
Suite 406
Landover, MD 20785
(301) 459-3700

Description: One-year research fellowships for graduate students interested in basic and clinical research in the biological, behavioral, and social sciences designed to advance the understanding, treatment, and prevention of epilepsy; tenable at United States institutions; recipients chosen on the basis of demonstrated competence in epilepsy research.
Restrictions: Funding must be used in the United States; no funding for capital equipment.
$ Given: A variable number of fellowships are awarded annually; support limited to $30,000.
Application Information: Write for details.
Deadline: September 1.
Contact Administrative Assistant, Research and Professional Education.

Eta Sigma Phi National Classics Honor Society
Eta Sigma Phi Summer Scholarships
University of South Dakota
Box 171
Vermillion, SD 57069
(605) 677-5468

Description: Summer scholarships for study at the American Academy in Rome or the American School of Classical Studies in Athens; for recent college graduates who majored in Latin, Greek, or the classics; recipients can earn six semester hours of graduate-level credit during summer session.
Restrictions: Preference for students planning to teach classics; membership in Eta Sigma Phi required; Ph.D. candidates ineligible; applicants must have graduated from college within the past five years.
$ Given: Two scholarships awarded annually; $2,400 to attend the American Academy in Rome, $2,600 to attend the American School of Classical Studies in Athens.

Application Information: Request application forms from Professor Thomas Sienkewicz, Department of Classics, Monmouth College, Monmouth, IL 61462.
Deadline: December 5.
Contact: Brent M. Froberg, Executive Secretary, Department of Classics.

**Florida Education Fund
McKnight Doctoral
Fellowships**
201 East Kennedy Boulevard
Suite 1525
Tampa, FL 33602
(813) 272-2772

Description: Fellowships for graduate study at one of eleven participating doctoral-degree-granting universities in Florida in the fields of business, engineering, agriculture, biology, computer science, mathematics, physical science, and psychology; recipients chosen on the basis of academic achievement.
Restrictions: Limited to African-American applicants only; B.A./B.S. degree required; United States citizenship required.
$ Given: Twenty-five fellowships awarded annually; each for a maximum of five years of study, with an annual $11,000 stipend plus up to $5,000 in tuition and fees.
Application Information: Write for details.
Deadline: January 15.
Contact: Dr. Israel Tribble, Jr.

**Foundation for
European Language and
Educational Centers
Intensive European Language
Courses Scholarships**
Scholarship Department
Eurocentres
Seestrasse 247
Zurich CH-8038
Switzerland
(01) 485-5251

Description: Partial scholarships for three-month foreign language courses in English, French, German, Italian, and Spanish; each course held in country where language is spoken; recipients chosen on the basis of financial need and prior knowledge of language to be studied.
Restrictions: Applicants must be ages 18-30 and must have at least two years of professional experience in any field.
$ Given: An unspecified number of scholarships are awarded annually; each for between $250 and $750, which covers only part of the course tuition.
Application Information: Write for details.
Deadlines: January 15, March 31, June 15, and October 15.
Contact: Eric Steenbergen, Students' Assistance Department.

**Foundation for Field Research
Field Research Grants**
P.O. Box 2010
Alpine, CA 92903
(619) 445-9264

Description: Research grants for graduate students, as well as field researchers, for work in the fields of archaeology, paleontology, anthropology, ornithology, primatology, folklore, historic preservation, museum studies, botany, plant sciences, entomology, marine sciences, and oceanography; tenable at projects worldwide; recipients chosen on the basis of proposed research.
Restrictions: Applicants must speak English.

$ Given: An unspecified number of grants for $1,000–$25,000 each are awarded annually; renewable.
Application Information: Submit two-page preliminary research proposal.
Deadline: Proposals accepted continuously.
Contact: Thomas J. Banks.

Gamma Theta Upsilon Buzzard Undergraduate and Graduate Scholarships
Department of Geography
University of Arkansas
Ozar 108A
Fayetteville, AR 72701

Description: Grants for undergraduate and graduate students in geography; recipients chosen on the basis of academic achievement (minimum 3.0 GPA) in accredited graduate geography program.
Restrictions: Membership in GTU required.
$ Given: Two grants of $500 each are awarded annually.
Application Information: Write for details.
Deadline: August 1.
Contact: Dr. O. O. Maxfield.

General Semantics Foundation Project Grants
14 Charcoal Hill
Westport, CT 06880
(203) 226-1394

Description: Grants for master's and doctoral candidates to conduct research in general semantics; recipients chosen on the basis of documentation of ongoing work.
Restrictions: N/A.
$ Given: An unspecified number of grants of $300–$4,500 are awarded annually.
Application Information: Write for details.
Deadline: Applications accepted continuously.
Contact: Harry E. Maynard, President.

German Academic Exchange Service
DAAD–American Institute for Contemporary German Studies Research Grants
950 Third Avenue
19th Floor
New York, NY 10022
(212) 758-3223
FAX (212) 755-5780

Description: Research grant for doctoral candidates and recent Ph.D.s studying postwar Germany; tenable at AICGS.
Restrictions: N/A.
$ Given: An unspecified number of grants are awarded annually; varying amounts.
Application Information: Write for details.
Deadline: April 15.
Contact: Barbara Motyka.

German Academic Exchange Service
German Studies Summer Seminar Grants for Graduate Students and Ph.D. Candidates
950 Third Avenue
19th Floor
New York, NY 10022
(212) 758-3223
FAX (212) 755-5780

Description: Six-week interdisciplinary seminars at the University of California, Berkeley, for advanced graduate students and doctoral candidates in the humanities and social sciences, including students of German intellectual and social history; for the study of Germany after World War II; recipients chosen on the basis of academic achievement; participants eligible for academic credit.
Restrictions: Working knowledge of German required; United States citizenship required.
$ Given: An unspecified number of grants are awarded annually; each with a $1,500 stipend, to be applied toward the $450 course fee and living expenses.
Application Information: Write for details.
Deadline: March 15.
Contact: Barbara Motyka.

German Academic Exchange Service
German Sur Place Grants
950 Third Avenue
19th Floor
New York, NY 10022
(212) 758-3223
FAX (212) 755-5780

Description: Grants for undergraduate upperclassmen and graduate students in German studies; for the study of German affairs from a multidisciplinary perspective.
Restrictions: Applicants must have completed at least two years college-level German and at least three courses in German studies.
$ Given: An unspecified number of grants are awarded annually; each offsets tuition and research costs or summer earnings requirements.
Application Information: Write for details.
Deadline: May 1, November 1.
Contact: Barbara Motyka.

German Academic Exchange Service
Short-Term Visits to Germany
Research Grants for Ph.D. Candidates and Recent Ph.D.s
950 Third Avenue
19th Floor
New York, NY 10022
(212) 758-3223
FAX (212) 755-5780

Description: Two to six months of grant funding for doctoral candidates and recent Ph.D.s to conduct research/study in Germany; for work in all fields; recipients chosen on the basis of academic achievement.
Restrictions: Maximum eligible age range of 32–35; working knowledge of German required; United States citizenship required; affiliation with United States university required.
$ Given: An unspecified number of grants are awarded annually; each with monthly stipend, travel allowance, and health insurance.
Application Information: Write for details.
Deadline: November 1.
Contact: Barbara Motyka.

German Academic Exchange Service Summer Language Study Grants at Goethe Institutes for Undergraduate and Graduate Students
950 Third Avenue
19th Floor
New York, NY 10022
(212) 758-3223
FAX (212) 755-5780

Description: Grants for two-month intensive German language course at the Goethe Institutes in Germany for undergraduate upperclassmen and graduate students; recipients chosen on the basis of academic achievement.
Restrictions: Basic knowledge of German required, three semesters of college-level German preferred; applicants must be between the ages of 18 and 32; United States citizenship required; full-time enrollment in United States university required; individuals with previous study experience in Germany ineligible; previous language scholarship recipients ineligible; majors in modern languages and literatures ineligible.
$ Given: An unspecified number of grants are awarded annually; each for tuition and fees, plus room and partial board; no travel allowance.
Application Information: Write for details.
Deadline: January 31.
Contact: Barbara Motyka.

Getty Center for the History of Art and the Humanities Getty Center Fellowships
401 Wilshire Boulevard
Suite 400
Santa Monica, CA 90401
(310) 458-9811
FAX (310) 458-6661

Description: Nine-month resident fellowships (October 1–June 30) at the Getty Center for doctoral candidates at dissertation level and recent Ph.D.s rewriting dissertations for publication; for work in art, art history, and interdisciplinary programs in the humanities and social sciences; recipients chosen on the basis of academic achievement, proposed research, and relevance of research topic to the interests and resources of the Getty Center.
Restrictions: N/A.
$ Given: One to two fellowship grants awarded annually; $18,000/year for predoctoral fellowship, $22,000/year for postdoctoral fellowship.
Application Information: Write for details.
Deadline: December 1.
Contact: Dr. Herbert H. Hymans, Department of Visiting Scholars and Conferences.

Harry Frank Guggenheim Foundation Dissertation Fellowships
527 Madison Avenue
New York, NY 10022-5304
(212) 644-4907

Description: Fellowships for doctoral candidates at dissertation level to conduct research on dominance, violence, and aggression; relevant disciplines include psychology, sociology, biology, history, anthropology, and political science; recipients chosen on the basis of academic achievement and quality of proposed research.
Restrictions: Open to all nationalities.
$ Given: Ten grants of $10,000 each are awarded annually.
Application Information: Write for details.
Deadline: February 1.
Contact: Program Officer.

Hagley Museum and Library
Grants-in-Aid
P.O. Box 3630
Wilmington, DE 19807
(302) 658-2400 ext 243

Description: Grants for two- to eight-week short-term research work conducted at the Hagley Museum and Library, using the imprint, manuscript, pictorial, and artifact collections; grants made available to degree candidates, advanced scholars, independent scholars, and professionals for study of American economic and technological history and French 18th-century history; recipients chosen on the basis of proposed research.
Restrictions: N/A.
$ Given: Several grants of up to $1,000/month each are awarded quarterly.
Application Information: Write for details.
Deadline: Applications accepted continuously.
Contact: Dr. Philip B. Scranton.

Hagley Museum and Library
Hagley-Winterthur Research
Fellowships in Arts and
Industries
Center for the History of
Business, Technology, and
Society
P.O. Box 3630
Wilmington, DE 19807
(302) 658-2400 ext 243

Description: One- to three-month short-term research fellowships for work using both the Hagley and the Winterthur collections and resources; fellowships made available to master's and doctoral candidates, as well as to independent scholars studying historical and cultural relationships of economic life and the arts, including design, architecture, crafts, and the fine arts; recipients chosen on the basis of research abilities and project relevance to both libraries' holdings.
Restrictions: N/A.
$ Given: Six fellowships awarded annually; each with $1,000/month stipend, plus seminar participation and use of both research collections.
Application Information: Write for details.
Deadline: November 15.

Harvard University
Center for International and
Area Studies Fellowships
Program
Center for International
Affairs
420 Coolidge Hall
1737 Cambridge Street
Cambridge, MA 02138
(617) 495-2137

Description: Grants for doctoral candidates at dissertation level and recent Ph.D.s to conduct research in several fields, including area and cultural studies, demography and population studies, economics, geography, history, languages, literatures and linguistics, political science and public policy, psychology, sociology, anthropology, archaeology, law, international affairs, and interdisciplinary programs in the humanities and social sciences; recipients chosen on the basis of academic achievement and proposed research.
Restrictions: Young applicants preferred; preference to individuals pursuing careers involving social science disciplines as relevant to specific geographic areas.
$ Given: A few grants are awarded annually; $22,000–$25,000 stipend for two years of predoctoral research, $30,000–$35,000 stipend for two years of postdoctoral research, plus travel and research allowance.

Application Information: Write for details.
Deadline: October 15.
Contact: Marisa Murtagh, Fellowship Coordinator.

Herb Society of America
Research and Education Grants
9019 Kirtland Chardon Road
Kirtland, OH 44094
(216) 256-0514

Description: Grants to graduate students for study/research in horticulture, science, literature, art, and economics—as related to herbs; recipients chosen on the basis of proposed research, which may be scientific or academic; research period may be up to one year.
Restrictions: N/A.
$ Given: One to two grants totaling $5,000 are awarded annually.
Application Information: Write for details.
Deadline: January 31.
Contact: Grants Administrator.

Herbert Hoover
Presidential Library
Association
Herbert Hoover Travel Grant
Competition
P.O. Box 696
West Branch, IA 52358
(319) 643-5327

Description: Travel grants to support scholarly use of the Herbert Hoover Presidential Library in West Branch, Iowa.
Restrictions: N/A.
$ Given: Several grants of $500–$1,500 each are awarded annually.
Application Information: Write for details.
Deadline: March 1.
Contact: Patricia Hand, Office Manager.

Hudson Institute
Herman Kahn Fellowship
5395 Emerson Way
P.O. Box 26919
Indianapolis, IN 46226-0919
(317) 545-1000

Description: Fellowships for one year of research/study in Indianapolis or Washington, DC, for doctoral candidates at dissertation level; relevant topics include education, economics, political economy, national security, policy issues, and political theory; recipients chosen on the basis of academic achievement, proposed research, and faculty recommendation.
Restrictions: United States citizenship required.
$ Given: Up to three fellowships awarded annually; each for $18,000 plus travel expenses.
Application Information: Write for details.
Deadline: April 15.
Contact: Director of Programs.

Huntington Library and Art
Gallery
W.M. Keck Foundation
Fellowship for Young Scholars
1151 Oxford Road
San Marino, CA 91108
(818) 405-2194

Description: Approximately ten-month residential research fellowships for graduate and postdoctoral scholars in British and American history, literature, and art; tenable at the Huntington Library.
Restrictions: N/A.
$ Given: A few fellowships awarded annually; each with $2,300/month stipend.

Application Information: Write for application form after October 1.
Deadline: December 15.
Contact: Robert C. Ritchie, Chairman, Committee on Awards.

Huntington Library and Art Gallery
Research Awards
1151 Oxford Road
San Marino, CA 91108
(818) 405-2116

Description: Residential fellowships at the Huntington Library for doctoral candidates in art and art history, geography, historic preservation and museum studies, history, languages, literatures and linguistics, liberal studies, library science, medieval and Renaissance studies, philosophy, and religion; most fellowships for one- to six-month period, longer tenures by special arrangement; recipients chosen on the basis of the value of proposed project, ability of researcher, and utilization of Huntington collections.
Restrictions: N/A.
$ Given: An unspecified number of fellowships awarded annually; each with $1,800/month stipend.
Application Information: Write for application form after October 1.
Deadline: December 15.
Contact: Robert C. Ritchie, Head of Research.

Institute for European History
Research Fellowships
Alte Universitaetsstrasse 19
Mainz 1
D–6500
Germany
(061) 31 39 93 60

Description: Residential fellowships at the Institute for doctoral candidates and postdoctoral scholars studying the history of Europe and European religion from the 16th to the 20th century; recipients chosen on the basis of academic achievement and proposed research.
Restrictions: Open to all nationalities; applicants must have thorough command of German.
$ Given: Twenty fellowships of DM13,080–DM17,280 each are awarded annually.
Application Information: Write for details.
Deadline: February, June, October.
Contact: For European History program, contact Professor Dr. Karl Otmar Freiherr von Aretin, (06131) 226143; for History of European Religion program, contact Professor Dr. Peter Manns, (06131) 224870.

Institute of Food Technologists
Graduate Fellowships
Scholarship Department
221 North LaSalle Street
Chicago, IL 60601
(312) 782-8424

Description: Fellowships for graduate students in fields of food science and technology; tenable at accredited institutions in the United States and Canada; recipients chosen on the basis of academic achievement.
Restrictions: Applicants must show interest/ability in research; students in such disciplines as genetics, nutrition, microbiology, and biochemistry are ineligible.
$ Given: 27 fellowships for $1,000–$10,000 each are awarded annually; renewable.

Application Information: Application forms are available from school department heads or IFT; individual application must be submitted to school department head.
Deadline: February 1.
Contact: Fellowship Administrator.

**Institute of International
Education
Colombian Government
Study and Research Grants**
U.S. Student Programs
Division
809 United Nations Plaza
New York, NY 10017-3580
(212) 984-5330

Description: Grants for B.S./B.A. holders to pursue up to two years of study/research at Colombian Universities; relevant disciplines include agriculture, biology, business administration, economics, chemistry, engineering, education, health services administration, economics, geography, history, Latin American literature, law, linguistics, political science, physics, regulatory development, public health, and remote sensing interpretation.
Restrictions: United States citizenship required.
$ Given: An unspecified number of grants awarded annually; each for modest monthly stipend, plus tuition and fees, health insurance, book/materials allowance, and one-way return airfare upon completion of study.
Application Information: Write for details.
Deadline: October 31.

**Institute of International
Education
Fulbright Fixed
Sum–Bulgarian Government
Grants**
U.S. Student Programs
Division
809 United Nations Plaza
New York, NY 10017-3580
(212) 984-5330

Description: Grants for B.A./B.S. holders in the humanities, physical sciences, and social sciences; for a six- to nine-month residency/exchange in Bulgaria (September–June).
Restrictions: Knowledge of Bulgarian language required; United States citizenship required; applicants must meet all Fulbright eligibility requirements.
$ Given: An unspecified number of grants awarded annually; Bulgarian government funds stipend, housing, and health/accident insurance; Fulbright provides fixed sum for round-trip transportation plus additional monthly stipend.
Application Information: Write for details.
Deadline: October 31.
Contact: United States Student Program Division.

**Institute of International
Education
Fulbright Fixed Sum–Syrian
Government Grants**
U.S. Student Programs
Division
809 United Nations Plaza
New York, NY 10017-3580
(212) 984-5330

Description: Grants for B.A./B.S. holders in Arabic language and culture, history, and geography; for study at the University of Damascus.
Restrictions: Applicants studying modern social sciences not eligible; minimum two years of Arabic language study or demonstrated proficiency required; United States citizenship required; applicants must meet all Fulbright funding.
$ Given: An unspecified number of grants awarded an-

nually; monthly stipend, tuition, and health insurance, supplemented by Fulbright funding.
Application Information: Write for details.
Deadline: October 31.
Contact: Campus Fulbright program advisor.

Institute of International Education Fulbright–Spanish Government Grants
U.S. Student Programs Division
809 United Nations Plaza
New York, NY 10017-3580
(212) 984-5330

Description: Grants for B.A./B.S. holders studying anthropology, archaeology, art history, ceramics, philology, economics, Hispano-American studies, history, law, Mediterranean studies, musicology, philosophy, political science, sociology, and Spanish language and literature; for study at a Spanish university.
Restrictions: Fluency in Spanish (written and spoken) required; United States citizenship required; applicants must meet all Fulbright eligibility requirements.
$ Given: An unspecified number of grants awarded annually; Spanish government funds tuition and stipend; Fulbright funds round-trip transportation, and expense allowance.
Application Information: Write for details.
Deadline: October 31.

Institute of International Education Fulbright Travel–Iceland Government Grants
U.S. Student Programs Division
809 United Nations Plaza
New York, NY 10017-3580
(212) 984-5330

Description: Grants for B.A./B.S. holders studying Icelandic language, literature, and history; for eight months of advanced study at the University of Iceland in Reykjavik.
Restrictions: Knowledge of Icelandic, Old Norse, or other Scandinavian language required for language/literature study; United States citizenship required; applicants must meet all Fulbright eligibility requirements .
$ Given: An unspecified number of grants awarded annually; cash stipend plus tuition.
Application Information: Write for details.
Deadline: October 31.

Institute of International Education Germanistic Society of America Fellowships
U.S. Student Programs Division
809 United Nations Plaza
New York, NY 10017-3580
(212) 984-5330

Description: Fellowships for master's degree holders and some B.A./B.S. holders studying German language and literature, art history, history, economics, philosophy, international law, political science, and public affairs; for one academic year of study in Germany.
Restrictions: United States citizenship required; applicants must meet all Fulbright eligibility requirements.
$ Given: Up to eight fellowships awarded annually; each for $10,000 plus consideration for a Fulbright Travel Grant.
Application Information: Write for details.
Deadline: October 31.

Institute of International Education Lusk Memorial Fellowships
U.S. Student Programs Division
809 United Nations Plaza
New York, NY 10017-3580
(212) 984-5330

Description: Grants for individuals in the creative and performing arts; for one academic year of study in the United Kingdom and Italy.
Restrictions: Written and spoken proficiency in Italian required for study in Italy; applicants must have completed at least four years of professional study; United States citizenship required.
$ Given: An unspecified number of grants awarded annually; maintenance allowance, health/accident insurance, and round-trip travel allowance.
Application Information: Write for details.
Deadline: October 31.

Institute of International Education Study and Research Grants for United States Citizens
U.S. Student Programs Division
809 United Nations Plaza
New York, NY 10017-3580
(212) 984-5330

Description: Grants to support study and research in all fields, as well as professional training in the creative and performing arts; tenable at institutions of higher learning outside of the United States for one year; list of participating countries in any given year may be obtained from IIE.
Restrictions: Open to United States citizens with B.A. or equivalent; acceptable plan of study and proficiency in host country's language required.
$ Given: A variable number of grants awarded annually; covers international transportation, language or orientation course (where appropriate), tuition, book and maintenance allowances, and health and accident insurance.
Application Information: If currently enrolled in a college or university, apply to the campus Fulbright Program Advisor; applications also available from IIE.
Deadline: October 31.

Institute of World Affairs International Affairs Seminars
375 Twin Lakes Road
Salisbury, CT 06068
(203) 824-5135
FAX (203) 824-7884

Description: Partial scholarships for master's and doctoral candidates to attend IWA summer seminars on topics of current and continuing international importance; funding made available to students of political science, economics, history, and finance; recipients chosen on the basis of financial need.
Restrictions: N/A.
$ Given: An unspecified number of partial scholarships are awarded annually.
Application Information: Write for details.
Deadline: Applications accepted continuously.
Contact: Bradford P. Johnson, Director.

International Foundation of Employee Benefit Systems Graduate Research Grants
18700 West Bluemound Road
P.O. Box 69
Brookfield, WI 53008-0069
(414) 786-6700

Description: Grants to support doctoral candidates conducting research on labor studies and employee benefit topics, such as health-care benefits, retirement, and income security; recipients chosen on the basis of proposed original research.
Restrictions: United States citizenship required.
$ Given: Five to seven grants of up to $5,000 each are awarded annually.
Application Information: Include 20-page proposal (or shorter), curriculum vitae, and two letters of recommendation (one from thesis/dissertation advisor) .
Deadline: Applications accepted continuously.
Contact: Director of Research.

International Research and Exchanges Board
IREX Developmental Fellowships
1616 H Street, N.W.
Washington, DC 20006
(202) 628-8188

Description: Individually designed fellowships for doctoral scholars to study within the United States in preparation for eventual field research in Eastern Europe; relevant disciplines include musicology, demography, economics, geography, political science, psychology, sociology, anthropology, archaeology, business, law, and international affairs; recipients chosen on the basis of proposed research.
Restrictions: United States citizenship required.
$ Given: An unspecified number of fellowships awarded annually; each for academic tuition, language training, stipend, or research allowance.
Application Information: Write for details.
Deadline: February 15.
Contact: Stan Zylowski, Program Officer.

International Research and Exchanges Board
IREX Research Exchange Program with Mongolia
1616 H Street, N.W.
Washington, DC 20006
(202) 628-8188

Description: Two- to ten-month exchange program for doctoral candidates to study in Mongolia; relevant disciplines include the humanities, social sciences, and natural sciences; recipients chosen on the basis of proposed research.
Restrictions: Command of host country's language required; United States citizenship required.
$ Given: An unspecified number of fellowships awarded annually; varying amounts.
Application Information: Write for details.
Deadline: October 15.
Contact: Cynthia Graves, Program Officer.

**International Research and Exchanges Board
IREX United States–Republics of the Former USSR Summer Exchange of Language Teachers**
1616 H Street, N.W.
Washington, DC 20006
(202) 628-8188

Description: Seven-week exchange program for language teachers and exceptional graduate students to study the Russian language at Moscow State University in Russia; recipients chosen on the basis of language ability.
Restrictions: Applicants must be employed as teachers of Russian at college level, and must have completed at least four years of college-level Russian courses and have at least two years of teaching experience; United States citizenship required.
$ Given: Twenty to twenty-five grants awarded annually; each for tuition, housing, stipend, travel, and other expenses.
Application Information: Write for details.
Deadline: December 15.
Contact: Myra Lee, Program Officer.

**Richard D. Irwin Foundation
Richard D. Irwin Doctoral Fellowships**
1333 Burr Ridge Pkwy
Burr Ridge, IL 60521

Description: One-year fellowships for doctoral candidates at dissertation level in business administration and economics; tenable at United States and Canadian institutions; preference to applicants with plans to teach business and/or economics.
Restrictions: Applicants must have completed all coursework and passed oral exams for degree.
$ Given: Twenty fellowships awarded annually; each with $2,000–$2,500 stipend.
Application Information: Applicants must be nominated by dean of school with accredited doctoral program.
Deadline: February 15.
Contact: Gail Ryba, Agent.

**Japan Foundation
Dissertation Fellowships**
142 West 57th Street
6th Floor
New York, NY 10019
(212) 949-6360

Description: Fellowships for two to 14 months of dissertation research in Japan; funding made available to doctoral candidates at dissertation level in the humanities and social sciences, with emphasis on political science, law, economics, business, and journalism—as related to Japan; recipients chosen on the basis of academic achievement and quality of proposed research.
Restrictions: Applicants must be proficient in Japanese; no funding for Japanese language study; recipients may not hold other fellowships concurrently.
$ Given: Thirteen fellowships awarded annually; each for ¥310,000 plus further allowances including one round-trip air ticket.
Application Information: Write for details.
Deadline: November 1.

Japan Ministry of Education, Science, and Culture Japanese Government (Monbusho) Scholarship Program
2-2 Kasumigaseki, 3-chome
Chiyoda-ku
Tokyo 100
Japan
03-581-4211

Description: Eighteen-month to two-year scholarships for non-Japanese graduate students to study at Japanese universities and research institutes; Research Students Program is specifically designed for graduate students (undergraduate program also available) in the humanities, social sciences, music, fine arts, and natural sciences; open to citiz ens of countries with educational exchange agreements with Japan.
Restrictions: Language proficiency required (12- to 18-month language training program required if language skills deemed insufficient); applicants must be under age 35.
$ Given: An unspecified number of scholarships awarded annually; each to cover monthly stipend, airfare, tuition, and expense allowance.
Application Information: For further information, contact Japanese Embassy or Consulate.
Deadlines: June 15, September 30.
Contact: Student Exchange Division.

Japanese American Citizens League National Scholarship and Student Aid Program
1765 Sutter Street
San Francisco, CA 94115
(415) 921-5225

Description: Scholarships for undergraduate and graduate students, as well as for individuals involved in performing and creative arts projects reflecting the Japanese American experience and culture.
Restrictions: Applicants must be of Japanese descent; membership in Japanese American Citizens League (or having parent who is member) preferred; United States citizenship required.
$ Given: An unspecified number of scholarships awarded annually; varying amounts.
Application Information: Application forms are available from local JACL chapters in September; write national office for list of local and regional chapters.
Deadline: April 1.

Lyndon Baines Johnson Foundation Grants-in-Aid of Research
2313 Red River Street
Austin, TX 78705
(512) 478-7829

Description: Grants for individuals to conduct research at the LBJ Library; relevant fields include communications, economics, environmental policy and resource management, history, political science, and public policy; recipients chosen on the proposed research.
Restrictions: N/A.
$ Given: A few grants awarded annually; each for $75/day plus travel costs.
Application Information: Contact the Chief Archivist regarding the availability of proposed material before applying.
Deadlines: January 31, July 31.
Contact: Assistant Executive Director.

**Kosciuszko Foundation
Graduate Studies and
Research in Poland Program**
15 East 65th Street
New York, NY 10021-6595
(212) 628-4552
FAX (212) 628-4552

Description: Grants to allow Americans to pursue
graduate and postgraduate studies in Poland in any subject.
Restrictions: Applicants must have strong command of
Polish language; United States citizenship required; Polish studies background required.
$ Given: An unspecified number of grants awarded an-
nually; each for tuition, room, board, and monthly
stipend for living expenses.
Application Information: Write for details.
Deadline: January 15.
Contact: Grants Office.

**Kosciuszko Foundation
Year Abroad at the
University of Cracow Program**
15 East 65th Street
New York, NY 10021-6595
(212) 628-4552
FAX (212) 628-4552

Description: Grants to support participation in one-year
program of academic study at the University of Cracow
(Jagiellonian University) in Poland; funding made available to undergraduate upperclassmen and graduate
students in the fields of Polish language, literature, history, and culture.
Restrictions: Applicants must have Polish background;
United States or Canadian citizenship required.
$ Given: An unspecified number of grants awarded
annually; each for tuition, housing, and monthly food/ex-
pense allowance; round-trip travel not covered.
Application Information: Write for details.
Deadline: November 15.
Contact: Grants Office.

**Samuel H. Kress Foundation
Art Conservation Advanced
Training Fellowships**
174 East 80th Street
New York, NY 10021
(212) 861-4993

Description: One-year fellowships in special areas of
fine arts conservation; tenable at appropriate institutions.
Restrictions: Applicants must have completed initial
conservation training; United States citizenship or enrollment in United States university required .
$ Given: Ten to twenty fellowships of $1,000–$10,000
each are awarded annually.
Application Information: Write for details.
Deadline: February 28.
Contact: Lisa Ackerman, Chief Administrative Officer.

**Samuel H. Kress Foundation
Art History Travel Fellowships**
174 East 80th Street
New York, NY 10021
(212) 861-4993

Description: Fellowships for doctoral candidates at dissertation level in art history to travel for the purpose of
viewing original materials/works; recipients chosen on
the basis of academic achievement, financial need, and
necessity of travel.
Restrictions: United States citizenship or enrollment in
United States university required.
$ Given: Fifteen to twenty fellowships awarded
annually; varying amounts.

Application Information: Applicants must be nominated by their art history departments.
Deadline: November 30.
Contact: Lisa Ackerman, Chief Administrative Officer.

Samuel H. Kress Foundation Dissertation Fellowship
174 East 80th Street
New York, NY 10021
(212) 861-4993

Description: Grants to support final preparation of doctoral dissertations in art history.
Restrictions: United States citizenship or enrollment in United States university required.
$ Given: Ten fellowships of $10,000 each are awarded annually.
Application Information: Applicants must be nominated by their art history departments.
Deadline: March 31.

Samuel H. Kress Foundation Predoctoral Fellowships for Research in Art History
174 East 80th Street
New York, NY 10021
(212) 861-4993

Description: Two-year fellowships for dissertation research in art history at Institutes in Florence, Jerusalem, Leiden, London, Munich, Nicosea, Paris, Rome, or Zurich; recipients chosen on the basis of academic achievement, financial need, and proposed research .
Restrictions: Affiliation with United States university required.
$ Given: Four fellowships of $15,000 are awarded annually.
Application Information: Write for details; applicants must be nominated by their department, one nomination per department.
Deadline: November 30.
Contact: Lisa Ackerman, Chief Administrative Officer.

Landscape Architecture Foundation
CLASS Fund Scholarships
4401 Connecticut Avenue, N.W.
5th Floor
Washington, DC 20008
(202) 686-0068

Description: Scholarships for undergraduate and graduate students in landscape architecture and ornamental horticulture; recipients chosen on the basis of financial need, commitment to and promise in profession, and plans for advanced study.
Restrictions: Applicants must be Southern California residents enrolled in programs for landscape architecture and ornamental horticulture.
$ Given: An unspecified number of scholarships awarded annually; varying amounts.
Application Information: Write for details.
Deadline: April 3.
Contact: David Bohardt, Acting Executive Director.

Landscape Architecture Foundation
Grace and Robert Fraser Landscape Heritage Fund Award
4401 Connecticut Avenue, N.W.
5th Floor
Washington, DC 20008
(202) 686-0068

Description: Award for new contribution to the field of landscape architecture; established professionals and outstanding students are eligible for consideration.
Restrictions: Applicants must be landscape architecture scholars pursuing research on new approaches to landscape architecture through horticulture.
$ Given: One award of $500 made annually.
Application Information: Write for details.
Deadline: May 4.
Contact: David Bohardt, Acting Executive Director.

Landscape Architecture Foundation
Edith H. Henderson Scholarship
4401 Connecticut Avenue, N.W.
5th Floor
Washington, DC 20008
(202) 686-0068

Description: Scholarship for undergraduate seniors and graduate students in landscape architecture; recipients chosen on the basis of academic achievement and commitment to developing practical client communication skills.
Restrictions: Limited to women applicants enrolled at the University of Georgia.
Given: One scholarship of $1,000 awarded annually.
Application Information: Personal essay addressing the importance of communication skills required for application.
Deadline: May 4.
Contact: David Bohardt, Acting Executive Director.

Landscape Architecture Foundation
LANDCADD Scholarship
4401 Connecticut Avenue, N.W.
5th Floor
Washington, DC 20008
(202) 686-0068

Description: Scholarship for undergraduate and graduate students in landscape architecture; recipients chosen on the basis of academic achievement and career plans for utilization of computer-aided design, video imaging, and/or telecommunications.
Restrictions: N/A.
$ Given: One scholarship awarded annually; for $500 in cash, plus $500-value LANDCADD software donated to winner's institution.
Application Information: Essay required.
Deadline: May 4.
Contact: David Bohardt, Acting Executive Director.

Landscape Architecture Foundation
Raymond E. Page Scholarships
4401 Connecticut Avenue, N.W.
5th Floor
Washington, DC 20008
(202) 686-0068

Description: Scholarships for undergraduate and graduate students in landscape architecture; recipients chosen on the basis of financial need alone.
Restrictions: N/A.
$ Given: Two scholarships of $500 each awarded annually.
Application Information: Write for details.
Deadline: May 4.
Contact: David Bohardt, Acting Executive Director.

Landscape Architecture Foundation Rain Bird Company Scholarship
4401 Connecticut Avenue, N.W.
5th Floor
Washington, DC 20008
(202) 686-0068

Description: Scholarship for undergraduate and graduate students in landscape architecture; recipients chosen on the basis of professional commitment as exemplified by extracurricular activities and academic achievements.
Restrictions: N/A.
$ Given: One scholarship of $1,000 awarded annually.
Application Information: Write for details.
Deadline: May 4.
Contact: David Bohardt, Acting Executive Director.

Landscape Architecture Foundation Student Research Grants
4401 Connecticut Avenue, N.W.
5th Floor
Washington, DC 20008
(202) 686-0068

Description: Grants for undergraduate and graduate students in landscape architecture; to support research projects; recipients chosen on the basis of research proposals and budgets.
Restrictions: N/A.
$ Given: Up to two grants awarded annually; each for $1,000.
Application Information: Write for details.
Deadline: May 4.
Contact: David Bohardt, Acting Executive Director.

Landscape Architecture Foundation Lester Walls III Endowment Scholarship
4401 Connecticut Avenue, N.W.
5th Floor
Washington, DC 20008
(202) 686-0068

Description: Scholarship for undergraduate and graduate students in landscape architecture; recipients chosen on the basis of personal disability or study of barrier-free design.
Restrictions: Preference for applicants who are visually handicapped, hearing impaired, or physically handicapped; no group projects.
$ Given: One scholarship for $500 awarded annually.
Application Information: Write for details.
Deadline: May 4.
Contact: David Bohardt, Acting Executive Director.

Landscape Architecture Foundation Harriet Barnhart Wimmer Scholarship
4401 Connecticut Avenue, N.W.
5th Floor
Washington, DC 20008
(202) 686-0068

Description: Scholarship to support final year of undergraduate or graduate studies in landscape architecture; recipients chosen on the basis of design excellence and environmental sensitivity of work submitted for consideration.
Restrictions: Limited to women applicants; group projects ineligible.
$ Given: One scholarship of $500 awarded annually.
Application Information: Write for details; assembled materials should be sent to Harriet Barnhart Wimmer Scholarship, c/o Wimmer, Yamada & Associates, 516 Fifth Avenue, San Diego, CA 92101, (619) 232-4004.
Deadline: May 4.
Contact: David Bohardt, Acting Executive Director.

L.S.B. Leakey Foundation Franklin Mosher Baldwin Memorial Fellowships
77 Jack London Square
Suite M
Oakland, CA 94607-3750
(510) 834-3636
FAX (510) 834-3640

Description: Fellowship for master's candidates in anthropology; tenable at any qualified institution in the world.
Restrictions: Limited to citizens of African nations.
$ Given: One fellowship of up to $8,500 awarded annually for nontuition expenses.
Application Information: Write for details.
Deadline: January 2.
Contact: D. Karla Savage, Ph.D., Program and Grants Officer.

L.S.B. Leakey Foundation Foraging Peoples Study Fellowships
77 Jack London Square
Suite M
Oakland, CA 94607-3750
(510) 834-3636
FAX (510) 834-3640

Description: Fellowship for doctoral candidates studying contemporary foraging peoples; recipients chosen on the basis of proposed research; preference for urgent research projects that might not ordinarily be funded by other agencies.
Restrictions: N/A.
$ Given: One occasional fellowship of up to $20,000 awarded for one to two years of field expenses.
Application Information: Write for details.
Deadlines: Preapplication and curriculum vitae due October 15; formal application due January 2.
Contact: D. Karla Savage, Ph.D., Program and Grants Officer.

L.S.B. Leakey Foundation General Grants
77 Jack London Square
Suite M
Oakland, CA 94607-3750
(510) 834-3636
FAX (510) 834-3640

Description: Fellowship for professional and doctoral candidates, if supported by faculty advisors, for the study of human evolution; priority to new projects in exploratory phases and novel opportunities to establish projects.
Restrictions: N/A.
$ Given: An unspecified number of grants for $3,000–$7,000 each are awarded annually.
Application Information: Write for details.
Deadlines: January 2, August 15.
Contact: D. Karla Savage, Ph.D., Program and Grants Officer.

Library and Information Technology Association Scholarship in Library and Information Technology
50 East Huron Street
Chicago, IL 60611
(312) 270-4270

Description: Scholarship for master's candidates in library science; recipients chosen on the basis of academic achievement, leadership qualities, commitment to career in library automation, and prior experience with library automation; financial need considered.
Restrictions: N/A.
$ Given: One scholarship of $2,500 is awarded annually.
Application Information: Write for details.
Deadline: April 1.
Contact: Nancy H. Evans, Program Officer

The Library Company of Philadelphia American History and Culture Research Fellowships
1314 Locust Street
Philadelphia, PA 19107
(215) 546-3181

Description: Residential research fellowships at the Library Company of Philadelphia for doctoral candidates and postdoctoral scholars in most disciplines as related to the history and culture of 18th- to 19th-century America; tenable for one or more months; recipients chosen on the basis of proposed research.
Restrictions: N/A.
$ Given: An unspecified number of fellowships awarded annually; each with $1,350/month stipend.
Application Information: Write for details.
Deadline: February 1.
Contact: James Green, Curator.

Charles A. Lindbergh Fund Lindbergh Grants Program
708 South 3rd Street
Suite 110
Minneapolis, MN 55415
(612) 338-1703
FAX (612) 338-6826

Description: Grants for individuals to conduct research into the balance of technology and the human/natural environment; relevant fields include humanities, biomedical research, conservation of natural resources, waste disposal management, wildlife preservation, intercultural communications, aviation, aeronautics, agriculture, astronautics, adaptive technology, the arts, health and population studies, and oceanography.
Restrictions: Open to all nationalities.
$ Given: Twenty or more grants of up to $10,580 each are awarded annually.
Application Information: Write for details.
Deadline: June 14.
Contact: Marlene K. White, Grants Coordinator.

Henry Luce Foundation Luce Scholars Program
111 West 50th Street
Rm. 3710
New York, NY 10020
(212) 489-7700

Description: Internship programs for graduate students in all disciplines relevant to Asian area and cultural studies to work in chosen disciplines in East and Southeast Asia; recipients chosen on the basis of academic achievement and leadership potential.
Restrictions: Maximum age 29; not intended for specialists in Asian affairs; United States citizenship required.
$ Given: Fifteen grants of $1,400–$1,700 each awarded annually.
Application Information: Applicants must be nominated by one of 67 participating colleges or universities.
Deadline: Early December.
Contact: Marlene K. White, Grants Coordinator.

Medical Library Association MLA Doctoral Fellowships
North Michigan Avenue
Suite 300
Chicago, IL 60602
(312) 419-9094

Description: One-year fellowships for doctoral candidates in health sciences librarianship, with emphasis on biomedical and health-related information science; funding intended to support research or travel, not tuition; recipients chosen on the basis of academic achievement.
Restrictions: Applicants must hold master's degrees

from ALA-accredited schools; United States or Canadian citizenship required.
$ Given: One fellowship for $1,000 is awarded annually; non-renewable.
Application Information: Write for details.
Deadline: February 1.
Contact: Assistant to the Director of Professional Development.

Medical Library Association
MLA Graduate Scholarships
6 North Michigan Avenue
Suite 300
Chicago, IL 60602
(312) 419-9094

Description: Scholarships for master's candidates in medical librarianship; recipients chosen on the basis of academic achievement and professional potential.
Restrictions: Applicants must be entering an ALA-accredited school or have at least one-half the academic requirements yet to complete during the scholarship year; United States or Canadian citizenship required.
$ Given: One scholarship for $2,000 is awarded annually.
Application Information: Write for details.
Deadline: February 1.
Contact: Assistant to the Director of Professional Development.

Medical Library Association
MLA Graduate Scholarships
for Minority Students
6 North Michigan Avenue
Suite 300
Chicago, IL 60602
(312) 419-9094

Description: Scholarships for master's candidates in health sciences librarianship; recipients chosen on the basis of academic achievement and professional potential.
Restrictions: Limited to minority group applicants only; applicants must be entering an ALA-accredited school or have at least one-half the academic requirements yet to complete during the scholarship year; United States or Canadian citizenship required.
$ Given: One scholarship for $2,000 is awarded annually.
Application Information: Write for details.
Deadline: February 1.
Contact: Assistant to the Director of Professional Development.

Memorial Foundation for
Jewish Culture
International Doctoral
Scholarship for Jewish Studies
15 East 26th Street
Room 1901
New York, NY 10010
(212) 679-4074

Description: Scholarships for doctoral candidates in Jewish studies; recipients chosen on the basis of academic achievement, financial need, and proposed research.
Restrictions: N/A.
$ Given: An unspecified number of scholarships awarded annually; each for $1,000–$4,000 per year; renewable for up to 4 years.

Application Information: Submit written request for application form; references required.
Deadline: October 31.
Contact: Executive Vice President.

**Metropolitan Museum of Art
Classical Fellowship**
Office of Academic Programs
Fifth Avenue and 82nd Street
New York, NY 10028
(212) 570-3710

Description: Fellowship for doctoral students studying Greek and Roman art at United States universities, for thesis-related work using the Metropolitan's Department of Greek and Roman Art resources; recipients chosen on the basis of academic achievement and proposed thesis topic.
Restrictions: Applicant's thesis topic must have been accepted by thesis advisor; fellowship not for exhibition projects.
$ Given: One fellowship awarded annually; $25,000 for senior fellow, $15,000 for predoctoral fellow, plus $2,500 travel allowance.
Application Information: Write for details.
Deadline: November 12.
Contact: Pia Quintano, Fellowships Coordinator.

**Metropolitan Museum of Art
Chester Dale Fellowships**
Office of Academic Programs
Fifth Avenue and 82nd Street
New York, NY 10028
(212) 570-3710

Description: Three-month to one-year residential fellowships for doctoral students studying fine art of the Western world, for research using the Metropolitan's resources; recipients chosen on the basis of academic achievement and proposed research.
Restrictions: Preferred maximum age 40; United States citizenship preferred; fellowships not for exhibition projects.
$ Given: An unspecified number of fellowships awarded annually; $25,000 for senior fellow, $15,000 for predoctoral fellow, plus $2,500 travel allowance.
Application Information: Write for details.
Deadline: November 12.
Contact: Pia Quintano, Fellowships Coordinator.

**Metropolitan Museum of Art
Andrew W. Mellon
Fellowships**
Office of Academic Programs
Fifth Avenue and 82nd Street
New York, NY 10028
(212) 570-3710

Description: Residential fellowships for doctoral students in art history, for research using the Metropolitan's collections; maximum one-year fellowship period; recipients chosen on the basis of academic achievement and proposed research.
Restrictions: Fellowships not for exhibition projects.
$ Given: An unspecified number of fellowships awarded annually; $25,000 for senior fellow, $15,000 for predoctoral fellow, plus $2,500 travel allowance.
Application Information: Write for details.
Deadline: November 12.
Contact: Pia Quintano, Fellowships Coordinator.

Metropolitan Museum of Art
Andrew W. Mellon
Fellowships in Conservation
Office of Academic Programs
Fifth Avenue and 82nd Street
New York, NY 10028
(212) 570-3710

Description: One-year residential fellowships for doctoral students in fine arts conservation, for work in specific departments of the Metropolitan, including Paintings Conservation, Objects Conservation, Musical Instruments, Arms and Armor, Paper Conservation, Costume Institute, Textile Conservation, and Asian Art Conservation; recipients chosen on the basis of training and proposed research.
Restrictions: Applicants must be planning employment in conservation.
$ Given: An unspecified number of fellowships awarded annually; stipends commensurate with training and experience; renewable for two more years.
Application Information: Write for details.
Deadline: January 12.
Contact: Pia Quintano, Fellowships Coordinator.

Metropolitan Museum of Art
J. Clawson Mills Scholarships
Office of Academic Programs
Fifth Avenue and 82nd Street
New York, NY 10028
(212) 570-3710

Description: One-year residential scholarships for doctoral students in fine arts, for study/research using the Metropolitan's collections; recipients chosen on the basis of academic achievement and proposed research.
Restrictions: N/A.
$ Given: An unspecified number of scholarships awarded annually; $25,000 for senior fellow; $15,000 for predoctoral fellow, plus $2,500 travel allowance.
Application Information: Write for details.
Deadline: November 12.
Contact: Pia Quintano, Fellowships Coordinator.

Metropolitan Museum of Art
Theodore Rousseau
Scholarships
Office of Academic Programs
Fifth Avenue and 82nd Street
New York, NY 10028
(212) 570-3710

Description: Fellowships for master's and doctoral candidates in art history, for study in Europe; intended to allow recipients first-hand examination of painting in major European collections.
Restrictions: Applicants must have completed at least one year of graduate training; applicants should be planning careers as museum curators of painting.
$ Given: An unspecified number of fellowships awarded annually; $25,000 for senior fellow; $15,000 for predoctoral fellow, plus $2,500 travel allowance.
Application Information: Write for details.
Deadline: November 12.
Contact: Pia Quintano, Fellowships Coordinator.

**Metropolitan Museum of Art
Norbert Schimmel
Fellowships for
Mediterranean Art and
Archaeology**
Office of Academic Programs
Fifth Avenue and 82nd Street
New York, NY 10028
(212) 570-3710

Description: Residential fellowships for doctoral candidates studying Near Eastern art and archaeology, Greek art, and/or Roman art at United States universities, for thesis-related research using the Metropolitan's art collection; recipients chosen on the basis of academic achievement, financial need, and proposed research.
Restrictions: N/A.
$ Given: One fellowship awarded annually; $25,000 for senior fellow, $15,000 for predoctoral fellow; plus $2,500 travel allowance.
Application Information: Write for details.
Deadline: November 2.
Contact: Pia Quintano, Fellowships Coordinator.

**Metropolitan Museum of Art
Summer Graduate Internships**
Office of Academic Programs
Fifth Avenue and 82nd Street
New York, NY 10028
(212) 879-5500
ext. 3306

Description: Nine-week internships to provide master's and doctoral candidates in museum studies with practical experience in various museum departments; recipients chosen on the basis of academic achievement and future career goals.
Restrictions: Applicants must have completed at least one year of museum studies and have strong art history background.
$ Given: An unspecified number of internships awarded annually; each with $2,500 honorarium.
Application Information: Write for details.
Deadline: January 28.
Contact: Coordinator of Internships

**Metropolitan Museum of Art
Polaire Weissman Fund
Fellowships**
Office of Academic Programs
Fifth Avenue and 82nd Street
New York, NY 10028
(212) 570-3710

Description: Fellowships for graduate students in fine arts and costume history, to provide experience with costume history and conservation at the Metropolitan Museum; preference for those interested in museum and teaching careers in these areas; fellowships offered in alternate years only.
Restrictions: N/A.
$ Given: An unspecified number of internships awarded in alternate years; $25,000 for senior fellow; $15,000 for predoctoral fellow; plus $2,500 travel allowance.
Application Information: Fellowships offered in academic years 92/93, 94/95, etc..
Deadline: November 12.
Contact: Pia Quintano, Fellowships Coordinator.

Metropolitan Museum of Art
Jane and Morgan Whitney
Fellowships
Office of Academic Programs
Fifth Avenue and 82nd Street
New York, NY 10028
(212) 570-3710

Description: One-year fellowships for graduate students in fine arts, for study/research in fields related to Metropolitan's collections; preference for decorative arts.
Restrictions: Applicants under age 40 preferred.
$ Given: An unspecified number of internships awarded annually; $25,000 for senior fellow; $15,000 for predoctoral fellow; plus $2,500 travel allowance; renewable.
Application Information: Write for details.
Deadline: November 12.
Contact: Pia Quintano, Fellowships Coordinator.

National Air and Space
Museum
Guggenheim Fellowships
6th and Independence
Avenue, S.W.
Washington, DC 20560
(202) 357-1529

Description: One-year residential fellowships for doctoral candidates at dissertation level, as well as recent Ph.D.s (within past seven years), for historical/scientific research on aviation and space; relevant disciplines include history, aerospace, and engineering.
Restrictions: N/A.
$ Given: An unspecified number of fellowships awarded annually; $14,000 predoctoral stipend, $25,000 postdoctoral stipend.
Application Information: Write for details.
Deadline: January 15.
Contact: Cheryl Bauer.

National Air and Space
Museum
Verville Fellowships
6th and Independence
Avenue, S.W.
Washington, DC 20560
(202) 357-1529

Description: Nine- to twelve-month fellowships for analysis of major developments, trends, and accomplishments in history of aviation/space studies; relevant disciplines include history, aerospace, and engineering.
Restrictions: Applicants must demonstrate skills in research and writing.
$ Given: An unspecified number of fellowships for $30,000 each are awarded annually.
Application Information: Write for details.
Deadline: January 15.
Contact: Cheryl Bauer.

National Association for Core
Curriculum
Bossing-Edwards Research
Scholarships
404 East White Hall
Kent State University
Kent, OH 44242
(216) 678-0006

Description: Scholarships for master's and doctoral candidates studying core curriculum, interdisciplinary studies, and integrated curriculum; intended as support for research promoting development of secondary education programs; recipients chosen on the basis of proposed research project's relevance to core curriculum.
Restrictions: Applicants must have been core teachers for at least one year; funding must be used at institution with adequate resources for core research; summary of research findings must be submitted to NACC.
$ Given: An unspecified number of scholarships for $100–$500 each are awarded annually.

Application Information: Write for details.
Deadline: October 1.
Contact: Dr. Gordon F. Vars, Executive Secretary-Treasurer.

National Association of Broadcasters
Grants for Research in Broadcasting
1771 N. Street, N.W.
Washington, DC 20036
(202) 429-5389

Description: Grants for graduate students to conduct research on the social, cultural, political, and economic aspects of the United States broadcast industry.
Restrictions: N/A.
$ Given: An unspecified number of grants of up to $5,000 each are awarded annually.
Application Information: Write for details.
Deadline: January 3.
Contact: Senior Vice President, NAB Grants for Research and Planning, Research and Information Group.

National Collegiate Athletic Association
NCAA Postgraduate Scholarships
6201 College Boulevard
Overland Park, KS 66211-2422
(913) 339-1906

Description: Scholarships for varsity college athletes in sports which NCAA conducts national championships; for full-time graduate study in any field; recipients chosen on the basis of academic achievement (minimum 3.0 GPA), athletic achievement, and capability for graduate study.
Restrictions: N/A.
$ Given: One hundred and twenty-five scholarships are awarded annually: 29 in football, 28 in basketball (14 to men, 14 to women), and 68 in other varsity sports (34 to men, 34 to women); varying amounts.
Application Information: Applicants must be nominated by college director of athletics during final season of NCAA eligibility; maximum two football, two basketball (one man, one woman), and four other sports (two men, two women) nominations per NCAA member school per year.
Deadlines: October 2 for football; March 4 for basketball; April 14 for other varsity sports.
Contact: Fannie B. Vaughan, Executive Assistant .

National Foundation for Jewish Culture
Doctoral Dissertation Fellowships in Jewish Studies
330 Seventh Avenue
21st Floor
New York, NY 10021
(212) 629-0500

Description: Fellowships for doctoral candidates at dissertation level in Jewish studies; recipients chosen on the basis of academic achievement and dissertation topic.
Restrictions: Preference for applicants planning careers in Jewish studies; United States citizenship or permanent resident status required.
$ Given: An unspecified number of fellowships of $6,000–$8,000 each are awarded annually.
Application Information: Write for details.
Deadline: December 31.
Contact: Graduate Administrator.

**National Gallery of Art
Chester Dale Predoctoral
Fellowships**
Center for Advanced Study in
the Visual Arts
4th and Constitution Avenue,
N.W.
Washington, DC 20565
(202) 842-6480
FAX (202) 408-8531

Description: One-year fellowships for doctoral candidates in history of art/architecture/urban design to advance their dissertation through research and/or travel; recipients chosen on the basis of academic achievement.
Restrictions: Applicants must be proficient in two foreign languages related to dissertation topic; recipients may not hold outside job during fellowship tenure; United States citizenship or enrollment in United States university required.
$ Given: Two fellowships for $11,000 each are awarded annually; non-renewable.
Application Information: Applicants must be sponsored by the chairperson of the art history graduate department.
Deadline: November 15.
Contact: Henry A. Millon, Dean.

**National Gallery of Art
Mary Davis Predoctoral
Fellowship**
Center for Advanced Study in
the Visual Arts
4th and Constitution Avenue,
N.W.
Washington, DC 20565
(202) 842-6480
FAX (202) 408-8531

Description: Two-year fellowships for doctoral candidates at dissertation level in history of art/architecture/urban design; to support one year of dissertation research within the United States or abroad, and one year in residence at the Center, working on research projects and gaining curatorial experience.
Restrictions: Applicants must have completed all preliminary coursework and exams for doctorate; applicants must be proficient in two foreign languages related to dissertation topic; United States citizenship or enrollment in United States university required.
$ Given: One fellowship for $11,000 per year (for two years) is awarded annually.
Application Information: Applicants must be sponsored by the chairperson of the art history graduate department.
Deadline: November 15.
Contact: Henry A. Millon, Dean.

**National Gallery of Art
David E. Finley Predoctoral
Fellowship**
Center for Advanced Study in
the Visual Arts
4th and Constitution Avenue,
N.W.
Washington, DC 20565
(202) 842-6480
FAX (202) 408-8531

Description: Three-year fellowships for doctoral candidates at dissertation level in history of art/architecture/urban design; for two years of dissertation-related research and travel, plus one year of residency at Center for Advanced Study in the Visual Arts; recipients chosen on the basis of academic achievement and proposed research.
Restrictions: Applicants must be proficient in two foreign languages related to dissertation topic; applicants must have significant interest in museum work; recipients may not hold outside job during fellowship tenure; United States citizenship or enrollment in United States university required.

$ Given: One fellowship for $11,000 per year (for three years) is awarded annually; non-renewable.
Application Information: Applicants must be sponsored by the chairperson of the art history graduate department.
Deadline: November 15.
Contact: Henry A. Millon, Dean.

**National Gallery of Art
Ittleson Predoctoral
Fellowship**
Center for Advanced Study in
the Visual Arts
4th and Constitution Avenue,
N.W.
Washington, DC 20565
(202) 842-6480
FAX (202) 408-8531

Description: Two-year fellowships for doctoral candidates at dissertation level in art and art history exclusive of Western art; for one year of dissertation-related research and travel, plus one year of residency at Center for Advanced Study in the Visual Arts; recipients chosen on the basis of academic achievement and proposed research.
Restrictions: United States citizenship or enrollment in United States university required.
$ Given: One fellowship for $11,000 per year (for two years) is awarded annually; non-renewable.
Application Information: Applicants must be sponsored by the chairperson of the art history graduate department.
Deadline: November 15.
Contact: Henry A. Millon, Dean.

**National Gallery of Art
Samuel H. Kress Predoctoral
Fellowship**
Center for Advanced Study in
the Visual Arts
4th and Constitution Avenue,
N.W.
Washington, DC 20565
(202) 842-6480
FAX (202) 408-8531

Description: Two-year fellowships for doctoral candidates at dissertation level in history of art/architecture/urban design; for one year of dissertation-related research and travel, plus one year of residency at Center for Advanced Study in the Visual Arts (half-time devoted to dissertation completion, half-time devoted to Gallery research projects); recipients chosen on the basis of academic achievement and proposed research.
Restrictions: Applicants must be proficient in two foreign languages related to dissertation topic; recipients may not hold outside job during fellowship tenure; United States citizenship or enrollment in United States university required.
$ Given: One fellowship for $11,000 per year (for two years) is awarded annually; non-renewable.
Application Information: Applicants must be sponsored by the chairperson of the art history graduate department.
Deadline: November 15.
Contact: Henry A. Millon, Dean.

National Gallery of Art
Andrew W. Mellon
Predoctoral Fellowship
Center for Advanced Study in
the Visual Arts
4th and Constitution Avenue,
N.W.
Washington, DC 20565
(202) 842-6480
FAX (202) 408-8531

Description: Two-year fellowships for doctoral candidates at dissertation level in art and art history, excluding Western art; to support one year of dissertation research within the United States or abroad, and one year in residence at the Center, completing dissertation.
Restrictions: Applicants must have completed all preliminary coursework and exams for doctorate; applicants must be proficient in two foreign languages related to dissertation topic; United States citizenship or enrollment in United States university required.
$ Given: One fellowship for $11,000 per year (for two years) is awarded annually; non-renewable.
Application Information: Applicants must be sponsored by the chairperson of the art history graduate department.
Deadline: November 15.
Contact: Henry A. Millon, Dean.

National Gallery of Art
Paul Mellon Fellowship
Center for Advanced Study in
the Visual Arts
4th and Constitution Avenue,
N.W.
Washington, DC 20565
(202) 842-6480
FAX (202) 408-8531

Description: Three-year fellowships for doctoral candidates at dissertation level in history of art/architecture/urban design; for two years of dissertation-related research and travel, plus one year of residency at Center for Advanced Study in the Visual Arts; recipients chosen on the basis of proposed research.
Restrictions: Applicants must be proficient in two foreign languages related to dissertation topic; recipients must have devoted at least six months full-time research to proposed dissertation topic before beginning fellowship; recipients may not hold outside job during fellowship tenure; United States citizenship or enrollment in United States university required.
$ Given: One fellowship for $11,000 per year (for three years) is awarded annually; non-renewable.
Application Information: Applicants must be sponsored by the chairperson of the art history graduate department.
Deadline: November 15.
Contact: Henry A. Millon, Dean.

National Gallery of Art
Predoctoral Fellowship
Center for Advanced Study in
the Visual Arts
4th and Constitution Avenue,
N.W.
Washington, DC 20565
(202) 842-6480
FAX (202) 408-8531

Description: One- to three-year fellowships for doctoral candidates at dissertation level in history of art/architecture/urban design; to support dissertation research.
Restrictions: Applicants must have completed all preliminary coursework and exams for doctorate; United States citizenship or enrollment in United States university required.
$ Given: Ten fellowships for $11,000 per year (for

one to three years) are awarded annually; non-renewable.

Application Information: Applicants must be sponsored by the chairperson of the art history graduate department.

Deadline: November 15.

Contact: Henry A. Millon, Dean.

National Gallery of Art
Robert H. and Clarice Smith
Predoctoral Fellowship
Center for Advanced Study in
the Visual Arts
4th and Constitution Avenue,
N.W.
Washington, DC 20565
(202) 842-6480
FAX (202) 408-8531

Description: One-year fellowship for doctoral candidates at dissertation level in Dutch or Flemish art history; for use within the United States or abroad; tenure at the Center not required; recipients chosen on the basis of academic achievement and proposed research.

Restrictions: Applicants must be proficient in two foreign languages related to dissertation topic; recipients may not hold outside job during fellowship tenure; United States citizenship or enrollment in United States university required.

$ Given: One fellowship for $11,000 is awarded annually; non-renewable.

Application Information: Applicants must be sponsored by the chairperson of the art history graduate department.

Deadline: November 15.

Contact: Henry A. Millon, Dean.

National Gallery of Art
Wyeth Predoctoral Fellowship
Center for Advanced Study in
the Visual Arts
4th and Constitution Avenue,
N.W.
Washington, DC 20565
(202) 842-6480
FAX (202) 408-8531

Description: Two-year fellowship for doctoral candidates at dissertation level in American art; for one year of dissertation-related research and travel, plus one year of residency at Center for Advanced Study in the Visual Arts; recipients chosen on the basis of academic achievement and proposed research.

Restrictions: Applicants must be proficient in two foreign languages related to dissertation topic; recipients may not hold outside job during fellowship tenure; United States citizenship or enrollment in United States university required.

$ Given: One fellowship for $11,000 per year (for two years) is awarded annually; non-renewable.

Application Information: Applicants must be sponsored by the chairperson of the art history graduate department.

Deadline: November 15.

Contact: Henry A. Millon, Dean.

National Geographic Society Research Grants
Committee for Research and Exploration
1145 17th Street, N.W.
Washington, DC 20036
(202) 857-7439

Description: Grants for research in anthropology, archaeology, astronomy, biology, glaciology, botany, ecology, physical and human geography, mineralogy, geology, oceanology, paleontology, zooology, and other sciences pertinent to geography; funding primarily for postdoctoral researchers, but occasionally awarded to exceptional doctoral candidates; recipients chosen on the basis of proposed research.
Restrictions: Open to all nationalities.
$ Given: An unspecified number of grants of $15,000–$20,000 average each are awarded annually.
Application Information: Write for details.
Deadline: Applications accepted continuously.
Contact: Committee for Research and Exploration.

National Historical Publications and Records Commission
NHPRC Historical Editing Fellowships
National Archives Building
Washington, DC 20408
(202) 501-5610

Description: Fellowships for doctoral candidates at dissertation level and postdoctoral scholars in United States history and editing, to participate in advanced editing of documentary sources for United States history; fellowship involves ten months of training, with concentration on one project; instruction in transcription, annotation, copyediting, and proofreading included.
Restrictions: United States citizenship or legal resident status required.
$ Given: A few fellowships awarded annually; varying amounts, average grant $39,000.
Application Information: Write for details.
Deadline: N/A.
Contact: Program Director.

National Historical Publications and Records Commission
NHPRC/The Andrew M. Mellon Foundation Fellowship in Archival Administration
National Archives Building
Washington, DC 20408
(202) 501-5610

Description: Nine- to twelve-month fellowships for master's degree holders in archival administration, to work at host archival institutions/organizations.
Restrictions: Applicants must have two to five years experience in an archival setting, performing archival work; United States citizenship or legal resident status required.
$ Given: Two fellowships awarded annually; average $39,000.
Application Information: Write for details.
Deadline: March 1.
Contact: Program Director.

National Italian American Foundation Scholarship Program
Vincent Visceglia General Graduate Scholarships
1860 19th Street, N.W.
Washington, DC 20009
(202) 638-2137
FAX (202) 638-0002

Description: Scholarships for master's and doctoral candidates in Italian studies; recipients chosen on the basis of academic achievement and financial need.
Restrictions: Applicants must be of Italian descent or be working on M.A. or Ph.D. in Italian studies.
$ Given: An unspecified number of scholarships for $1,000 each are awarded annually.
Application Information: Application must be filled in triplicate; write for details.
Deadline: May 31.
Contact: Dr. Maria Lombardo, Education Director.

National Italian American Foundation Scholarship Program
Silvio Conte Internship
1860 19th Street, N.W.
Washington, DC 20009
(202) 638-2137
FAX (202) 683-0002

Description: Internship for undergraduate and graduate students to work for one semester in Congressman Conte's Washington, DC office.
Restrictions: Applicants must be of Italian descent; recipient must write paper about the internship experience and its expected benefit to recipient's future career.
$ Given: One internship paying $1,000 is awarded annually.
Application Information: Send SASE for details.
Deadline: May 31.
Contact: Dr. Maria Lombardo, Education Director.

National Italian American Foundation Scholarship Program
Italian American Regional Scholarships
1860 19th Street, N.W.
Washington, DC 20009
(202) 638-2137
FAX (202) 683-0002

Description: Scholarships for high school, undergraduate, and graduate students in all fields; regions are East Coast, Midwest, Southwest, and Mid-Atlantic; recipients chosen on the basis of academic achievement and financial need.
Restrictions: Applicants must be of Italian descent.
$ Given: Fifteen scholarships awarded annually; each for $500–$2,500.
Application Information: Send SASE for details.
Deadline: May 31.
Contact: Dr. Maria Lombardo, Education Director.

National Research Council
NRC/Ford Predoctoral and Dissertation Fellowships for Minorities
Fellowships Office
2101 Constitution Avenue, N.W.
Washington, DC 20418
(202) 334-2872

Description: Fellowships for graduate students in the humanities, social sciences, biological and agricultural sciences, physical sciences and mathematics, and engineering and applied sciences; recipients chosen on the basis of academic achievement and proposed research.
Restrictions: Limited to members of minority groups; United States citizenship or legal residency required.
$ Given: Fifty-five fellowships awarded; $11,500 for fellow, $6,000 for institution; 20 dissertation fellowships available for $18,000.
Application Information: Write for details.
Deadline: November 5.

National Right to Work Committee
William B. Ruggles Journalism Scholarship
8001 Braddock Road
Suite 500
Springfield, VA 22160
(703) 321-9820

Description: Scholarship for undergraduate and graduate students in journalism, mass media, and mass communications; award for best 500-word essay on the right to work principle.
Restrictions: Applicant must be enrolled in accredited United States journalism schools; scholarship must be used within the United States.
$ Given: One scholarship for $2,000 awarded annually.
Application Information: Submit application between January 1 and March 31.
Deadline: March 31.
Contact: Public Relations Director.

National Scholarship Trust Fund Printing, Publishing, and Packaging Industry Graduate Fellowships
4615 Forbes Avenue
Pittsburgh, PA 15213
(412) 621-6941 ext. 229

Description: One-year research/study fellowships for graduate students (and graduating college seniors) in graphic communications; recipients chosen on the basis of academic achievement (minimum 3.0 GPA) and proposed research.
Restrictions: N/A.
$ Given: An unspecified number of fellowships for $1,500–$3,000 each are awarded annually.
Application Information: Write for details.
Deadline: January 10.
Contact: Margaret Dimperio, Business Manager.

National Science Foundation Behavioral and Neural Sciences Research Grants
4201 Wilson Boulevard
Arlington, VA 22230
(703) 306-1416

Description: Grants to support research on nervous systems and human/animal behavior; awarded in the following subprogram categories: cultural/physical anthropology, archaeology, animal behavior, behavioral neuroendocrinology, cellular neuroscience, developmental neuroscience, human cognition/perception, linguistics, neural mechanisms of behavior, neurobiology of learning/memory, sensory system, and social psychology; recipients chosen on the basis of proposed research.
Restrictions: N/A.
$ Given: An unspecified number of grants awarded annually; varying amounts.
Application Information: Write for subprogram details.
Deadlines: accepted continuously; January 15, July 15 .
Contact: Dr. Christopher Comer, Division of Integrative Biology and Neuroscience.

**National Women's Studies Association
NAIAD-NWSA Graduate Scholarships in Lesbian Studies**
7100 Baltimore Avenue
Suite 304
College Park, MD 20742
(301) 403-0525

Description: Scholarships for master's and doctoral candidates in lesbian studies; recipients chosen on the basis of financial need and thesis/dissertation topic.
Restrictions: Membership in NWSA preferred.
$ Given: One scholarship for $1,000 awarded annually.
Application Information: Write for details.
Deadline: February 15.
Contact: Loretta Younger, Office Manager.

**National Women's Studies Association
NWSA Scholarship in Jewish Women's Studies**
7100 Baltimore Avenue
Suite 301
College Park, MD 20742
(301) 403-0525

Description: Scholarship for graduate students in Jewish women's studies; recipients chosen on the basis of financial need and academic achievement.
Restrictions: N/A.
$ Given: One scholarship awarded annually.
Application Information: Write for details.
Deadline: February 15.
Contact: Loretta Younger, Office Manager.

**National Women's Studies Association
Pergamon–NWSA Graduate Scholarships in Women's Studies**
7100 Baltimore Avenue
Suite 301
College Park, MD 20742
(301) 403-0525

Description: Scholarship for master's and doctoral candidates in women's studies; recipients chosen on the basis of financial need and proposed research; preference for research project on women of color, Third World women, or women and class.
Restrictions: Membership in NWSA preferred.
$ Given: Two scholarships awarded annually; one for $1,000, one for $500.
Application Information: Write for details.
Deadline: February 15.
Contact: Loretta Younger, Office Manager.

**Natural Sciences and Engineering Research Council of Canada
NSERC Postgraduate Scholarships in Science Librarianship and Documentation**
200 Kent Street
Ottawa, Ontario K1A 1H5
Canada
(613) 992-8203

Description: One-year scholarships for first- and second-year study toward M.L.S. degree in library science; recipients chosen on the basis of academic achievement, commitment to field, and relevant experience.
Restrictions: Applicants must have B.S. degree in science or engineering; Canadian citizenship or permanent resident status required.
$ Given: A few scholarships awarded annually; each for $13,500 Canadian plus travel allowance.
Application Information: Write for details.
Deadline: December 1.
Contact: Nadine Bohan; Information Officer.

New Jersey Historical Commission Governor Alfred E. Driscoll Publications Prize
4 North Broad Street
CN 305
Trenton, NJ 08625
(609) 292-6062

Description: Award for best dissertation by a doctoral candidate on the history of New Jersey.
Restrictions: Dissertation must have been accepted by graduate department.
$ Given: One prize awarded annually; $500 cash to author, plus up to $6,000 as publication subvention (paid to press).
Application Information: Write for details.
Deadline: June 15.
Contact: Mary R. Murrin, Grants and Prizes.

New Jersey Historical Commission Grants-in-Aid Program
4 North Broad Street
CN 305
Trenton, NJ 08625
(609) 292-6062

Description: Grants to support research on the history of New Jersey; funding made available to individuals and organizations planning research that will contribute to knowledge of New Jersey history.
Restrictions: N/A.
$ Given: An unspecified number of grants of $1,000–$6,000 each are awarded annually; renewable.
Application Information: Write for details.
Deadline: February 1.
Contact: Mary R. Murrin, Grants and Prizes.

New Jersey Historical Commission Minigrants
4 North Broad Street
CN 305
Trenton, NJ 08625
(609) 292-6062.

Application Information: Grants to help inexpensive projects on the history of New Jersey with the rules and procedures of a grant request.
Restrictions: N/A.
$ Given: An unspecified number of grants for $1,000 each are awarded annually.
Application Information: Write for details.
Deadline: Applications accepted continuously.
Contact: Mary R. Murrin, Grants and Prizes.

New York State Senate Richard J. Roth Journalism Fellowships
State Capitol
Room 500A
Albany, NY 12247
(518) 445-2611
FAX (518) 432-5470

Description: One-year fellowships for master's and doctoral candidates in all disciplines to work full-time in the office of the press secretary of the New York State Senate; recipients chosen on the basis of academic achievement, strong commitment to public service, established skills, and outstanding ability and versatility.
Restrictions: New York state residency and full-time enrollment in accredited graduate program at a New York state university required; United States citizenship required.
$ Given: One fellowship position filled annually; $22,575 stipend.
Application Information: Write for details.
Deadline: May 10.
Contact: Senate Student Program Office.

**New York State Senate
Senate Legislative
Fellows Program**
State Capitol
Room 500A
Albany, NY 12247
(518) 445-2611
FAX (518) 432-5470

Description: One-year fellowships for master's and doctoral candidates in political science and public policy to work in the New York State Senate; recipients chosen on the basis of academic achievement, strong commitment to public service, and a good understanding of the legislative process.
Restrictions: Applicants must demonstrate suitability for placement in high-level leadership office; New York state residency or full-time enrollment in accredited graduate program at a New York state university required.
$ Given: Fourteen fellowship positions filled annually; each with $22,575 stipend, paid biweekly over the year, plus benefits.
Application Information: Write for details.
Deadline: May 6.
Contact: Senate Student Program Office.

**New York University
AEJMC Summer Internship
for Minorities in Journalism**
269 Mercer Street
Suite 601
New York, NY 10003
(212) 998-2130

Description: Summer internships for college upperclassmen and graduate students; participation includes actual work, journalism courses, workshops, and on-site visits; media worksites include TV Guide, New York Times, radio stations, public relations companies, advertising firms, and broadcasting companies.
Restrictions: Limited to minority group members only, especially African-American, Hispanic, Native American, Eskimo, and Asian-American applicants.
$ Given: An unspecified number of internships awarded annually; each pays at least $200/week.
Application Information: Request form by December 3.
Deadline: December 11.
Contact: Glenda Noel-Doyle, AEJMC Internship Coordinator, Institute of Afro-American Affairs .

**New York University
Publishing Studies Fellowships**
715 Broadway
6th Floor
New York, NY 10003
(212) 998-7370

Description: Fellowships sponsored by North American publishing houses to train graduate students in book/magazine publishing; participation requires enrollment in two-year M.A. program (first year, full-time coursework; second year, paid internship in New York City).
Restrictions: Applicants must be college graduates with minimum 3.0 GPA.
$ Given: Nine fellowships for $5,500 each are awarded annually.

Application Information: Application requires college transcripts, two letters of recommendation, and interview.
Deadline: March 1.
Contact: Mary Witty, Publishing Studies Program Coordinator, Gallatin Division.

Newberry Library
Frances C. Allen Fellowships
Committee on Awards
60 West Walton Street
Chicago, IL 60610-3380
(312) 943-9090

Description: One-month to one-year research fellowships for master's and doctoral candidates in the humanities and social sciences; tenable primarily at the D'Arcy McNickle Center for the History of the American Indian.
Restrictions: Limited to female Native American applicants.
$ Given: An unspecified number of fellowships awarded annually; each with stipend for living and travel expenses.
Application Information: Write for details.
Deadlines: February 1, August 1.

Newberry Library
Short-Term Resident
Fellowships for Individual
Research
Committee on Awards
60 West Walton Street
Chicago, IL 60610-3380
(312) 943-9090 ext. 267

Description: Two- to three-month research fellowships for Ph.D.s and doctoral candidates at dissertation level in any field appropriate to the Newberry Library collections, including history and the humanities in Western civilization, from the Middle Ages through the early 20th century; recipients chosen on the basis of proposed research.
Restrictions: Preference to applicants needing to use Newberry facilities; preference to individuals living outside the Chicago area; open to all nationalities.
$ Given: An unspecified number of fellowships awarded annually; each with $800 monthly stipend.
Application Information: Write for details.
Deadlines: March 1, October 15.

Newberry Library
Herman Dunlap Smith Center
for the History of Cartography
Research Fellowships
Committee on Awards
60 West Walton Street
Chicago, IL 60610-3380
(312) 943-9090

Description: Short-term (up to three months) and long-term (6–12 months) residential research fellowships for doctoral candidates and postdoctoral scholars in the history of cartography; tenable at the Newberry Library; recipients chosen on the basis of proposed research and its applicability to Library's holdings.
Restrictions: N/A.
$ Given: An unspecified number of fellowships awarded annually; each with $800 monthly stipend for living and travel expenses, reaching a maximum $30,000 stipend for long-term projects.
Application Information: Write for details.
Deadlines: March 1 for long- and short-term projects; October 15 for short-term projects only.

Norwegian Information Service in the United States Norwegian Emigration Fund of 1975 Scholarships and Grants for Americans
825 Third Avenue
17th Floor
New York, NY 10022
(212) 421-7333

Description: Grants for American master's and doctoral candidates to visit Norway to study emigration history and relations between the United States and Norway.
Restrictions: United States citizenship or permanent resident status required.
$ Given: An unspecified number of grants of NKr5,000–NKr40,000 each are awarded annually.
Application Information: Write for details.
Deadline: July 1.
Contact: Grants and Scholarships Section.

Norwegian Information Service in the United States Norwegian Marshall Fund Grants
825 Third Avenue
17th Floor
New York, NY 10022
(212) 421-7333

Description: Grants for American master's and doctoral candidates in science and the humanities to conduct research abroad.
Restrictions: United States citizenship required.
$ Given: An unspecified number of grants of up to $5,000 each are awarded annually.
Application Information: Request application forms from Norway-American Association, Drammensveien 20 C, Oslo 2, 0255, Norway, (02) 44.76.83.
Deadline: March 15.
Contact: Grants and Scholarships Section.

Norwegian Information Service in the United States SASS Travel Grants
825 Third Avenue
17th Floor
New York, NY 10022
(212) 421-7333

Description: Grants for master's and doctoral candidates who have passed preliminary exams, as well as for Norwegian language/culture teachers, for study/research in Norway.
Restrictions: United States citizenship or permanent resident status required; membership in SASS (Society for the Advancement of Scandinavian Study) required.
$ Given: An unspecified number of grants of $750–$1,500 each are awarded annually.
Application Information: Write for details.
Deadline: April 15.
Contact: Grants and Scholarships Section.

Oak Ridge Institute for Science and Education Department of Energy Research Participation Program
P.O. Box 117
Oak Ridge, TN 37831
(615) 576-3421

Description: Program for undergraduate and graduate students, as well as faculty members, to conduct/participate in research programs at seven Department of Energy facilities; summer and academic-year programs available; research programs are related to energy production, utilization, and conservation.
Restrictions: Applicants must have done degree work in life/physical/social sciences, mathematics, toxicology, or engineering; United States citizenship or permanent resident status required.

$ Given: An unspecified number of fellowships awarded annually; each with $20,000–$48,000 stipend, based on degree, program, and area of research.
Application Information: Write for application forms.
Deadline: Early January.
Contact: Al Wohlpart, Science and Engineering Education Division.

Omega Psi Phi Fraternity George E. Meares Memorial Scholarships
1004 Spencer Avenue
Gastonia, NC 28052

Description: Scholarships for graduate students in social work, social sciences, and criminal justice; recipients chosen on the basis of academic achievement (transcripts).
Restrictions: United States citizenship required.
$ Given: An unspecified number of $1,000 scholarships are awarded annually.
Application Information: Write for details.
Deadline: April 1.
Contact: Minnie Meares Draughn.

Pacific Cultural Foundation Grants for Chinese Studies
Palace Office Building
Suite 807
346 Nanking East Road
Section 3
Taipei, Taiwan 10567
Republic of China
(02) 752-7424 through -7429
(six phone lines)

Description: Grants for master's degree holders for research in Chinese studies; four types of studies grants: research, writing, publication, and seminar; recipients chosen on the basis of proposed work/research.
Restrictions: Applicants must be residents of the free world.
$ Given: Approximately 80 grants of $2,000–$5,000 each are awarded annually.
Application Information: Separate application for travel grant available.
Deadlines: March 1, September 1.

Parapsychology Foundation Eileen J. Garrett Scholarship
228 East 71st Street
New York, NY 10021
(212) 628-1550

Description: Scholarship for research and study in parapsychology; funding made available to students at accredited universities; recipients chosen on the basis of academic achievement, quality of proposed research, and plans to pursue career in parapsychology.
Restrictions: N/A.
$ Given: One scholarship for $3,000 is awarded annually.
Application Information: Write for details.
Deadline: July 15.

Phi Alpha Theta International Honor Society in History Journalism Prizes for Graduate Students in History
2333 Liberty Street
Allentown, PA 18104
(610) 433-4140

Description: Prizes for best undergraduate and graduate history essays; judged on combination of original research and good composition.
Restrictions: Membership in PAT required.
$ Given: Six prizes awarded annually - one Hammond Prize of $200 for best graduate essay; one Turner Prize of $150 for best undergraduate essay; four additional un-

named prizes of $100 each, open to both undergraduate and graduate students.
Application Information: Submit manuscript and letter of faculty recommendation to Dr. Marsha L. Frey, Kansas State University, Manhattan, KS 66506.
Deadline: July 1.
Contact: Dr. Marsha L. Frey, Secretary.

Phi Alpha Theta International Honor Society in History Scholarships
2333 Liberty Street
Allentown, PA 18104
(610) 433-4140

Description: Scholarships for graduate study in history; Zimmerman Scholarship for individuals entering graduate school for M.A. degree in history; Pine Memorial Scholarship for advanced graduate study; and a number of other smaller graduate scholarships.
Restrictions: Membership in PAT required.
$ Given: Zimmerman Scholarship, $1,250; Pine Memorial Scholarship, $1,000; other scholarships, $750 each—all awarded annually.
Application Information: Write for details.
Deadline: March 15.
Contact: Donald B. Hoffman, Ph.D., Secretary-Treasurer.

Phi Beta Kappa Society Mary Isabel Sibley Fellowship
1811 Q. Street, N.W.
Washington, DC 20009
(202) 265-3808

Description: One-year fellowship for postdoctoral scholars and doctoral candidates at dissertation level for research on French language and literature or Greek language, literature, history and archaeology; recipients chosen on the basis of academic achievement and quality of proposed research during fellowship year.
Restrictions: Limited to unmarried women ages 25–35 only; recipients must devote full-time efforts to research.
$ Given: One fellowship for $10,000 is awarded annually; non-renewable.
Application Information: French fellowship awarded in even-numbered years; Greek fellowship awarded in odd-numbered years.
Deadline: January 15.
Contact: Linda D. Surles, Program Officer.

Philip Morris Fellowships for Artists of Color
Maryland Institute College of Art
1300 West Mount Royal Avenue
Baltimore, MD 21217
(410) 225-2255

Description: Two-year fellowships for master's degree candidates in the fine arts; to support work toward M.F.A. degree in painting, printmaking, sculpture, graphic design, or photography at the following participating schools: California Institute of the Arts, Cranbrook Academy of Art, Maryland Institute College of Art, School of Art Institute of Chicago, and Yale School of Art; recipients chosen on the basis of financial need.
Restrictions: Limited to African-American, Hispanic, Asian-American, and Native American applicants, as well as other applicants of color.

$ Given: Four fellowships awarded at each school annually; each for $10,000/year (for two years), supplementing financial aid offered by art schools.
Application Information: Write for details.
Deadline: February 1–March 1 (varies).
Contact: Dr. Leslie King-Hammond, Program Director.

Pitt Rivers Museum
James A. Swan Fund
Oxford University
South Parks Road
Oxford, England OX1 3PP
0865-270927

Description: Grants for individuals to travel to Africa to pursue study/research on the hunter-gatherer peoples of Africa; recipients chosen on the basis of proposed research.
Restrictions: N/A.
$ Given: Ten grants of 1,000 pounds–2,000 pounds each are awarded annually; renewable.
Application Information: No form; submit research proposal and proposed budget.
Deadline: Accepted continuously.
Contact: Dr. Schuyler Jones, Curator.

Population Council
Population Council
Fellowships in the Social
Sciences
1 Dag Hammarskjold Plaza
New York, NY 10017
(212) 339-0667

Description: Fellowships for doctoral candidates at dissertation level and mid-career professionals seeking master's degrees; for study/research combining population studies and such other social science disciplines as anthropology, sociology, economics, geography, public health, and public administration; recipients chosen on the basis of academic achievement and proposed research.
Restrictions: Research/study must be carried out at institution with strong program in population studies; preference to applicants with employment experience in population studies or family planning; strong preference for nationals of developing countries who are committed to returning to their home countries in population-related careers.
$ Given: An unspecified number of fellowships awarded annually; monthly stipend based on place of study and other factors.
Application Information: Women encouraged to apply.
Deadline: November 15.
Contact: Manager, Fellowships Program.

Presbyterian Church U.S.A.
Presbyterian Graduate Study
Grants
100 Witherspoon Street,
Mezzanine
Office of Financial Aid for
Studies
Church Vocations Unit
Louisville, KY 40202
(502) 569-5760

Description: Grants for graduate students and Presbyterian seminarians pursuing a first professional degree; recipients chosen on the basis of financial need.
Restrictions: Applicants must be communicant members of churches of the Presbyterian Church U. S.A. who are enrolled full-time in accredited seminaries or theological institutes; no funding for doctoral studies; United States citizenship or permanent resident status required.
$ Given: An unspecified number of grants for $500–$1,500 each are awarded annually.
Application Information: Write for details.
Deadline: accepted continuously.
Contact: Financial Aid Administrator.

Presbyterian Church U.S.A.
Racial/Ethnic Leadership
Supplemental Grants
100 Witherspoon Street,
Mezzanine
Office of Financial Aid for
Studies
Church Vocations Unit
Louisville, KY 40202
(502) 569-5760

Description: Grants for graduate students in religious studies pursuing a first professional degree and planning career in the church; recipients chosen on the basis of financial need.
Restrictions: Limited to Asian, African-American, Hispanic, and Native American applicants only; applicants must be communicant members of churches of the Presbyterian Church U.S.A. who are enrolled at least half-time in program of study approved by the presbytery; United States citizenship or permanent resident status required.
$ Given: An unspecified number of grants for up to $1,000 each are awarded annually.
Application Information: Write for details.
Deadline: Applications accepted continuously.
Contact: Financial Aid Administrator

President's Commission on
White House Fellowships
White House
Fellowships
712 Jackson Place, N.W.
Washington, DC 20503
(202) 395-4522

Description: Twelve-month appointments as special assistants to the Vice President, Cabinet members, and the Presidential staff; fellowships include participation in educational program; positions available for students in public affairs, education, the sciences, business, and the professions; recipients chosen on the basis of leadership qualities, commitment to community service, and career/academic achievement.
Restrictions: Limited to young adults, ages 30–39; civilian federal employees are ineligible; recipients may not hold official state or local office while serving as White House fellows; United States citizenship required.
$ Given: Eleven to nineteen wage-earning fellowships for up to a maximum of $65,000 are awarded annually.

Application Information: Write for details.
Deadline: December 15.
Contact: Phyllis A. Williams

Radcliffe College
Jeanne Humphrey Block
Dissertation Awards
Henry A. Murray Research
Center
10 Garden Street
Cambridge, MA 02138
(617) 495-8140
FAX (617) 495-8422

Description: Grants to doctoral candidates at dissertation level for research on the psychological development of girls and women; recipients chosen on the basis of proposed research; preference for proposals emphasizing use of Murray Center resources.
Restrictions: Limited to women applicants.
$ Given: An unspecified number of grants of $2,500 each are awarded annually.
Application Information: Write for details.
Deadline: April 1.

REFORMA, The National
Association to Promote
Library Services to the
Spanish Speaking
REFORMA Scholarships in
Library and Information
Science
Auroria Library
Lawrence at 11th Street
Denver, CO 80204-2096
(303) 556-3526

Description: Scholarships for individuals studying library and information science; recipients chosen on the basis of academic achievement and financial need.
Restrictions: Applicants must speak Spanish and must demonstrate a desire to serve the Spanish-speaking community.
$ Given: An unspecified number of $1,000 scholarships are awarded annually.
Application Information: Write for details.
Deadline: May 15.
Contact: Orlando Archibeque, Scholarship Committee Chair

Rockefeller University
Rockefeller Archive Center
Research Grants
15 Dayton Avenue
Pocantico Hills
North Tarrytown, NY
10591-1598
(914) 631-4505

Description: Residential research fellowships for graduate students and postdoctoral scholars pursuing research using Archive Center resources; relevant disciplines including philanthropy, education, science, medicine, black history, agriculture, labor, social welfare, social sciences, politics, religion, population, economic development, and the arts; recipients chosen on the basis of proposed research and necessity of using Archive Center resources.
Restrictions: N/A.
$ Given: An unspecified number of grants awarded annually; each for up to $1,500 for travel, lodging, and research expenses.
Application Information: Write for details.
Deadline: December 31.
Contact: Dr. Darwin H. Stapleton, Director.

**School of American Research
Katrin H. Lamon Resident
Scholar Program for Native
Americans**
P.O. Box 2188
Santa Fe, NM 87504
(505) 982-2919

Description: Nine-month residential fellowship for post-doctoral scholars and doctoral candidates at dissertation level in anthropology and related social sciences; intended to provide recipients with intellectual stimulation of campus life plus time to write up results of compiled field work/research.
Restrictions: Limited to Native American applicants.
$ Given: One fellowship awarded annually; maximum $29,000 stipend plus housing and office; non-renewable.
Application Information: Write for details.
Deadline: December 1.
Contact: Resident Scholar Coordinator.

**School of American Research
Resident Scholar Fellowships**
P.O. Box 2188
Santa Fe, NM 87504
(505) 982-2919

Description: Nine-month residential fellowship for post-doctoral scholars and doctoral candidates at dissertation level in anthropology and related humanities and social sciences; National Endowment for the Humanities funds three fellowships for Ph.D.s; Weatherhead Foundation funds two fellowships for doctoral candidates working on their dissertations.
Restrictions: Preference to applicants who have completed research and need time to write up results; United States citizenship required.
$ Given: Six fellowships awarded annually; each with minimum $28,000 stipend plus housing, office and medical insurance.
Application Information: Send registered mail.
Deadline: December 1.
Contact: Resident Scholar Coordinator.

**Scripps Howard Foundation
Ellen Browning Scripps
Fellowships in Journalism**
1100 Central Trust Tower
P.O. Box 5380
Cincinnati, OH 45201
(513) 977-3035

Description: Fellowships for working journalists pursuing graduate study in any field (business, science, law, etc.) as a specialty of journalism; tenable at any university with an accredited graduate-level program in the field of choice; recipients chosen on the basis of academic achievement and financial need.
Restrictions: Applicants must be intending to return to employment in journalism and communications; United States citizenship or resident alien status required.
$ Given: An unspecified number of fellowships awarded annually; each for up to $3,000.
Application Information: Write to request before December 20.
Deadline: February 25.
Contact: Executive Director.

**Scripps Howard Foundation
Scripps Howard Foundation
Scholarships**
1100 Central Trust Tower
P.O. Box 5380
Cincinnati, OH 45201
(513) 977-3035

Description: Scholarships for undergraduate upperclassmen and graduate students in journalism and communications; recipients chosen on the basis of academic achievement and financial need.
Restrictions: Applicants must be full-time students planning employment in journalism and communications; preference to applicants with experience in journalism, to prior recipients, and to students in areas served by Scripps Howard; United States citizenship or resident alien status required.
$ Given: An unspecified number of grants awarded annually; each for up to $3,000; renewable.
Application Information: Write to request before December 20.
Deadline: February 25.
Contact: Executive Director.

**Scripps Howard Foundation
Scripps Howard Graphic Arts
Grants**
1100 Central Trust Tower
P.O. Box 5380
Cincinnati, OH 45201
(513) 977-3035

Description: Grants for undergraduates and other students of graphic arts as related to the newspaper industry; recipients chosen on the basis of academic achievement and financial need.
Restrictions: Applicants must be planning employment in newspaper production; United States citizenship or resident alien status required.
$ Given: An unspecified number of grants awarded annually; each for up to $3,000.
Application Information: Write to request before December 20.
Deadline: February 25.
Contact: Executive Director.

**Sinfonia Foundation Research
Assistance Grants**
10600 Old State Road
Evansville, IN 47711
(812) 867-2433

Description: Grants for musicians and music teachers to pursue post-graduate research in American music and music education; recipients chosen on the basis of financial need.
Restrictions: Applicants must demonstrate competence in writing and research; open to all nationalities.
$ Given: An unspecified number of grants averaging $1,000 each are awarded annually.
Application Information: Write for details.
Deadline: April 1.
Contact: Dr. Gary Ingle.

**Smithsonian Institution
Graduate Student Research
Fellowships**
Office of Fellowships and
Grants
955 L'Enfant Plaza
Suite 7300
Washington, DC 20560
(202) 287-3271

Description: Ten-week residential fellowships for
graduate students to pursue research at the Smithsonian;
relevant disciplines include art history, anthropology,
ecology, biology, environmental science, astrophysics,
history of science, Oriental art, natural history, African
art and culture, and American cultural/sociological history; recipients chosen on the basis of proposed research.
Restrictions: N/A.
$ Given: Approximately 38 fellowships are awarded an-
nually; each with maximum $3,000 stipend.
Application Information: Write for details.
Deadline: January 15.
Contact: Program Assistant.

**Smithsonian Institution
Minority Students Internships**
Office of Fellowships and
Grants
955 L'Enfant Plaza
Suite 7300
Washington, DC 20560
(202) 287-3271

Description: Nine- to twelve-week internships for undergraduate upperclassmen and graduate students in the
humanities, social sciences, natural sciences, and physical
sciences; internship program includes participation in ongoing research or activities at the Museum plus
supervised independent research in any bureau; recipients chosen on the basis of academic achievement and
proposed research.
Restrictions: Limited to minority group applicants.
$ Given: An unspecified number of internship positions
are awarded annually; $250/week undergraduate sti-
pend, $300/week graduate stipend.
Application Information: Write for details.
Deadlines: February 15, June 15, and October 15.

**Smithsonian Institution
Predoctoral Research
Fellowships in Anthropology**
Office of Fellowships and
Grants
955 L'Enfant Plaza
Suite 7300
Washington, DC 20560
(202) 287-3271

Description: One-year residential fellowships for doctoral candidates at dissertation level in anthropology to
pursue independent research using the Smithsonian's collections, resources, and staff expertise; relevant
disciplines include anthropology, ethnology, ethnohistory, archaeology, and carbon-14 dating; recipients
chosen on the basis of proposed research.
Restrictions: Applicants must have completed all
preliminary coursework and exams for degree.
$ Given: An unspecified number of fellowships are
awarded annually; each with $14,000 stipend.
Application Information: Write for details.
Deadline: January 15.
Contact: Program Assistant.

Smithsonian Institution Predoctoral Research Fellowships in Cultural History
Office of Fellowships and Grants
955 L'Enfant Plaza
Suite 7300
Washington, DC 20560
(202) 287-3271

Description: One-year residential fellowships for doctoral candidates at dissertation level in cultural history to pursue independent research using the Smithsonian's collections, resources, and staff expertise; recipients chosen on the basis of proposed research.
Restrictions: Applicants must have completed all preliminary coursework and exams for degree.
$ Given: An unspecified number of fellowships are awarded annually; each with $14,000 stipend.
Application Information: Write for details.
Deadline: January 15.
Contact: Program Assistant.

Smithsonian Institution Predoctoral Research Fellowships in the History of Art
Office of Fellowships and Grants
955 L'Enfant Plaza
Suite 7300
Washington, DC 20560
(202) 287-3271

Description: One-year residential fellowships for doctoral candidates at dissertation level in art history to pursue independent research using the Smithsonian's collections, resources, and staff expertise; recipients chosen on the basis of proposed research.
Restrictions: Applicants must have completed all preliminary coursework and exams for degree.
$ Given: An unspecified number of fellowships are awarded annually; each with $14,000 stipend.
Application Information: Write for details.
Deadline: January 15.
Contact: Program Assistant.

Smithsonian Institution Predoctoral Research Fellowships in the History of Science and Technology
Office of Fellowships and Grants
955 L'Enfant Plaza
Suite 7300
Washington, DC 20560
(202) 287-3271

Description: One-year residential fellowships for doctoral candidates at dissertation level in the history of science and technology, to pursue independent research using the Smithsonian's collections, resources, and staff expertise; relevant disciplines include history of mathematics, physical sciences, pharmacy, medicine, civil and mechanical engineering, electrical technology, and history of American science; recipients chosen on the basis of proposed research.
Restrictions: Applicants must have completed all preliminary coursework and exams for degree.
$ Given: An unspecified number of fellowships are awarded annually; each with $14,000 stipend.
Application Information: Write for details.
Deadline: January 15.
Contact: Program Assistant.

Smithsonian Institution
James Renwick Fellowships
Office of Fellowships and
Grants
955 L'Enfant Plaza
Suite 7300
Washington, DC 20560
(202) 357-2531

Description: Three- to twelve-month fellowships for
doctoral candidates and postdoctoral scholars to pursue
study/research on modern American crafts, including
20th century art, craft and design; preference for work
with post-1930 crafts.
Restrictions: N/A.
$ Given: An unspecified number of fellowships are
awarded annually; $13,000 for predoctoral fellow;
$21,000 for postdoctoral fellow, plus travel allowance.
Application Information: Write for details.
Deadline: January 15.
Contact: Renwick Gallery.

Smithsonian Institution
Libraries
Dibner Library
Resident Scholar Program
Grants
NHB 24
Mail Stop 154
Washington, DC 20560

Description: Grants for doctoral candidates, postdoctoral scholars, and professionals studying the history of
science and technology, to support one to three months
of research/study at Dibner Library of the History of Science and Technology and other libraries of the
Smithsonian.
Restrictions: N/A.
$ Given: An unspecified number of grants awarded an-
nually; each with $1,500/month stipend to cover
expenses.
Application Information: Write for details.
Deadline: November 1.

Social Science Research
Council
Advanced German and
European Studies Doctoral
Dissertation Fellowships
605 Third Avenue
New York, NY 10158
(212) 661-0280

Description: Nine- to 24-month residential fellowships
for doctoral candidates at dissertation level to study at
Free University of Berlin; for dissertation work addressing the economic, political, and social aspects of modern
and contemporary German and European affairs; recipients chosen on the basis of academic achievement and
proposed research.
Restrictions: Good command of German required;
United States citizenship or permanent resident status required.
$ Given: An unspecified number of fellowships
awarded annually; each covers monthly stipend and
travel expenses.
Application Information: Write for details.
Deadline: January 1.

Social Science Research
Council
Africa Doctoral Dissertation
Research Fellowships
605 Third Avenue
New York, NY 10158
(212) 661-0280

Description: Nine- to 18-month fellowships for doctoral
candidates at dissertation level to conduct field work on
humanities/social sciences topic as related to sub-Saharan Africa; recipients chosen on the basis of academic
achievement, proposed research, and fluency in project-
relevant African/European languages.

Restrictions: Good command of project-relevant languages required; no funding for coursework; United States citizenship or enrollment in United States university required.
$ Given: An unspecified number of fellowships awarded annually; each for up to $25,000.
Application Information: Write for details.
Deadline: November 1.

Social Science Research Council
Africa Predissertation
Research Fellowships
605 Third Avenue
New York, NY 10158
(212) 661-0280

Description: Fellowships for doctoral candidates to take short-term field trips to Africa for preliminary dissertation research; for dissertation work in the humanities and social sciences; Africanist and non-Africanist students encouraged to apply in such underrepresented disciplines as economics, psychology, sociology, and the humanities; recipients chosen on the basis of academic achievement and proposed research.
Restrictions: Applicants must have completed one year of graduate study and been accepted into full-time Ph.D. program; United States citizenship or full-time enrollment in United States university required.
$ Given: An unspecified number of fellowships awarded annually; each for up to $25,000.
Application Information: Write for details.
Deadline: November 1.

Social Science Research Council
Africa Training and Dissertation Research Fellowships on Agricultural and Health
605 Third Avenue
New York, NY 10158
(212) 661-0280

Description: Fellowships to support doctoral candidates for up to 12 months of natural/technical science training and 9-18 months of field research and write-up in Africa; for dissertation work in the social sciences as related to African agriculture and health; recipients chosen on the basis of academic achievement and proposed research.
Restrictions: United States citizenship or full-time enrollment in United States university required.
$ Given: An unspecified number of fellowships awarded annually; maximum award $45,000.
Application Information: Proposal should state dissertation topic, proposed research site, and preliminary plans for training.
Deadline: November 1.
Contact: Africa Program.

Social Science Research Council International Predissertation Research Fellowships
605 Third Avenue
New York, NY 10158
(212) 661-0280

Description: Fellowships for doctoral candidates in the early stages of Ph.D. programs in the social sciences, to promote internationalization of graduate training and to focus research on the developing world; relevant disciplines include political science, economics, and sociology; tenable for 12 months of support over two-year period, for domestic and overseas study.
Restrictions: Applicants must be full-time students in Ph.D. degree-granting programs at the following schools: University of California at Berkeley, UCLA, University of California at San Diego, University of Chicago, Columbia, Cornell, Duke, Harvard, Indiana University at Bloomington, University of Michigan, University of Minnesota at Twin Cities, Northwestern, University of Pennsylvania, Princeton, Stanford, University of Texas at Austin, University of Washington, University of Wisconsin at Madison, and Yale; no funding for dissertation research.
$ Given: An unspecified number of fellowships awarded annually; each $1,500 for domestic study plus allowance for overseas expenses.
Application Information: Write for details.
Deadline: N/A.
Contact: Dr. Ellen Perecman, Program Director.

Social Science Research Council Japan Doctoral Dissertation Fellowships
605 Third Avenue
New York, NY 10158
(212) 661-0280

Description: Fellowships for doctoral candidates who have completed dissertation research to write dissertation on Japanese topic in the humanities or social sciences; recipients chosen on the basis of academic achievement.
Restrictions: No funding for travel, fellowships for use within United States; United States citizenship or full-time enrollment in United States university required.
$ Given: An unspecified number of fellowships awarded annually; varying amounts.
Application Information: Write for details.
Deadline: January 1.

Social Science Research Council Korea Doctoral Dissertation Fellowships
605 Third Avenue
New York, NY 10158
(212) 661-0280

Description: Nine- to 18-month fellowships for doctoral candidates at dissertation level in the humanities and social sciences to pursue research in Korea and/or other country justified by research; recipients chosen on the basis of academic achievement, proposed research, and proficiency in Korean.
Restrictions: Good command of Korean required; United States citizenship or full-time enrollment in United States university required.

$ Given: An unspecified number of fellowships awarded annually; each for $9,000–$10,000.
Application Information: Write for details.
Deadline: January 1.

Social Science Research Council
Latin America and the Caribbean Doctoral Dissertation Research Fellowships
605 Third Avenue
New York, NY 10158
(212) 661-0280

Description: Nine- to 18-month fellowships for doctoral candidates at dissertation level to conduct field research on humanities/social sciences topics as related to Latin America or the Caribbean; recipients chosen on the basis of academic achievement and proposed research.
Restrictions: Open to all nationalities; full-time enrollment in United States university graduate program required.
$ Given: An unspecified number of fellowships awarded annually; varying amounts.
Application Information: Write for details.
Deadline: November 1.
Contact: Eric Hershberg.

Social Science Research Council
MacArthur Foundation Fellowships on International Peace and Security in a Changing World
605 Third Avenue
New York, NY 10158
(212) 661-0280

Description: Fellowship support for up to two years of research in the setting and nation of the recipient's choice; funding made available to doctoral candidates at dissertation level, postdoctoral scholars, and professionals studying international peace and security (in disciplines of humanities, social sciences, physical sciences, and natural sciences); recipients chosen on the basis of proposed research.
Restrictions: Open to all nationalities.
$ Given: Approximately eight fellowships awarded annually; $12,500–$17,500 per year predoctoral fellow; $25,000–$30,000 per year postdoctoral fellow.
Application Information: Write for details.
Deadline: December 1.
Contact: Felicia Sullivan.

Social Science Research Council
Near and Middle East Doctoral Dissertation Research Fellowships
605 Third Avenue
New York, NY 10158
(212) 661-0280

Description: Nine- to 18-month fellowships for doctoral candidates at dissertation level to conduct field research in one or more countries in North Africa, Turkey, Iran, Afghanistan, and the Middle East; for dissertation work in the humanities and social sciences as related to the Near and Middle East since the beginning of Islam; recipients chosen on the basis of academic achievement and proposed research.
Restrictions: United States citizenship or full-time enrollment in United States university required.
$ Given: Up to five fellowships awarded annually; varying amounts.
Application Information: Write for details.
Deadline: November 1.

Social Science Research Council
Russia and the Soviet Union and its Successor States
Doctoral Dissertation Write-Up Fellowships
605 Third Avenue
New York, NY 10158
(212) 661-0280

Description: One-year fellowships for doctoral candidates in the final year of dissertation writing to complete their dissertations; for dissertation topics in the humanities and social sciences as related to Russia and the Soviet Union and its successor states; recipients chosen on the basis of academic achievement.
Restrictions: United States citizenship required.
$ Given: An unspecified number of fellowships for $15,000 each are awarded annually.
Application Information: Write for details.
Deadline: December 1.

Social Science Research Council
Russia and the Soviet Union and its Successor States
Graduate Training Fellowships
605 Third Avenue
New York, NY 10158
(212) 661-0280

Description: Twelve-month fellowships for graduate students in the social sciences and humanities to support their third, fourth, or fifth year of graduate study, for pursuit of Russian and Soviet studies, possibly including support for intensive language training; recipients chosen on the basis of academic achievement.
Restrictions: Applicants must have completed two years of graduate work, not necessarily in Russian studies; United States citizenship required.
$ Given: An unspecified number of fellowships awarded annually; each for $15,000/year.
Application Information: Write for details.
Deadline: December 1.
Contact: Robert Huber.

Social Science Research Council
South Asia Doctoral Dissertation and Advanced Research Fellowships
605 Third Avenue
New York, NY 10158
(212) 661-0280

Description: Nine- to 18-month fellowships for doctoral candidates to conduct dissertation-related or advanced field research in Bangladesh, Nepal, Sri Lanka, Pakistan, Bhutan, or Maldives for dissertation work in the humanities and social sciences, business administration, and management; recipients chosen on the basis of academic achievement, proposed research, and proficiency in a major South Asian language.
Restrictions: United States citizenship or full-time enrollment in United States university required.
$ Given: Up to 15 fellowships awarded annually; varying amounts.
Application Information: Write for details.
Deadline: November 1.

Social Science Research Council
Southeast Asia Doctoral Dissertation and Advanced Research Fellowships
605 Third Avenue
New York, NY 10158
(212) 661-0280

Description: Nine- to 18-month fellowships for doctoral candidates to conduct dissertation-related or advanced field research in Brunei, Burma, Indonesia, Laos, Kampuchea, Malaysia, Thailand, Singapore, the Philippines, or Vietnam; for dissertation work in the humanities and social sciences, including law, public health, and public planning; recipients chosen on the basis of academic achievement, proposed research, and proficiency in a major Southeast Asian language.
Restrictions: United States citizenship or full-time enrollment in United States university required.
$ Given: An unspecified number of fellowships awarded annually; varying amounts.
Application Information: Write for details.
Deadline: November 1.

Social Science Research Council
Western Europe Doctoral Dissertation Research Fellowships
605 Third Avenue
New York, NY 10158
(212) 661-0280

Description: Nine- to 18-month fellowships for doctoral candidates to conduct dissertation field research in Western Europe; for dissertation work in the humanities and social sciences as related to Western Europe; recipients chosen on the basis of academic achievement and proposed research.
Restrictions: United States citizenship or full-time enrollment in United States university required.
$ Given: Twelve to fifteen fellowships awarded annually; varying amounts.
Application Information: Write for details.
Deadline: November 1.

Social Sciences and Humanities Research Council of Canada
Jules and Gabrielle Leger Fellowships
Fellowships Division
350 Albert Street
Box 1610
Ottawa, Ontario K1P 6G4
Canada
(613) 992-0525

Description: One-year fellowships for university-affiliated and private scholars at graduate level in the humanities and social sciences, to support research and writing on the historical/contemporary contribution of the Crown and its representatives; tenable at recognized university/institution for at least eight months of full-time work; recipients chosen on the basis of academic achievement.
Restrictions: Canadian citizenship required.
$ Given: An unspecified number of fellowships awarded in alternate years; each for $40,000 Canadian plus $10,000 Canadian for research/travel expenses.
Application Information: Fellowships offered in odd-numbered years.
Deadline: October 1.
Contact: Helene Regnier, Fellowships Division.

**Social Sciences and
Humanities Research Council
of Canada
SSHRC Doctoral Fellowships**
Fellowships Division
350 Albert Street
Box 1610
Ottawa, Ontario K1P 6G4
Canada
(613) 992-3145

Description: Two-year renewable fellowships for doctoral candidates in the humanities, and social sciences;
tenable in Canada or abroad; recipients chosen on the
basis of academic achievement and proposed research.
Restrictions: Applicants must have completed one year
of doctoral study; Canadian citizenship or permanent
resident status required.
$ Given: Six hundred fellowships awarded annually,
plus 600 annual renewables; each for up to $14,436 Cana-
dian per year plus relocation costs.
Application Information: Write for details.
Deadline: October 15.

**Social Sciences and
Humanities Research Council
of Canada
SSHRC Queen's Fellowships**
Fellowships Division
350 Albert Street
Box 1610
Ottawa, Ontario K1P 6G4
Canada
(613) 992-3145

Description: One-year fellowships for graduate students in social sciences and humanities, to support study
toward Ph.D. in Canadian studies at Canadian institutions.
Restrictions: Canadian citizenship required; must have
completed one year of graduate study.
$ Given: One to two fellowships awarded annually;
each for up to $14,436 Canadian plus tuition and travel
allowance; non-renewable.
Application Information: Applicants automatically
eligible if currently studying Canadian studies at Canadian University; no application.
Deadline: October 15.
Contact: Heather Steele, Director, Fellowships Division Society for Historians of American Foreign
Relations.

**W. Stull Holt Dissertation
Fellowship**
Wright State University
Department of History
Dayton, OH 45435
(513) 873-2838

Description: Fellowship for doctoral candidate to conduct dissertation research on topic relevant to the
history of American foreign relations; recipients chosen
on the basis of proposed research.
Restrictions: N/A.
$ Given: One fellowship of $1,500 is awarded annually.
Application Information: Application information and
materials from Katherine Siegel, Department of History,
St. Josephs University, 5600 City Avenue, Philadelphia,
PA 19131.
Deadline: April 1.

Society of Architectural Historians Rosann Berry Fellowship
1232 Pine Street
Philadelphia, PA 19107
(215) 735-0224 or
(215) 735-0246

Description: Fellowship to allow one doctoral student to attend the Society's annual meeting; relevant disciplines includes history of architecture, city planning, decorative arts, and historic preservation; recipients chosen on the basis of academic achievement and quality of work.
Restrictions: N/A.
$ Given: One fellowship awarded annually; Society fees waived, plus $500 to cover travel/lodging; meals reimbursed.
Application Information: Write for details.
Deadline: N/A.
Contact: Assistant to the Executive Director.

Sourisseau Academy for California State and Local History
Sourisseau Academy Research Grants
History Department
San Jose State University
San Jose, CA 95192
(408) 924-6510 or
(408) 227-2657

Description: Grants to support research related to any aspect of California and Santa Clara County history.
Restrictions: N/A.
$ Given: Up to ten grants for $500 each are awarded annually.
Application Information: Write for details.
Deadlines: April 1, November 1.
Contact: Glory Anne Laffey, Executive Secretary.

Special Libraries Association Affirmative Action Scholarship
1700 Eighteenth Street, N.W.
Washington, DC 20009
(202) 234-4700

Description: Scholarship for master's candidates and graduating college seniors; tenable at United States or Canadian institution of library and information science; preference to students with interest in special librarianship; recipients chosen on the basis of academic achievement and financial need.
Restrictions: Limited to minority group applicants only; United States or Canadian citizenship required.
$ Given: One scholarship for $6,000 is awarded annually.
Application Information: Write for details.
Deadline: October 31.

Special Libraries Association ISI Scholarship
1700 Eighteenth Street, N.W.
Washington, DC 20009
(202) 234-4700

Description: Scholarship for beginning doctoral candidates in library science, information science, and related fields; tenable at United States or Canadian institution of library and information science; preference to students with interest in special librarianship; recipients chosen on the basis of academic achievement and financial need.
Restrictions: Applicants must have work experience in special librarianship at M.A. level; preference to SLA members; United States or Canadian citizenship required; must show financial need.

$ Given: One scholarship for $1,000 is awarded annually.
Application Information: Write for details.
Deadline: October 31.

Special Libraries Association
Plenum Scholarships
1700 Eighteenth Street, N.W.
Washington, DC 20009
(202) 234-4700

Description: Research scholarships for doctoral candidates with approved dissertation topics; tenable at United States or Canadian institution of library and information science; preference to students with interest in special librarianship; recipients chosen on the basis of academic achievement, financial need, and proposed research.
Restrictions: United States or Canadian citizenship required.
$ Given: One scholarship for $1,000 is awarded annually.
Application Information: Write for details.
Deadline: October 31.

Special Libraries Association
Special Libraries Association
Scholarships
1700 Eighteenth Street, N.W.
Washington, DC 20009
(202) 234-4700

Description: Scholarships for master's candidates and graduating college seniors studying library science; tenable at United States or Canadian institution of library and information science; preference to students with interest in special librarianship; recipients chosen on the basis of academic achievement and financial need.
Restrictions: United States or Canadian citizenship required.
$ Given: Three scholarships for $6,000 each are awarded annually.
Application Information: Write for details.
Deadline: October 31.

State Historical Society of
Wisconsin
Alice E. Smith Fellowship
816 State Street
Madison, WI 53706
(608) 264-6464

Description: Research fellowship for master's and doctoral candidates studying American history, especially that of Wisconsin or the Midwest; recipients chosen on the basis of proposed research.
Restrictions: Limited to women only.
$ Given: One fellowship for $2,000 is awarded annually.
Application Information: Write for details.
Deadline: July 15.
Contact: Michael E. Stevens, State Historian.

Swann Foundation for
Caricature and Cartoon
Fellowships for the Study of
Caricature and Cartoon
641 Lexington Avenue
New York, NY 10022
(212) 838-2424

Description: Fellowships for doctoral candidates at dissertation level in any university discipline as related to caricature and cartoon; recipients chosen on the basis of academic achievement, financial need, and quality of proposed research.
Restrictions: Enrollment at United States or Canadian university required.

$ Given: One fellowship for $10,000 is awarded annually.
Application Information: Write for details.
Deadline: February 15.
Contact: Henry J. Goldschmidt, President.

Swann Foundation for Caricature and Cartoon Grants-in-Aid
641 Lexington Avenue
New York, NY 10022
(212) 838-2424

Description: Funding for projects involving the study, preservation, and evaluation of original works of comic art; recipients chosen on the basis of academic achievement, financial need, and quality of ongoing projects.
Restrictions: N/A.
$ Given: An unspecified number of grants are awarded annually; varying amounts.
Application Information: Write for details.
Deadline: Varies.
Contact: Rosemarie Guarieri.

Swedish Institute International Summer Courses Scholarships
P.O. Box 7434
Stockholm S-103 91
Sweden
46-8-789 20 00

Description: Scholarships for four-week summer courses (July–August) at Swedish folk high schools throughout Sweden, for study in Swedish language, culture, society and literature; instruction in Swedish; classes six hours/day, five days/week.
Restrictions: Minimum age 18; language proficiency requirement, dependent on level of study.
$ Given: A few scholarships awarded annually; varying amounts.
Application Information: Write for details.
Deadline: March 31.
Contact: Brita Holm, Course Director; or Pernilla Eldblom, Course Secretary.

Swedish Women's Educational Association International Swedish Women's Educational Association International Scholarships
P.O. Box 2585
La Jolla, CA 92038-2585
(619) 587-0807

Description: Scholarships for graduate students in Swedish literature and language; tenable for graduate-level study at Scandinavian institutions.
Restrictions: Limited to women only; all nationalities may apply.
$ Given: An unspecified number of scholarships for $5,000 each are awarded annually.
Application Information: Write for details.
Deadline: April 1.
Contact: Boel Alkdal, Administrator.

Harry S. Truman Library Institute Dissertation-Year Fellowships
24 Highway and Delaware
Independence, MO 64050
(816) 833-1400

Description: One-year fellowships for doctoral candidates who have completed their dissertation research; to support the writing of dissertations on Truman's public career and administration; Library residency not required.
Restrictions: Recipients must provide the Library with copies of finished dissertations.

$ Given: Two fellowships for $16,000 each are awarded annually.
Application Information: Write for details.
Deadline: February 1.
Contact: Secretary.

**Harry S. Truman Library Institute
Research Grants**
24 Highway and Delaware
Independence, MO 64050
(816) 833-1400

Description: Grants to support one to three weeks of research at the Library on projects concerning Truman's public career or administration; for master's and doctoral candidates, as well as postdoctoral scholars; recipients chosen on the basis of proposed research.
Restrictions: N/A.
$ Given: An unspecified number of grants for up to $2,500 each are awarded annually; intended to cover round-trip airfare and living expenses.
Application Information: Submit written proposal.
Deadline: Applications accepted continuously.
Contact: Secretary.

**United Daughters of the Confederacy
Mrs. Simon Baruch University Award**
328 North Boulevard
Richmond, VA 23220
(804) 355-1636

Description: Award for best submitted scholarly book or monograph on Southern history and the Confederacy; open to master's degree holders, doctoral candidates, and postdoctoral scholars.
Restrictions: Submitted work must be unpublished.
$ Given: One author's award of $500, plus $2,000 to aid publication of the manuscript.
Application Information: Offered only in even-numbered years.
Deadline: May 1 of even-numbered years.

**United Methodist Communications
Stoody-West Fellowship for Graduate Study in Religious Journalism**
475 Riverside Drive
Suite 1901
New York, NY 10115
(212) 663-8900

Description: One-year fellowship to support graduate study in religious journalism at accredited university or department of journalism; open to master's candidates, B.S./B.A. holders, and graduating college seniors; recipients chosen on the basis of academic achievement, Christian commitment and involvement in the church, journalistic experience or evidence of talent, and clarity of purpose/goals.
Restrictions: Applicants must be Christians; no funding for summer sessions.
$ Given: One fellowship awarded annually; $6,000 paid in two equal installments.
Application Information: Write for details.
Deadline: February 1.
Contact: Fellowship Committee.

**U.S. Air Force Historical Foundation
AFHF Fellowship in Aviation History**
Department of the Air Force
Building 1413, Stop 44
Andrews AFB, MD
20331-5064
(301) 736-1959

Description: Annual fellowship for dissertation level doctoral candidates and postdoctoral scholars, to support research in the history of aviation; recipients chosen on the basis of research capabilities.
Restrictions: United States citizenship or legal residency required.
$ Given: One fellowship to support research at the foundation archives.
Application Information: Applicants must demonstrate ability to produce publishable material.
Deadline: December 1.
Contact: Col. Cummings, Executive Director.

**U.S. Arms Control and Disarmament Agency
Hubert H. Humphrey Doctoral Fellowships in Arms Control and Disarmament**
Office of Public Affairs
The State Department
320 21st Street
Washington, DC 20451
(202) 647-8677

Description: Fellowships for doctoral candidates at dissertation level, as well as third-year law students; to support up to 12 months of research on arms control and disarmament; recipients chosen on the basis of academic achievement and proposed research.
Restrictions: United States citizenship or legal residency required.
$ Given: An unspecified number of fellowships awarded annually; each with $5,000 stipend, plus up to $3,400 paid to institution to cover tuition and fees.
Application Information: Write for details.
Deadline: March 15.
Contact: Robert Waters.

U.S. Army Center of Military History Dissertation Year Fellowships
Pulaski Building
20 Massachusetts Avenue, N.W.
Washington, DC 20314
(202) 272-0293

Description: One-year fellowships for doctoral candidates at dissertation level studying the history of war on land, especially the history of the United States Army; recipients chosen on the basis of academic achievement and proposed research.
Restrictions: Open to civilians only; United States citizenship or legal residency required.
$ Given: An unspecified number of fellowships for $8,000 each are awarded annually.
Application Information: Write for details.
Deadline: January 10.
Contact: Morris MacGregor, Acting Chief Historian.

U.S. Army Military History Institute Advanced Research Grant Program
Carlisle Barracks, PA
17013-5008
(717) 245-3631

Description: Grants to graduate degree holders and professionals to support on-site Institute research on any topic related to military history, within the Institute's scope of holdings; recipients chosen on the basis of proposed research, use of Institute's holdings, and potential benefit to United States Army.
Restrictions: N/A.
$ Given: An unspecified number of grants up to $1,500 each are awarded annually; renewable.

Application Information: Write for details.
Deadline: January 1.
Contact: Dr. James Williams, Director for Educational Services.

U.S. Department of Education
FLAS Fellowships
Center for International Education
400 Maryland Avenue, S.W.
Washington, DC 20202
(202) 732-3283

Description: Fellowships for graduate students at accredited United States institutions studying foreign languages and area studies; recipients chosen on the basis of academic achievement and proposed research.
Restrictions: Applicants must be preparing for careers as specialists in uncommon languages and area studies; United States citizenship or permanent resident status required.
$ Given: Six hundred fellowships awarded annually; each covers tuition and fees ($17,863 academic year; $3,726 summer), plus $5,000 stipend; renewable.
Application Information: Write for details.
Deadline: Varies.

U.S. Department of Education
Jacob K. Javits Fellows Program
400 Maryland Avenue, S.W.
Washington, DC 20202
(202) 260-3574

Description: Fellowships for doctoral candidates with fewer than 20 semester hours; relevant disciplines include most humanities, arts, and social sciences; recipients chosen on the basis of academic achievement and proposed research.
Restrictions: United States citizenship or permanent resident status required.
$ Given: Approximately 80 fellowships awarded annually; average award of $14,000 per year; renewable for up to 48 months.
Application Information: Write for details.
Deadline: Applications accepted December 20–February 3.
Contact: Andre Smith, Director.

U.S. General Accounting Office
Doctoral Research Program
441 G Street, N.W.
Room 7822
Washington, DC 20548
(202) 275-8674

Description: Ten- to twelve-month program that provides doctoral candidates at dissertation level with opportunities to work/conduct research in Washington, DC; relevant disciplines include government, public policy, public administration, economics, political science, public health, international affairs, environmental policy, and resource management; recipients chosen on the basis of proposed research.
Restrictions: Recipients must sever all ties that violate conflict-of-interest laws applicable to federal employees; United States citizenship required.
$ Given: An unspecified number of grants awarded annually; each for $25,000–$30,000.

Application Information: Applicants must be recommended for the program by a member of the GAO Research and Education Advisory Panel.
Deadline: February 2.
Contact: Kenneth W. Hunter, Coordinator, Doctoral Research Program.

University of Illinois at Urbana-Champaign
Kate Neal Kinley Memorial Fellowship
College of Fine and Applied Arts
110 Architecture Building
608 East Lorado Taft Drive
Champaign, IL 61820
(217) 333-1661

Description: One-year fellowships for B.S./B.A. holders in the fields of applied arts and design, architecture, art, and music; recipients chosen on the basis of artistic talent and academic achievement.
Restrictions: Limited to graduates of the College of Fine and Applied Arts of the University of Illinois at Urbana-Champaign or similar institutions; preference for applicants under age 25.
$ Given: One fellowship for $7,000 awarded annually.
Application Information: Write for details.
Deadline: March 15.
Contact: R. Wilcoxon, Secretary.

University of North Carolina at Chapel Hill
Gilbert Chinard French History and Literature Research Grants
Romance Languages Department
CB3170
Chapel Hill, NC 27599

Description: Grants for doctoral candidates at dissertation level and recent Ph.D.s (within past six years) for two months' study of French history and literature in France; recipients chosen on the basis of academic achievement and proposed work.
Restrictions: Applicants must be affiliated with United States universities; United States citizenship or permanent resident status required.
$ Given: Two to three grants for $750 each are awarded annually.
Application Information: Write for details.
Deadline: January 15.
Contact: Catherine Maley, President, Institut Français de Washington.

University of Oslo
International Summer School
University of Oslo
International Summer School (ISS) Scholarships
c/o Saint Olaf College
1520 Saint Olaf College
Northfield, MN 55057
(507) 663-3269

Description: Scholarships for undergraduate upperclassmen and master's degree candidates studying Norwegian medical care/health services, and Norwegian literature, peace research, and energy/environment issues; to attend six-week summer school (June-August) in Oslo; recipients chosen on the basis of academic achievement and financial need.
Restrictions: N/A.
$ Given: A large number of scholarships; normally cover room, board, incidental expenses; no tuition fee.

Application Information: Application forms available from Norwegian Embassy or the North American Admissions Office (address below).
Deadline: March 1.
Contact: JoAnn Kleber, Administrator, North American Admissions Office.

Virginia State Council of Higher Education
Virginia Tuition Assistance Grant Program
101 North 14th Street
James Monroe Building
9th Floor
Richmond, VA 23219
(804) 371-7941

Description: Grants for full-time undergraduates and graduate students, including medical and law school students; tenable at eligible private universities in Virginia; some recipients chosen without regard to financial need.
Restrictions: Limited to Virginia residents.
$ Given: An unspecified number of grants awarded annually; each for up to $1,440 per academic year.
Application Information: Write for details.
Deadline: July 31; late applications accepted until September 10.
Contact: Elizabeth J. Waddy, Student Aid Program Specialist.

Wellesley College
Anne Louise Barett
Fellowship
Office of Financial Aid
106 Central Street
Wellesley, MA 02181
(617) 235-0320

Description: Fellowship for B.S./B.A. holders and graduating college seniors in the fields of music theory, composition and history; tenable for full-time graduate study in the United States or abroad at institutions other than Wellesley; recipients chosen on the basis of merit and financial need.
Restrictions: Limited to Wellesley graduates.
$ Given: One fellowship of up to $3,000 is awarded annually.
Application Information: Request application form before November 25.
Deadline: December 11.
Contact: Secretary to the Committee on Graduate Fellowships.

Wellesley College
Ruth Ingersoll Goldmark
Fellowship
Office of Financial Aid
106 Central Street
Wellesley, MA 02181
(617) 235-0320

Description: Fellowship for B.S./B.A. holders and graduating college seniors in the fields of English literature, composition, and the classics; tenable for full-time graduate study in the United States or abroad at institutions other than Wellesley; recipients chosen on the basis of merit and financial need.
Restrictions: Limited to women graduates of Wellesley.
$ Given: One fellowship of up to $3,000 is awarded annually.
Application Information: Request application form before November 25.
Deadline: December 11.
Contact: Secretary to the Committee on Graduate Fellowships.

Wellesley College
Edna V. Moffett Fellowship
Office of Financial Aid
106 Central Street
Wellesley, MA 02181
(617) 235-0320

Description: Fellowship for B.S./B.A. holders and graduating college seniors in the field of history; tenable for full-time graduate study in the United States or abroad at institutions other than Wellesley; preference for individuals entering their first year of graduate study; recipients chosen on the basis of merit and financial need.
Restrictions: Limited to women graduates of Wellesley.
$ Given: One fellowship of up to $2,500 is awarded annually.
Application Information: Request application form before November 25.
Deadline: December 11.
Contact: Secretary to the Committee on Graduate Fellowships.

Wellesley College
Mary McEwin Schimke
Scholarships
Office of Financial Aid
Box GR
106 Central Street
Wellesley, MA 02181
(617) 235-0320

Description: Scholarships for B.S./B.A. in the fields of literature, history, and American studies; recipients chosen on the basis of merit and financial need; tenable for graduate study at institutions other than Wellesley; intended to afford relief from costs of household and child care during graduate study.
Restrictions: Limited to women applicants; minimum age 30; applicants must have received their bachelor's degrees from United States institutions.
$ Given: An unspecified number of scholarships of up to $1,000 each are awarded annually.
Application Information: Request application form before November 25.
Deadline: December 11.
Contact: Secretary to the Committee on Graduate Fellowships.

Wellesley College
Vida Dutton Scudder
Fellowship
Office of Financial Aid
106 Central Street
Wellesley, MA 02181
(617) 235-0320

Description: Fellowship for B.S./B.A. holders and graduating college seniors in the fields of literature, political science, and the social sciences; tenable for full-time graduate study in the United States or abroad at institutions other than Wellesley; recipients chosen on the basis of merit and financial need.
Restrictions: Limited to Wellesley graduates.
$ Given: One fellowship of up to $2,000 is awarded annually.
Application Information: Request application form before November 25.
Deadline: December 11.
Contact: Secretary to the Committee on Graduate Fellowships.

Wellesley College
Harriet A. Shaw Fellowship
Office of Financial Aid
106 Central Street
Wellesley, MA 02181
(617) 235-0320

Description: Fellowship for B.S./B.A. in the fields of music and allied arts; tenable for full-time graduate study in the United States or abroad; recipients chosen on the basis of academic achievement and financial need.
Restrictions: Limited to Wellesley graduates.
$ Given: One fellowship of up to $3,000 is awarded annually.
Application Information: Request application form before November 25.
Deadline: December 11.
Contact: Secretary to the Committee on Graduate Fellowships.

Wenner-Gren Foundation for Anthropological Research Developing Countries Training Fellowships
220 Fifth Avenue
16th Floor
New York, NY 10001
(212) 683-5000

Description: Six-month to three-year training fellowships for doctoral candidates and nondegree scholars in anthropology.
Restrictions: Applicants must be residents of developing countries, and must be able to demonstrate unavailability of adequate training programs in home countries; applicants from the following places are not eligible: Abu-Dhabi, Australia, Bahrain, Brunei, Canada, Hong Kong, Israel, Japan, Kuwait, Libya, New Caledonia, New Zealand, Puerto Rico, Qatar, Saudi Arabia, United Arab Emirates, United States, Commonwealth of Independent States, and Western European countries; recipients must plan to return and work in home countries.
$ Given: An unspecified number of fellowships awarded annually; each for up to $12,500 per year.
Application Information: Applicants must be sponsored by home institution and host country institution.
Deadline: Nine months prior to anticipated start of training program.
Contact: Dr. Sydel Silverman, President.

Wenner-Gren Foundation for Anthropological Research Predoctoral Grants
220 Fifth Avenue
16th Floor
New York, NY 10001
(212) 683-5000

Description: Research fellowships for doctoral candidates at dissertation level in anthropology, including cultural/social and biological/physical anthropology, ethnology, archaeology, linguistics, and related disciplines concerned with human origins; recipients chosen on the basis of proposed dissertation research.
Restrictions: N/A.
$ Given: An unspecified number of fellowships awarded annually; each for up to $12,000 per year.
Application Information: Write for details.
Deadlines: May 1, November 1.
Contact: Dr. Sydel Silverman, President.

Whatcom Museum of History and Art
Jacobs Research Fund Small Grants Program
121 Prospect Street
Bellingham, WA 98225
(206) 676-6981

Description: Grants to support field research on living Native Americans; relevant disciplines include folklore, languages, literatures and linguistics, music, dance, drama, sociocultural anthropology, and ethnoscience; preference for Pacific Northwest focus; recipients chosen on the basis of proposed research.
Restrictions: Native American applicants encouraged.
$ Given: Ten grants of up to $1,200 each are awarded annually.
Application Information: Write for details.
Deadline: February 15.
Contact: Rebecca Schlotterback, Administrator.

Williams College
Gaius Charles Bolin
Fellowships for Minority Graduate Students
Hopkins Hall
Williamstown, MA 01267
(413) 597-4352

Description: One-year residential fellowships at Williams College for doctoral candidates at dissertation level in the humanities, natural sciences, social sciences, or behavioral sciences; fellowships tenure includes teaching responsibilities for only one semester course; recipients chosen on the basis of academic achievement and promise as college teachers.
Restrictions: Limited to minority group applicants.
$ Given: Two fellowships awarded annually; each for $25,000 plus up to $2,500 for research expenses.
Application Information: Write for details.
Deadline: January 15.
Contact: Michael McPherson, Dean of the Faculty.

Woodrow Wilson National Fellowship Foundation
Mellon Fellowships in the Humanities
CN 5329
Princeton, NJ 08543
(609) 452-7007

Description: Two-year fellowships for graduating college seniors and recent college graduates planning to pursue Ph.D. degrees in the humanities; tenable at any United States or Canadian institution, subject to cost ceiling; recipients chosen on the basis of outstanding academic achievement.
Restrictions: United States or Canadian citizenship or permanent resident status required.
$ Given: Eighty fellowships awarded annually; each for $13,250 plus tuition and fees for the first year; comparable stipend plus 2/3 tuition and fees for the second year.
Application Information: Application by faculty nomination only.
Deadline: November 4 for nomination; December 2 for application.
Contact: Dr. Alvin Kernan, Director.

Woodrow Wilson National Fellowship Foundation Charlotte W. Newcombe Doctoral Dissertation Fellowships
CN 5281
Princeton, NJ 08543
(609) 452-7007

Description: Research fellowships for doctoral candidates at dissertation level, for dissertation research on ethical or religious values in all fields of social sciences, humanities, and education.
Restrictions: Applicants must be enrolled in United States graduate schools.
$ Given: Fourty fellowships for $12,500 each are awarded annually.
Application Information: Write for details.
Deadline: Early December.
Contact: Program Officer.

Woodrow Wilson National Fellowship Foundation Women's Studies Doctoral Research Grants
CN 5281
Princeton, NJ 08543
(609) 452-7007

Description: Research grants for doctoral candidates at dissertation level in women's studies; recipients chosen on the basis of proposed dissertation research.
Restrictions: Applicants should have completed all Ph.D. requirements except dissertation at United States graduate schools.
$ Given: Fifteen research grants for $1,200 each are awarded annually.
Application Information: Write for details.
Deadline: November 5.
Contact: Carolyn Q. Wilson, Director, Women's Studies Program.

Winterthur Museum, Garden and Library Winterthur Museum Visiting Research Scholars
Office of Advanced Studies
Winterthur, DE 19735
(302) 888-4649

Description: One-month to one-year residential fellowships for doctoral candidates in all disciplines related to the Winterthur collections; intended for scholars who have been granted awards from other institutions but need a place to work/research; fellowship tenure features full access to museum resources and rental housing on Winterthur grounds; recipients chosen on the basis of proposed research.
Restrictions: N/A.
$ Given: An unspecified number of positions available; no stipend.
Application Information: Write for details.
Deadline: December 1.
Contact: Research Fellowship Program.

Women's Research and Education Institute Congressional Fellowships on Women and Public Policy
1700 Eighteenth Street, N.W.
Suite 400
Washington, DC 20009
(202) 328-7070

Description: Congressional fellowship program designed to train women as potential public policy leaders; fellowship runs September through April and involves 30 hrs/wk work in a United States Congress office as a legislative aide on policy issues affecting women; open to master's and doctoral candidates at United States institutions; relevant disciplines include humanities, social sciences, biology and biomedical sciences, engineering and applied sciences, biomedical engineering, technology management and policy, business administration and management, health services management and hospital administration, education, allied health professionals, medicine, nursing, public and community health, and law; recipients chosen on the basis of political/civic activity and interest in women's issues.

Restrictions: Limited to women applicants; nine hours previous graduate coursework preferred; United States citizenship preferred.

$ Given: Eight to fifteen fellowships awarded annually; each with $9,500 stipend plus $500 for health insurance and up to $1,500 toward six hours tuition at home institution.

Application Information: Request application after November 1.

Deadline: February 14.

Contact: Alison Dineen, Fellowship Director.

Yale University
John D. Rockefeller III
Summer Graduate Research
Fellowships
Institute for Social and Policy
Studies
P.O. Box 208253
88 Trumbull Street
New Haven, CT 06520
(203) 432-2121

Description: Residential summer fellowships at Yale for doctoral candidates in history, social sciences, American studies, religious studies, women's studies, management, public health, and divinity; to support research on philanthropy, voluntarism, and non-profit organizations; fellowship tenure runs mid-June through mid-August; fellows expected to produce publishable papers on their summer work.

Restrictions: Preference to applicants with body of written work; preference to applicants whose work will take full advantage of Yale's resources.

$ Given: Six fellowships awarded annually; each with $3,000 stipend plus office space, library privileges, and support services.

Application Information: Write for details.

Deadline: March 30.

Contact: Peter Hall, Coordinator

Biological and Agricultural Sciences

American Association for the Advancement of Science Mass Media Science and Engineering Fellows Program
1333 H Street, N.W.
Washington, DC 20005
(202) 326-6760

Description: Ten-week summer fellowships for science graduate students to work as journalists (print, radio, or television) to increase their understanding of the news media; available to students at any graduate level of study in the natural and social sciences, as well as engineering; recipients chosen on the basis of academic achievement and demonstrated commitment of conveying to the public a better understanding and appreciation of science and technology.
Restrictions: No funding to non-technical applicants; United States citizenship required; no concurrent funding allowed.
$ Given: Twenty fellowships awarded annually; weekly living stipend for 10 weeks plus travel costs.
Application Information: Write for details and application form; minorities and individuals with disabilities encouraged to apply.
Deadline: January 15.
Contact: Amie Hubbard, Program Manager.

American Association of University Women Educational Foundation AAUW Selected Professions Fellowships
P.O. Box 4030
Iowa City, IA 52243-4030
(319) 337-1716

Description: Fellowships for graduate students entering their final year of study in fields with traditionally low female representation, including architecture, business administration, computer science, dentistry, engineering, law, mathematics/statistics, medicine, and veterinary medicine; recipients chosen on the basis of academic achievement; tenable for full-time study at accredited United States institutions.
Restrictions: Limited to women who are members of minority groups; United States citizenship or permanent resident status required.
$ Given: An unspecified number of fellowships of $5,000–$9,500 each are awarded annually.
Application Information: Application forms available August 1 through November 1.
Deadline: December 15, February 1 for MBA.

**American Fishing Tackle
Manufacturers Association
A.J. Boehm Fellowships**
1250 Grove Avenue, Suite 300
Barrington, IL 60010
(708) 381-9490

Description: One-year fellowships for master's and doctoral candidates at thesis/dissertation level for research in fisheries management; recipients chosen on the basis of academic achievement (minimum 3.0 GPA) and proposed research.
Restrictions: Applicants must be committed to careers in fisheries management or related research.
$ Given: An unspecified number of fellowships awarded annually; each for $1,000–$10,000; paid directly to sponsor university on behalf of student research project.
Application Information: Application must be submitted by supervising professor.
Deadline: March 15.
Contact: Robert G. Kavanaugh, President.

**American Geological Institute
AGI Minority Geoscience
Scholarships**
4220 King Street
Alexandria, VA 22302-1507
(703) 379-2480

Description: Scholarships for undergraduate and graduate students who are geoscience and geoscience education majors at accredited institutions; relevant disciplines included geology, geophysics, geochemistry, hydrology, oceanography, planetary geology, and geoscience education; tenable in the United States; recipients chosen on the basis of academic achievement and financial need.
Restrictions: Limited to minority group applicants; United States citizenship required.
$ Given: An unspecified number of scholarships awarded annually; each for up to $4,000 at graduate level, up to $10,000 at undergraduate level; renewable.
Application Information: Application for required.
Deadline: February 1.
Contact: Marilyn J. Suiter, Administrator, Special Programs.

**American Geophysical Union
Horton Research Grant in
Hydrology and Water
Resources**
2000 Florida Avenue, N.W.
Washington, DC 20009
(202) 462-6900

Description: Grants for doctoral candidates, to support research projects in hydrology and water resources; relevant disciplines include physical/chemical/biological aspects of hydrology, as well as water resources policy sciences (economies, sociology, and law).
Restrictions: Membership in American Geophysical Union required.
$ Given: One or more grants awarded annually; approximately $9,000 plus travel allowance to ensure attendance at awards luncheon.
Application Information: Proposal must be signed by faculty advisor; application forms required.
Deadline: March 1.

**American Institute of
Pakistan Studies
American Institute of
Pakistan Studies Fellowships**
P.O. Box 7568
Wake Forest University
Winston-Salem, NC 27109
(919) 759-5453

Description: Fellowships for doctoral candidates, post-doctoral scholars, and professional researchers to undertake study/research in Pakistan; for students of humanities and social sciences, especially rural development, agriculture, local government, economics, demography, history, and culture; recipients chosen on the basis of proposed research.
Restrictions: Doctoral candidates must have completed all preliminary Ph.D. requirements; United States citizenship required.
$ Given: An unspecified number of fellowships awarded annually; each to cover air travel, maintenance, rental allowance, research allowance, internal travel, and excess baggage allowance.
Application Information: Write for details.
Deadline: January 1.
Contact: Dr. Charles H. Kennedy, Director.

**American Museum of Natural
History
Frank M. Chapman Memorial
Grants for Ornithological
Research**
Ornithology Department
Central Park West
at 79th Street
New York, NY 10024
(212) 769-5775

Description: Grants to support advanced graduate and postdoctoral scholars in research in both neontological and paleontological ornithology from a broad, international perspective; tenable at the American Museum of Natural History or elsewhere.
Restrictions: N/A.
$ Given: An unspecified number of grants awarded annually; each for $200–$1,000.
Application Information: Write for details.
Deadline: January 15.

**American Museum of Natural
History Collection Study Grants**
Office of Grants and
Fellowships
Central Park West
at 79th Street
New York, NY 10024
(212) 769-5040

Description: Grants to support four or more days of residential study at the American Museum of Natural History; for doctoral candidates and recent postdoctoral scholars studying vertebrate and invertebrate zoology, paleozoology, anthropology, and mineral sciences.
Restrictions: Limited to investigators living more than daily commute distance from the American Museum of Natural History.
$ Given: An unspecified number of grants awarded annually; each for up to $400 toward travel and subsistence; no funding for tuition; non-renewable.
Application Information: Write for details.
Deadline: Applications accepted continuously.
Contact: Grants Administrator.

American Museum of Natural History
Lerner-Gray Grants for Marine Research
Office of Grants and Fellowships
Central Park West
at 79th Street
New York, NY 10024
(212) 769-5040

Description: Grants to support advanced graduate students and postdoctoral scholars in marine zoology in early career research projects involving systematics, evolution, ecology, evolution, and field studies of behavior of marine animals; tenable at the American Museum of Natural History or elsewhere.
Restrictions: N/A.
$ Given: An unspecified number of grants awarded annually; each for $200–$1,000.
Application Information: Write for details.
Deadline: March 15.
Contact: Grants Administrator.

American Museum of Natural History
Theodore Roosevelt Memorial Grants
Office of Grants and Fellowships
Central Park West
at 79th Street
New York, NY 10024
(212) 769-5040

Description: Short-term grants to support advanced graduate students and postdoctoral scholars in paleontology research of the fauna of North America related to wildlife conservation or natural history; recipients chosen on the basis of academic achievement and proposed research.
Restrictions: N/A.
$ Given: An unspecified number of grants awarded annually; each for $200–$1,000 toward continuing research; no funding for tuition.
Application Information: Write for details.
Deadline: February 15.
Contact: Grants Administrator.

American Orchid Society
Orchid Research Fellowships
6000 South Olive Avenue
West Palm Beach, FL 33405
(407) 585-8666

Description: Long-term fellowships for doctoral candidates in orchidology, to support fundamental and applied research on orchids; tenable for up to three years of work on orchid-related dissertation project leading to Ph.D. from accredited United States institution; research should address the biology of the orchid: physiology, molecular biology, structure, cytology, ecology, systematics, or evolution; women, minorities, and the disabled are encouraged to apply.
Restrictions: Applicant must be enrolled full-time in a doctoral program at an accredited United States school.
$ Given: An unspecified number of grants awarded annually; each for $9,000/year for up to three consecutive years; funds paid directly to sponsor institution on behalf of individual researcher; may not be used for institution's indirect expenses.
Application Information: Write for details.
Deadline: January 1.
Contact: Lee Cooke, Executive Director.

**American Orchid Society
Research Grants**
6000 South Olive Avenue
West Palm Beach, FL 33405
(407) 585-8666

Description: One-year grant support for master's and doctoral candidates, as well as other qualified researchers, for experimental research projects involving fundamental and applied research on orchids; relevant disciplines include taxonomy, genetics, cytogenics, physiology, pathology, and conservation; recipients chosen on the basis of academic achievement and proposed research.
Restrictions: Applicants must be affiliated with accredited educational institutions or research facilities.
$ Given: An unspecified number of grants awarded annually; each for $500–$12,000; renewable up to three years.
Application Information: Write for details.
Deadlines: January 1, August 1.
Contact: Lee S. Cooke, Executive Director.

**American Philosophical
Society Library
Mellon Resident Research
Fellowships**
104 South Fifth Street
Philadelphia, PA 19106
(215) 440-3400

Description: One- to three-month residential fellowships for doctoral candidates at dissertation level and postdoctoral scholars studying the history of American history and culture; tenable at the Society Library, for short-term research using the library's collections.
Restrictions: United States citizenship required.
$ Given: An unspecified number of fellowships awarded annually; each for $1,800/month.
Application Information: Write for details.
Deadline: March 1.
Contact: Assistant Librarian for Research Programs.

**American Psychological
Association
APA Minority Fellowship
Program in Neuroscience**
750 First Street, NE
Washington, DC 20002-4242
(202) 336-6027 or
(202) 336-6012

Description: Ten-month fellowships for doctoral candidates in neuroscience; recipients chosen on the basis of academic achievement, financial need, and commitment to future career in neuroscience research.
Restrictions: African-American, Hispanic, Native American, Alaskan Native, Asian-American, and Pacific Islander applicants preferred; applicants must be planning careers in neuroscience; United States or Canadian citizenship or permanent resident status required.
$ Given: An unspecified number of fellowships awarded annually; each for $7,084 plus cost-sharing arrangement for full tuition scholarship; renewable for up to three years if recipient maintains good academic standing.
Application Information: Write for details.
Deadline: January 15.
Contact: Dr. James M. Jones, Director; or Ernesto Guerra, Minority Fellowship Program.

American Schools of Oriental Research
George A. Barton Fellowship at the Albright Institute for Archaeological Research, Jerusalem
3301 North Charles Street
Baltimore, MD 21218
(401) 516-3498

Description: Residential fellowships for doctoral study in humanistic disciplines of the Middle East; for one to five months of study/research at the Albright Institute in Jerusalem; recipients chosen on the basis of proposed research.
Restrictions: Fellowship may not be used for summer study.
$ Given: An unspecified number of fellowships are awarded annually; each with a $2,000 stipend plus room and half-board.
Application Information: Write for details.
Deadlines: September 15, October 15.
Contact: Dr. Rudolph H. Dornemann, Administrative Director.

American Schools of Oriental Research
Endowment for Biblical Research
Summer Research Grants & Travel Scholarships
3301 North Charles Street
Baltimore, MD 21218
(401) 516-3498

Description: Grants and scholarships for graduate and seminary students; for study of archaeology, linguistics, natural sciences, and anthropology in the Holy Land; recipients chosen on the basis of proposed study/research.
Restrictions: Membership in ASOR required; citizenship in any country outside the Middle East required.
$ Given: Two one- to three-month research grants of $1,500 each are awarded annually; 16 summer travel scholarships of $1,000 each are awarded annually.
Application Information: Write for details.
Deadline: February 1.
Contact: Dr. Rudolph H. Dornemann, Administrative Director.

American Society for Engineering Education
Office of Naval Research
Graduate Fellowships
1818 N Street, N.W., Suite 600
Washington, DC 20036
(202) 331-3525

Description: Thirty-six-month fellowships (tenable over five years) for college seniors in engineering, mathematics, and science to support graduate work toward Ph.D. beginning the following September; fellowship includes summer work at Navy laboratory; relevant disciplines include biology/biomedical sciences, oceanography, mathematics, computer science, electrical engineering, material science, cognitive and neural sciences, naval architecture and ocean engineering, physics, chemistry, and aerospace/mechanical engineering; recipients chosen on the basis of academic achievement.
Restrictions: United States citizenship required; applicants already in graduate school ineligible.
$ Given: Up to 50 fellowships awarded annually; each for $15,000 for the first 12 months, $16,000 for the second 12 months, and $17,000 for the third 12 months, plus full tuition paid directly to the United States university, plus $1,800/month summer stipend during summer work at Navy laboratory.
Application Information: Write for details.
Deadline: January 19.
Contact: Projects Officer.

American Society for Enology and Viticulture Scholarship
P.O. Box 1855
Davis, CA 95617
(916) 753-3142

Description: Scholarship for undergraduate and graduate students interested in enology and viticulture (wine-making and grape-growing); recipients chosen on the basis of academic achievement, financial need, and educational/career pursuits.
Restrictions: Limited to residents of North America who are enrolled in accredited universities in North America.
$ Given: One scholarship of $1,000–$3,000 is awarded annually; renewable.
Application Information: Write for details.
Deadline: March 1.

American Statistical Association
ASA and USDA/NASS Research Fellow and Associate Program
1429 Duke Street
Alexandria, VA 22314-3402

Description: Nine- to twelve-month fellowships and associateships for doctoral candidates and postdoctoral researchers in agricultural statistics, for residential research/work at the National Agricultural Statistics Service; recipients chosen on the basis of academic achievement and proposed research.
Restrictions: N/A.
$ Given: An unspecified number of fellowship/associateship positions awarded annually; each with stipend.
Application Information: Write for details.
Deadline: March 1.
Contact: Marie Argana, Fellowship Programs Director.

American Water Works Association
LARS Scholarships
6666 West Quincy Avenue
Denver, CO 80235
(303) 794-7711

Description: Scholarships for outstanding graduate students in fields of water treatment, corrosion control, and aquatic/analytic/environmental chemistry.
Restrictions: Applicants must be graduate students at institutions in the United States, Canada, Guam, Puerto Rico, or Mexico who will complete their degree requirements after August 31 of the deadline year.
$ Given: Two scholarships awarded annually; $3,000 for M.S. candidate; $5,000 for Ph.D. candidate.
Application Information: Write for details.
Deadlines: December 15 for M.S. candidate; February 15 for Ph.D. candidate.
Contact: Administrative Coordinator, Education Department.

American Water Works Association
Abel Wolman Doctoral Fellowships
6666 West Quincy Avenue
Denver, CO 80235
(303) 794-7711

Description: Twelve-month fellowships for outstanding doctoral candidates, to support research and training in water supply and treatment.
Restrictions: Applicants must be within two years of completing Ph.D. requirements; United States, Canadian, or Mexican citizenship required.

$ Given: One fellowship awarded annually; $10,000 stipend plus $1,000 research supplies/equipment allowance and up to $4,000 for tuition and fees.
Application Information: Write for details.
Deadline: February 15.
Contact: Administrative Coordinator, Education Department.

Arctic Institute of North America
Grant-in-Aid Program
University of Calgary
2500 University Drive, N.W.
Calgary, Alberta T2N 1N4
Canada
(403) 220-7515

Description: Grants for graduate students for natural/social sciences field work in the northern regions; recipients chosen on the basis of academic achievement and quality of proposed research.
Restrictions: N/A.
$ Given: An unspecified number of grants of up to $5,000 Canadian are awarded annually.
Application Information: Write for details.
Deadline: January 15.
Contact: Mike Robinson, Executive Director.

Argonne National Laboratory
Graduate Research
Appointments
9700 South Cass Avenue
Argonne, IL 60439-4845
(708) 252-3371

Description: One-year research appointments for graduate students to conduct thesis/dissertation research at Argonne National Laboratory in the fields of physical/life sciences, computer science, engineering, mathematics, fission/fusion energy, conservation, and the environment; recipients chosen on the basis of academic achievement, proposed research, and relevance of research to ANL projects.
Restrictions: Enrollment in United States university graduate program required.
$ Given: An unspecified number of appointments available annually; each with stipend plus up to $4,000/year for tuition and travel; renewable.
Application Information: Preliminary contact with ANL researchers recommended.
Deadline: Applicants accepted continuously.
Contact: Graduate Student Programs Office.

Argonne National Laboratory
Graduate Thesis Parts
Research Appointments
9700 South Cass Avenue
Argonne, IL 60439-4845
(708) 252-3371

Description: Short-term appointments (a few days to a few months) for graduate students to conduct thesis/dissertation research at Argonne National Laboratory in the fields of physical/life sciences, computer science, engineering, mathematics, fission/fusion energy, conservation, and the environment; recipients chosen on the basis of academic achievement, proposed research.
Restrictions: Enrollment at United States university required.
$ Given: An unspecified number of appointments available annually; each with per diem and travel expenses.

Application Information: Write for details.
Deadline: Applications accepted continuously.
Contact: Graduate Student Programs Office.

**Arthritis Foundation
Doctoral Dissertation Awards
for Nonphysician Health
Professionals**
1314 Spring Street, N.W.
Atlanta, GA 30309
(404) 872-7100

Description: One to two years of grant support for doctoral candidates conducting dissertation-level research related to arthritis; recipients chosen on the basis of proposed research.
Restrictions: Applicants must be planning careers in arthritis research; membership in or eligibility for professional organization required.
$ Given: An unspecified number of grants awarded annually; each for up to $10,000/year.
Application Information: Applicant's doctoral chairperson must approve the project.
Deadline: September 1.
Contact: Administrative Assistant, Research Administrator.

**Arthritis Foundation
Doctoral Dissertation
Physician Scientist
Development Award**
1314 Spring Street, N.W.
Atlanta, GA 30309
(404) 872-7100

Description: Two years of grant support for medical students in M.D. or M.D./Ph.D. programs at accredited United States medical schools pursuing arthritis-related research; recipients chosen on the basis of proposed research and potential as biomedical investigators.
Restrictions: Applicants must be planning careers in medicine; applicants must have research advisors who agree to provide the necessary space, facilities, and guidance for the proposed research.
$ Given: An unspecified number of grants awarded annually; each for $27,000–$32,000/year.
Application Information: Write for details.
Deadline: September 1.
Contact: Research Department.

**Association for Women in
Science Educational
Foundation
AWIS Predoctoral Award**
1522 K Street, N.W.
Suite 820
Washington, DC 20005
(202) 408-0742

Description: Awards for doctoral candidates in life sciences, physical sciences, social sciences, engineering, mathematics, and behavioral sciences; recipients chosen on the basis of academic achievement and quality of proposed research.
Restrictions: Limited to women only; United States citizenship and enrollment in United States institution required.
$ Given: An unspecified number of grants of $500 each are awarded annually.
Application Information: Write for details.
Deadline: January 15.
Contact: Catherine Didion.

**Atlantic Salmon Federation
Bensinger-Liddle Salmon
Fellowship**
P.O. Box 429
Saint Andrews,
New Brunswick
EOG 2X0
Canada
(506) 529-4581

Description: Fellowship to support individual research overseas on Atlantic salmon conservation and management; recipients chosen on the basis of research capability and benefit of proposed research.
Restrictions: United States or Canadian citizenship required in even-numbered years; United Kingdom citizenship required in odd-numbered years.
$ Given: One fellowship for $10,000 Canadian awarded annually.
Application Information: For application form, contact the United States office, Atlantic Salmon Federation, P.O. Box 807, Calais, ME 04619.
Deadline: March 1.
Contact: Cheryl Carter.

**Atlantic Salmon Federation
Olin Fellowships**
P.O. Box 429
Saint Andrews, New Brunswick
EOG 2X0
Canada
(506) 529-4581

Description: Fellowship to support research on Atlantic salmon conservation and management; tenable at any accredited university or research laboratory; recipients chosen on the basis of academic achievement and benefit of proposed research.
Restrictions: United States or Canadian citizenship required
Given: Two to six fellowships awarded annually; each for $1,000–$3,000 Canadian.
Application Information: For application form, contact the United States office, Atlantic Salmon Federation, P.O. Box 807, Calais, ME 04619.
Deadline: March 15.
Contact: Cheryl Carter.

**Canadian Federation of
University Women
CFUW Memorial Grant**
55 Parkdale Avenue
Ottawa, Ontario K1Y 1E5
Canada
(613) 722-8732

Description: Grant for B.S./B.A. holders, to support graduate study in science and technology; recipients chosen on the basis of academic achievement, personal qualities, and potential.
Restrictions: Limited to women only; applicants must be accepted at intended places of study; Canadian citizenship or one-year landed immigrant status required.
$ Given: One grant of $1,000 Canadian awarded annually.
Application Information: Request application between July 1 and November 13.
Deadline: November 30.
Contact: Chair, Fellowships Committee.

Carnegie Institution of Washington
Carnegie Developmental Biology Research Fellowships
1530 P Street, N.W.
Washington, DC 20005
(202) 387-6411

Description: One-year residential research fellowships at the Department of Embryology in Baltimore, Maryland, for doctoral candidates at dissertation level and postdoctoral scholars studying developmental biology and embryology; recipients chosen on the basis of academic achievement and proposed research.
Restrictions: N/A.
$ Given: An unspecified number of fellowships awarded annually; varying amounts; renewable for two additional years.
Application Information: Applicants should establish contact with staff member with whom they plan to study; application materials include educational record, record of work experience, list of publications, essay, and three letters of recommendation; completed applications should be sent to Director, Carnegie Institution, Department of Embryology, 115 West University Parkway, Baltimore, MD 21210-3301.
Deadline: One year in advance of fellowship.
Contact: Publications Officer.

Carnegie Institution of Washington
Carnegie Plant Biology Fellowships
1530 P Street, N.W.
Washington, DC 20005
(202) 387-6411

Description: One-year residential research fellowship at the Department of Plant Biology in Stanford, California, for doctoral candidates at dissertation level and postdoctoral scholars studying plant biology; recipients chosen on the basis of academic achievement and proposed research.
Restrictions: N/A.
$ Given: Ten to twelve fellowships awarded annually; varying amounts; renewable for two additional years.
Application Information: Applicants should establish contact with staff member with whom they plan to study; application materials include educational record, record of work experience, list of publications, essay, and three letters of recommendation; completed applications should be sent to Director, Carnegie Institution, Department of Plant Biology, 290 Panama Street, Stanford, CA 94305-4101.
Deadline: January 1.
Contact: Publications Officer.

Council for the Advancement of Science Writing
Nate Haseltine Memorial Fellowships in Science Writing
P.O. Box 404
Greenlawn, NY 11740

Description: Fellowships for the study of science writing, available to B.S./B.A. holders in science of journalism, as well as to professional reporters and graduate students; recipients chosen on the basis of academic achievement, quality of writing, and commitment to writing career.

Restrictions: Preference to journalists with two years professional experience who want to specialize in science writing.
$ Given: An unspecified number of grants of up to $2,000 each are awarded annually.
Application Information: Write for details.
Deadline: June 1.
Contact: Executive Director.

Deafness Research Foundation
Research Grants
9 East 38th Street
New York, NY 10016
(212) 684-6556

Description: Grant for doctoral candidates, faculty and staff members, to support research on any aspect of the ear—its function, physiology, biochemistry, genetics, anatomy, pathology, or rehabilitation; recipients chosen on the basis of proposed research.
Restrictions: Funding must be used at United States or Canadian facility; applicants must disclose any other sources of funding for the project.
$ Given: An unspecified number of grants of up to $15,000 are awarded annually; renewable for one to two additional years.
Application Information: Write for details.
Deadline: July 15.
Contact: Medical Director.

Epilepsy Foundation of America
EFA Behavioral Sciences
Student Research Fellowships
4351 Garden City Drive
Suite 406
Landover, MD 20785
(301) 459-3700

Description: One-year research fellowships for graduate students interested in basic and clinical research in the biological, behavioral, and social sciences designed to advance the understanding, treatment, and prevention of epilepsy; tenable at United States institutions; recipients chosen on the basis of demonstrated competence in epilepsy research.
Restrictions: Funding must be used in the United States; no funding for capital equipment.
$ Given: Fifteen to twenty fellowships awarded annually; each for $1,500.
Application Information: Write for details.
Deadline: March 1.
Contact: Ruby Gerald, Program Assistant, Research and Professional Education.

Epilepsy Foundation of America
Medical Student Fellowships
4351 Garden City Drive
Suite 406
Landover, MD 20785
(301) 459-3700

Description: Short-term fellowships (three months) for medical students interested in careers in epilepsy research; tenable for research at United States institutions with ongoing epilepsy research/service projects; recipients chosen on the basis of submitted statement addressing relevant experiences and interest.
Restrictions: End-of-project report required.
$ Given: An unspecified number of fellowships for $2,000 each are awarded annually.

Application Information: Submit outline of proposed 8- to 12-week program of research, plus personal statement addressing interest in epilepsy research.
Deadline: March 1.
Contact: Ruby Gerald, Administrative Assistant, Research and Professional Education.

Florida Education Fund McKnight Doctoral Fellowships
201 East Kennedy Boulevard
Suite 1525
Tampa, FL 33602
(813) 272-2772

Description: Fellowships for graduate study at one of eleven participating doctoral-degree-granting universities in Florida in the fields of business, engineering, agriculture, biology, computer science, mathematics, physical science, and psychology; recipients chosen on the basis of academic achievement.
Restrictions: Limited to African-American applicants only; B.A./B.S. degree required; United States citizenship required.
$ Given: Twenty-five fellowships awarded annually; each for a maximum of five years of study, with an annual $11,000 stipend plus up to $5,000 in tuition and fees.
Application Information: Write for details.
Deadline: January 15.
Contact: Dr. Israel Tribble, Jr.

Foundation for Field Research Field Research Grants
P.O. Box 2010
Alpine, CA 92903
(619) 445-9264

Description: Research grants for graduate students, as well as field researchers, for work in the fields of archaeology, paleontology, anthropology, ornithology, primatology, folklore, historic preservation, museum studies, botany, plant sciences, entomology, marine sciences, and oceanography; tenable at projects worldwide; recipients chosen on the basis of proposed research.
Restrictions: Applicants must speak English.
$ Given: An unspecified number of grants for $1,000–$25,000 each are awarded annually; renewable.
Application Information: Submit two-page preliminary research proposal.
Deadline: Proposals accepted continuously.
Contact: Thomas J. Banks.

French Embassy Scientific Services
Chateaubriand Research Scholarships for the Exact Sciences, Engineering, and Medicine
Department of Science and Technology
4101 Reservoir Road, N.W.
Washington, DC 20007
(202) 944-6241

Description: Six- to twelve-month research scholarship for doctoral candidates at dissertation level, as well as postdoctoral scholars, to conduct research in France at French universities, engineering schools, and private laboratories; language training sessions provided; relevant disciplines include biological and agricultural sciences, physical sciences and mathematics, engineering and applied sciences, medicine, nutrition, optometry and vision sciences, pharmacy and pharmaceuticals sciences, and veterinary medicine and sciences; recipients chosen on the basis of proposed research.

Restrictions: Each applicant must be registered at United States university and already in contact with French host institution; United States citizenship required.
$ Given: Twenty to thirty scholarships awarded annually; each for 9,000 francs per month plus airfare and health insurance.
Application Information: Application forms must be submitted with faculty recommendation.
Deadline: January 31.

Golf Course Superintendents Association of America GCSAA Scholarships
1421 Research Park Drive
Lawrence, KS 66049
(913) 841-2240

Description: Scholarships for undergraduate upperclassmen and graduate students, as well as second-year students in two-year technical programs; for study of turf grass management; recipients chosen on the basis of academic achievement, financial need, and character.
Restrictions: Applicants must be planning careers in golf course supervision or related research.
$ Given: Five to ten scholarships awarded annually; each for $1,000–$5,000.
Application Information: Application forms must be submitted with faculty recommendation.
Deadline: October 1.
Contact: Chair, Scholarship and Research Committee.

Grass Foundation Grass Fellowships in Neurophysiology
77 Reservoir Road
Quincy, MA 02170
(617) 773-0002

Description: Ten- to fourteen-week summer residential research fellowships at the Marine Biological Laboratory in Woods Hole, Massachusetts, for doctoral candidates and postdoctoral researchers in neurophysiology, electrophysiology, experimental neuroanatomy, neurochemistry, cellular neurobiology, developmental neurobiology, tissue culture, and behavioral analysis; recipients chosen on the basis of academic achievement and commitment to research career.
Restrictions: Recipients may not attempt to combine this fellowship with dissertation work; open to all nationalities.
$ Given: An unspecified number of fellowships awarded annually; each for housing, board, research space rental, and expense budget.
Application Information: Write for bulletin.
Deadline: December 1.
Contact: Secretary.

**Herb Society of America
Research and Education
Grants**
9019 Kirtland Chardon Road
Kirtland, OH 44094
(216) 256-0514

Description: Grants to graduate students for study/research in horticulture, science, literature, art, and economics—as related to herbs; recipients chosen on the basis of proposed research, which may be scientific or academic; research period may be up to one year.
Restrictions: N/A.
$ Given: One to two grants totaling $5,000 are awarded annually.
Application Information: Write for details.
Deadline: January 31.
Contact: Grants Administrator.

Horticultural Research Institute
HRI Grants
1250 I Street, N.W.
Suite 500
Washington, DC 20005
(202) 789-2900

Description: Research grants to support work on improving the efficiency of the landscape/nursery trade; recipients chosen on the basis of proposed research.
Restrictions: N/A.
$ Given: Fifteen to twenty grants for $500–$10,000 each are awarded annually.
Application Information: Write for details.
Deadline: May 1.
Contact: Ashby P. Ruden, Administrator.

**Howard Hughes Medical
Institute
Predoctoral Fellowships in
Biological Sciences**
National Research Council
2101 Constitution Ave, N.W.
Washington, DC 20418
(202) 334-2872

Description: Three-year international fellowships to support full-time study toward Ph.D. degree in biological sciences; intended for students at or near the beginning of graduate studies; relevant fields include biochemistry, biophysics, biostatistics, mathematical biology, cell biology, developmental biology, epidemiology, genetics, immunology, microbiology, molecular biology, neuroscience, pharmacology, physiology, structural biology, and virology; tenable at United States institutions; recipients chosen on the basis of academic achievement and future promise in biomedical research; women and minorities encouraged to apply.
Restrictions: Open to all nationalities.
$ Given: Sixty-six fellowships awarded annually; each with $14,500/year stipend and $14,000 annual cost-of-education allowance in lieu of tuition and fees; renewable for two additional years.
Application Information: Write for details.
Deadline: November 3.
Contact: Fellowship Office, National Research Council.

Howard Hughes Medical Institute
HHMI-NIH Cloister Research Scholars Program
One Cloister Court,
Department G
Bethesda, MD 20814-1460
(301) 951-6770
(800) 424-9924

Description: One-year research scholar positions for medical students to participate in laboratory research at the National Institutes of Health in Bethesda, Maryland; sponsored by HHMI and NIH.
Restrictions: Applicants must be attending medical school (usually in second year) in the United States or Puerto Rico; United States citizenship or permanent resident status required.
$ Given: An unspecified number of positions given annually; each with $16,800 stipend, plus fringe benefits.
Application Information: Kits and brochures available from medical school deans' offices.
Deadline: January 10.
Contact: Program Officer.

Edmund Niles Huyck
Preserve Graduate and Postgraduate Research Grants
P.O. Box 189
Rensselaerville, NY 12147

Description: Grants for graduate students, as well as postdoctoral investigators, to support up to one year of research in animal behavior, evolution, and forest biology; research to be conducted using the Biological Station of the Huyck Preserve; recipients chosen on the basis of proposed research.
Restrictions: N/A.
$ Given: Ten grants awarded annually; each for up to $2,500, plus housing and laboratory space.
Application Information: Write for details.
Deadline: February 1.
Contact: Grants Administrator.

Institute of International Education
Colombian Government Study and Research Grants
U.S. Student Programs Division
809 United Nations Plaza
New York, NY 10017-3580
(212) 984-5330

Description: Grants for B.S./B.A. holders to pursue up to two years of study/research at Colombian universities; relevant disciplines include agriculture, biology, business administration, economics, chemistry, engineering, education, health services administration, economics, chemistry, engineering, education, geography, history, Latin American literature, law, linguistics, political science, physics, regulatory development, public health, and remote sensing interpretation.
Restrictions: United States citizenship required.
$ Given: An unspecified number of grants awarded annually; each for modest monthly stipend, plus tuition and fees, health insurance, book/materials allowance, and one-way return airfare upon completion of study.
Application Information: Write for details.
Deadline: October 31.

Institute of International Education Study and Research Grants for US Citizens
U.S. Student Programs Division
809 United Nations Plaza
New York, NY 10017-3580
(212) 984-5330

Description: Grants to support study and research in all fields, as well as professional training in the creative and performing arts; tenable at institutions of higher learning outside of the United States for one year; list of participating countries in any given year may be obtained from IIE.
Restrictions: Open to United States citizens with B.A. or equivalent; acceptable plan of study and proficiency in host country's language required.
$ Given: A variable number of grants awarded annually; covers international transportation, language or orientation course (where appropriate), tuition, book and maintenance allowances, and health and accident insurance.
Application Information: If currently enrolled in a college or university, apply to the campus Fulbright Program Advisor; applications also available from IIE.
Deadline: October 31.

International Research and Exchanges Board
IREX Research Exchange Program with Mongolia
1616 H Street, N.W.
Washington, DC 20006
(202) 628-8188

Description: Two- to ten-month exchange program for doctoral candidates to study in Mongolia; relevant disciplines include the humanities, social sciences, and natural sciences; recipients chosen on the basis of proposed research.
Restrictions: Command of host country's language required; United States citizenship required.
$ Given: An unspecified number of fellowships awarded annually; varying amounts.
Application Information: Write for details.
Deadline: October 15.
Contact: Cynthia Graves, Program Officer.

International Society of Arborculture
Shade Tree Research Grants
Shade Tree Laboratories
Department of Botany
Ohio Wesleyan University
Delaware, OH 43015
(614) 368-3508

Description: Grants to support scientific and educational research on shade trees; relevant disciplines include horticulture, plant pathology, entomology, and soil studies; recipients chosen on the basis of proposed research.
Restrictions: Open to all nationalities.
$ Given: An unspecified number of grants for $5,000 each are awarded annually.
Application Information: Submit two-page outline of project (in English) and respond to eleven questions from evaluation committee.
Deadline: November 1.
Contact: Dr. Bruce Roberts, Chairperson, Research Committee.

International Women's Fishing Association Scholarships
P.O. Drawer 3125
Palm Beach, FL 33480
(407) 746-0547

Description: Scholarships for graduate students in marine science; recipients chosen on the basis of academic achievement and financial need.
Restrictions: Applicants must be enrolled at United States universities; both sexes eligible.
$ Given: Up to ten scholarships awarded annually; each for up to $3,000.
Application Information: Write for details.
Deadline: March 1.
Contact: Scholarship Trust Chairperson.

Japan Ministry of Education, Science, and Culture Japanese Government (Monbusho) Scholarship Program
2-2 Kasumigaseki, 3-chome
Chiyoda-ku
Tokyo 100
Japan
03-581-4211

Description: Eighteen-month to two-year scholarships for non-Japanese graduate students to study at Japanese universities and research institutes; Research Students Program is specifically designed for graduate students (undergraduate program also available) in the humanities, social sciences, music, fine arts, and natural sciences; open to citizens of countries with educational exchange agreements with Japan.
Restrictions: Language proficiency required (12- to 18-month language training program required if language skills deemed insufficient); applicants must be under age 35.
$ Given: An unspecified number of scholarships awarded annually; each to cover monthly stipend, airfare, tuition, and expense allowance.
Application Information: For further information, contact Japanese Embassy or Consulate.
Deadlines: June 15, September 30.
Contact: Student Exchange Division.

Landscape Architecture Foundation CLASS Fund Scholarships
4401 Connecticut Avenue, N.W.
5th Floor
Washington, DC 20008
(202) 686-0068

Description: Scholarships for undergraduate and graduate students in landscape architecture and ornamental horticulture; recipients chosen on the basis of financial need, commitment to and promise in profession, and plans for advance study.
Restrictions: Applicants must be Southern California residents enrolled in programs for landscape architecture and ornamental horticulture.
$ Given: An unspecified number of scholarships awarded annually; varying amounts.
Application Information: Write for details.
Deadline: April 3.
Contact: David Bohardt, Acting Executive Director.

**Landscape Architecture
Foundation
Grace and Robert Fraser
Landscape Heritage Fund
Award**
4401 Connecticut Avenue,
N.W.
5th Floor
Washington, DC 20008
(202) 686-0068

Description: Award for new contribution to the field of
landscape architecture; established professionals and outstanding students are eligible for consideration.
Restrictions: Applicants must be landscape architecture
scholars pursuing research on new approaches to landscape architecture through horticulture.
$ Given: One award of $500 made annually.
Application Information: Write for details.
Deadline: May 4.
Contact: David Bohardt, Acting Executive Director.

**Landscape Architecture
Foundation
Edith H. Henderson
Scholarship**
4401 Connecticut Avenue,
N.W.
5th Floor
Washington, DC 20008
(202) 686-0068

Description: Scholarship for undergraduate seniors and
graduate students in landscape architecture; recipients
chosen on the basis of academic achievement and commitment to developing practical client communication
skills.
Restrictions: Limited to women applicants enrolled at
the University of Georgia.
$ Given: One scholarship of $1,000 awarded annually.
Application Information: Personal essay addressing the
importance of communication skills required for application.
Deadline: May 4.
Contact: David Bohardt, Acting Executive Director.

**Landscape Architecture
Foundation
LANDCADD Scholarship**
4401 Connecticut Avenue, N.W.
5th Floor
Washington, DC 20008
(202) 686-0068

Description: Scholarship for undergraduate and graduate students in landscape architecture; recipients chosen
on the basis of academic achievement and career plans
for utilization of computer-aided design, video imaging,
and/or telecommunications.
Restrictions: N/A.
$ Given: One scholarship awarded annually; for $500 in
cash, plus $500-value LANDCADD software donated to
winner's institution.
Application Information: Essay required.
Deadline: May 4.
Contact: David Bohardt, Acting Executive Director.

**Landscape Architecture
Foundation
Raymond E. Page
Scholarships**
4401 Connecticut Ave, N.W.
5th Floor
Washington, DC 20008
(202) 686-0068

Description: Scholarships for undergraduate and graduate students in landscape architecture; recipients chosen
on the basis of financial need alone.
Restrictions: N/A.
$ Given: Two scholarships of $500 each awarded annu-
ally.
Application Information: Write for details.
Deadline: May 4.
Contact: David Bohardt, Acting Executive Director.

Landscape Architecture Foundation Rain Bird Company Scholarship
4401 Connecticut Ave, N.W.
5th Floor
Washington, DC 20008
(202) 686-0068

Description: Scholarship for undergraduate and graduate students in landscape architecture; recipients chosen on the basis of professional commitment as exemplified by extracurricular activities and academic achievements.
Restrictions: N/A.
$ Given: One scholarship of $1,000 awarded annually.
Application Information: Write for details.
Deadline: May 4.
Contact: David Bohardt, Acting Executive Director.

Landscape Architecture Foundation Student Research Grants
4401 Connecticut Ave, N.W.
5th Floor
Washington, DC 20008
(202) 686-0068

Description: Grants for undergraduate and graduate students in landscape architecture; to support research projects; recipients chosen on the basis of research proposals and budgets.
Restrictions: N/A.
$ Given: Up to two grants awarded annually; each for $1,000.
Application Information: Write for details.
Deadline: May 4.
Contact: David Bohardt, Acting Executive Director.

Landscape Architecture Foundation Lester Walls III Endowment Scholarship
4401 Connecticut Ave, N.W.
5th Floor
Washington, DC 20008
(202) 686-0068

Description: Scholarship for undergraduate and graduate students in landscape architecture; recipients chosen on the basis of personal disability or study of barrier-free design.
Restrictions: Preference for applicants who are visually handicapped, hearing impaired, or physically handicapped; no group projects.
$ Given: One scholarship for $500 awarded annually.
Application Information: Write for details.
Deadline: May 4.
Contact: David Bohardt, Acting Executive Director.

Landscape Architecture Foundation Harriet Barnhart Wimmer Scholarship
4401 Connecticut Ave, N.W.
5th Floor
Washington, DC 20008
(202) 686-0068

Description: Scholarship to support final year of undergraduate or graduate studies in landscape architecture; recipients chosen on the basis of design excellence and environmental sensitivity of work submitted for consideration.
Restrictions: Limited to women applicants; group projects ineligible.
$ Given: One scholarship of $500 awarded annually.
Application Information: Write for details; assembled materials should be sent to Harriet Barnhart Wimmer Scholarship, c/o Wimmer, Yamada & Associates, 516 Fifth Avenue, San Diego, CA 92101, (619) 232-4004.
Deadline: May 4.
Contact: David Bohardt, Acting Executive Director.

The Library Company of Philadelphia
American History and Culture Research Fellowships
1314 Locust Street
Philadelphia, PA 19107
(215) 546-3181

Description: Residential research fellowships at the Library Company of Philadelphia for doctoral candidates and postdoctoral scholars in most disciplines as related to the history and culture of 18th- to 19th- century America; tenable for one or more months; recipients chosen on the basis of proposed research.
Restrictions: N/A.
$ Given: An unspecified number of fellowships awarded annually; each with $1,350/month stipend.
Application Information: Write for details.
Deadline: February 1.
Contact: James Green, Curator.

Charles A. Lindbergh Fund
Lindbergh Grants Program
708 South 3rd Street
Suite 110
Minneapolis, MN 55415
(612) 338-1703
FAX (612) 338-6826

Description: Grants for individuals to conduct research into the balance of technology and the human/natural environment; relevant fields include humanities, biomedical research, conservation of natural resources, waste disposal management, wildlife preservation, intercultural communications, aviation, aeronautics, agriculture, astronautics, adaptive technology, the arts, health and population studies, and oceanography.
Restrictions: Open to all nationalities.
$ Given: Twenty or more grants of up to $10,580 each are awarded annually.
Application Information: Write for details.
Deadline: June 14.
Contact: Marlene K. White, Grants Coordinator.

National Geographic Society
Research Grants
Committee for Research and Exploration
1145 17th Street, N.W.
Washington, DC 20036
(202) 857-7439

Description: Grants for research in anthropology, archaeology, astronomy, biology, glaciology, botany, ecology, physical and human geography, mineralogy, geology, oceanology, paleontology, zoology, and other sciences pertinent to geography; funding primarily for postdoctoral researchers, but occasionally awarded to exceptional doctoral candidates; recipients chosen on the basis of proposed research.
Restrictions: Open to all nationalities.
$ Given: An unspecified number of grants of $15,000–$20,000 average each are awarded annually.
Application Information: Write for details.
Deadline: Applications accepted continuously.
Contact: Committee for Research and Exploration.

National Medical Fellowships, Inc.
The Commonwealth Fund Medical Fellowships for Minorities
110 West 32nd Street
8th Floor
New York, NY 10001
(212) 714-1007

Description: Eight- to twelve-week fellowships for second- and third-year medical students to work in major research laboratories under the supervision/tutelage of prominent biomedical scientists; recipients chosen on the basis of academic achievement.
Restrictions: Limited to minority group members only; applicants must attend accredited United States medical schools and must be interested in careers in research/academic medicine.
$ Given: Thirty-five fellowship awarded annually; each for $6,000.
Application Information: Applicants must be nominated by medical school deans.
Deadlines: September for nomination; application deadline follows.
Contact: Programs Department.

National Science Foundation Behavioral and Neural Sciences Research Grants
4201 Wilson Boulevard
Arlington, VA 22230
(703) 306-1416

Description: Grants to support research on nervous systems and human/animal behavior; awarded in the following subprogram categories- cultural/physical anthropology, archaeology, animal behavior, behavioral neuroendocrinology, cellular neuroscience, developmental neuroscience, human cognition/perception, linguistics, neural mechanisms of behavior, neurobiology of learning/memory, sensory system, and social psychology; recipients chosen on the basis of proposed research.
Restrictions: N/A.
$ Given: An unspecified number of grants awarded annually; varying amounts.
Application Information: Write for subprogram details.
Deadline: Applications accepted continuously; January 15, July 15.
Contact: Dr. Christopher Comer, Division of Integrative Biology and Neuroscience.

National Society to Prevent Blindness
Student Fellowships
500 East Remington Rd.
Schaumburg, IL 60173
(708) 843-2020

Description: Short-term (60-90 days) fellowships for undergraduate, graduate, and medical students, to support eye-related clinical or basic science research; fellowship involves full-time residence, usually in summer.
Restrictions: N/A.
$ Given: An unspecified number of fellowships awarded annually; each for up to $500/month ($1,500 maximum total).
Application Information: Write for details.
Deadline: March 1.
Contact: Director, Program Services, Fight for Sight Research Division.

**National Speleological Society
Ralph W. Stone Award in
Speleology**
Ames Research Center
MS 239-4
Moffett Field, CA 94035

Description: Grants to registered graduate students for research in geology, biology, speleology, geochemistry, hydrology, and other cave-related sciences; recipients chosen on the basis of financial need and proposed research.
Restrictions: NSS membership required.
$ Given: One grant for $1,500 is awarded annually.
Application Information: Write for details.
Deadline: May 1.
Contact: David Des Marais.

**Natural Sciences and
Engineering Research
Council of Canada NSERC
Postgraduate Scholarships in
Science Librarianship and
Documentation**
200 Kent Street
Ottawa, Ontario K1A 1H5
Canada
(613) 992-8203

Description: One-year scholarships for first- and second-year study toward M.L.S. degree in library science; recipients chosen on the basis of academic achievement, commitment to field, and relevant experience.
Restrictions: Applicants must have B.S. degree in science or engineering; Canadian citizenship or permanent resident status required.
$ Given: A few scholarships awarded annually; each for $13,500 Canadian plus travel allowance.
Application Information: Write for details.
Deadline: December 1.
Contact: Nadine Bohan; Information Officer.

**Parenteral Drug Association
Foundation for
Pharmaceutical Sciences
Foundation Grant in
Biotechnology**
P.O. Box 242
Garden City, NY 11530
(516) 248-6713

Description: One- to three-year grant for research in developing biotechnology analytical methodology; recipients chosen on the basis of proposed research.
Restrictions: No geographic restrictions.
$ Given: One grant of $15,000 is awarded annually.
Application Information: Application form and eight copies of proposal required.
Deadline: June 15.
Contact: Grants Administrator.

**Parenteral Drug Association
Foundation for
Pharmaceutical Sciences
PDAF Research Grants**
P.O. Box 242
Garden City, NY 11530
(516) 248-6713

Description: One-year grants to support research in parenteral technology and related fields; recipients chosen on the basis of proposed research.
Restrictions: United States citizenship required.
$ Given: Two grants of $15,000 each are awarded annually; renewable once.
Application Information: Write for details.
Deadline: June 15.
Contact: Grants Administrator.

Parenteral Drug Association Foundation for Pharmaceutical Sciences Charles P. Schaufus Parenteral Processing Technology Research Grant
P.O. Box 242
Garden City, NY 11530
(516) 248-6713

Description: One- to three-year grants to support research in parenteral technology; recipients chosen on the basis of proposed research.
Restrictions: United States citizenship required.
$ Given: One grant of $10,000 is awarded annually; renewable.
Application Information: Write for details.
Deadline: June 15.
Contact: Grants Administrator.

President's Commission on White House Fellowships White House Fellowships
712 Jackson Place, N.W.
Washington, DC 20503
(202) 395-4522

Description: Twelve-month appointments as special assistants to the Vice President, Cabinet members, and the Presidential staff; fellowships include participation in educational program; positions available for students in public affairs, education, the sciences, business, and the professions; recipients chosen on the basis of leadership qualities, commitment to community service, and career/academic achievement.
Restrictions: Limited to young adults, ages 30–39; civilian federal employees are ineligible; recipients may not hold official state or local office while serving as White House fellows; United States citizenship required.
$ Given: Eleven to nineteen wage-earning fellowships for up to a maximum of $65,000 are awarded annually.
Application Information: Write for details.
Deadline: December 15.
Contact: Phyllis A. Williams.

Purina Mills Company Purina Mills Research Fellowships
Purina Research Awards Committee
P.O. Box 66812
St. Louis, MO 63166-6812

Description: Fellowships for graduate students at agricultural colleges, for nutrition and physiology research as related to dairy, poultry, and animal sciences; recipients chosen on the basis of academic achievement and proposed research.
Restrictions: N/A.
$ Given: Four fellowships awarded annually; each for $12,500/year.
Application Information: Write for guidelines.
Deadline: February 5.
Contact: Mary E. Timpe–2E.

Rockefeller University
Rockefeller Archive Center
Research Grants
15 Dayton Avenue
Pocantico Hills
North Tarrytown, NY
10591-1598
(914) 631-4505

Description: Residential research fellowships for graduate students and postdoctoral scholars pursuing research using Archive Center resources; relevant disciplines including philanthropy, education, science, medicine, black history, agriculture, labor, social welfare, social sciences, politics, religion, population, economic development, and the arts; recipients chosen on the basis of proposed research and necessity of using Archive Center resources.
Restrictions: N/A.
$ Given: An unspecified number of grants awarded annually; each for up to $1,500 for travel, lodging, and research expenses.
Application Information: Write for details.
Deadline: December 31.
Contact: Dr. Darwin H. Stapleton, Director.

Sigma Delta Epsilon/
Graduate Women in Science
Eloise Gerry Fellowships
P.O. Box 19947
San Diego, CA 92159

Description: One-year research fellowships for graduate students and postdoctoral scholars in the biological and chemical sciences; recipients chosen on the basis of academic achievement, financial need, and proposed research.
Restrictions: Limited to women applicants only; funding may not be used for tuition; applicants may not apply simultaneously for other SDE fellowships.
$ Given: Three to six fellowships awarded annually; each for $1,500–$4,000.
Application Information: Write for details.
Deadline: December 1.
Contact: Helen D. Haller, Secretary.

Sigma Xi, The Scientific
Research Society
Grants-in-Aid of Research
P.O. Box 13975
Research Triangle Park, NC
27709

Description: Research grants to graduate and undergraduate students in science and engineering, to support research projects; recipients chosen on the basis of proposed research.
Restrictions: Open to all nationalities.
$ Given: An unspecified number of grants awarded annually; each for up to $1,000 (average $600).
Application Information: Application forms required.
Deadlines: February 1, May 1, and November 1.
Contact: Committee on Grants-in-Aid of Research.

Slocum-Lunz Foundation
Scholarships and Grants
Scholarship and Grant
Committee
P.O. Box 12559
Charleston, SC 29412
(803) 795-6350

Description: Grants for graduating college seniors and graduate students; support for research in marine biology and closely related natural species; recipients chosen on the basis of academic achievement and proposed research.
Restrictions: Residents of southeastern United States preferred; applicants planning careers in South Carolina

preferred; funding may not be used for living expenses or tuition.
$ Given: An unspecified number of grants awarded annually; each for up to $1,500.
Application Information: Write for details.
Deadline: April 1.
Contact: Scholarship and Grant Committee Chair.

Smithsonian Institution Graduate Student Research Fellowships
Office of Fellowships and Grants
955 L'Enfant Plaza
Suite 7300
Washington, DC 20560
(202) 287-3271

Description: Ten-week residential fellowships for graduate students to pursue research at the Smithsonian; relevant disciplines include art history, anthropology, ecology, biology, environmental science, astrophysics, history of science, Oriental art, natural history, African art and culture, and American cultural/sociological history; recipients chosen on the basis of proposed research.
Restrictions: N/A.
$ Given: Approximately 38 fellowships are awarded annually; each with maximum $3,000 stipend.
Application Information: Write for details.
Deadline: January 15.
Contact: Program Assistant.

Smithsonian Institution Minority Students Internships
Office of Fellowships and Grants
955 L'Enfant Plaza
Suite 7300
Washington, DC 20560
(202) 287-3271

Description: Nine- to twelve-week internships for undergraduate upperclassmen and graduate students in the humanities, social sciences, natural sciences, and physical sciences; internship program includes participation in ongoing research or activities at the Museum plus supervised independent research in any bureau; recipients chosen on the basis of academic achievement and proposed research.
Restrictions: Limited to minority group applicants.
$ Given: An unspecified number of internship positions are awarded annually; $250/week undergraduate stipend, $300/week graduate stipend.
Application Information: Write for details.
Deadlines: February 15, June 15, and October 15.

Smithsonian Institution Predoctoral Research Fellowships in the History of Science and Technology
Office of Fellowships and Grants
955 L'Enfant Plaza
Suite 7300
Washington, DC 20560
(202) 287-3271

Description: One-year residential fellowships for doctoral candidates at dissertation level in the history of science and technology, to pursue independent research using the Smithsonian's collections, resources, and staff expertise; relevant disciplines include history of mathematics, physical sciences, pharmacy, medicine, civil and mechanical engineering, electrical technology, and history of American science; recipients chosen on the basis of proposed research.
Restrictions: Applicants must have completed all preliminary coursework and exams for degree.

$ Given: An unspecified number of fellowships are awarded annually; each with $14,000 stipend.
Application Information: Write for details.
Deadline: January 15.
Contact: Program Assistant.

Social Science Research Council
Africa Training and Dissertation Research Fellowships on Agricultural and Health
605 Third Avenue
New York, NY 10158
(212) 661-0280

Description: Fellowships to support doctoral candidates for up to 12 months of natural/technical science training and 9–18 months of field research and write-up in Africa; for dissertation work in the social sciences as related to African agriculture and health; recipients chosen on the basis of academic achievement and proposed research.
Restrictions: United States citizenship or full-time enrollment in United States university required.
$ Given: An unspecified number of fellowships awarded annually; maximum award $45,000.
Application Information: Proposal should state dissertation topic, proposed research site, and preliminary plans for training.
Deadline: November 1.
Contact: Africa Program.

Social Science Research Council
MacArthur Foundation Fellowships on International Peace and Security in a Changing World
605 Third Avenue
New York, NY 10158
(212) 661-0280

Description: Fellowship support for up to two years of research in the setting and nation of the recipient's choice; funding made available to doctoral candidates at dissertation level, postdoctoral scholars, and professionals studying international peace and security (in disciplines of humanities, social sciences, physical sciences, and natural sciences); recipients chosen on the basis of proposed research.
Restrictions: Open to all nationalities.
$ Given: Approximately eight fellowships awarded annually; $12,500–$17,500 per year predoctoral fellow; $25,000–$30,000 per year postdoctoral fellow.
Application Information: Write for details.
Deadline: December 1.
Contact: Felicia Sullivan.

Soil and Water Conservation Society
Kenneth E. Grant Research Awards
7515 N.E. Ankeny Road
Ankeny, IA 50021
(515) 289-2331
(800) 843-7645

Description: Awards for graduate students to conduct research (thesis/dissertation related or other) on good land use; relevant disciplines include agronomy and soil sciences, natural resources, water resources, and economics; recipients chosen on the basis of academic achievement and financial need.
Restrictions: SWCS membership required.
$ Given: An unspecified number of awards of up to $1,400 each are awarded annually.

Application Information: Request application from university department head or SWCS.
Deadline: April 1.
Contact: Max Schnepf, Director of Public Affairs.

Southern Illinois University at Carbondale
Minority Doctoral Fellowships in Science and Engineering Graduate School
Woody Hall, B-114
Carbondale, IL 62901
(618) 536-7791

Description: Three-year fellowships for doctoral candidates in the life sciences, physical sciences, and engineering; recipients chosen on the basis of GRE or other national standardized test scores.
Restrictions: Limited to minority group applicants; applicants of Mexican or Puerto Rican descent preferred; United States citizenship required.
$ Given: Ten to twenty fellowships awarded annually; each for $15,000/year plus full tuition & fees (for three years).
Application Information: Write for details.
Deadline: February 2.
Contact: Dr. Harry Daniels, Associate Dean.

Sport Fishing Institute Fund
Sport Fishing Research Program Fellowships and Grants
1010 Massachusetts Avenue, N.W.
Suite 320
Washington, DC 20001
(202) 898-0770

Description: Grants for graduate students to support research in aspects of fish life history, aquatic ecology, environmental biology, zoology, and natural resource sciences.
Restrictions: N/A.
$ Given: Ten to twenty-five grants awarded annually; each for $500–$5,000 per year; renewable.
Application Information: Application must be submitted by supervising professor.
Deadline: March 1.
Contact: Christine Altman.

Rob and Bessie Welder Wildlife Foundation
Welder Graduate Wildlife Research Scholarships
P.O. Drawer 1400
Sinton, TX 78387-1400
(512) 364-2643

Description: One-year scholarships for graduate students at accredited universities for research in wildlife-related issues; some scholarships tenable at the Welder Refuge; recipients chosen on the basis of academic achievement and proposed research.
Restrictions: N/A.
$ Given: Fifteen to twenty scholarships awarded annually; each for $750/month (master's) to $800/month (doctoral); renewable; money paid directly to sponsor university.
Application Information: Application letter must be signed by qualified faculty member of applicant's university.
Deadline: October 15.
Contact: Director.

**Williams College
Gaius Charles Bolin
Fellowships for Minority
Graduate Students**
Hopkins Hall
Williamstown, MA 01267
(413) 597-4352

Description: One-year residential fellowships at Williams College for doctoral candidates at dissertation level in the humanities, natural sciences, social sciences, or behavioral sciences; fellowships tenure includes teaching responsibilities for only one semester course; recipients chosen on the basis of academic achievement and promise as college teachers.
Restrictions: Limited to minority group applicants.
$ Given: Two fellowships awarded annually; each for $25,000 plus up to $2,500 for research expenses.
Application Information: Write for details.
Deadline: January 15.
Contact: Michael McPherson, Dean of the Faculty.

**Wilson Ornithological Society
Louis Agassiz Fuertes and
Margaret Morse Nice**
Ornithological Research
Awards
University of Michigan
Museum of Zoology
Ann Arbor, MI 48109
(313) 764-0457

Description: Grants for graduate students in ornithology to conduct avian research; recipients chosen on the basis of financial need and proposed research.
Restrictions: Recipients must report their research results at society's annual meeting.
$ Given: Two grants of $200 each are awarded annually.
Application Information: Application form required.
Deadline: January 15.

**Wilson Ornithological Society.
Paul A. Stewart
Ornithological Research
Awards**
University of Michigan
Museum of Zoology
Ann Arbor, MI 48109
(313) 764-0457

Description: Grants for ornithologists to conduct avian research; recipients chosen on the basis of financial need and proposed research.
Restrictions: Recipients must report their research at society's annual meeting.
$ Given: Several grants of $200 each are awarded annually.
Application Information: Application form required.
Deadline: January 15.

**Women's Research and
Education Institute
Congressional Fellowships on
Women and Public Policy**
1700 18th Street, N.W.
Suite 400
Washington, DC 20009
(202) 328-7070

Description: Congressional fellowship program designed to train women as potential public policy leaders; fellowship runs September through April and involves 30 hrs/wk work in a United States Congress office as a legislative aide on policy issues affecting women; open to master's and doctoral candidates at United States institutions; relevant disciplines include humanities, social sciences, biology and biomedical sciences, engineering and applied sciences, biomedical engineering, technology management and policy, business administration and management, health services management and hospital administration, education, allied health professionals, medicine, nursing, public and community health, and law; recipients chosen on the basis of political/civic activity and interest in women's issues.

Restrictions: Limited to women applicants; nine hours previous graduate coursework preferred; United States citizenship preferred.

$ Given: Eight to fifteen fellowships awarded annually; each with $9,500 stipend plus $500 for health insurance and up to $1,500 toward six hours tuition at home institution.

Application Information: Request application after November 1.

Deadline: February 14.

Contact: Alison Dineen, Fellowship Director.

Physical Sciences and Mathematics

**American Association of
Petroleum Geologists
AAPG Grants-in-Aid of
Research**
P.O. Box 979
Tulsa, OK 74101-0979
(918) 584-2555

Description: Grants for master's and doctoral candidates at thesis/dissertation level, for field work on research project leading to degree; relevant disciplines include sedimentology, stratigraphy, paleontology, mineralogy, structural geology, geochemistry, geophysics, environmental geology, and the search for hydrocarbons and economic sedimentary minerals; special named grants also available.
Restrictions: No funding for the purchase of capital equipment.
$ Given: An unspecified number of grants awarded annually; maximum $2,000.
Application Information: Write for application form.
Deadline: January 15.
Contact: W.A. Morgan, Chairman, Grants-in-Aid Committee.

**American Association of
University Women
Educational Foundation
AAUW Selected Professions
Fellowships**
P.O. Box 4030
Iowa City, IA 52243-4030
(319) 337-1716

Description: Fellowships for graduate students entering their final year of study in fields with traditionally low female representation, including architecture, business administration, computer science, dentistry, engineering, law, mathematics/statistics, medicine, and veterinary medicine; recipients chosen on the basis of academic achievement; tenable for full-time study at accredited United States institutions.
Restrictions: Limited to women who are members of minority groups; United States citizenship or permanent resident status required.
$ Given: An unspecified number of fellowships of $5,000–$9,500 each are awarded annually.
Application Information: Application forms available August 1 through November 1.
Deadlines: December 15, February 1 for M.B.A.

**American Geological Institute
AGI Minority Geoscience
Scholarships**
4220 King Street
Alexandria, VA 22303
(703) 379-2480

Description: Scholarships for undergraduate and graduate students who are geoscience and geoscience education majors at accredited institutions; relevant disciplines include geology, geophysics, geochemistry, hydrology, oceanography, planetary geology, and geoscience education; tenable in the United States; recipients chosen on the basis of academic achievement and financial need.

Restrictions: Limited to minority group applicants; United States citizenship required.
$ Given: An unspecified number of scholarships awarded annually; each for up to $4,000 at graduate level, up to $10,000 at undergraduate level; renewable.
Application Information: Application form required.
Deadline: February 1.
Contact: Marilyn J. Suiter, Administrator, Special Programs.

American Geophysical Union Horton Research Grant in Hydrology and Water Resources
2000 Florida Avenue, N.W.
Washington, DC 20009
(202) 462-6900

Description: Grants for doctoral candidates, to support research projects in hydrology and water resources; relevant disciplines include physical/chemical/biological aspects of hydrology, as well as water resources policy sciences (economics, sociology, and law).
Restrictions: Membership in American Geophysical Union required.
$ Given: One or more grants awarded annually; approximately $9,000 plus travel allowance to ensure attendance at awards luncheon.
Application Information: Proposal must be signed by faculty advisor; application forms required.
Deadline: March 1.

American Philosophical Society
John Clarke Slater Fellowships
104 South Fifth Street
Philadelphia, PA 19106
(215) 440-3403

Description: Fellowships for doctoral candidates writing dissertations on the history of physical sciences in the twentieth century; recipients chosen on the basis of academic achievement and quality of proposed dissertation research.
Restrictions: Applicants must have completed all Ph.D. degree requirements except dissertation.
$ Given: An unspecified number of fellowships of $12,000 are awarded annually.
Application Information: Write for details.
Deadline: December 1.

American Philosophical Society Library Mellon Resident Research Fellowships
104 South Fifth Street
Philadelphia, PA 19106
(215) 440-3400

Description: One- to three-month residential fellowships for doctoral candidates at dissertation level and postdoctoral scholars studying the history of American science and technology, its European roots, and its relation to American history and culture; tenable at the Society Library for short-term research using the library's collections.
Restrictions: United States citizenship required.
$ Given: An unspecified number of fellowships awarded annually; each for $1,800/month; tenable at Society for one to three months.
Application Information: Write for details.
Deadline: March 1.

American Society for Engineering Education Office of Naval Research Graduate Fellowships
1818 N Street, N.W.
Suite 600
(202) 331-3525

Description: Thirty-six-month fellowships (tenable over five years) for college seniors in engineering, mathematics, and science to support graduate work toward Ph.D. beginning the following September; fellowship includes summer work at Navy laboratory; relevant disciplines include biology/biomedical sciences, oceanography, mathematics, computer science, electrical engineering, material science, cognitive and neural sciences, naval architecture and ocean engineering, physics, chemistry, and aerospace/mechanical engineering; recipients chosen on the basis of academic achievement.
Restrictions: United States citizenship required; applicants already in graduate school ineligible.
$ Given: Up to 50 fellowships awarded annually; each for $15,000 for the first 12 months, $16,000 for the second 12 months, and $17,000 for the third 12 months, plus full tuition paid directly to the United States university, plus $1,800/month summer stipend during summer work at Navy laboratory.
Application Information: Write for details.
Deadline: January 19.

American Statistical Association ASA/NSF/BLS Senior Research Fellow and Associate Program
1429 Duke Street
Alexandria, VA 22314 (703) 684-1221

Description: Fellowships/associateships for doctoral candidates and recent Ph.D.s in economics, business, and labor studies; for participation in research at the Bureau of Labor Statistics; recipients chosen on the basis of academic achievement and quality of proposed research.
Restrictions: Significant computer experience required.
$ Given: An unspecified number of associateships are awarded annually; stipend is commensurate with qualifications and experience; fringe benefits and travel allowance also included.
Application Information: Write for details.
Deadline: January 14.
Contact: Carolee Bush, Fellowship Program Director.

American Statistical Association ASA/NSF Census Research Fellow and Associate Program
1429 Duke Street
Alexandria, VA 22314
(703) 684-1221

Description: Fellowships/associateship for doctoral candidates and recent Ph.D.s in demography and population studies; for participation in research at the United States bureau of Census; recipients chosen on the basis of academic achievement and quality of proposed research.
Restrictions: Significant computer experience required.
$ Given: An unspecified number of associateships are awarded annually; stipend is commensurate with qualifications and experience; fringe benefits and travel allowance also included.
Application Information: Write for details.
Deadline: January 14.
Contact: Carolee Bush, Fellowship Program Director.

American Statistical Association
ASA and USDA/NASS Research Fellow and Associate Program
1429 Duke Street
Alexandria, VA 22314
(703) 684-1221

Description: Nine- to twelve-month fellowships and associateships for doctoral candidates and postdoctoral researchers in agricultural statistics, for residential research/work at the National Agricultural Statistics Service; recipients chosen on the basis of academic achievement and proposed research.
Restrictions: N/A.
$ Given: An unspecified number of fellowships/associateship positions awarded annually; each with stipend.
Application Information: Write for details.
Deadline: March 1.
Contact: Marie Argana, Fellowship Program Director.

American Water Works Association
LARS Scholarships
6666 West Quincy Avenue
Denver, CO 80235
(303) 794-7711

Description: Scholarships for outstanding graduate students in fields of water treatment, corrosion control, and aquatic/ analytic/ environmental chemistry.
Restrictions: Applicants must be graduate students at institutions in the United States, Canada, Guam, Puerto Rico, or Mexico who will complete their degree requirements after August 31 of the deadline year.
$ Given: Two scholarships awarded annually; $3,000 for M.S. candidate; $5,000 for Ph.D. candidate.
Application Information: Write for details.
Deadlines: December 15 for M.S. candidate; February 15 for Ph.D. candidate.
Contact: Administrative Coordinator, Education Department.

American Water Works Association
Abel Wolman Doctoral Fellowships
6666 West Quincy Avenue
Denver, CO 80235
(303) 794-7711

Description: Twelve-month fellowships for outstanding doctoral candidates, to support research and training in water supply and treatment.
Restrictions: Applicants must be within two years of completing Ph.D. requirements; United States, Canadian, or Mexican citizenship required.
$ Given: One fellowship awarded annually; $10,000 stipend plus $1,000 research supplies/equipment allowance and up to $4,000 for tuition and fees.
Application Information: Write for details.
Deadline: February 15.
Contact: Administrative Coordinator, Education Department.

Argonne National Laboratory Graduate Research Appointments
9700 South Cass Avenue
Argonne, IL 60439-4845
(708) 252-3371

Description: One-year research appointments for graduate students to conduct thesis/dissertation research at Argonne National Laboratory in the fields of physical/life sciences, computer science, engineering, mathematics, fission/fusion energy, conservation, and the environment; recipients chosen on the basis of aca

demic achievement, proposed research, and relevance of research to ANL projects.
Restrictions: Enrollment in United States university graduate program required.
$ Given: An unspecified number of appointments available annually; each with stipend plus up to $4,000/year for tuition and travel; renewable.
Application Information: Preliminary contact with ANL researchers recommended.
Deadline: Applicants accepted continuously.
Contact: Graduate Student Programs Office.

Argonne National Laboratory
Graduate Thesis Parts
Research Appointments
9700 South Cass Avenue
Argonne, IL 60439-4845
(708) 252-3371

Description: Short-term appointments (a few days to a few months) for graduate students to conduct thesis/dissertation research at Argonne National Laboratory in the fields of physical/life sciences, computer science, engineering, mathematics, fission/fusion energy, conservation, and the environment; recipients chosen on the basis of academic achievement, proposed research.
Restrictions: Enrollment at United States university required.
$ Given: An unspecified number of appointments available annually; each with per diem and travel expenses.
Application Information: Write for details.
Deadline: Applications accepted continuously.
Contact: Graduate Student Programs Office.

Association for Women in
Science Educational
Foundation
AWIS Predoctoral Award
1522 K Street, N.W.
Suite 820
Washington, DC 20005
(202) 408-0742

Description: Awards for doctoral candidates in life sciences, physical sciences, social sciences, engineering, mathematics, and behavioral sciences; recipients chosen on the basis of academic achievement and quality of proposed research.
Restrictions: Limited to women only; United States citizenship and enrollment in United States institution required.
$ Given: An unspecified number of grants of $500 each are awarded annually.
Application Information: Write for details.
Deadline: January 15.
Contact: Catherine Didion.

AT&T Bell Laboratories
Cooperative Research
Fellowships for Minorities
600 Mountain Avenue
Murray Hill, NJ 07974
(201) 582-4822

Description: Fellowships for graduate study toward Ph.D. degree, for graduating college seniors with the potential to become professional research scientists or engineers; relevant disciplines include chemistry, communications science, computer science, engineering, information science, materials science, mathematics, operations research, physics, and statistics; fellowship tenure includes one summer of work at AT&T; recipients chosen on the basis of academic achievement and proposed research.

Restrictions: Limited to African-American, Hispanic, and Native American applicants only; GRE exam scores required; United States citizenship or permanent resident status required.

$ Given: An unspecified number of fellowships awarded annually; each for $13,200/year plus tuition and fees and expenses.

Application Information: Write for details.

Deadline: January 15.

Contact: Special Programs Manager, CRFP.

AT&T Bell Laboratories Graduate Research Program for Women
600 Mountain Avenue
Murray Hill, NJ 07974
(201) 582-4822

Description: Fellowships and grants for graduate study toward Ph.D. degree, for graduating college seniors with the potential to become professional research scientists or engineers; relevant disciplines include chemistry, chemical engineering, communications science, computer science, electrical engineering, information science, materials science, mathematics, operations research, physics, and statistics; fellowship tenure includes summer work at AT&T; recipients chosen on the basis of academic achievement and proposed research.

Restrictions: Limited to women applicants only; applicants must be admitted for full-time study in approved doctoral program; United States citizenship or permanent resident status required.

$ Given: An unspecified number of fellowships awarded annually; fellowships and grants are renewable annually.

Application Information: Application forms required.

Deadline: January 15.

Contact: Special Programs Manager, GRPW.

AT&T Bell Laboratories Ph.D. Scholarship Program
600 Mountain Avenue
Murray Hill, NJ 07974
(201) 582-4822

Description: Fellowships for doctoral candidates in the fields of chemistry, communications science, manufactural engineering, electrical engineering, and materials science; recipients chosen on the basis of academic achievement and proposed research.

Restrictions: United States citizenship or permanent resident status required.

$ Given: An unspecified number of fellowships awarded annually; each for $13,200/year plus $500 for tuition, books, and fees and up to $1,000 for travel.

Application Information: Applicants must be nominated by faculty member or department chair.

Deadline: January 15.

Contact: University Relations.

**Canadian Federation of
University Women
CFUW Memorial Grant**
55 Parkdale Avenue
Ottawa, Ontario K1Y 1E5
Canada
(613) 722-8732

Description: Grant for B.S./B.A. holders, to support graduate study in science and technology; recipients chosen on the basis of academic achievement, personal qualities, and potential.
Restrictions: Limited to women only; applicants must be accepted at intended places of study; Canadian citizenship or one-year landed immigrant status required.
$ Given: One grant of $1,000 Canadian awarded annually.
Application Information: Request application between July 1 and November 13.
Deadline: November 30.
Contact: Chair, Fellowships Committee.

**Canadian Federation of
University Women
CFUW Memorial Grant**
55 Parkdale Avenue
Ottawa, Ontario K1Y 1E5
Canada
(613) 722-8732

Description: Grant for B.S./B.A. holders, to support graduate study in science and technology; recipients chosen on the basis of academic achievement, personal qualities, and potential.
Restrictions: Limited to women only; applicants must be accepted at intended places of study; Canadian citizenship or one-year landed immigrant status required.
$ Given: One grant of $1,000 Canadian awarded annually.
Application Information: Request application between July 1 and November 13.
Deadline: November 30.
Contact: Chair, Fellowships Committee.

**Council for the Advancement
of Science Writing
Nate Haseltine Memorial
Fellowships in Science Writing**
P.O. Box 404
Greenlawn, NY 11740

Description: Fellowships for the study of science writing, available to B.S./B.A. holders in science of journalism, as well as to professional reporters and graduate students; recipients chosen on the basis of academic achievement, quality of writing, and commitment to writing career.
Restrictions: Preference to journalists with two years professional experience who want to specialize in science writing.
$ Given: An unspecified number of grants of up to $2,000 each are awarded annually.
Application Information: Write for details.
Deadline: June 1.
Contact: Executive Director.

Florida Education Fund
McKnight Doctoral **Fellowships**
201 East Kennedy Boulevard
Suite 1525
Tampa, FL 33602
(813) 272-2772

Description: Fellowships for graduate study at one of eleven participating doctoral-degree-granting universities in Florida in the fields of business, engineering, agriculture, biology, computer science, mathematics, physical science, and psychology; recipients chosen on the basis of academic achievement.

Restrictions: Limited to African-American applicants only; B.A./B.S. degree required; United States citizenship required.
$ Given: 25 fellowships awarded annually; each for a maximum of five years of study, with an annual $11,000 stipend plus up to $5,000 in tuition and fees.
Application Information: Write for details.
Deadline: January 15.
Contact: Dr. Israel Tribble, Jr.

**French Embassy
Scientific Services
Chateaubriand Research
Scholarships for the Exact
Sciences, Engineering, and
Medicine**
Department of Science
and Technology
4101 Reservoir Road, N.W.
Washington, DC 20007
(202) 944-6241

Description: Six- to twelve-month research scholarship for doctoral candidates at dissertation level, as well as postdoctoral scholars, to conduct research in France at French universities, engineering schools, and private laboratories; language training sessions provided; relevant disciplines include biological and agricultural sciences, physical sciences and mathematics, engineering and applied sciences, medicine, nutrition, optometry and vision sciences, pharmacy and pharmaceuticals sciences, and veterinary medicine and sciences; recipients chosen on the basis of proposed research.
Restrictions: Each applicant must be registered at United States university and already in contact with French host institution; United States citizenship required.
$ Given: Twenty to thirty scholarships awarded annually; each for 9,000 Francs per month plus airfare and health insurance.
Application Information: Application forms must be submitted with faculty recommendation.
Deadline: January 31.

**Geological Society of America
GSA Penrose Research
Grants**
P.O. Box 9140
Boulder, CO 80301
(303) 447-2020

Description: Grants to support master's and doctoral candidates in thesis/dissertation research in geology; recipients chosen on the basis of academic achievement, financial need, and proposed research.
Restrictions: Enrollment at university in Canada, Mexico, or the United States required.
$ Given: Approximately 240 grants awarded annually; average award range $200–$2,000.
Application Information: Request current GSA application form from university geology department.
Deadline: February 15.
Contact: June R. Forstrom, Administrator, Research Grants Program.

Fannie and John Hertz Foundation
Fannie and John Hertz Foundation Graduate Fellowship Program
P.O. Box 5032
Livermore, CA 94551-5032
(415) 373-1642

Description: Fellowships to provide B.S./B.A. holders with support for academic study through graduate school in the applied physical sciences, including engineering, applied physics, mathematics, and chemistry; tenable at one of 26 participating schools; recipients chosen on the basis of outstanding academic achievement (minimum 3.5 GPA in last two years of undergraduate work).
Restrictions: Applicants must have completed at least two years of college-level physics and college-level math courses, plus one year of college-level chemistry; recipients must agree to respond in time of national emergency; United States citizenship required.
$ Given: An unspecified number of fellowships awarded annually; each for $15,000 plus up to $10,000 for tuition and fees.
Application Information: Write for details.
Deadline: October 21.
Contact: Dr. Wilson K. Talley.

Hughes Aircraft Company Doctoral Fellowships
7200 Hughes Terrace
Los Angeles, CA 90045
(213) 568-7200

Description: Fellowships for doctoral candidates and master's degree holders in aerospace, electrical/mechanical/systems engineering, computer science, physics, and mathematics; work-study and full-study programs offered, with work-study involving 20–36 hours/week employment at Hughes facility; participation in both programs includes initial full-time summer (10–13 weeks) employment at Hughes facility; most fellows attend UCLA, USC, CalTech, MIT, Cornell, Purdue, Stanford, Georgia Tech, University of Arizona, University of Illinois, etc.; recipients chosen on the basis of academic achievement (minimum 3.0 GPA).
Restrictions: United States citizenship and good health required.
$ Given: An unspecified number of fellowships awarded annually; each for tuition, stipend, academic expenses, relocation allowance, and salary/benefits during employment.
Application Information: Write for application packet; include university, field of interest, year of graduation, and GPA in query letter.
Deadline: February 1.
Contact: Kimberly J. Everett, Educational Coordinator.

**Hughes Aircraft Company
Master of Science Fellowships**
7200 Hughes Terrace
Los Angeles, CA 90045
(213) 568-7200

Description: Fellowships for B.S. degree holders in aerospace, physics, computer science, mathematics, and electrical/mechanical/systems engineering; work-study and full-study programs offered, with work-study involving 20–36 hours/week employment at Hughes facility (80% of participants are work-study and attend southern California schools); participation in both programs includes initial full-time summer (10–13 weeks) employment at Hughes facility; most fellows attend UCLA, USC, CalTech, MIT, Cornell, Purdue, Stanford, Georgia Tech, University of Arizona, University of Illinois, etc.; recipients chosen on the basis of academic achievement (minimum 3.0 GPA).
Restrictions: Applicants must have B.S. degree from institution accredited by the Accrediting Board of Engineering Technology; United States citizenship and good health required.
$ Given: An unspecified number of fellowships awarded annually; each for tuition, stipend, academic expenses, relocation allowance, and salary/benefits during employment.
Application Information: Write for application packet; include university, field of interest, year of graduation, and GPA in query letter.
Deadline: March 15.
Contact: Kimberly J. Everett, Educational Coordinator.

**Institute of International
Education
Colombian Government
Study and Research Grants**
U.S. Student Programs
Division
809 United Nations Plaza
New York, NY 10017-3580
(212) 984-5330

Description: Grants for B.S./B.A. holders to pursue up to two years of study/research at Colombian universities; relevant disciplines include agriculture, biology, business administration, economics, chemistry, engineering, education, health services administration, economics, chemistry, engineering, education, health services administration, geography, history, Latin American literature, law, linguistics, political science, physics, regulatory development, public health, and remote sensing interpretation.
Restrictions: United States citizenship required.
$ Given: An unspecified number of grants awarded annually; each for modest monthly stipend, plus tuition and fees, health insurance, book/materials allowance, and one-way return airfare upon completion of study.
Application Information: Write for details.
Deadline: October 31.

**Institute of International
Education
Fulbright Fixed
Sum–Bulgarian Government
Grants**
U.S. Student Programs
Division
809 United Nations Plaza
New York, NY 10017-3580
(212) 984-5330

Description: Grants for B.A./B.S. holders in the humanities, physical sciences, and social sciences; for a six-to nine-month residency/exchange in Bulgaria (September - June).
Restrictions: Knowledge of Bulgarian language required; United States citizenship required; applicants must meet all Fulbright eligibility requirements.
$ Given: An unspecified number of grants awarded annually; Bulgarian government funds stipend, housing, and health/accident insurance; Fulbright provides fixed sum for round-trip transportation plus additional monthly stipend.
Application Information: Write for details.
Deadline: October 31.
Contact: U.S. Student Program Division.

**Institute of International
Education
Study and Research Grants
for US Citizens**
U.S. Student Programs
Division
809 United Nations Plaza
New York, NY 10017-3580
(212) 984-5330

Description: Grants to support study and research in all fields, as well as professional training in the creative and performing arts; tenable at institutions of higher learning outside of the United States for one year; list of participating countries in any given year may be obtained from IIE.
Restrictions: Open to United States citizens with B.A. or equivalent; acceptable plan of study and proficiency in host country's language required.
$ Given: A variable number of grants awarded annually; covers international transportation, language or orientation course (where appropriate), tuition, book and maintenance allowances, and health and accident insurance.
Application Information: If currently enrolled in a college or university, apply to the campus Fulbright Program Advisor; applications also available from IIE.
Deadline: October 31.

**International Union for
Vacuum Science, Technique,
and Applications
Welch Foundation Scholarship**
Advanced Technology
Laboratory
Bell North Research
Box 3511, Station C
Ottawa, Ontario K1Y 4H7
Canada
(613) 763-3248
FAX (613) 763-2404

Description: One-year scholarship for the study of vacuum sciences, preferably for study in a foreign laboratory; funding made available to scholars with B.S., M.S., or Ph.D. degrees; recipients chosen on the basis of proposed research.
Restrictions: Fluency in foreign language may be required; midterm and final research reports required for funding.
$ Given: One scholarship for $12,500 is awarded annually; paid in three installments.
Application Information: Write for details.
Deadline: April 15.
Contact: Dr. W. D. Westwood, Administrator.

Japan Ministry of Education, Science, and Culture Japanese Government (Monbusho) Scholarship Program
2-2 Kasumigaseki, 3-chome
Chiyoda-ku
Tokyo 100
Japan
03-581-4211

Description: Eighteen-month to two-year scholarships for non-Japanese graduate students to study at Japanese universities and research institutes; Research Students Program is specifically designed for graduate students (undergraduate program also available) in the humanities, social sciences, music, fine arts, and natural sciences; open to citizens of countries with educational exchange agreements with Japan.
Restrictions: Language proficiency required (12- to 18-month language training program required if language skills deemed insufficient); applicants must be under age 35.
$ Given: An unspecified number of scholarships awarded annually; each to cover monthly stipend, airfare, tuition, and expense allowance.
Application Information: For further information, contact Japanese Embassy or Consulate.
Deadlines: June 15, September 30.
Contact: Student Exchange Division.

The Library Company of Philadelphia American History and Culture Research Fellowships
1314 Locust Street
Philadelphia, PA 19107
(215) 546-3181

Description: Residential research fellowships at the Library Company of Philadelphia for doctoral candidates and postdoctoral scholars in most disciplines as related to the history and culture of 18th to 19th century America; tenable for one or more months; recipients chosen on the basis of proposed research.
Restrictions: N/A.
$ Given: An unspecified number of fellowships awarded annually; each with $1,350/month stipend.
Application Information: Write for details.
Deadline: February 1.
Contact: James Green, Curator.

National Aeronautics and Space Administration Space Science Dissertation Research Fellowships
University Programs Branch
Educational Affairs Division
NASA Headquarters
Code FEH
600 Independence Ave, S.W.
Washington, DC 20546
(202) 453-8344

Description: One-year fellowships for doctoral candidates at dissertation level in aeronautics and space science, for research using NASA facilities; recipients chosen on the basis of academic achievement, relevance of proposed research to NASA, and planned utilization of NASA facilities.
Restrictions: United States citizenship required.
$ Given: An unspecified number of fellowships awarded annually; each for $22,000 per year; renewable for up to three years.
Application Information: Write for details.
Deadline: February 1.

National Air and Space Museum
Guggenheim Fellowships
6th and Independence
Avenue, S.W.
Washington, DC 20560
(202) 357-1529

Description: One-year residential fellowships for doctoral candidates at dissertation level, as well as recent Ph.D.s (within past 7 years), for historical/scientific research on aviation and space; relevant disciplines include history, aerospace, and engineering.
Restrictions: N/A.
$ Given: An unspecified number of fellowships awarded annually; $14,000 predoctoral stipend, $25,000 postdoctoral stipend.
Application Information: Write for details.
Deadline: January 15.
Contact: Cheryl Bauer.

National Air and Space Museum
Verville Fellowships
6th and Independence
Avenue, S.W.
Washington, DC 20560
(202) 357-1529

Description: Nine- to twelve-month fellowships for analysis of major developments, trends, and accomplishments in history of aviation/space studies; relevant disciplines include history, aerospace, and engineering.
Restrictions: Applicants must demonstrate skills in research and writing.
$ Given: An unspecified number of fellowships for $30,000 each are awarded annually.
Application Information: Write for details.
Deadline: January 15.
Contact: Cheryl Bauer.

National Center for Atmospheric Research
NCAR Graduate Research Assistantships
P.O. Box 3000
Boulder, CO 80307-3000
(303) 497-1601

Description: Research positions for doctoral candidates at dissertation level in the atmospheric sciences and related fields; recipients chosen on the basis of academic achievement, financial need, and proposed research.
Restrictions: Proposed thesis work must coincide with NCAR program.
$ Given: An unspecified number of positions available annually; $13,900 stipend if recipient has passed comprehensive exam; $13,100 stipend if recipient has not yet passed comprehensive exam; renewable for one year.
Application Information: Proposals must be submitted jointly by university scientist and NCAR scientist; graduate student will work under supervision of both scientists.
Deadlines: January 1, April 1, July 1, October 1.
Contact: Barbara McDonald, Administrator, Advanced Study Program.

**National Geographic Society
Research Grants**
Committee for Research and
Exploration
1145 17th Street, N.W.
Washington, DC 20036
(202) 857-7439

Description: Grants for research in anthropology, archaeology, astronomy, biology, glaciology, botany, ecology, physical and human geography, mineralogy, geology, oceanology, paleontology, zooology, and other sciences pertinent to geography; funding primarily for post-doctoral researchers, but occasionally awarded to exceptional doctoral candidates; recipients chosen on the basis of proposed research.
Restrictions: Open to all nationalities.
$ Given: An unspecified number of grants of $15,000–$20,000 average each are awarded annually.
Application Information: Write for details.
Deadline: Applications accepted continuously.
Contact: Committee for Research and Exploration.

**National Research Council
NRC/Ford Predoctoral and
Dissertation Fellowships for
Minorities**
Fellowships Office
2101 Constitution Avenue, N.W.
Washington, DC 20418
(202) 334-2872

Description: Fellowships for graduate students in the humanities, social sciences, biological and agricultural sciences, physical sciences and mathematics, and engineering and applied sciences; recipients chosen on the basis of academic achievement and proposed research.
Restrictions: Limited to members of minority groups; United States citizenship or legal residency required.
$ Given: Fifty-five predoctoral fellowships awarded; $11,500 for fellow, $6,000 for Institution; 20 dissertation fellowships available for $18,000.
Application Information: Write for details.
Deadline: November 5.

**National Science Foundation
Minority Graduate Research
Fellowships**
Office of Research and Career
Development
Directorate for Education
and Human Resources
1800 G Street, N.W.
Washington, DC 20550
(202) 357-7856

Description: Fellowships to support master's and doctoral candidates for three years of full-time study (over a five-year period) in mathematics, engineering, physical, biological, and social sciences, and history/philosophy of science.
Restrictions: Limited to members of ethnic minority groups; United States citizenship or residency required.
$ Given: One hundred and fifty fellowships awarded annually, ten of them for Women in Engineering; each for $12,900/year (for three years), plus $6,000 institutional allowance in lieu of tuition and fees.
Application Information: Write for details.
Deadline: November 8.
Contact: Dr. Susan Sherman.

**National Speleological Society
Ralph W. Stone Award in
Speleology**
Ames Research Center
MS 239-4
Moffet Field, CA 94035

Description: Grants to registered graduate students for research in geology, biology, speleology, geochemistry, hydrology, and other cave-related sciences; recipients chosen on the basis of financial need and proposed research.
Restrictions: NSS membership required.

$ Given:	One grant for $1,500 is awarded annually.
Application Information:	Write for details.
Deadline:	May 1.
Contact:	David Des Marais.

**Natural Sciences and
Engineering Research
Council of Canada NSERC
Postgraduate Scholarships in
Science Librarianship and
Documentation**
200 Kent Street
Ottawa, Ontario K1A 1H5
Canada
(613) 992-8203

Description:	One-year scholarships for first- and second-year study toward MLS degree in library science; recipients chosen on the basis of academic achievement, commitment to field, and relevant experience.
Restrictions:	Applicants must have B.S. degree in science or engineering; Canadian citizenship or permanent resident status required.
$ Given:	A few scholarships awarded annually; each for $13,500 Canadian plus travel allowance.
Application Information:	Write for details.
Deadline:	December 1.
Contact:	Nadine Bohan; Information Officer.

**Oak Ridge Institute for
Science and Education
Department of Energy
Research Participation
Program**
P.O. Box 117
Oak Ridge, TN 37831-0117

Description:	Program for undergraduate and graduate students, as well as faculty members, to conduct/participate in research programs at seven Department of Energy facilities; summer and academic-year programs available; research programs are related to energy production, utilization, and conservation.
Restrictions:	Applicants must have done degree work in life/physical/social sciences, mathematics, toxicology, or engineering; United States citizenship or permanent resident status required.
$ Given:	An unspecified number of fellowships awarded annually; each with $20,000–$48,000 stipend, based on degree, program, and area of research.
Application Information:	Write for application forms.
Deadline:	Early January.
Contact:	William E. Felling, Executive Director, (615) 576-3300; or Al Wohlpart, General University Activities Contact, (615) 576-3421.

**Oak Ridge Institute for
Science and Education
Nuclear Engineering and
Health Physics Fellowships**
P.O. Box 117
Oak Ridge, TN 37831-0117
(615) 576-3428

Description:	One-year fellowship for graduate students studying nuclear science and engineering or health physics at participating Oak Ridge Associated Universities with practicum at various DOE facilities; recipients chosen on the basis of academic achievement, career goals, and interests.
Restrictions:	N/A.

$ **Given:** An unspecified number of fellowships awarded annually; each with $14,400 stipend, plus $300/month during practicum, and travel, tuition and fees; renewable for up to four years.
Application Information: Write for details.
Deadline: January 25.

Oak Ridge Institute for Science and Education Nuclear Regulatory Commission Graduate Fellowships Program
P.O. Box 117
Oak Ridge, TN 37831-0117
(615) 576-9279
FAX (615) 576-0202

Description: Fellowships for master's candidates studying nuclear engineering and health physics; participation includes work/orientation prefellowship; recipients chosen on the basis of academic achievement.
Restrictions: United States citizenship or permanent resident status required.
$ **Given:** An unspecified number of fellowships awarded annually; each for cost-of-education (paid directly to university) plus $1,800/month stipend.
Application Information: Write for details.
Deadline: January 29.

Optical Society of America Newport Research Awards
2010 Massachusetts Avenue, N.W.
Washington, DC 20036
(202) 416-1404

Description: Grants to doctoral candidates for one year of research on electro-optics and laser technology.
Restrictions: Applicants must be enrolled at United States universities.
$ **Given:** Three new grants and three renewals awarded annually; each with up to $12,000 stipend plus $4,000 research expense allowance.
Application Information: Write for application forms.
Deadline: February 15.
Contact: Doreen Weinberger, Chair, Newport Research Award Committee.

President's Commission on White House Fellowships White House Fellowships
712 Jackson Place, N.W.
Washington, DC 20503
(202) 395-4522

Description: Twelve-month appointments as special assistants to the Vice President, Cabinet members, and the Presidential staff; fellowships include participation in educational program; positions available for students in public affairs, education, the sciences, business, and the professions; recipients chosen on the basis of leadership qualities, commitment to community service, and career/academic achievement.
Restrictions: Limited to young adults, ages 30–39; civilian federal employees are ineligible; recipients may not hold official state or local office while serving as White House fellows; United States citizenship required.
$ **Given:** Eleven to nineteen wage-earning fellowships for up to a maximum of $65,000 are awarded annually.
Application Information: Write for details.
Deadline: December 15.
Contact: Phyllis A. Williams.

Rockefeller University
Rockefeller Archive Center
Research Grants
15 Dayton Avenue
Pocantico Hills
North Tarrytown, NY 10591
(914) 631-4505

Description: Residential research fellowships for graduate students and postdoctoral scholars pursuing research using Archive Center resources; relevant disciplines including philanthropy, education, science, medicine, black history, agriculture, labor, social welfare, social sciences, politics, religion, population, economic development, and the arts; recipients chosen on the basis of proposed research and necessity of using Archive Center resources.
Restrictions: N/A.
$ Given: An unspecified number of grants awarded annually; each for up to $1,500 for travel, lodging, and research expenses.
Application Information: Write for details.
Deadline: December 31.
Contact: Dr. Darwin H. Stapleton, Director.

Sigma Delta Epsilon/
Graduate Women in Science
Eloise Gerry Fellowships
P.O. Box 19947
San Diego, CA 92159

Description: One-year research fellowships for graduate students and postdoctoral scholars in the biological and chemical sciences; recipients chosen on the basis of academic achievement, financial need, and proposed research.
Restrictions: Limited to women applicants only; funding may not be used for tuition; applicants may not apply simultaneously for other SDE fellowships.
$ Given: Three to six fellowships awarded annually; each for $1,500–$4,000.
Application Information: Write for details.
Deadline: December 1.
Contact: Helen D. Haller, Secretary.

Sigma Xi, The Scientific
Research Society
Grants-in-Aid of Research
P.O. Box 13975
Research Triangle Park, NC
27709

Description: Research grants to graduate and undergraduate students in science and engineering, to support research projects; recipients chosen on the basis of proposed research.
Restrictions: Open to all nationalities.
$ Given: An unspecified number of grants awarded annually; each for up to $1,000 (average $600).
Application Information: Application forms required.
Deadlines: February 1, May 1, and November 1.
Contact: Committee on Grants-in-Aid of Research.

Smithsonian Institution Graduate Student Research Fellowships
Office of Fellowships and Grants
955 L'Enfant Plaza
Suite 7300
Washington, DC 20560
(202) 287-3271

Description: Ten-week residential fellowships for graduate students to pursue research at the Smithsonian; relevant disciplines include art history, anthropology, ecology, biology, environmental science, astrophysics, history of science, Oriental art, natural history, African art and culture, and American cultural/sociological history; recipients chosen on the basis of proposed research.
Restrictions: N/A.
$ Given: Approximately 38 fellowships are awarded annually; each with maximum $3,000 stipend.
Application Information: Write for details.
Deadline: January 15.
Contact: Program Assistant.

Smithsonian Institution Minority Students Internships
Office of Fellowships and Grants
955 L'Enfant Plaza
Suite 7300
Washington, DC 20560
(202) 287-3271

Description: Nine- to twelve-week internships for undergraduate upperclassmen and graduate students in the humanities, social sciences, natural sciences, and physical sciences; internship program includes participation in ongoing research or activities at the Museum plus supervised independent research in any bureau; recipients chosen on the basis of academic achievement and proposed research.
Restrictions: Limited to minority group applicants.
$ Given: An unspecified number of internship positions are awarded annually; $250/week undergraduate stipend, $300/week graduate stipend.
Application Information: Write for details.
Deadlines: February 15, June 15, and October 15.

Smithsonian Institution Predoctoral Research Fellowships in Astrophysics and Related Topics
Smithsonian Astrophysical Observatory
60 Garden Street
Mail Stop 47
Cambridge, MA 02138
(617) 495-7103

Description: One-year fellowships for doctoral candidates in astrophysics and related topics to conduct independent dissertation research, working with Smithsonian staff and using Smithsonian resources; recipients chosen on the basis of academic achievement and proposed research.
Restrictions: Applicants must have completed all preliminary coursework and examinations.
$ Given: An unspecified number of fellowships awarded annually; each for $14,000/year; renewable for one year.
Application Information: Write for details.
Deadline: April 15.
Contact: Secretary, Predoctoral Fellowship Committee.

**Smithsonian Institution
Predoctoral Research
Fellowships in the History of
Science and Technology**
Office of Fellowships and
Grants
955 L'Enfant Plaza
Suite 7300
Washington, DC 20560
(202) 287-3271

Description: One-year residential fellowships for doctoral candidates at dissertation level in the history of science and technology, to pursue independent research using the Smithsonian's collections, resources, and staff expertise; relevant disciplines include history of mathematics, physical sciences, pharmacy, medicine, civil and mechanical engineering, electrical technology, and history of American science; recipients chosen on the basis of proposed research.
Restrictions: Applicants must have completed all preliminary coursework and exams for degree.
$ Given: An unspecified number of fellowships are awarded annually; each with $14,000 stipend.
Application Information: Write for details.
Deadline: January 15.
Contact: Program Assistant.

**Smithsonian Institution
Libraries
Dibner Library
Resident Scholar Program
Grants**
NHB 24
Mail Stop 154
Washington, DC 20560

Description: Grants for doctoral candidates, postdoctoral scholars, and professionals studying the history of science and technology, to support one to three months of research/study at Dibner Library of the History of Science and Technology and other libraries of the Smithsonian.
Restrictions: N/A.
$ Given: An unspecified number of grants awarded annually; each with $1,500/month stipend to cover expenses.
Application Information: Write for details.
Deadline: November 1.

**Social Science Research
Council
MacArthur Foundation
Fellowships on International
Peace and Security in a
Changing World**
605 Third Avenue
New York, NY 10158
(212) 661-0280

Description: Fellowship support for up to two years of research in the setting and nation of the recipient's choice; funding made available to doctoral candidates at dissertation level, postdoctoral scholars, and professionals studying international peace and security (in disciplines of humanities, social sciences, physical sciences, and natural sciences); recipients chosen on the basis of proposed research.
Restrictions: Open to all nationalities.
$ Given: Approximately eight fellowships awarded annually; $12,500–$17,500 per year predoctoral fellow; $25,000–$30,000 per year postdoctoral fellow.
Application Information: Write for details.
Deadline: December 1.
Contact: Felicia Sullivan.

Society of Exploration Geophysicists
SEG Foundation Scholarship Program
P.O. Box 702740
Tulsa, OK 74170
(918) 493-3516

Description: One year scholarships for undergraduate and graduate students in geophysics; recipients chosen on the basis of academic achievement and commitment to career in exploration geophysics.
Restrictions: N/A.
$ Given: An unspecified number of scholarships awarded annually; each for $500–$3,000; renewable.
Application Information: Write for details.
Deadline: March 1.
Contact: Marge Gerhart.

Southern Illinois University at Carbondale
Minority Doctoral Fellowships in Science and Engineering
Graduate School
Woody Hall, B-114
Carbondale, IL 62901
(618) 536-7791

Description: Three-year fellowships for doctoral candidates in the life sciences, physical sciences, and engineering; recipients chosen on the basis of GRE or other national standardized test scores.
Restrictions: Limited to minority group applicants; applicants of Mexican or Puerto Rican descent preferred; United States citizenship required.
$ Given: Ten to twenty fellowships awarded annually; each for $15,000/year plus full tuition and fees (for three years).
Application Information: Write for details.
Deadline: February 2.
Contact: Dr. Harry Daniels, Associate Dean.

Women's Research and Education Institute
Congressional Fellowships on Women and Public Policy
1700 Eighteenth Street, N.W.
Suite 400
Washington, DC 20009
(202) 328-7070

Description: Congressional fellowship program designed to train women as potential public policy leaders; fellowship runs September through April and involves 30 hrs/wk work in a United States Congress office as a legislative aide on policy issues affecting women; open to master's and doctoral candidates at United States institutions; relevant disciplines include humanities, social sciences, biology and biomedical sciences, engineering and applied sciences, biomedical engineering, technology management and policy, business administration and management, health services management and hospital administration, education, allied health professionals, medicine, nursing, public and community health, and law; recipients chosen on the basis of political/civic activity and interest in women's issues.
Restrictions: Limited to women applicants; nine hours previous graduate coursework preferred; United States citizenship preferred.
$ Given: Eight to fifteen fellowships awarded annually; each with $9,500 stipend plus $500 for health insurance and up to $1,500 toward six hours tuition at home institution.
Application Information: Request application after November 1.
Deadline: February 14.
Contact: Alison Dineen, Fellowship Director.

Engineering and Applied Sciences

American Association for the Advancement of Science Mass Media Science and Engineering Fellows Program
1333 H Street, N.W.
Washington, DC 20005
(202) 326-6760

Description: Ten-week summer fellowships for science graduate students to work as journalists (print, radio, or television) to increase their understanding of the news media; available to students at any graduate level of study in the natural and social sciences, as well as engineering; recipients chosen on the basis of academic achievement and demonstrated commitment of conveying to the public a better understanding and appreciation of science and technology.
Restrictions: No funding to non-technical applicants; United States citizenship required; no concurrent funding allowed.
$ Given: Twenty fellowships awarded annually; weekly living stipend for 10 weeks plus travel costs.
Application Information: Write for details and application form; minorities and individuals with disabilities encouraged to apply.
Deadline: January 15.
Contact: Amie Hubbard, Program Manager.

American Association of University Women Educational Foundation AAUW Selected Professions Fellowships
P.O. Box 4030
Iowa City, IA 52243-4030
(319) 337-1716

Description: Fellowships for graduate students entering their final year of study in fields with traditionally low female representation, including architecture, business administration, computer science, dentistry, engineering, law, mathematics/statistics, medicine, and veterinary medicine; recipients chosen on the basis of academic achievement; tenable for full-time study at accredited United States institutions.
Restrictions: Limited to women who are members of minority groups; United States citizenship or permanent resident status required.
$ Given: An unspecified number of fellowships of $5,000 –$9,500 each are awarded annually.
Application Information: Application forms available August 1 through November 1.
Deadlines: December 15, February 1 for M.B.A.

American Association of University Women Educational Foundation AAUW Selected Professions Program Dissertation Fellowships in Engineering
P.O. Box 4030
Iowa City, IA 52243-4030
(319) 337-1716

Description: Fellowships for doctoral candidates in engineering; to support dissertation work.
Restrictions: Limited to women applicants; applicants must have completed all coursework and exams for Ph.D.; United States citizenship or permanent resident status required.
$ Given: An unspecified number of fellowships awarded annually; each for $14,500.
Application Information: Application forms available August 1 through November 1.
Deadline: November 15.
Contact: Selected Professions Fellowship Program.

American Indian Graduate Center Native American Graduate Student Fellowships
4520 Montgomery Boulevard, N.E.
Suite 1-B
Albuquerque, NM 87109
(505) 881-4584

Description: Fellowships for full-time graduate study in all fields; recipients chosen on the basis of financial need, academic achievement, and desire to perform community service after graduation; preference for graduate studies in health, law, education, natural resources, and engineering.
Restrictions: Applicants must have 1/4 or more Indian blood from federally recognized Alaskan Native or Native American tribe; United States citizenship required.
$ Given: An unspecified number of fellowships awarded annually; each for $250 –$10,000 per year, average award $4,000; renewable.
Application Information: Write for details.
Deadline: April 30.
Contact: Oran LaPointe, Executive Director.

American Philosophical Society Library Mellon Resident Research Fellowships
104 South Fifth Street
Philadelphia, PA 19106-3386
(215) 440-3400

Description: One- to three-month residential fellowships for doctoral candidates at dissertation level and postdoctoral scholars studying the history of American science and technology, its European roots, and its relation to American history and culture; tenable at the Society Library for short-term research using the library's collections.
Restrictions: United States citizenship required.
$ Given: An unspecified number of fellowships awarded annually; each for $1800/month; tenable at Society for one to three months.
Application Information: Write for details.
Deadline: March 1.

**American Society for
Engineering Education
Helen Carr Minority
Fellowships**
1818 North Street, N.W.
Suite 600
Washington, DC 20036
(202) 331-3525

Description: One-year fellowships for doctoral candidates in engineering at the following schools: Hampton University, Morgan State University, Howard University, North Carolina A&T State University, Prairie View A&M University, Tennessee State University, Tuskegee University, and Southern University; recipients chosen on the basis of financial need.
Restrictions: Limited to African-American applicants only; applicants must intend to return to one of the historically black engineering colleges to teach; United States citizenship required.
$ Given: An unspecified number of fellowships awarded annually; each for up to $10,000/year; renewable.
Application Information: Write for details.
Deadlines: January 5, May 5

**American Society for
Engineering Education
Office of Naval Research
Graduate Fellowships**
1818 North Street, N.W.
Suite 600
Washington, DC 20036
(202) 331-3525 or
(202) 331-3500

Description: Thirty-six-month fellowships (tenable over five years) for college seniors in engineering, mathematics, and science to support graduate work toward Ph.D. beginning the following September; fellowship includes summer work at Navy laboratory; relevant disciplines include biology/biomedical sciences, oceanography, mathematics, computer science, electrical engineering, material science, cognitive and neural sciences, naval architecture and ocean engineering, physics, chemistry, and aerospace/mechanical engineering; recipients chosen on the basis of academic achievement.
Restrictions: United States citizenship required.
$ Given: Up to 50 fellowships awarded annually; each for $15,000 for the first 12 months, $16,000 for the second 12 months, and $17,000 for the third 12 months, plus full tuition paid directly to the United States university, plus $1,800/month summer stipend during summer work at Navy laboratory.
Application Information: Write for details.
Deadline: January 16.
Contact: Projects Officer.

**American Society of Civil
Engineers
O.H. Ammann Research
Fellowship in Structural
Engineering**
345 East 47th Street
New York, NY 10017-2398
(212) 705-7885

Description: Fellowships for master's and doctoral candidates studying structural design and construction; recipients chosen on the basis of proposed research.
Restrictions: Membership in ASCE required; recipients expected to produce publishable report by end of tenure.
$ Given: One fellowship awarded annually; each with $5,000/year stipend; renewable.
Application Information: Write for details.
Deadline: February 15.
Contact: Assistant Manager of Student Services

American Society of Civil Engineers Freeman Fellowships
345 East 47th Street
New York, NY 10017-2398
(212) 705-7885

Description: Fellowships for researchers studying civil engineering, especially hydraulics; traveling scholarships available to researchers under age 45; recipients chosen on the basis of proposed research.
Restrictions: Membership in ASCE required.
$ Given: An unspecified number of fellowships awarded annually; based on funds available.
Application Information: Write for details.
Deadline: February 15.
Contact: Assistant Manager of Student Services.

American Society of Civil Engineers J. Waldo Smith Hydraulic Fellowship
345 East 47th Street
New York, NY 10017-2398
(212) 705-7885

Description: One-year fellowship for master's and doctoral candidates studying experimental hydraulics, to support practical research experiments; recipients chosen on the basis of proposed research.
Restrictions: Associate membership in ASCE preferred.
$ Given: One fellowship awarded every third year (1994, 1997, etc.); each for $4,000 plus up to $1,000 for equipment.
Application Information: Write for application packet.
Deadline: February 15.
Contact: Assistant Manager of Student Services.

American Society of Civil Engineers Arthur S. Tuttle Memorial Scholarships
345 East 47th Street
New York, NY 10017-2398
(212) 705-7885

Description: One-year scholarships providing tuition assistance for first-year graduate students studying civil engineering; recipients chosen on the basis of academic achievement and financial need.
Restrictions: National student membership in ASCE required.
$ Given: One to two scholarships awarded annually; each for $1,000 –$2,000, applicable for tuition only.
Application Information: Write for details.
Deadline: February 15.
Contact: Assistant Manager of Student Services.

American Society of Heating, Refrigerating and Air Conditioning Engineers ASHRAE Graduate Student Grant-in-Aid Program
1791 Tullie Circle, N.E.
Atlanta, GA 30329
(404) 636-8400

Description: Grants for full-time graduate students of technologies and environmental effects related to heating, refrigerating, and air-conditioning engineering.
Restrictions: N/A.
$ Given: Twelve to eighteen grants awarded annually; each for up to $7,500; non-renewable.
Application Information: Write for details.
Deadline: December 15.
Contact: Manager of Research.

American Water Works Association Academic Achievement Awards
6666 West Quincy Avenue
Denver, CO 80235
(303) 794-7711

Description: Awards for best master's theses and doctoral dissertations addressing potable water, in any discipline.
Restrictions: N/A.
$ Given: Four awards annually, 1st and 2nd in each category (thesis and dissertation); 1st place awards each $1,000; 2nd place awards each $500.
Application Information: Write for announcement and application form.
Deadline: October 1.
Contact: Scholarships Coordinator.

Argonne National Laboratory Graduate Research Appointments
9700 South Cass Avenue
Argonne, IL 60439-4845
(708) 252-3371

Description: One-year research appointments for graduate students to conduct thesis/dissertation research at Argonne National Laboratory in the fields of physical/life sciences, computer science, engineering, mathematics, fission/fusion energy, conservation, and the environment; recipients chosen on the basis of academic achievement, proposed research, and relevance of research to ANL projects.
Restrictions: Enrollment in United States university graduate program required.
$ Given: An unspecified number of appointments available annually; each with stipend plus up to $4,000/year for tuition and travel; renewable.
Application Information: Preliminary contact with ANL researchers recommended.
Deadline: Applicants accepted continuously.
Contact: Graduate Student Programs Office.

Argonne National Laboratory Graduate Thesis Parts Research Appointments
9700 South Cass Avenue
Argonne, IL 60439-4845
(708) 252-3371

Description: Short-term appointments (a few days to a few months) for graduate students to conduct thesis/dissertation research at Argonne National Laboratory in the fields of physical/life sciences, computer science, engineering, mathematics, fission/fusion energy, conservation, and the environment; recipients chosen on the basis of academic achievement, proposed research.
Restrictions: Enrollment at United States university required.
$ Given: An unspecified number of appointments available annually; each with per diem and travel expenses.
Application Information: Write for details.
Deadline: Applications accepted continuously.
Contact: Graduate Student Programs Office.

Association for Women in Science Educational Foundation
AWIS Predoctoral Award
1522 K Street, N.W., Ste. 820
Washington, DC 20005
(202) 408-0742

Description: Awards for doctoral candidates in life sciences, physical sciences, social sciences, engineering, mathematics, and behavioral sciences; recipients chosen on the basis of academic achievement and quality of proposed research.
Restrictions: Limited to women only; United States citizenship and enrollment in United States institution required.
$ Given: An unspecified number of grants of $500 each are awarded annually.
Application Information: Write for details.
Deadline: January 15.

AT&T Bell Laboratories Cooperative Research Fellowships for Minorities
600 Mountain Avenue
Murray Hill, NJ 07974
(201) 582-4822

Description: Fellowships for graduate study toward Ph.D. degree, for graduating college seniors with the potential to become professional research scientists or engineers; relevant disciplines include chemistry, communications science, computer science, engineering, information science, materials science, mathematics, operations research, physics, and statistics; fellowship tenure includes one summer of work at AT&T; recipients chosen on the basis of academic achievement and proposed research.
Restrictions: Limited to African-American, Hispanic, and Native American applicants only; GRE exam scores required; United States citizenship or permanent resident status required.
$ Given: An unspecified number of fellowships awarded annually; each for $13,200/year plus tuition and fees and expenses.
Application Information: Write for details.
Deadline: January 15.
Contact: Special Programs Manager, CRFP.

AT&T Bell Laboratories Graduate Research Program for Women
600 Mountain Avenue
Murray Hill, NJ 07974
(201) 582-4822

Description: Fellowships and grants for graduate study toward Ph.D. degree, for graduating college seniors with the potential to become professional research scientists or engineers; relevant disciplines include chemistry, chemical engineering, communications science, computer science, electrical engineering, information science, materials science, mathematics, operations research, physics, and statistics; fellowship tenure includes summer work at AT&T; recipients chosen on the basis of academic achievement and proposed research.
Restrictions: Limited to women applicants only; applicants must be admitted for full-time study in approved doctoral program; United States citizenship or permanent resident status required.

$ Given: An unspecified number of fellowships awarded annually; fellowships and grants are renewable annually.
Application Information: Application forms required.
Deadline: January 15.
Contact: Special Programs Manager, GRPW.

AT&T Bell Laboratories
Ph.D. Scholarship Program
600 Mountain Avenue
Murray Hill, NJ 07974
(201) 582-4822

Description: Fellowships for doctoral candidates in the fields of chemistry, communications science, manufactural engineering, electrical engineering, and materials science; recipients chosen on the basis of academic achievement and proposed research.
Restrictions: United States citizenship or permanent resident status required.
$ Given: An unspecified number of fellowships awarded annually; each for $13,200/year plus $500 for tuition, books, and fees and up to $1,000 for travel.
Application Information: Applicants must be nominated by faculty member or department chair.
Deadline: January 15.
Contact: University Relations.

Canadian Federation of
University Women
CFUW Memorial Grant
55 Parkdale Avenue
Ottawa, Ontario K1Y 1E5
Canada
(613) 722-8732

Description: Grant for B.S./B.A. holders, to support graduate study in science and technology; recipients chosen on the basis of academic achievement, personal qualities, and potential.
Restrictions: Limited to women only; applicants must be accepted at intended places of study; Canadian citizenship or one-year landed immigrant status required.
$ Given: One grant of $1,000 Canadian awarded annually.
Application Information: Request application between July 1 and November 13.
Deadline: November 30.
Contact: Chair, Fellowships Committee.

Electrical Women's Round
Table, Inc.
Julia Kiene Fellowship/Lyle
Mamer Fellowship
P.O. Box 292793
Nashville, TN 37229
(615) 890-1272

Description: One-year research fellowship for graduate students in communications, education, research, advertising, home economics, electrical and power engineering, and business administration; recipients chosen on the basis of academic achievement, financial need, and quality of proposed research.
Restrictions: Limited to women only; United States citizenship or legal residency required.
$ Given: One Julia Kiene Fellowship for $2,000 and one Lyle Mamer Fellowship for $1,000 are awarded annually; renewable.
Application Information: Write for details.
Deadline: March 1.
Contact: Fellowships Administrator.

**Florida Education Fund
McKnight Doctoral
Fellowships**
201 East Kennedy Blvd
Suite 1525
Tampa, FL 33602
(813) 272-2772

Description: Fellowships for graduate study at one of eleven participating doctoral-degree-granting universities in Florida in the fields of business, engineering, agriculture, biology, computer science, mathematics, physical science, and psychology; recipients chosen on the basis of academic achievement.
Restrictions: Limited to African-American applicants only; B.A./B.S. degree required; United States citizenship required.
$ Given: Twenty-five fellowships awarded annually; each for a maximum of five years of study, with an annual $11,,000 stipend plus up to $5,000 in tuition and fees.
Application Information: Write for details.
Deadline: January 15.
Contact: Dr. Israel Tribble, Jr.

**French Embassy Scientific
Services
Chateaubriand Research
Scholarships for the Exact
Sciences, Engineering, and
Medicine**
Department of Science and
Technology
4101 Reservoir Road, N.W.
Washington, DC 20007
(202) 944-6241

Description: Six- to twelve-month research scholarships for doctoral candidates at dissertation level, as well as postdoctoral scholars, to conduct research in France at French universities, engineering schools, and private laboratories; language training sessions provided; relevant disciplines include biological and agricultural sciences, physical sciences and mathematics, engineering and applied sciences, medicine, nutrition, optometry and vision sciences, pharmacy and pharmaceutical sciences, and veterinary medicine and sciences; recipients chosen on the basis of proposed research.
Restrictions: Each applicant must be registered at United States university and already in contact with French host institution; United States citizenship required.
$ Given: Twenty to thirty scholarships awarded annually; each for F9,000 per month plus airfare and health insurance.
Application Information: Request application forms after September.
Deadline: January 31.
Contact: Anne Bartheleny.

**Fannie and John Hertz
Foundation
Fannie and John Hertz
Foundation Graduate
Fellowship Program**
P.O. Box 5032
Livermore, CA 94551-5032
(415) 373-1642

Description: Fellowships to provide B.S./B.A. holders with support for academic study through graduate school in the applied physical sciences, including engineering, applied physics, mathematics, and chemistry; tenable at one of 26 participating schools; recipients chosen on the basis of outstanding academic achievement (minimum 3.5 GPA in last two years of undergraduate work).
Restrictions: Applicants must have completed at least two years of college-level physics and college-level math

courses, plus one year of college-level chemistry; recipients must agree to respond in time of national emergency; United States citizenship required.
$ Given: An unspecified number of fellowships awarded annually; each for $15,000 plus up to $10,000 for tuition and fees.
Application Information: Write for details.
Deadline: October 21.
Contact: Dr. Wilson K. Talley.

Hughes Aircraft Company Doctoral Fellowships
7200 Hughes Terrace
Los Angeles, CA 90045
(213) 568-7200

Description: Fellowships for doctoral candidates and master's degree holders in aerospace, electrical/mechanical/systems engineering, computer science, physics, and mathematics; work-study and full-study programs offered, with work-study involving 20–36 hours/week employment at Hughes facility; participation in both programs includes initial full-time summer (10–13 weeks) employment at Hughes facility; most fellows attend UCLA, USC, CalTech, MIT, Cornell, Purdue, Stanford, Georgia Tech, University of Arizona, University of Illinois, etc.; recipients chosen on the basis of academic achievement (minimum 3.0 GPA).
Restrictions: United States citizenship and good health required.
$ Given: An unspecified number of fellowships awarded annually; each for tuition, stipend, academic expenses, relocation allowance, and salary/benefits during employment.
Application Information: Write for application packet; include university, field of interest, year of graduation, and GPA in query letter.
Deadline: February 1.
Contact: Kimberly J. Everett, Educational Coordinator.

Hughes Aircraft Company Engineering Fellowships
7200 Hughes Terrace
Los Angeles, CA 90045
(213) 568-7200

Description: Fellowships for doctoral candidates and master's degree holders aerospace or electrical/mechanical/systems engineering; work-study and full-study programs offered, with work-study involving 20–36 hours/week employment at Hughes facility (most fellows attend southern California schools as work-study participants); participation in both programs includes initial full-time summer (10–13 weeks) employment at Hughes facility; most fellows attend UCLA, USC, CalTech, MIT, Cornell, Purdue, Stanford, Georgia Tech, University of Arizona, University of Illinois, etc.; recipients chosen on the basis of academic achievement (minimum 3.0 GPA).
Restrictions: United States citizenship and good health required.

$ Given: An unspecified number of fellowships awarded annually; each for tuition, stipend, academic expenses, relocation allowance, and salary/benefits during employment.
Application Information: Write for application packet; include university, field of interest, year of graduation, and GPA in query letter.
Deadline: March 15.
Contact: Kimberly J. Everett, Educational Coordinator.

Hughes Aircraft Company
Master of Science Fellowships
7200 Hughes Terrace
Los Angeles, CA 90045
(213) 568-7200

Description: Fellowships for B.S. degree holders in aerospace, physics, computer science, mathematics, and electrical/mechanical/systems engineering; work-study and full-study programs offered, with work-study involving 20–36 hours/week employment at Hughes facility (80% of participants are work-study and attend southern California schools); participation in both programs includes initial full-time summer (10–13 weeks) employment at Hughes facility; most fellows attend UCLA, USC, CalTech, MIT, Cornell, Purdue, Stanford, Georgia Tech, University of Arizona, University of Illinois, etc.; recipients chosen on the basis of academic achievement (minimum 3.0 GPA).
Restrictions: Applicants must have B.S. degree from institution accredited by the Accrediting Board of Engineering Technology; United States citizenship and good health required.
$ Given: An unspecified number of fellowships awarded annually; each for tuition, stipend, academic expenses, relocation allowance, and salary/benefits during employment.
Application Information: Write for application packet; include university, field of interest, year of graduation, and GPA in query letter.
Deadline: March 15.
Contact: Kimberly J. Everett, Educational Coordinator.

Institute of Electrical and
Electronics Engineers
Charles LeGeyt Fortescue
Fellowship
445 Hoes Lane
Piscataway, NY 08855
(908) 562-3839

Description: One-year fellowship for graduate study in electronics engineering; tenable at United States or Canadian school; preference to applicants beginning first year of graduate work.
Restrictions: Applicants must hold B.S. in electronics engineering.
$ Given: One fellowship for $24,000 is awarded annually.
Application Information: Write for details.
Deadline: January 15.
Contact: Staff Secretary, Fellowship Committee.

**Institute of International
Education
Colombian Government
Study and Research Grants**
U.S. Student Programs
Division
809 United Nations Plaza
New York, NY 10017-3580
(212) 984-5330

Description: Grants for B.S./B.A. holders to pursue up
to two years of study/research at Colombian universities;
relevant disciplines include agriculture, biology, business
administration, economics, chemistry, engineering, education, health services administration, geography,
history, Latin American literature, law, linguistics, political science, physics, regulatory development, public
health, and remote sensing interpretation.
Restrictions: United States citizenship required.
$ Given: An unspecified number of grants awarded annu-
ally; each for modest monthly stipend, plus tuition and
fees, health insurance, book/materials allowance, and
one-way return airfare upon completion of study.
Application Information: Write for details.
Deadline: October 31.

**Institute of International
Education Study and
Research Grants for US
Citizens**
U.S. Student Programs
Division
809 United Nations Plaza
New York, NY 10017-3580
(212) 984-5330

Description: Grants to support study and research in all
fields, as well as professional training in the creative and
performing arts; tenable at institutions of higher learning
outside of the United States for one year; list of participating countries in any given year may be obtained from
IIE.
Restrictions: Open to United States citizens with B.A.
or equivalent; acceptable plan of study and proficiency
in host country's language required.
$ Given: A variable number of grants awarded annually;
covers international transportation, language or orientation course (where appropriate), tuition, book and
maintenance allowances, and health and accident insurance.
Application Information: If currently enrolled in a college or university, apply to the campus Fulbright
Program Advisor; applications also available from IIE.
Deadline: October 31.

**International Union for
Vacuum Science, Technique,
and Applications
Welch Foundation Scholarship**
Advanced Technology
Laboratory
Bell North Research
Box 3511
Station C
Ottawa, Ontario K1Y 4H7
Canada
(613) 763-3248
FAX (613) 763-2404

Description: One-year scholarship for the study of vacuum sciences, preferably for study in a foreign
laboratory; funding made available to scholars with B.S.,
M.S., or Ph.D. degrees; recipients chosen on the basis of
proposed research.
Restrictions: Fluency in foreign language may be
required; midterm and final research reports required
for funding.
$ Given: One scholarship for $12,500 is awarded
annually; paid in three installments.
Application Information: Write for details.
Deadline: April 15.
Contact: Dr. W.D. Westwood, Administrator.

Charles A. Lindbergh Fund
Lindbergh Grants Program
708 South 3rd Street
Suite 110
Minneapolis, MN 55415
(612) 338-1703
FAX (612) 338-6826

Description: Grants for individuals to conduct research into the balance of technology and the human/natural environment; relevant fields include humanities, biomedical research, conservation of natural resources, waste disposal management, wildlife preservation, intercultural communications, aviation, aeronautics, agriculture, astronautics, adaptive technology, the arts, health and population studies, and oceanography.
Restrictions: Open to all nationalities.
$ Given: Twenty or more grants of up to $10,580 each are awarded annually.
Application Information: Write for details.
Deadline: June 14.
Contact: Marlene K. White, Grants Coordinator.

National Air and Space
Museum
Guggenheim Fellowships
6th and Independence
Avenue, S.W.
Washington, DC 20560
(202) 357-1529

Description: One-year residential fellowships for doctoral candidates at dissertation level, as well as recent Ph.D.s (within past seven years), for historical/scientific research on aviation and space; relevant disciplines include history, aerospace, and engineering.
Restrictions: N/A.
$ Given: An unspecified number of fellowships awarded annually; $14,000 predoctoral stipend, $25,000 postdoctoral stipend.
Application Information: Write for details.
Deadline: January 15.
Contact: Cheryl Bauer.

National Air and Space
Museum
Verville Fellowships
6th and Independence
Avenue S.W.
Washington, DC 20560
(202) 357-1529

Description: Nine- to twelve-month fellowships for analysis of major developments, trends, and accomplishments in history of aviation/space studies; relevant disciplines include history, aerospace, and engineering.
Restrictions: Applicants must demonstrate skills in research and writing.
$ Given: An unspecified number of fellowships for $30,000 each are awarded annually.
Application Information: Write for details.
Deadline: January 15.
Contact: Cheryl Bauer.

National Association of
Purchasing Management
Doctoral Dissertation Grant
Center for Advanced
Purchasing Studies
2055 East Centennial Circle
P.O. Box 22160
Tempe, AZ 85285-2160
(602) 752-2277

Description: Grants for doctoral candidates to conduct dissertation research on purchasing and materials management; open to individuals seeking Ph.D. or M.B.A. in business, economics, industrial engineering, management, and purchasing logistics; tenable at accredited United States institutions; recipients chosen on the basis of proposed research; preference for applicants planning careers in college teaching and research.

Restrictions: United States citizenship or permanent resident status required.
$ Given: Four grants awarded annually; each for $10,000 per academic year, paid in three equal installments.
Application Information: Write for details.
Deadline: January 31.
Contact: Richard Boyle, Assistant Director.

National Consortium for Graduate Degrees for Minorities in Engineering and Science, Inc.
Graduate Engineering for Minorities (GEM) Fellowships
P.O. Box 537
Notre Dame, IN 46556
(219) 287-1097

Description: Fellowships for master's candidates in engineering, physical and life sciences; recipients chosen on the basis of academic achievement.
Restrictions: Limited to African-American, Native American, Mexican-American, and Puerto Rican applicants only; United States citizenship required.
$ Given: Two hundred and twenty-five master's, 30 Ph.D. (English) and 30 Ph.D. (science) fellowships awarded annually; each for tuition and fees at member institution plus $6,000/year living stipend and summer employment.
Application Information: Write for details.
Deadline: December 1.
Contact: Betty Jean Valdez.

National Italian American Foundation Scholarship Program
Michael and Francesca Marinelli Scholarships
1860 19th Street, N.W.
Washington, DC 20009
(202) 638-2137
FAX (202) 638-0002

Description: Scholarships for graduate students in the DC area and for undergraduates at Nova University in Florida; relevant disciplines limited to science and business; recipients chosen on the basis of academic achievement and financial need.
Restrictions: Applicants must be of Italian descent.
$ Given: Two scholarships for $1,000–$2,000 each are awarded annually.
Application Information: Essay required.
Deadline: May 31.
Contact: Dr. Maria Lombardo, Education Director.

National Research Council
NRC/Ford Predoctoral and Dissertation Fellowships for Minorities
Fellowships Office
2101 Constitution Avenue, N.W.
Washington, DC 20418
(202) 334-2872

Description: Fellowships for graduate students in the humanities, social sciences, biological and agricultural sciences, physical sciences and mathematics, and engineering and applied sciences; recipients chosen on the basis of academic achievement and proposed research.
Restrictions: Limited to members of minority groups; United States citizenship or legal residency required.
$ Given: Fifty-five fellowships awarded; $11,500 for fellow, $6,000 for institution; 20 dissertation fellowships available for $18,000.
Application Information: Write for details.
Deadline: November 5.

Natural Sciences and Engineering Research Council of Canada NSERC Postgraduate Scholarships in Science Librarianship and Documentation
200 Kent Street
Ottawa, Ontario K1A 1H5
Canada
(613) 992-8203

Description: One-year scholarships for first- and second-year study toward M.L.S. degree in library science; recipients chosen on the basis of academic achievement, commitment to field, and relevant experience.
Restrictions: Applicants must have B.S. degree in science or engineering; Canadian citizenship or permanent resident status required.
$ Given: A few scholarships awarded annually; each for $13,500 Canadian plus travel allowance.
Application Information: Write for details.
Deadline: December 1.
Contact: Nadine Bohan; Information Officer.

Oak Ridge Institute for Science and Education Department of Energy Participation Program
P.O. Box 117
Oak Ridge, TN 37831-0117
(615) 576-3428

Description: Program for undergraduate and graduate students, as well as faculty members, to conduct/participate in research programs at seven Department of Energy facilities; summer and academic-year programs available; research programs are related to energy production, utilization, and conservation.
Restrictions: Applicants must have done degree work in life/physical/social sciences, mathematics, toxicology, or engineering; United States citizenship or permanent resident status required.
$ Given: An unspecified number of fellowships awarded annually; each with $20,000–$48,000 stipend, based on degree, program, and area of research.
Application Information: Write for application forms.
Deadline: Early January.
Contact: William E. Felling, Executive Director, (615) 576-3300; or Al Wohlpart, General University Activities Contact, (615) 576-3421.

Oak Ridge Institute for Science and Education Nuclear Engineering and Health Physics Fellowships
P.O. Box 117
Oak Ridge, TN 37831-0117
(615) 576-3428

Description: One-year fellowship for graduate students studying nuclear science and engineering or health physics at participating Oak Ridge Associated Universities with practicum at various DOE facilities; recipients chosen on the basis of academic achievement, career goals, and interests.
Restrictions: N/A.
$ Given: An unspecified number of fellowships awarded annually; each with $14,400 stipend, plus $300/month during practicum, and travel, tuition and fees; renewable for up to four years.
Application Information: Write for details.
Deadline: January 25.

Oak Ridge Institute for Science and Education Nuclear Regulatory Commission Graduate Fellowships Program
P.O. Box 117
Oak Ridge, TN 37831-0117
(615) 576-9279
FAX (615) 576-0202

Description: Fellowships for master's candidates studying nuclear engineering and health physics; participation includes work/orientation prefellowship; recipients chosen on the basis of academic achievement.
Restrictions: United States citizenship or permanent resident status required.
$ Given: An unspecified number of fellowships awarded annually; each for cost-of-education (paid directly to university) plus $1,800/month stipend
Application Information: Write for details.
Deadline: January 29.

President's Commission on White House Fellowships White House Fellowships
712 Jackson Place, N.W.
Washington, DC 20503
(202) 395-4522

Description: Twelve-month appointments as special assistants to the Vice President, Cabinet members, and the Presidential staff; fellowships include participation in educational program; positions available for students in public affairs, education, the sciences, business, and the professions; recipients chosen on the basis of leadership qualities, commitment to community service, and career/academic achievement.
Restrictions: Limited to young adults, ages 30–39; civilian federal employees are ineligible; recipients may not hold official state or local office while serving as White House fellows; United States citizenship required.
$ Given: Eleven to nineteen wage-earning fellowships for up to a maximum of $65,000 are awarded annually.
Application Information: Write for details.
Deadline: December 15.
Contact: Phyllis A. Williams.

Radio Technical Commission for Aeronautics William E. Jackson Award
655 15th Street, N.W.
Suite 300
Washington, DC 20005
(202) 639-4006

Description: Award for best technical paper by a graduate student in the field of aviation electronics or telecommunications; project reports, theses, and technical journal articles accepted.
Restrictions: Paper must be in English and must have been completed within the past three years.
$ Given: One award of $1,500 is given annually.
Application Information: Submit two copies of the following: paper, one to two page summary, biographical sketch of author, and faculty letter of endorsement.
Deadline: June 30.
Contact: Jackson Award Committee.

Rockefeller University
Rockefeller Archive Center
Research Grants
15 Dayton Avenue
Pocantico Hills
North Tarrytown, NY
10591-1598
(914) 631-4505

Description: Residential research fellowships for graduate students and postdoctoral scholars pursuing research using Archive Center resources; relevant disciplines including philanthropy, education, science, medicine, black history, agriculture, labor, social welfare, social sciences, politics, religion, population, economic development, and the arts; recipients chosen on the basis of proposed research and necessity of using Archive Center resources.
Restrictions: N/A.
$ Given: An unspecified number of grants awarded annually; each for up to $1,500 for travel, lodging, and research expenses.
Application Information: Write for details.
Deadline: December 31.
Contact: Dr. Darwin H. Stapleton, Director.

Sigma Xi, The Scientific
Research Society
Grants-in-Aid of Research
P.O. Box 13975
Research Triangle Park, NC
27709

Description: Research grants to graduate and undergraduate students in science and engineering, to support research projects; recipients chosen on the basis of proposed research.
Restrictions: Open to all nationalities.
$ Given: An unspecified number of grants awarded annually; each for up to $1,000 (average $600).
Application Information: Application forms required.
Deadlines: February 1, May 1, and November 1.
Contact: Committee on Grants-in-Aid of Research.

Smithsonian Institution
Predoctoral Research
Fellowships in Astrophysics
and Related Topics
Smithsonian Astrophysical
Observatory
60 Garden Street
Mail Stop 47
Cambridge, MA 02138
(617) 495-7103

Description: One-year fellowships for doctoral candidates in astrophysics and related topics to conduct independent dissertation research, working with Smithsonian staff and using Smithsonian resources; recipients chosen on the basis of academic achievement and proposed research.
Restrictions: Applicants must have completed all preliminary coursework and examinations.
$ Given: An unspecified number of fellowships awarded annually; each for $14,000/year; renewable for one year.
Application Information: Write for details.
Deadline: April 15.
Contact: Secretary, Predoctoral Fellowship Committee.

Smithsonian Institution Predoctoral Research Fellowships in the History of Science and Technology
Office of Fellowships and Grants
955 L'Enfant Plaza
Suite 7300
Washington, DC 20560
(202) 287-3271

Description: One-year residential fellowships for doctoral candidates at dissertation level in the history of science and technology, to pursue independent research using the Smithsonian's collections, resources, and staff expertise; relevant disciplines include history of mathematics, physical sciences, pharmacy, medicine, civil and mechanical engineering, electrical technology, and history of American science; recipients chosen on the basis of proposed research.
Restrictions: Applicants must have completed all preliminary coursework and exams for degree.
$ Given: An unspecified number of fellowships are awarded annually; each with $14,000 stipend.
Application Information: Write for details.
Deadline: January 15.
Contact: Program Assistant.

Southern Illinois University at Carbondale Minority Doctoral Fellowships in Science and Engineering
Graduate School
Woody Hall, B-114
Carbondale, IL 62901
(618) 536-7791

Description: Three-year fellowships for doctoral candidates in the life sciences, physical sciences, and engineering; recipients chosen on the basis of GRE or other national standardized test scores.
Restrictions: Limited to minority group applicants; applicants of Mexican or Puerto Rican descent preferred; United States citizenship required.
$ Given: Ten to twenty fellowships awarded annually; each for $15,000/year plus full tuition and fees (for three years).
Application Information: Write for details.
Deadline: February 2.
Contact: Dr. Harry Daniels, Associate Dean.

Tau Beta Pi Association Tau Beta Pi Fellowship Program
P.O. Box 2697
Knoxville, TN 37901-2697
(423) 546-4578

Description: One-year fellowships to support graduate study in engineering; tenable at the recipient's engineering institution of choice; recipients chosen on the basis of academic achievement.
Restrictions: Membership in United States or Puerto Rican chapter of Tau Beta Pi required; applicants must hold undergraduate degree.
$ Given: An unspecified number of fellowships awarded annually; each for $10,000.
Application Information: Application forms available in September.
Deadline: January 19.
Contact: James D. Froula, Secretary-Treasurer.

Transportation Research Board
Graduate Research Award Program on Public-Sector Aviation Issues
National Research Council
2101 Constitution Ave, N.W.
Washington, DC 20418
(202) 334-3206

Description: Awards for gifted graduate students for developing research papers on public sector aviation issues; final selection by expert panel; intended to attract students to policy and management positions.
Restrictions: N/A.
$ Given: Up to five awards made annually; each for $6,000.
Application Information: Write for details.
Deadline: October 25.
Contact: Joseph Breen, Research Award Program, Air Transport Section.

Women's Research and Education Institute
Congressional Fellowships on Women and Public Policy
1700 Eighteenth Street, N.W.
Suite 400
Washington, DC 20009
(202) 328-7070

Description: Congressional fellowship program designed to train women as potential public policy leaders; fellowship runs September through April and involves 30 hrs/wk work in a United States Congress office as a legislative aide on policy issues affecting women; open to master's and doctoral candidates at United States institutions; relevant disciplines include humanities, social sciences, biology and biomedical sciences, engineering and applied sciences, biomedical engineering, technology management and policy, business administration and management, health services management and hospital administration, education, allied health professionals, medicine, nursing, public and community health, and law; recipients chosen on the basis of political/civic activity and interest in women's issues.
Restrictions: Limited to women applicants; nine hours previous graduate coursework preferred; United States citizenship preferred.
$ Given: Eight to fifteen fellowships awarded annually; each with $9,500 stipend plus $500 for health insurance and up to $1,500 toward six hours tuition at home institution.
Application Information: Request application after November 1.
Deadline: February 14.
Contact: Alison Dineen, Fellowship Director.

Zonta International
Zonta Amelia Earhart
Fellowship Awards
557 West Randolph Street
Chicago, IL 60661-2206
(312) 930-5848

Description: Fellowships to support advanced study/research in aerospace engineering; funding made available to graduating college seniors and graduate students; recipients chosen on the basis of outstanding academic achievement (4.0 GPA preferred).

Restrictions: Limited to women only; applicant must hold B.S. in science and be accepted at accredited graduate school for advanced degree work in aerospace science or engineering.

$ Given: Approximately 40 fellowships of $6,000 are awarded annually.

Application Information: Request application forms from Zonta or from appropriate United States and Canadian graduate schools.

Deadline: December 1.

Contact: Ana L. Ubides.

Business, Education, Health, and Law

American Association for the Advancement of Science Mass Media Science and Engineering Fellows Program
1333 H Street, N.W.
Washington, DC 20005
(202) 326-6760

Description: Ten-week summer fellowships for science graduate students to work as journalists (print, radio, or television) to increase their understanding of the news media; available to students at any graduate level of study in the natural and social sciences, as well as engineering; recipients chosen on the basis of academic achievement and demonstrated commitment to conveying to the public a better understanding and appreciation of science and technology.
Restrictions: No funding to non-technical applicants; United States citizenship required; no concurrent funding allowed.
$ Given: Twenty fellowships awarded annually; weekly living stipend for 10 weeks plus travel costs.
Application Information: Write for details and application form; minorities and individuals with disabilities encouraged to apply.
Deadline: January 15.
Contact: Amie Hubbard, Program Manager.

American Association of University Women Educational Foundation AAUW Selected Professions Fellowships
P.O. Box 4030
Iowa City, IA 52243-4030
(319) 337-1716

Description: Fellowships for graduate students entering their final year of study in fields with traditionally low female representation, including architecture, business administration, computer science, dentistry, engineering, law, mathematics/statistics, medicine, and veterinary medicine; recipients chosen on the basis of academic achievement; tenable for full-time study at accredited United States institutions.
Restrictions: Limited to women who are members of minority groups; United States citizenship or permanent resident status required.
$ Given: An unspecified number of fellowships of $5,000–$9,500 each are awarded annually.
Application Information: Application forms available August 1 through November 1.
Deadline: December 15, February 1 for M.B.A.

**American Association of
Women Dentists
Colgate-Palmolive Award**
401 N. Michigan Avenue
Chicago, IL 60611
(312) 644-6610

Description: Grants for dental school students, to support senior year of study; recipients chosen on the basis of financial need.
Restrictions: Limited to women dental students only.
$ Given: Ten awards made annually; each for $500.
Application Information: Ten dental schools participate annually; the ten schools are selected on a rotating basis; each school's dean chooses one student to receive the award.
Deadline: Varies.
Contact: Deene Alongi.

**American Dental Hygienists'
Association Institute for Oral
Health
ADHA Institute for Oral
Health Graduate Scholarships**
444 North Michigan Avenue
Suite 3400
Chicago, IL 60611
(312) 440-8900

Description: Scholarships for full-time master's and doctoral candidates in dental hygiene studies; recipients chosen on the basis of academic achievement (minimum 3.0 GPA in dental hygiene curriculum) and financial need.
Restrictions: Applicants must be licensed dental hygienists with at least B.S./B.A. degree; applicants must be accepted by graduate program.
$ Given: Approximately 20 scholarships are awarded annually; each for up to $1,500.
Application Information: Write for application packet.
Deadline: May 1.
Contact: Beatrice Pedersen.

**American Dental Hygienists'
Association Institute for Oral
Health
ADHA Institute for Oral
Health Research Grants
Program**
444 North Michigan Avenue
Suite 3400
Chicago, IL 60611
(312) 440-8900

Description: Research grants for dental hygienists pursuing associate, baccalaureate, master's or doctoral degree, as well as for licensed dental hygienists, for conducting research related to dental hygiene.
Restrictions: Applicants must be licensed dental hygienists or students pursuing license; ADHA membership or student scholarship by ADHA member required.
$ Given: An unspecified number of scholarships are awarded annually; each for $1,000–$5,000.
Application Information: Write for application packet.
Deadline: January 15.
Contact: Research Grants Program.

**American Foundation for
Aging Research
AFAR Grants**
North Carolina State
University
128 Polk Hall; Box 7622
Raleigh, NC 27695
(919) 515-5679

Description: Grants for master's and doctoral candidates, to support biomedical or basic biological research on aging or cancer.
Restrictions: Applicant must already be involved in relevant research.
$ Given: Five to ten grants awarded annually; each for $500–$1,000 per semester or summer session; renewable.

Application Information: Application must be submitted by United States university on behalf of student.
Deadline: Applications accepted continuously.
Contact: Dr. Paul F. Agris, President.

American Foundation for the Blind
TSI/VTEK Scholarship
15 West 16th Street
New York, NY 10011
(212) 620-2064

Description: Scholarships for undergraduate and graduate students studying rehabilitation and/or education of the blind/visually impaired; tenable within the United States
Restrictions: Limited to legally blind applicants; United States citizenship required.
$ Given: An unspecified number of scholarships for $1,000 each are awarded annually.
Application Information: Write for details.
Deadline: April 1.
Contact: Leslye S. Piqueras, National. Consultant in Low Vision.

American Geophysical Union
Horton Research Grant in Hydrology and Water Resources
2000 Florida Avenue, N.W.
Washington, DC 20009
(202) 462-6900

Description: Grants for doctoral candidates, to support research projects in hydrology and water resources; relevant disciplines include physical/chemical/biological aspects of hydrology, as well as water resources policy sciences (economics, sociology, and law).
Restrictions: Membership in American Geophysical Union required.
$ Given: One or more grants awarded annually; each for $4,500–$9,500 plus travel allowance to ensure attendance at awards luncheon.
Application Information: Proposal must be signed by faculty advisor; application forms required.
Deadline: March 1.

American Indian Graduate Center
Native American Graduate Student Fellowships
4520 Montgomery Boulevard, N.E.
Suite 1-B
Albuquerque, NM 87109
(505) 881-4584

Description: Fellowships for full-time graduate study in all fields; recipients chosen on the basis of financial need, academic achievement, and desire to perform community service after graduation; preference for graduate studies in health, law, education, natural resources, and engineering.
Restrictions: Applicants must have ¼ or more Indian blood from federally recognized Alaskan Native or Native American tribe; United States citizenship required.
$ Given: An unspecified number of fellowships awarded annually; each for $250–$10,000 per year; average award $4,000; renewable.
Application Information: Write for details.
Deadline: April 30.
Contact: Oran LaPointe, Executive Director.

**American Institute of
Certified Public Accountants
AICPA Doctoral Fellowships**
1211 Avenue of the Americas
New York, NY 10036-8775
(212) 596-6221

Description: Fellowships for full-time students entering
accredited doctoral degree programs in accounting.
Restrictions: Doctoral program must be accredited by
the American Assembly of Collegiate Schools of Business; applicant must have CPA certificate; United States
citizenship preferred.
$ Given: An unspecified number of fellowships
awarded annually; each for $5,000/year; renewable for
up to three years.
Application Information: Request application forms
from the Institute.
Deadline: April 1.
Contact: Leticia B. Romeo.

**American Institute of
Certified Public Accountants
John L. Carey Scholarships in
Accounting**
1211 Avenue of the Americas
New York, NY 10036-8775
(212) 596-6221

Description: Scholarships for college liberal arts majors
to study accounting on the graduate level; tenable at
United States graduate schools.
Restrictions: Applicants must be college seniors who
are liberal arts majors at Yale, University of Georgia, or
University of Illinois; recipients must plan careers in accounting.
$ Given: An unspecified number of scholarships
awarded annually; each for $4,000/year; renewable for
second year.
Application Information: Request application forms
from the Institute.
Deadline: April 1.

**American Institute of
Certified Public Accountants
Minority Accounting
Scholarships**
1211 Avenue of the Americas
New York, NY 10036-8775
(212) 596-6200

Description: Scholarships for undergraduate and graduate students majoring in accounting; recipients chosen
on the basis of academic achievement.
Restrictions: Limited to minority group members only;
United States citizenship or permanent resident status required.
$ Given: An unspecified number of scholarships
awarded annually; varying amounts up to $5,000.
Application Information: Request application forms
from the Institute.
Deadlines: July 1, December 1.

**American Institute of Real
Estate Appraisers Student
Scholarships**
875 North Michigan Avenue
Suite 2400
Chicago, IL 60611
(312) 335-4100

Description: Scholarships for undergraduate and graduate students in land economics, real estate, real estate
appraising, and allied fields; recipients chosen on the basis of academic achievement.
Restrictions: N/A.
$ Given: Fifteen scholarships awarded annually; $2,000
per undergraduate fellowship; $3,000 per graduate fel-
lowship; renewable.

Application Information: Application forms available October 1 through March 15.
Deadline: March 15.
Contact: Education Department.

American Legion National Headquarters Eight and Forty Nurses Scholarships
P.O. Box 1055
Indianapolis, IN 46206
(317) 634-1804

Description: One-year scholarships for registered nurses pursuing undergraduate or graduate study in lung and respiratory diseases; recipients chosen on the basis of academic achievement and leadership qualities.
Restrictions: Applicants must be employed full-time and attending courses full-time at an accredited nursing school; minimum age 22; United States citizenship required.
$ Given: An unspecified number of $2,500 scholarships awarded annually; renewable.
Application Information: Write for details.
Deadline: May 15.

American Nurses' Foundation Nursing Research Grants
600 Maryland Ave, S.W.
Suite 100W
Washington, DC 20024
(202) 651-7231

Description: Grants for United States registered nurses to conduct research related to nursing; recipients chosen on the basis of proposed one-year research project.
Restrictions: N/A.
$ Given: An unspecified number of grants awarded annually; each for up to $2,700.
Application Information: Write for details.
Deadline: May 1.
Contact: Grants Administrator.

American Psychological Association APA Minority Fellowship Program in Neuroscience
1200 Seventeenth Street, N.W.
Washington, DC 20036
(202) 955-7761

Description: Ten-month fellowships for doctoral candidates in neuroscience; recipients chosen on the basis of academic achievement, financial need, and commitment to future career in neuroscience research.
Restrictions: African-American, Hispanic, Native American, Alaskan Native, Asian-American, and Pacific Islander applicants preferred; applicants must be planning careers in neuroscience; United States or Canadian citizenship or permanent resident status required.
$ Given: An unspecified number of fellowships awarded annually; each for $7,084 plus cost-sharing arrangement for full tuition scholarship; renewable for up to three years if recipient maintains good academic standing.
Application Information: Write for details.
Deadline: January 15.
Contact: Dr. James M. Jones, Director; or Ernesto Guerra, Minority Fellowship Program.

American Psychological Association APA Minority Fellowship Program in Psychology
1200 Seventeenth Street, N.W.
Washington, DC 20036
(202) 955-7761

Description: Fellowship for doctoral candidates in psychology; one program to support the training of clinicians, another program to support the training of researchers; recipients chosen on the basis of academic achievement and financial need.
Restrictions: African-American, Hispanic, Native American, Alaskan Native, Asian-American, and Pacific Islander applicants preferred; United States citizenship or legal residency required; applicants must be planning careers in psychology.
$ Given: An unspecified number of fellowships awarded annually; $7084 for ten months; renewable for up to three years.
Application Information: Write for details.
Deadline: January 15.
Contact: Dr. James M. Jones, Director; or Ernesto Guerra, Minority Fellowship Program.

American Psychological Association Psychology Dissertation Research Awards
750 First Street, N.E.
Washington, DC 20002
(202) 336-6000

Description: Awards for doctoral candidates at dissertation level in psychology; to fund dissertation research.
Restrictions: Dissertation topics must be pre-approved; applicants must be APA-student affiliates enrolled in APA-approved psychology graduate programs.
$ Given: One hundred awards for $500 each are awarded annually.
Application Information: Write for details.
Deadlines: February 15; September 15.
Contact: APA, Science Directorate.

American Statistical Association ASA/NSF/BLS Senior Research Fellow and Associate Program
1429 Duke Street
Alexandria, VA 22314
(703) 684-1221

Description: Fellowships/associateships for doctoral candidates and recent Ph.D.s in economics, business, and labor studies; for participation in research at the Bureau of Labor Statistics; recipients chosen on the basis of academic achievement and quality of proposed research.
Restrictions: Significant computer experience required.
$ Given: An unspecified number of associateships are awarded annually; stipend is commensurate with qualifications and experience; fringe benefits and travel allowance also included.
Application Information: Write for details.
Deadline: January 14.
Contact: Carolee Bush, Fellowship Program Director.

Armenian General Benevolent Union Excellence Grant
585 Saddle River Road
Saddle Brook, NJ 07662
(201) 797-7600

Description: Grant for graduate students in Armenian Studies, international affairs, education, public administration, and journalism; recipients chosen on the basis of outstanding academic achievement and competence in subject area.

Restrictions: Limited to individuals of Armenian descent who are enrolled at Columbia University, Harvard University, University of Michigan, or UCLA.
$ Given: One grant of $5,000 is awarded annually.
Application Information: Write for details.
Deadline: April 30.

Armenian General Benevolent Union Graduate Scholarship Program
585 Saddle River Road
Saddle Brook, NJ 07662
(201) 797-7600

Description: Scholarships for graduate students in law, medicine, international relations, and Armenian studies; recipients chosen on the basis of academic achievement, financial need, and involvement in the Armenian community.
Restrictions: Limited to individuals of Armenian descent who are enrolled in accredited United States institutions.
$ Given: Seventy grants of $1,000 are awarded annually; renewable.
Application Information: Write for details.
Deadline: April 30.

Arthritis Foundation Doctoral Dissertation Awards for Nonphysician Health Professionals
1314 Spring Street, N.W.
Atlanta, GA 30309
(404) 872-7100

Description: One to two years of grant support for doctoral candidates conducting dissertation-level research related to arthritis; recipients chosen on the basis of proposed research.
Restrictions: Applicants must be planning careers in arthritis research; membership in or eligibility for professional organization required.
$ Given: An unspecified number of grants awarded annually; each for up to $10,000/year.
Application Information: Applicant's doctoral chairperson must approve the project.
Deadline: September 1.
Contact: Leigh Hoffner, Administrative Assistant, Research Administration

Arthritis Foundation Medical Student Research Awards
1314 Spring Street, N.W.
Atlanta, GA 30309
(404) 872-7100

Description: One year of grant support for medical students in M.D. or M.D./Ph.D. programs at accredited United States medical schools, for arthritis-related research in the fields of biochemistry, microbiological science, immunology, and medicine; recipients chosen on the basis of proposed research and potential as biomedical investigators.
Restrictions: Applicants must be planning careers in medicine; applicants must have research advisors who agree to provide the necessary space, facilities, and guidance for the proposed research.
$ Given: An unspecified number of grants awarded annually; each for $11,000 in year one; renewable for $11,500 in year two and $12,000 in year three.

Application Information: Write for details.
Deadlines: March 1, November 1.
Contact: Leigh Hoffner, Administrative Assistant, Research Administration.

**Atlantic Salmon Federation
Bensinger-Liddle Salmon
Fellowship**
P.O. Box 429
Saint Andrews,
New Brunswick
EOG 2X0
Canada
(506) 529-4581

Description: Fellowship to support individual research overseas on Atlantic salmon conservation and management; recipients chosen on the basis of research capability and benefit of proposed research.
Restrictions: United States or Canadian citizenship required in even-numbered years; United Kingdom citizenship required in odd-numbered years.
$ Given: One fellowship for $10,000 Canadian awarded annually.
Application Information: For application form, contact the United States office, Atlantic Salmon Federation, P.O. Box 807, Calais, ME 04619.
Deadline: March 1.
Contact: Cheryl Carter.

**Atlantic Salmon Federation
Olin Fellowships**
P.O. Box 429
Saint Andrews, New
Brunswick
EOG 2X0
Canada
(506) 529-8889

Description: Fellowship to support research on Atlantic salmon conservation and management; tenable at any accredited university or research laboratory; recipients chosen on the basis of academic achievement and benefit of proposed research.
Restrictions: United States or Canadian residency required.
$ Given: Two to six fellowships awarded annually; each for $1,000–$3,000 Canadian.
Application Information: For application form, contact the United States office, Atlantic Salmon Federation, P.O. Box 807, Calais, ME 04619.
Deadline: March 15.
Contact: Dr. J.M. Anderson, Director of Operations.

**Business and Professional
Women's Clubs—New York
State
Grace LeGendre Fellowships
and Endowment Fund**
239 Genesee Street
Mayro Building, Suite 212
Utica, NY 13501
(315) 735-3114

Description: Fellowships and grants for master's and doctoral candidates in all fields of study; tenable at accredited New York State institutions.
Restrictions: Limited to women applicants who are residents of New York State; United States citizenship or legal residency required.
$ Given: An unspecified number of $1,000 grants are awarded annually.
Application Information: Write for details.
Deadline: February 28.

Business and Professional Women's Foundation
BPW Career Advancement Scholarships
2012 Massachusetts Avenue, N.W.
Washington, DC 20036
(202) 296-9118

Description: One-year scholarships for undergraduate and graduate study in all disciplines, with emphasis on computer science, education, science, and paralegal training; scholarships are awarded within 24 months of the applicant's completing an undergraduate or graduate program in the United States; recipients chosen on the basis of financial need; funding designed to improve recipients' chances for career advancement/success.
Restrictions: Limited to women only; applicants must be at least 30 years old; no funding for Ph.D. studies, study abroad, or correspondence courses; United States citizenship required.
$ Given: One hundred and fifty scholarships of up to $1,000 each are awarded annually.
Application Information: Request application materials between October 1 and April 1.
Deadline: April 15.
Contact: Assistant Director, Education and Training.

Business and Professional Women's Foundation
BPW/Sears-Roebuck Loan Fund for Women in Graduate Business Studies
2012 Massachusetts Avenue, N.W.
Washington, DC 20036
(202) 293-1200

Description: Loans for master's degree candidates studying business administration at accredited institutions.
Restrictions: Limited to women only; BPW and Sears Foundation employees ineligible; United States citizenship required.
$ Given: An unspecified number of loans of up to $2,500 each are awarded annually.
Application Information: Request application materials between October 1 and April 1.
Deadline: May 1.
Contact: Education Department.

California Western School of Law
Law Scholarship Program for Librarians
225 Cedar Street
San Diego, CA 92101
(619) 239-0391

Description: Scholarships for librarians holding M.L.S. degrees from ALA-accredited schools to study law at California Western School of Law; recipients chosen on the basis of academic achievement, LSAT scores, and personal interview; preference for applicants planning careers in law librarianship.
Restrictions: Applicants must have already been accepted by California Western School of Law.
$ Given: An unspecified number of full-tuition scholarships are awarded annually.
Application Information: Contact Admissions Office for details.
Deadline: None.
Contact: Admissions Office.

Canadian Association of University Teachers J.H. Stewart Reid Memorial Fellowship for Doctoral Studies
2675 Queensview Drive
Ottawa, Ontario K2B 8K2
Canada
(613) 820-2270

Description: Fellowship for doctoral candidates in all fields; tenable at Canadian institutions; recipients chosen on the basis of outstanding academic achievement.
Restrictions: Canadian citizenship or minimum one-year landed immigrant status required.
$ Given: One fellowship for $5,000 Canadian is awarded annually.
Application Information: Write for details.
Deadline: April 30.
Contact: Awards Officer.

Canadian Embassy Canadian Studies Graduate Student Fellowships
501 Pennsylvania Avenue, N.W.
Washington, DC 20001
(202) 682-1740

Description: Fellowships for doctoral candidates in the humanities, social sciences, fine arts, business, law, or environmental studies who are working on dissertation topics related in substantial part to Canada; funding for dissertation research in Canada over a three- to nine-month fellowship period.
Restrictions: Applicants must be doctoral students at accredited institutions in Canada or the United States; applicants must have completed all degree requirements other than the dissertation; United States citizenship or permanent resident status required.
$ Given: An unspecified number of fellowships with $850/month stipends are awarded annually; non-renewable.
Application Information: Write for details.
Deadline: October 30.
Contact: Dr. Norman T. London, Academic Relations Officer.

Canadian Institute of Ukrainian Studies Doctoral Thesis Fellowships
352 Athabasca Hall
University of Alberta
Edmonton, Alberta T6G 2E8
Canada
(403) 492-2972

Description: Fellowships for doctoral candidates at dissertation level studying education, law, history, humanities, social sciences, or library sciences as related to Ukrainian or Ukrainian-Canadian topics; recipients chosen on the basis of academic achievement and dissertation topic; tenable in Canada or elsewhere.
Restrictions: Canadian citizenship or landed immigrant status required.
$ Given: An unspecified number of grants, each for $8,000 Canadian, are awarded annually; renewable.
Application Information: Write for details.
Deadline: May 1

Canadian Institute of Ukrainian Studies Thesis Fellowships
352 Athabasca Hall
University of Alberta
Edmonton, Alberta T6G 2E8
Canada
(403) 492-2972

Description: Fellowships for master's candidates studying education, law, history, humanities, social sciences, or library sciences as related to Ukrainian or Ukrainian-Canadian topics; recipients chosen on the basis or academic achievement and thesis topic; tenable in Canada or elsewhere.
Restrictions: Canadian citizenship or landed immigrant status required.
$ Given: An unspecified number of one-year grants, each for $4,500 Canadian, are awarded annually.
Application Information: Write for details.
Deadline: May 1.

CDS International Robert Bosch Foundation Fellowships
330 Seventh Avenue
19th Floor
New York, NY 10001
(212) 760-1400
FAX (212) 268-1288

Description: Nine-month internships at German government and business institutions (September–May) for master's degree holders and professionals in communications, journalism, economics, political science, public affairs, business administration, law, and German studies; German internships provided in a framework of government and commerce; recipients chosen on the basis of academic achievement, evidence of leadership, and community participation.
Restrictions: Recipients must be proficient in German by the start of the internship (fees for language courses reimbursed); United States citizenship required.
$ Given: Fifteen fellowships awarded annually; each with DM3,500/month stipend plus travel expenses and possible spouse stipend.
Application Information: Write for details.
Deadline: October 15.
Contact: Rick Blanckmeister, Program Officer.

Council for Advancement and Support of Education John Grenzebach Outstanding Doctoral Dissertation Award
11 Dupont Circle
Suite 400
Washington, DC 20036
(202) 328-5985

Description: Award for outstanding doctoral dissertation addressing philanthropy for education.
Restrictions: N/A.
$ Given: One award of $2,000 for the author, plus travel and lodging expenses for the author and a faculty member to attend the CASE annual assembly.
Application Information: Write for details.
Deadline: February 28.
Contact: Judy Grace, Grenzebach Research Awards.

Deafness Research Foundation Research Grants
9 East 38th Street
New York, NY 10016
(212) 684-6556

Description: Grant for doctoral candidates, faculty, and staff members, to support research on any aspects of the ear—its function, physiology, biochemistry, genetics, anatomy, pathology, or rehabilitation; recipients chosen on the basis of proposed research.

Restrictions: Funding must be used at United States or Canadian facility; applicants must disclose any other sources of funding for the project.
$ Given: An unspecified number of grants of up to $15,000 are awarded annually; renewable for one to two additional years.
Application Information: Write for details.
Deadline: July 15.
Contact: Medical Director.

Deafness Research Foundation Otological Research Fellowships for Medical Students
9 East 38th Street
New York, NY 10016
(212) 684-6556

Description: One-year fellowship following the third year of medical school, for research in otolaryngology, or immunology; participation requires a one-year leave of absence from medical school curriculum; recipients chosen on the basis of proposed research.
Restrictions: Funding must be used at a sponsor facility in the United States or Canada.
$ Given: One fellowship awarded annually; $10,000 plus up to $3,500 for laboratory and consumable supplies.
Application Information: Candidate and sponsor facility must submit application materials.
Deadline: November 15.
Contact: Medical Director.

Educational Foundation of the National Restaurant Association Heinz Graduate Degree Fellowships
250 South Wacker Drive
Suite 1400
Chicago, IL 60606
(312) 715-1010

Description: Fellowships for master's and doctoral candidates in food service management and education; recipients chosen on the basis of academic achievement and ability to improve teaching/administration skills.
Restrictions: Applicants must be employed full-time as teachers or administrators of food service education, and must be pursuing full-time or part-time graduate study.
$ Given: Seven fellowships awarded annually; one for $2,000; one for $1200; five for $1,000 each.
Application Information: Write for details.
Deadline: March 15.
Contact: Scholarship Services.

Educational Testing Service Second/Foreign Language Dissertation Research Grants
P.O. Box 6155
Princeton, NJ 08541
(609) 921-9000

Description: Annual awards for research on second/foreign language testing conducted as part of dissertation work for doctoral degree.
Restrictions: Dissertation level students only.
$ Given: An unspecified number of grants of $2,500 each are awarded annually.
Application Information: Write for details.
Deadline: N/A.
Contact: Dr. Carol Taylor, Director, TOEFL Research Program.

Electrical Women's Round Table, Inc.
Julia Kiene Fellowship/Lyle Mamer Fellowship
P.O. Box 292793
Nashville, TN 37229
(615) 890-1272

Description: One-year research fellowship for graduate students in communications, education, research, advertising, home economics, electrical and power engineering, and business administration; recipients chosen on the basis of academic achievement, financial need, and quality of proposed research.
Restrictions: Limited to women only; United States citizenship or legal residency required.
$ Given: One Julia Kiene Fellowship for $2,000 and one Lyle Mamer Fellowship for $1,000 are awarded annually; renewable.
Application Information: Write for details.
Deadline: March 1.
Contact: Fellowships Administrator.

Epilepsy Foundation of America
EFA Behavioral Sciences Student Research Fellowships
4351 Garden City Drive
Suite 406
Landover, MD 20785
(301) 459-3700

Description: One-year research fellowship for graduate students interested in basic and clinical research in the biological, behavioral, and social sciences designed to advance the understanding, treatment, and prevention of epilepsy; tenable at United States institutions; recipients chosen on the basis of demonstrated competence in epilepsy research.
Restrictions: Funding must be used in the United States; no funding for capital equipment.
$ Given: Fifteen to twenty fellowships awarded annually; varying amounts.
Application Information: Write for details.
Deadline: March 1.
Contact: Ruby Gerald, Administrative Assistant, Research and Professional Education.

Epilepsy Foundation of America
Medical Student Fellowships
4351 Garden City Drive
Suite 406
Landover, MD 20785
(301) 459-3700

Description: Short-term fellowships (three months) for medical students interested in careers in epilepsy research; tenable for research at United States institutions with ongoing epilepsy research/service projects; recipients chosen on the basis of submitted statement addressing relevant experiences and interest.
Restrictions: End-of-project report required.
$ Given: An unspecified number of fellowships for $2,000 each are awarded annually.
Application Information: Submit outline of proposed eight-to 12-week program of research, plus personal statement addressing interest in epilepsy research.
Deadline: March 1.
Contact: Ruby Gerald, Administrative Assistant, Research and Professional Education.

**Florida Education Fund
McKnight Doctoral
Fellowships**
201 East Kennedy Blvd
Suite 1525
Tampa, FL 33602
(813) 272-2772

Description: Fellowships for graduate study at one of eleven participating doctoral-degree-granting universities in Florida in the fields of business, engineering, agriculture, biology, computer science, mathematics, physical science, and psychology; recipients chosen on the basis of academic achievement.
Restrictions: Limited to African-American applicants only; B.A./B.S. degree required; United States citizenship required.
$ Given: Twenty-five fellowships awarded annually; each for a maximum of five years of study, with an annual $11,000 stipend plus up to $5,000 in tuition and fees.
Application Information: Write for details.
Deadline: January 15.
Contact: Dr. Israel Tribble, Jr.

**French Embassy Scientific
Services
Chateaubriand Research
Scholarships for the Exact
Sciences, Engineering, and
Medicine**
Department of Science and
Technology
4101 Reservoir Road, N.W.
Washington, DC 20007
(202) 944-6241

Description: Six- to twelve-month research scholarships for doctoral candidates at dissertation level, as well as postdoctoral scholars, to conduct research in France at French universities, engineering schools, and private laboratories; language training sessions provided; relevant disciplines include biological and agricultural sciences, physical sciences and mathematics, engineering and applied sciences, medicine, nutrition, optometry and vision sciences, pharmacy and pharmaceutical sciences, and veterinary medicine and sciences; recipients chosen on the basis of proposed research.
Restrictions: Each applicant must be registered at United States university and already in contact with French host institution; United States citizenship required.
$ Given: Twenty to thirty scholarships awarded annually; each for F9,000 per month plus airfare and health insurance.
Application Information: Request application forms after September.
Deadline: January 31.
Contact: Anne Bartheleny.

**Grass Foundation
Grass Foundation in
Neurophysiology**
77 Reservoir Road
Quincy, MA 02170
(617) 773-0002

Description: Ten- to fourteen-week summer residential fellowships at the Marine Biological Laboratory in Woods Hole, Massachusetts, for doctoral candidates and postdoctoral researchers in neurophysiology, electrophysiology, experimental neuroanatomy, neurochemistry, cellular neurobiology, developmental neurobiology, tissue culture, and behavioral analysis; recipients chosen on the basis of academic achievement and commitment to research career.
Restrictions: Recipients may not attempt to combine

this fellowship with dissertation work; open to all nationalities.
$ Given: An unspecified number of fellowships awarded annually; each for housing, board, research space rental, and expense budget.
Application Information: Write for bulletin.
Deadline: December 1.
Contact: Secretary.

Hagley Museum and Library Grants-in-Aid
P.O. Box 3630
Wilmington, DE 19807
(302) 658-2400 ext 243

Description: Grants for two- to eight-week short-term research work conducted at the Hagley Museum and Library, using the imprint, manuscript, pictorial, and artifact collections; grants made available to degree candidates, advanced scholars, independent scholars, and professionals for study of American economic and technological history and French 18th century history; recipients chosen on the basis of proposed research.
Restrictions: N/A.
$ Given: Several grants of up to $1,000/month each are awarded quarterly.
Application Information: Write for details.
Deadline: Applications accepted continuously.
Contact: Dr. Philip B. Scranton.

Hagley Museum and Library Hagley-Winterthur Research Fellowships in Arts and Industries
P.O. Box 3630
Wilmington, DE 19807
(302) 658-2400 ext 243

Description: One- to three-month short-term research fellowships for work using both the Hagley and the Winterthur collections and resources; fellowships made available to master's and doctoral candidates, as well as to independent scholars studying historical and cultural relationships of economic life and the arts, including design, architecture, crafts, and the fine arts; recipients chosen on the basis of research abilities and project relevance to both libraries' holdings.
Restrictions: N/A.
$ Given: Six fellowships awarded annually; each with $1,000/month stipend, plus seminar participation and use of both research collections.
Application Information: Write for details.
Deadline: November 15.

Harvard University Center for International and Area Studies Fellowships Program
Center for International Affairs
420 Coolidge Hall
1737 Cambridge Street
Cambridge, MA 02138
(617) 495-2137

Description: Grants for doctoral candidates at dissertation level and recent Ph.D.s to conduct research in several fields, including area and cultural studies, demography and population studies, economics, geography, history, languages, literatures and linguistics, political science and public policy, psychology, sociology, anthropology, archaeology, law, international affairs, and interdisciplinary programs in the humanities and social sciences; recipients chosen on the basis of academic achievement and proposed research.

Restrictions: Young applicants preferred; preference to individuals pursuing careers involving social science disciplines as relevant to specific geographic areas.

$ Given: A few grants are awarded annually; $22,000–$25,000 stipend for two years of predoctoral research, $30,000–$35,000 stipend for two years of postdoctoral research, plus travel and research allowance.

Application Information: Write for details.

Deadline: October 15.

Contact: Marisa Murtagh, Fellowship Coordinator.

Herb Society of America Research and Education Grants
9019 Kirtland Chardon Road
Kirtland, OH 44094
(216) 256-0514

Description: Grants to graduate students for study/research in horticulture, science, literature, art, and economics—as related to herbs; recipients chosen on the basis of proposed research, which may be scientific or academic; research period may be up to one year.

Restrictions: N/A.

$ Given: One to two grants totaling $5,000 are awarded annually.

Application Information: Write for details.

Deadline: January 31.

Contact: Grants Administrator.

Horticultural Research Institute
HRI Grants
12501 Street, N.W.
Suite 500
Washington, DC 20005
(202) 789-2900

Description: Research grants to support work on improving the efficiency of the landscape/nursery trade; recipients chosen on the basis of proposed research.

Restrictions: N/A.

$ Given: Fifteen to twenty grants for $500–$10,000 each are awarded annually.

Application Information: Write for details.

Deadline: May 1.

Contact: Ashby P. Ruden.

Hudson Institute
Herman Kahn Fellowship
5395 Emerson Way
P.O. Box 26919
Indianapolis, IN 46226
(317) 545-1000

Description: Fellowships for one year of research/study in Indianapolis or Washington, DC, for doctoral candidates at dissertation level; relevant topics include education, economics, political economy, national security, policy issues, and political theory; recipients chosen on the basis of academic achievement, proposed research, and faculty recommendation.

Restrictions: United States citizenship required.

$ Given: Up to three fellowships awarded annually; each for $18,000 plus travel expenses.

Application Information: Write for details.

Deadline: April 15.

Contact: Director of Programs.

**Howard Hughes Medical Institute
Doctoral Fellowships in
Biological Sciences**
National Research Council
2101 Constitution Ave, N.W.
Washington, DC 20418
(202) 334-2872

Description: Three-year international fellowships to support full-time study toward Ph.D. or Sc.D. degree in biological sciences; intended for students at or near the beginning of graduate studies; relevant fields include biochemistry, biophysics, biostatistics, mathematical biology, cell biology, developmental biology, epidemiology, genetics, immunology, microbiology, molecular biology, neuroscience, pharomacology, physiology, structural biology, and virology; tenable at United States institutions; recipients chosen on the basis of academic achievement and future promise in biomedical research; women and minorities encouraged to apply.
Restrictions: Open to all nationalities.
$ Given: Sixty-six fellowships awarded annually; each with $14,000/year stipend and $11,700 annual cost-of-education allowance in lieu of tuition and fees; renewable for two additional years.
Application Information: Write for details.
Deadline: November 9.
Contact: Fellowship Office, National Research Council.

Howard Hughes Medical Institute
**HHMI-NIH Research
Scholars** Awards
One Cloister Court
Bethesda, MD 20814-1460
(301) 951-6710

Description: One-year research scholar position for medical students to participate in laboratory research at the National Institutes of Health in Bethesda, Maryland; sponsored by HHMI and NIH.
Restrictions: Applicants must be attending medical school (usually in second year) in the United States or Puerto Rico; United States citizenship or permanent resident status required.
$ Given: An unspecified number of positions filled annually; recipients paid as HHMI employees and housed on NIH campus.
Application Information: Kits and brochures available from medical school deans' offices.
Deadline: January 15.
Contact: Donald H. Harter, M.D., Senior Scientific Officer and Director, Research Scholars Program.

**Howard Hughes Medical
Institute Research Training
Fellowships for Medical
Students**
Grants and Special Programs
4000 Jones Bridge Road
Chevy Chase, MD 20815
(301) 215-8889

Description: Fellowships for medical students to participate in a one-year program of intensive, fundamental, full-time research in the biomedical sciences at an academic or research institution in the United States; recipients chosen on the basis of academic achievement, quality of proposed research, and future research potential.
Restrictions: Applicants must be enrolled at United States medical schools; Ph.D. and M.D./Ph.D. candidates are ineligible.

$ Given: Up to 60 fellowships for $20,000 each are awarded annually.
Application Information: Write for details.
Deadline: March 15.

Institute of International Education Colombian Government Study and Research Grants
U.S. Student Programs Division
809 United Nations Plaza
New York, NY 10017-3580
(212) 984-5330

Description: Grants for B.S./B.A. holders to pursue up to two years of study/research at Colombian universities; relevant disciplines include agriculture, biology, business administration, economics, chemistry, engineering, education, health services administration, geography, history, Latin American literature, law, linguistics, political science, physics, regulatory development, public health, and remote sensing interpretation.
Restrictions: United States citizenship required.
$ Given: An unspecified number of grants awarded annually; each for modest monthly stipend, plus tuition and fees, health insurance, book/materials allowance, and one-way return airfare upon completion of study.
Application Information: Write for details.
Deadline: October 31.

Institute of International Education Fulbright–Spanish Government Grants
U.S. Student Programs Division
809 United Nations Plaza
New York, NY 10017
(212) 984-5330

Description: Grants for B.A./B.S. holders studying anthropology, archaeology, art history, ceramics, philology, economics, Hispano-American studies, history, law, Mediterranean studies, musicology, philosophy, political science, sociology, and Spanish language and literature; for study at a Spanish university.
Restrictions: Fluency in Spanish (written and spoken) required; United States citizenship required; applicants must meet all Fulbright eligibility requirements.
$ Given: An unspecified number of grants awarded annually; Spanish government funds tuition and stipend; Fulbright funds round-trip transportation, and expense allowance.
Application Information: Write for details.
Deadline: October 31.

Institute of International Education Germanistic Society of America Fellowships
U.S. Student Programs Division
809 United Nations Plaza
New York, NY 10017-3580
(212) 984-5330

Description: Fellowships for master's degree holders and some B.A./B.S. holders studying German language and literature, art history, history, economics, philosophy, international law, political science, and public affairs; for one academic year of study in Germany.
Restrictions: United States citizenship required; applicants must meet all Fulbright eligibility requirements.

$ **Given:** Up to eight fellowships awarded annually; each for $10,000 plus consideration for a Fulbright Travel Grant.
Application Information: Write for details.
Deadline: October 31.

Institute of International Education Study and Research Grants for US Citizens
U.S. Student Programs Division
809 United Nations Plaza
New York, NY 10017-3580
(212) 984-5330

Description: Grants to support study and research in all fields, as well as professional training in the creative and performing arts; tenable at institutions of higher learning outside of the United States for one year; list of participating countries in any given year may be obtained from IIE.
Restrictions: Open to United States citizens with B.A. or equivalent; acceptable plan of study and proficiency in host country's language required.
$ **Given:** A variable number of grants awarded annually; covers international transportation, language or orientation course (where appropriate), tuition, book and maintenance allowances, and health and accident insurance.
Application Information: If currently enrolled in a college or university, apply to the campus Fulbright Program Advisor; applications also available from IIE.
Deadline: October 31.

International Foundation of Employee Benefit Systems Graduate Research Grants
18700 W. Bluemound Rd
P.O. Box 69
Brookfield, WI 53008
(414) 786-6700

Description: Grants to support doctoral candidates conducting research on labor studies and employee benefit topics, such as health-care benefits, retirement, and income security; recipients chosen on the basis of proposed original research.
Restrictions: United States citizens with thesis/dissertation topics approved by advisor.
$ **Given:** Five to seven grants of up to $5,000 each are awarded annually.
Application Information: Include 20-page proposal (or shorter), curriculum vitae, and two letters of recommendation (one from thesis/dissertation advisor).
Deadline: Applications accepted continuously.
Contact: Director of Research.

International Research and Exchanges Board IREX Developmental Fellowships
1616 H Street, N.W.
Washington, DC 20006
(202) 628-8188

Description: Individually designed fellowships for doctoral scholars to study within the United States in preparation for eventual field research in Eastern Europe; relevant disciplines include musicology, demography, economics, geography, political science, psychology, sociology, anthropology, archaeology, business, law, and international affairs; recipients chosen on the basis of proposed research.
Restrictions: United States citizenship required.

<mark>190</mark>

$ Given: An unspecified number of fellowships awarded annually; each for academic tuition, language training, stipend, or research allowance.
Application Information: Write for details.
Deadline: February 15.
Contact: Stan Zylowski, Program Officer.

Richard D. Irwin Foundation
Richard D. Irwin Doctoral
Fellowships
1333 Burr Ridge Pkwy
Burr Ridge, IL 60521

Description: One-year fellowships for doctoral candidates at dissertation level in business administration and economics; tenable at United States and Canadian institutions; preference to applicants with plans to teach business and/or economics.
Restrictions: Applicants must have completed all coursework and passed oral exams for degree.
$ Given: Twenty fellowships awarded annually; each with $2,000–$2,500 stipend.
Application Information: Applicants must be nominated by dean of school with accredited doctoral program.
Deadline: February 15.
Contact: Gail Ryba, Agent.

Japan Foundation
Dissertation Fellowships
142 West 57th Street
6th Floor
New York, NY 10019
(212) 949-6360

Description: Fellowships for two to 14 months of dissertation research in Japan; funding made available to doctoral candidates at dissertation level in the humanities and social sciences, with emphasis on political science, law, economics, business, and journalism—as related to Japan; recipients chosen on the basis of academic achievement and quality of proposed research.
Restrictions: Applicants must be proficient in Japanese; no funding for Japanese language study; recipients may not hold other fellowships concurrently.
$ Given: Thirteen fellowships awarded annually; each for ¥310,000 plus further allowances including one round-trip air ticket.
Application Information: Write for details.
Deadline: November 1.

Lyndon Baines Johnson
Foundation
Grants-in-Aid of Research
2313 Red River Street
Austin, TX 78705
(512) 478-7829

Description: Grants for individuals to conduct research at the LBJ Library; relevant fields include communications, economics, environmental policy and resource management, history, political science, and public policy; recipients chosen on the proposed research.
Restrictions: N/A.
$ Given: A few grants awarded annually; each for $75/day plus travel costs.

Application Information: Contact the Chief Archivist regarding the availability of proposed material before applying.
Deadlines: January 31, July 31.
Contact: Assistant Executive Director.

Medical Library Association
MLA Doctoral Fellowships
6 North Michigan Avenue
Suite 300
Chicago, IL 60602
(312) 419-9094

Description: One-year fellowships for doctoral candidates in health sciences librarianship, with emphasis on biomedical and health-related information science; funding intended to support research or travel, not tuition; recipients chosen on the basis of academic achievement.
Restrictions: Applicants must hold master's degrees from ALA-accredited schools; United States or Canadian citizenship required.
$ Given: One fellowship for $1,000 is awarded annually; non-renewable.
Application Information: Write for details.
Deadline: February 1.
Contact: Assistant to the Director of Professional Development.

Medical Library Association
MLA Graduate Scholarships
6 North Michigan Avenue
Suite 300
Chicago, IL 60602
(312) 419-9094

Description: Scholarships for master's candidates in medical librarianship; recipients chosen on the basis of academic achievement and professional potential.
Restrictions: Applicants must be entering an ALA-accredited school or have at least one-half the academic requirements yet to complete during the scholarship year; United States or Canadian citizenship required.
$ Given: One scholarship for $2,000 is awarded annually.
Application Information: Write for details.
Deadline: February 1.
Contact: Assistant to the Director of Professional Development.

Medical Library Association
MLA Graduate Scholarships
for Minority Students
6 North Michigan Avenue
Suite 300
Chicago, IL 60602
(312) 419-9094

Description: Scholarships for master's candidates in health sciences librarianship; recipients chosen on the basis of academic achievement and professional potential.
Restrictions: Limited to minority group applicants only; applicants must be entering an ALA-accredited school or have at least one-half the academic requirements yet to complete during the scholarship year; United States or Canadian citizenship required.
$ Given: One scholarship for $2,000 is awarded annually.

Application Information: Write for details.
Deadline: February 1.
Contact: Assistant to the Director of Professional Development.

Mexican American Legal Defense and Educational Fund
Law School Scholarships for Hispanics
634 South Spring Street
11th Floor
Los Angeles, CA 90014
(213) 629-2512

Description: One-year scholarships tenable at any accredited law school; recipients chosen on the basis of academic achievement and financial need.
Restrictions: Limited to Hispanic American applicants only; applicants must be enrolled full-time in law school; United States citizenship required.
$ Given: Twenty scholarships awarded annually; 19 for $1,000 each, one for $2,000; non-renewable but re-application is allowed.
Application Information: Application form required.
Deadline: May 30.

Myasthenia Gravis Foundation
Viets Medical Student
Myasthenia Gravis Research Fellowships
222 South Riverside Plaza
Suite 1540
Chicago, IL 60606
(312) 427-6252 or
(800) 541-5454

Description: Fellowships for medical students, for training in myasthenia gravis research; recipients chosen on the basis of proposed research.
Restrictions: Applicants must find scientist with established research program to supervise fellowship training and research.
$ Given: A few fellowships awarded annually; varying amounts.
Application Information: Application materials include personal background, program of study, research description, and sponsor endorsement.
Deadline: March 15.
Contact: Anna El-Oudsi, Executive Administrator.

National Association of Purchasing Management
Doctoral Dissertation Grant
Center for Advanced Purchasing Studies
2055 East Centennial Circle
P.O. Box 22160
Tempe, AZ 85285-2160
(602) 752-2277

Description: Grants for doctoral candidates to conduct dissertation research on purchasing and materials management; open to individuals seeking Ph.D. or D.B.A. in business, economics, industrial engineering, management, and purchasing logistics; tenable at accredited United States institutions; recipients chosen on the basis of proposed research; preference for applicants planning careers in college teaching and research.
Restrictions: United States citizenship or permanent resident status required.
$ Given: Four grants awarded annually; each for $10,000 per academic year, paid in three equal installments.
Application Information: Write for details.
Deadline: January 31.
Contact: Richard Boyle, Assistant Director.

National Italian American Foundation Scholarship Program
Oresto A. and Maddalena Giargiari Endowment Medical Scholarships
1860 19th Street, N.W.
Washington, DC 20009
(202) 638-2137
FAX (202) 638-0002

Description: Scholarships for second-, third-, and fourth-year medical students at approved United States medical schools; recipients chosen on the basis of academic achievement and financial need.
Restrictions: Applicants must be of Italian descent.
$ Given: An unspecified number of scholarships for $5,000 each are awarded annually.
Application Information: Application materials must be submitted in triplicate.
Deadline: May 31.
Contact: Dr. Maria Lombardo, Education Director.

National Italian American Foundation Scholarship Program
Michael and Francesca Marinelli Scholarships
1860 19th Street, N.W.
Washington, DC 20009
(202) 638-2137
FAX (202) 638-0002

Description: Scholarships for graduate students in the DC area and for undergraduates at Nova University in Florida; relevant disciplines limited to science and business; recipients chosen on the basis of academic achievement and financial need.
Restrictions: Applicants must be of Italian descent.
$ Given: Two scholarships for $2,000 each are awarded annually.
Application Information: Essay required.
Deadline: May 31.
Contact: Dr. Maria Lombardo, Education Director.

National Italian American Foundation Scholarship Program
Matching Law Fellowships
1860 19th Street, N.W.
Washington, DC 20009
(202) 638-2137
FAX (202) 638-0002

Description: Fellowships for graduate law students; recipients chosen on the basis of 750-word essay describing the contributions of Italian-Americans to the American judicial system.
Restrictions: N/A.
$ Given: Five fellowships for $1,000 each are awarded annually.
Application Information: Send SASE for details.
Deadline: May 31.
Contact: Dr. Maria Lombardo, Education Director.

National Italian American Foundation Scholarship Program
Stella Business Scholarship
1860 19th Street, N.W.
Washington, DC 20009
(202) 638-2137
FAX (202) 638-0002

Description: Scholarship for undergraduate and graduate students in business; recipients chosen on the basis of academic achievement and financial need.
Restrictions: Applicants must be of Italian descent.
$ Given: One scholarship for $1,000 is awarded annually.
Application Information: Send SASE for details.
Deadline: May 31.
Contact: Dr. Maria Lombardo, Education Director.

National Medical Fellowships, Inc.
William and Charlotte Cadbury Award
110 West 32nd Street
8th Floor
New York, NY 10001
(212) 714-1007

Description: Award for senior medical student; recipients chosen on the basis of academic achievement, leadership, and community service.
Restrictions: Limited to minority group members only; applicants must attend United States medical schools.
$ Given: One award made annually; for $2,000 plus certificate of merit.
Application Information: Applicants must be nominated by medical school deans; medical schools must provide letters of recommendation and transcripts for nominees.
Deadline: June 30 for nomination.
Contact: Programs Department.

National Medical Fellowships, Inc.
The Commonwealth Fund Medical Fellowships for Minorities
110 West 32nd Street
8th Floor
New York, NY 10001
(212) 714-1007

Description: Eight- to twelve-week fellowships for second- and third-year medical students to work in major research laboratories under the supervision/tutelage of prominent biomedical scientists; recipients chosen on the basis of academic achievement.
Restrictions: Limited to minority group members only; applicants must attend accredited United States medical schools and must be interested in careers in research/academic medicine.
$ Given: Thirty-five fellowships awarded annually; each for $6,000.
Application Information: Applicants must be nominated by medical school deans.
Deadline: September for nomination; application deadline follows.
Contact: Programs Department.

National Medical Fellowships, Inc.
Irving Graef Memorial Scholarship
110 West 32nd Street
8th Floor
New York, NY 10001
(212) 714-1007

Description: Two-year scholarship for rising third-year medical students; recipients chosen on the basis of academic achievement, leadership, and community service.
Restrictions: Limited to minority group members only; applicants must have received NMF assistance during second year of medical school.
$ Given: One scholarship for $2,000 is awarded annually.
Application Information: Applicants must be nominated by medical school deans.
Deadline: July for nomination; August 25 for application.
Contact: Programs Department.

National Medical Fellowships, Inc.
Henry G. Halladay Awards
110 West 32nd Street
8th Floor
New York, NY 10001
(212) 714-1007

Description: Supplemental scholarships for individuals accepted into the first year of medical school despite significant obstacles; recipients chosen on the basis of recommendations, personal statement, and financial need.
Restrictions: Limited to black male applicants only; applicants must be accepted at accredited United States medical schools.
$ Given: Five scholarships for $760 each are awarded annually.
Application Information: Recipients chosen from General Scholarship applicants.
Deadline: August 31.
Contact: Programs Department.

National Medical Fellowships, Inc.
George Hill Memorial Scholarship
110 West 32nd Street
8th Floor
New York, NY 10001
(212) 714-1007

Description: Scholarship for incoming first-year medical students; recipients chosen on the basis of financial need, academic achievement, leadership, and community service.
Restrictions: Limited to African-American applicants only; applicants must be residents of Westchester County, New York, and must be accepted at accredited United States medical schools.
$ Given: One scholarship for $4,000/year is awarded annually; renewable annually.
Application Information: Application forms included with General Scholarship application forms.
Deadline: N/A.
Contact: Programs Department.

National Medical Fellowships, Inc.
Franklin C. McLean Award
110 West 32nd Street
8th Floor
New York, NY 10001
(212) 714-1007

Description: Award for senior medical students; recipients chosen on the basis of academic achievement, leadership, and community service.
Restrictions: Limited to minority group members only; applicants must be enrolled in accredited United States medical schools.
$ Given: One award for $3,000 is made annually.
Application Information: Applicants must be nominated by medical school deans; medical schools must provide letters of recommendation and transcripts for nominees.
Deadline: June 30 for nomination.
Contact: Programs Department.

National Medical Fellowships, Inc.
Metropolitan Life Foundation Awards Program for Academic Excellence in Medicine
110 West 32nd Street
8th Floor
New York, NY 10001
(212) 714-1007

Description: Awards for second- and third-year medical students; recipients chosen on the basis of academic achievement, leadership, financial need, and potential for contribution to the field of medicine.
Restrictions: Limited to minority group members only; applicants must attend medical schools in or be residents of the following areas: San Francisco, CA; Tampa, FL; Atlanta, GA; Aurora, IL; Wichita, KS; New York, NY; Tulsa, OK; Pittsburgh, PA; Scranton, PA; Warwick, RI; Greenville, SC; and San Antonio, TX.
$ Given: Up to ten awards made annually; each for $2,500.
Application Information: Applicants must be nominated by medical school deans.
Deadline: August for nomination.
Contact: Programs Department.

National Medical Fellowships, Inc.
National General Medical Scholarships for Minorities
110 West 32nd Street
8th Floor
New York, NY 10001
(212) 714-1007

Description: Scholarships for second- and third-year medical students in M.D. programs at accredited United States medical schools.
Restrictions: Limited to minority group members only.
$ Given: Seven hundred and sixty scholarships awarded annually; each for $500–$4,000.
Application Information: Write for details.
Deadline: May 31.
Contact: Scholarships Department.

National Medical Fellowships, Inc.
National Medical Association Special Awards Program
110 West 32nd Street
8th Floor
New York, NY 10001
(212) 714-1007

Description: Need-based awards for medical students; recipients chosen on the basis of academic achievement, leadership, and potential for contribution to the field of medicine, as well as financial need; NMA Merit Scholarship (four per year), Slack Award for Medical Journalism (one per year), Beecham/NMA Scholarship (one per year), and Ford/NMA Scholarship (one per year).
Restrictions: Limited to African-American applicants only; applicants must attend accredited M.D. or D.O. degree-granting United States medical schools.
$ Given: Seven awards made annually; each for $1,350–$2,500.
Application Information: Applicants must be nominated by medical school deans.
Deadline: May for nomination.
Contact: NMA Special Awards Program.

National Medical Fellowships, Inc.
NMF-Gerber Pediatrics Fellowship
110 West 32nd Street
8th Floor
New York, NY 10001
(212) 714-1007

Description: Fellowship for senior-year medical students who plan careers in pediatric medicine; recipients chosen on the basis of academic achievement, leadership, and financial need.
Restrictions: Limited to minority group members only; applicants must match for pediatric residencies; applicants must attend the following schools: University of Michigan Medical School, Michigan State University School of Human Medicine, or Wayne State University School of Medicine.
$ Given: One fellowship awarded annually; $2,000 stipend plus certificate of merit.
Application Information: Applicants must be nominated by medical school deans and chairs of departments of pediatrics.
Deadline: January for nomination.
Contact: Pediatrics Fellowship Administrator.

National Medical Fellowships, Inc.
James H. Robinson Memorial Prizes in Surgery
110 West 32nd Street
8th Floor
New York, NY 10001
(212) 714-1007

Description: Prizes to senior medical students for outstanding performance in surgery.
Restrictions: Limited to minority group members only; applicants must attend accredited United States medical schools; good academic standing required.
$ Given: Two prizes of $500 each are awarded annually.
Application Information: Applicants must be nominated by medical school deans and chairs of departments of surgery.
Deadline: December for nomination; January 12 for application.
Contact: Programs Department.

National Medical Fellowships, Inc.
Aura E. Severinghaus Award
110 West 32nd Street
8th Floor
New York, NY 10001
(212) 714-1007

Description: Award to senior medical students for outstanding academic achievement, leadership, and community service.
Restrictions: Limited to minority group members only; applicants must attend Columbia University's College of Physicians and Surgeons.
$ Given: One award for $2,000 is made annually.
Application Information: Recipients chosen by committee of faculty and administrators at Columbia.
Deadline: N/A.
Contact: Programs Department.

National Science Foundation
Behavioral and Neural Sciences Research Grants
4201 Wilson Boulevard
Arlington, VA 22230
(703) 306-1416

Description: Grants to support research on nervous systems and human/animal behavior; awarded in the following subprogram categories: cultural/physical anthropology, archaeology, animal behavior, behavioral neuroendocrinology, cellular neuroscience, developmental neuroscience, human cognition/perception,

linguistics, neural mechanisms of behavior, neurobiology of learning/memory, sensory system, and social psychology; recipients chosen on the basis of proposed research.
Restrictions: N/A.
$ Given: An unspecified number of grants awarded annually; varying amounts.
Application Information: Write for subprogram details.
Deadline: Applications accepted continuously; January 15, July 15.
Contact: Dr. Christopher Comer, Division of Integrative Biology and Neuroscience.

New York University
Publishing Studies Fellowships
715 Broadway
6th Floor
New York, NY 10003
(212) 998-7370

Description: Fellowships sponsored by North American publishing houses to train graduate students in book/magazine publishing; participation requires enrollment in two-year M.A. program (first year, full-time coursework; second year, paid internship in New York City).
Restrictions: Applicants must be college graduates with minimum 3.0 GPA.
$ Given: Nine fellowships for $5,500 each are awarded annually.
Application Information: Application requires college transcripts, two letters of recommendation, and interview.
Deadline: March 1.
Contact: Mary Witty, Publishing Studies Program Coordinator, Gallatin Division.

New York University
Student Affairs and Services
Graduate Assistantships and
Internships
239 Greene Street
New York, NY 10003
(212) 998-5656

Description: Graduate internships and assistantships for master's and doctoral candidates in higher education who are planning careers in student affairs and services.
Restrictions: N/A.
$ Given: An unspecified number of positions filled annually; varying amount.
Application Information: Write for details.
Deadline: February 1.
Contact: Judith Casey, Coordinator of Internship Program.

Nurses Educational Funds
NEF Scholarships
555 West 57th Street
13th Floor
New York, NY 10019
(212) 582-8820

Descriptions: Scholarships for master's and doctoral candidates in nursing; to support full-time study toward a master's degree or full- or part-time study toward a doctorate.
Restrictions: Applicants must be registered nurses enrolled in programs approved by the National League for Nursing; membership in national professional nursing organization required; United States citizenship required.

$ Given: An unspecified number of scholarships awarded annually; each for $2,500–$10,000; non-renewable.
Application Information: Write for details.
Deadline: March 1.
Contact: Barbara Butler, Administrative Assistant.

Oak Ridge Institute for Science and Education Nuclear Regulatory Commission Engineering and Health Physics Graduate Fellowships
P.O. Box 117
Oak Ridge, TN 37831-0117
(615) 576-9279
FAX (615) 576-0202

Description: Fellowships for master's candidates studying nuclear engineering and health physics; participation includes work/orientation prefellowship; recipients chosen on the basis of academic achievement.
Restrictions: United States citizenship or permanent resident status required.
$ Given: An unspecified number of fellowships awarded annually; each for cost-of-education (paid directly to university) plus $1,500/month stipend.
Application Information: Write for details.
Deadline: January 27.

Parenteral Drug Association Foundation for Pharmaceutical Sciences Nina Dale Demuth Research Grant
P.O. Box 242
Garden City, NJ 11530
(516) 248-6713

Description: Research grant for master's and doctoral candidates who are parenteral nutrition majors; recipients chosen on the basis of proposed research.
Restrictions: No geographical restrictions.
$ Given: One grant of $15,000 is awarded annually.
Application Information: Application form and eight copies of proposal required.
Deadline: June 15.
Contact: Grants Administrator.

Parenteral Drug Association Foundation for Pharmaceutical Sciences Parenteral Drug Association Foundation Research Grants
P.O. Box 242
Garden City, NJ 11530
(516) 248-6713

Description: Grants to support research in parenteral technology and related fields; recipients chosen on the basis of proposed research.
Restrictions: United States citizenship required.
$ Given: Two grants of $15,000 each are awarded annually; renewable once.
Application Information: Write for details.
Deadline: June 15.
Contact: Nina L. Demuth.

Parenteral Drug Association Foundation for Pharmaceutical Sciences Charles P. Schaufus Parenteral Processing Technology Research Grant
P.O. Box 242
Garden City, NJ 11530
(516) 248-6713

Description: Grants to support parenteral processing technology research; recipients chosen on the basis of proposed research.
Restrictions: United States citizenship required.
$ Given: One grant of $10,000 is awarded annually; renewable.
Application Information: Write for details.
Deadline: June 15.
Contact: Nina L. Demuth.

Pharmaceutical Manufacturers Association Foundation PMA Fellowships for Advanced Predoctoral Training in Pharmaceuticals
1100 Fifteenth Street, N.W.
Washington, DC 20005
(202) 835-3565

Description: One- to two-year fellowships for full-time doctoral candidates in pharmaceutics, to support thesis work/research.
Restrictions: Applicants must be enrolled in schools of pharmacy accredited by the American Council on Pharmaceutical Education; applicants must hold Pharm.D. or B.S. in pharmacy or related discipline (biology, chemistry) from accredited United States schools.
$ Given: Eight fellowships awarded annually; each for $10,000/year.
Application Information: Write for details.
Deadline: October 1.
Contact: President.

Pharmaceutical Manufacturers Association Foundation PMA Fellowships for Advanced Predoctoral Training in Pharmacology/ Toxicology
1100 Fifteenth Street, N.W.
Washington, DC 20005
(202) 835-3470

Description: One- to two-year fellowships for full-time doctoral candidates in pharmacology and toxicology, to support pharmacological research.
Restrictions: Applicants must be enrolled in schools of medicine, dentistry, or veterinary medicine and have completed all pre-thesis requirements; applicants should expect to receive Ph.D. within two years.
$ Given: Twelve fellowships awarded annually; each for $10,000/year plus $500/year for thesis research expenses; paid directly to universities on behalf of fellows.
Application Information: Write for details.
Deadline: September 15 (pharmacology); October 1 (pharmaceuticals).
Contact: Maurice E. Bectel, President.

Pharmaceutical Manufacturers Association Foundation PMA Medical Student Research Fellowship in Pharmacology–Clinical Pharmacology
1100 Fifteenth Street, N.W.
Washington, DC 20005
(202) 835-3565

Description: Three-month to two-year fellowships for full-time medical, dental, and veterinary students to conduct research in pharmacology and clinical pharmacology.
Restrictions: Applicants must be enrolled in schools of medicine, dentistry, or veterinary medicine and have completed at least one year of study.

$ **Given:** Six fellowships awarded annually; each for $10,000/year; paid directly to universities on behalf of fellows.
Application Information: Write for details.
Deadline: January 15.

President's Commission on White House Fellowships
White House Fellowships
712 Jackson Place, N.W.
Washington, DC 20503
(202) 395-4522

Description: Twelve-month appointments as special assistants to the Vice President, Cabinet members, and the Presidential staff; fellowships include participation in educational program; positions available for students in public affairs, education, the sciences, business, and the professions; recipients chosen on the basis of leadership qualities, commitment to community service, and career/academic achievement.
Restrictions: Limited to young adults, ages 30–39; civilian federal employees are ineligible; recipients may not hold official state or local office while serving as White House fellows; United States citizenship required.
$ **Given:** Eleven to ninieteen wage-earning fellowships for up to a maximum of $65,000 are awarded annually.
Application Information: Write for details.
Deadline: December 15.
Contact: Phyllis A. Williams.

Purina Mills Company
Purina Mills Research Fellowships
Purina Research Awards Committee
P.O. Box 66812
St. Louis, MO 63166-6812

Description: Fellowships for graduate students at agriculture colleges, for nutrition and physiology research as related to dairy, poultry, and animal sciences; recipients chosen on the basis of academic achievement and proposed research.
Restrictions: N/A.
$ **Given:** Five fellowships awarded annually, at least one in each of these categories; dairy science, animal science, poultry science; each for $10,000 per academic year; renewable for one additional year.
Application Information: Write for guidelines.
Deadline: February 5.
Contact: Dolores M. Adams–1E.

Rockefeller University
Rockefeller Archive Center
Research Grants
15 Dayton Avenue
Pocantico Hills
North Tarrytown, NY
10591-1598
(914) 631-4505

Description: Residential research fellowships for graduate students and postdoctoral scholars pursuing research using Archive Center resources; relevant disciplines including philanthropy, education, science, medicine, black history, agriculture, labor, social welfare, social sciences, politics, religion, population, economic development, and the arts; recipients chosen on the basis of proposed research and necessity of using Archive Center resources.
Restrictions: N/A.

$ Given: An unspecified number of grants awarded annually; each for up to $1,500 for travel, lodging, and research expenses.
Application Information: Write for details.
Deadline: December 31.
Contact: Dr. Darwin H. Stapleton, Director.

Smithsonian Institution Predoctoral Research Fellowships in the History of Science and Technology
Office of Fellowships and Grants
955 L'Enfant Plaza
Suite 7300
Washington, DC 20560
(202) 287-3271

Description: One-year residential fellowships for doctoral candidates at dissertation level in the history of science and technology, to pursue independent research using the Smithsonian's collections, resources, and staff expertise; relevant disciplines include history of mathematics, physical sciences, pharmacy, medicine, civil and mechanical engineering, electrical technology, and history of American science; recipients chosen on the basis of proposed research.
Restrictions: Applicants must have completed all preliminary coursework and exams for degree.
$ Given: An unspecified number of fellowships are awarded annually; each with $14,000 stipend.
Application Information: Write for details.
Deadline: January 15.
Contact: Program Assistant.

The Spencer Foundation Spencer Dissertation Fellowships for Research Related to Education
900 N. Michigan Avenue
Suite 2800
Chicago, IL 60611-1542
(312) 337-7000

Description: Fellowships for doctoral candidates at dissertation level in education, to support final year of dissertation research and writing; preference for candidates interested in careers in education research.
Restrictions: Applicants must be enrolled in United States graduate schools and must have completed all coursework and field work for dissertation; United States or Canadian citizenship or permanent resident status required.
$ Given: Thirty fellowships for $17,000 awarded annually.
Application Information: Write for details.
Deadline: October 25.

Social Science Research Council South Asia Doctoral Dissertation and Advanced Research Fellowships
605 Third Avenue
New York, NY 10158
(212) 661-0280

Description: Nine- to 18-month fellowships for doctoral candidates to conduct dissertation-related or advanced field research in Bangladesh, Nepal, Sri Lanka, Pakistan, Bhutan, or Maldives for dissertation work in the humanities and social sciences, business administration, and management; recipients chosen on the basis of academic achievement, proposed research, and proficiency in a major South Asian language.
Restrictions: United States citizenship or full-time enrollment in United States university required.

$ Given: Up to 15 fellowships awarded annually; varying amounts.
Application Information: Write for details.
Deadline: November 1.

Social Science Research Council
Southeast Asia Doctoral Dissertation and Advanced Research Fellowships
605 Third Avenue
New York, NY 10158
(212) 661-0280

Description: Nine- to 18-month fellowships for doctoral candidates to conduct dissertation-related or advanced field research in Brunei, Burma, Indonesia, Laos, Kampuchea, Malaysia, Thailand, Singapore, the Philippines, or Vietnam; for dissertation work in the humanities and social sciences, including law, public health, and public planning; recipients chosen on the basis of academic achievement, proposed research, and proficiency in a major Southeast Asian language.
Restrictions: United States citizenship or full-time enrollment in United States university required.
$ Given: An unspecified number of fellowships awarded annually; varying amounts.
Application Information: Write for details.
Deadline: November 1.

U.S. Arms Control and Disarmament Agency
Hubert H. Humphrey Doctoral Fellowships in Arms Control and Disarmament
Office of Public Affairs
The State Department
320 21st Street
Washington, DC 20451
(202) 647-8677

Description: Fellowship for doctoral candidates at dissertation level, as well as third-year law students; to support up to 12 months of research on arms control and disarmament; recipients chosen on the basis of academic achievement and proposed research.
Restrictions: United States citizenship or legal residency required.
$ Given: An unspecified number of fellowships awarded annually; each with $5,000 stipend, plus up to $3,400 paid to institution to cover tuition and fees.
Application Information: Write for details.
Deadline: March 15.
Contact: Robert Waters.

University of Oslo
International Summer School
University of Oslo
International Summer School (ISS) Scholarships
c/o Saint Olaf College
1520 Saint Olaf College
Northfield, MN 55057
(507) 663-3269

Description: Scholarships for undergraduate upperclassmen and master's degree candidates studying Norwegian medical care/health services, and Norwegian literature, peace research, and energy/environment issues; to attend six-week summer school (June–August) in Oslo; recipients chosen on the basis of academic achievement and financial need.
Restrictions: N/A.
$ Given: A large number of scholarships; normally cover room, board, incidental expenses; no tuition fee.

Application Information: Application forms available from Norwegian Embassy or the North American Admissions Office (address below).
Deadline: March 1.
Contact: JoAnn Kleber, Administrator, North American Admissions Office.

Wellesley College
M.A. Carland Shackford
Medical Fellowship
106 Central Street
Office of Financial Aid
Wellesley, MA 02181

Description: Fellowship for medical students pursuing general medical practice (not psychiatry); recipients chosen on the basis of academic achievement and financial need.
Restrictions: Limited to women only; applicants may be graduates of any United States undergraduate academic institution.
$ Given: One fellowship for up to $3,500 awarded annually.
Application Information: Application forms available after November 20.
Deadline: Mid-December.
Contact: Secretary to the Committee on Graduate Fellowships.

Woodrow Wilson National
Fellowship Foundation
Charlotte W. Newcombe
Doctoral Dissertation
Fellowships
CN 5281
Princeton, NJ 08543
(609) 452-7007

Description: Research fellowships for doctoral candidates at dissertation level, for dissertation research on ethical or religious values in all fields of social sciences, humanities, and education.
Restrictions: Applicants must be enrolled in United States graduate schools.
$ Given: Forty fellowships for $12,500 each are awarded annually.
Application Information: Write for details.
Deadline: Early December.
Contact: Program Officer.

Women's Research and
Education Institute
Congressional Fellowships on
Women and Public Policy
1700 Eighteenth Street, N.W.
Suite 400
Washington, DC 20009
(202) 328-7070

Description: Congressional fellowship program designed to train women as potential public policy leaders; fellowship runs September through April and involves 30 hrs/wk work in a United States Congress office as a legislative aide on policy issues affecting women; open to master's and doctoral candidates at United States institutions; relevant disciplines include humanities, social sciences, biology and biomedical sciences, engineering and applied sciences, biomedical engineering, technology management and policy, business administration and management, health services management and hospital administration, education, allied health professionals, medicine, nursing, public and community health, and law; recipients chosen on the basis of political/civic activity and interest in women's issues.

Restrictions: Limited to women applicants; nine hours previous graduate coursework preferred; United States citizenship preferred.
$ Given: Eight to fifteen fellowships awarded annually; each with $9,500 stipend plus $500 for health insurance and up to $1,500 toward six hours tuition at home institution.
Application Information: Request application after November 1.
Deadline: February 14.
Contact: Alison Dineen, Fellowship Director.

World Health Organization
WHO Fellowships
525 23rd Street, N.W.
Washington, DC 20037
(202) 861-3200

Description: One-year or shorter fellowships for individual or group health training/study in another country; intended for training/study not available in recipient's own country; relevant disciplines include public health administration, environmental health, medical social work, maternal and child health, communicable diseases, laboratory services, clinical medicine, basic medical sciences, and medical/allied education; recipients chosen on the basis of academic achievement and proposed study/training.
Restrictions: Applicants must be planning careers in public health; language proficiency required, as appropriate.
$ Given: An unspecified number of fellowships awarded annually; each to cover monthly stipend, tuition, and books.
Application Information: Contact WHO for detailed information booklet; application forms are available from national health administrations.
Deadline: At least 6 months prior to study.

Yale Law School
Fellowships for Journalists
401A Yale Station
New Haven, CT 06520
(203) 432-1681

Description: One-year fellowships for experienced professional journalists to participate in intensive program leading to Master of Studies in Law degree.
Restrictions: N/A.
$ Given: Five fellowships awarded annually; each for $22,500 stipend plus tuition.
Application Information: Write for details.
Deadline: January 15.
Contact: Judy Couture, Director of Public Affairs.

Yale University
John D. Rockefeller, III
Summer Graduate Research
Fellowships
Institute for Social and Policy
Studies
P.O. Box 208253
88 Trumbull Street
New Haven, CT 06520
(203) 432-2121

Description: Residential summer fellowships at Yale for doctoral candidates in history, social sciences, American studies, religious studies, women's studies, management, public health, and divinity; to support research on philanthropy, voluntarism, and non-profit organizations; fellowship tenure runs mid-June through mid-August; fellows expected to produce publishable papers on their summer work.

Restrictions: Preference to applicants with body of written work; preference to applicants whose work will take full advantage of Yale's resources.

$ Given: Six fellowships awarded annually; each with $3,000 stipend plus office space, library privileges, and support services.

Application Information: Write for details.

Deadline: March 30.

Contact: Peter Hall, Coordinator.

Women Only, Women Preferred, Women's Studies

American Association of University Women Educational Foundation AAUW American Fellowships
P.O. Box 4030
Iowa City, IA 52243-4030
(319) 337-1716

Description: Fellowships for full-time doctoral students and postdoctoral scholars, for research in all disciplines; recipients chosen on the basis of academic achievement and commitment to women's issues in professional career.
Restriction: Limited to women applicants; United States citizenship or permanent resident status required.
$ Given: Eight fellowships awarded annually, one for a senior fellow and seven for less experienced researchers; each for $20,000–$25,000.
Application Information: Write for details.
Deadline: November 1.
Contact: American Fellowship Program.

American Association of University Women Educational Foundation AAUW Dissertation Fellowships
P.O. Box 4030
Iowa City, IA 52243-4030
(319) 337-1716

Description: Fellowships to support doctoral candidates in full-time dissertation work for at least twelve months in any field.
Restrictions: Limited to women applicants; applicants must have completed all coursework and exams for Ph.D. by November; United States citizenship required.
$ Given: An unspecified number of fellowships awarded annually; each for $13,500 which may not be used for tuition or loan repayment.
Application Information: Application forms must be requested in writing.
Deadline: November 15.
Contact: Dissertation Fellowship Program.

American Association of University Women Educational Foundation AAUW International Fellowships
P.O. Box 4030
Iowa City, IA 52243-4030
(319) 337-1716

Description: Fellowships for one year of graduate study/research at an approved institution in the United States; recipients chosen on the basis of professional potential and importance of project to home country.
Restriction: Limited to women applicants; applicants must be citizens of countries other than the United States; applicants must hold B.A./B.S. or equivalent; proficiency in English required; recipients must return to home countries to work after fellowships are completed.
$ Given: An unspecified number of fellowships awarded annually; each for $15,065.

Application Information: Write for details.
Deadline: December 1.
Contact: International Fellowship Program.

American Association of University Women Educational Foundation AAUW Selected Professions Fellowships
P.O. Box 4030
Iowa City, IA 52243-4030
(319) 337-1716

Description: Fellowships for graduate students entering their final year of study in fields with traditionally low female representation, including architecture, business administration, computer science, dentistry, engineering, law, mathematics/statistics, medicine, and veterinary medicine; recipients chosen on the basis of academic achievement; tenable for full-time study at accredited United States institutions.
Restrictions: Limited to women who are members of minority groups; United States citizenship or permanent resident status required.
$ Given: An unspecified number of fellowships of $5,000–$9,500 each are awarded annually.
Application Information: Application forms available August 1 through November 1.
Deadline: December 15, February 1 for M.B.A.

American Association of University Women Educational Foundation AAUW Selected Professions Program Dissertation Fellowships in Engineering
P.O. Box 4030
Iowa City, IA 52243-4030
(319) 337-1716

Description: Fellowships for doctoral candidates in engineering; to support dissertation work.
Restrictions: Limited to women applicants; applicants must have completed all coursework and exams for Ph.D.; United States citizenship or permanent resident status required.
$ Given: An unspecified number of fellowships awarded annually; each for $14,500.
Application Information: Application forms available August 1 through November 1.
Deadline: November 15.
Contact: Selected Professions Fellowship Program.

American Association of Women Dentists Colgate-Palmolive Award
401 N. Michigan Avenue
Chicago, IL 60611
(312) 644-6610

Description: Grants for dental school students, to support senior year of study; recipients chosen on the basis of financial need.
Restrictions: Limited to women dental students only.
$ Given: Ten awards made annually; each for $500.
Application Information: Ten dental schools participate annually; the ten schools are selected on a rotating basis; each school's dean chooses one student to receive the award.
Deadline: Varies.
Contact: Deene Alongi.

Association for Women in Science Educational Foundation
AWIS Predoctoral Award
1522 K Street, N.W., Ste. 820
Washington, DC 20005
(202) 408-0742

Description: Awards for doctoral candidates in life sciences, physical sciences, social sciences, engineering, mathematics, and behavioral sciences; recipients chosen on the basis of academic achievement and quality of proposed research.
Restrictions: Limited to women only; United States citizenship and enrollment in United States institution required.
$ Given: An unspecified number of grants of $500 each are awarded annually.
Application Information: Write for details.
Deadline: January 15.

AT&T Bell Laboratories Graduate Research Program for Women
600 Mountain Avenue
Murray Hill, NJ 07974
(201) 582-4822

Description: Fellowships and grants for graduate study toward Ph.D. degree, for graduating college seniors with the potential to become professional research scientists or engineers; relevant disciplines include chemistry, chemical engineering, communications science, computer science, electrical engineering, information science, materials science, mathematics, operations research, physics, and statistics; fellowship tenure includes summer work at AT&T; recipients chosen on the basis of academic achievement and proposed research.
Restrictions: Limited to women applicants only; applicants must be admitted for full-time study in approved doctoral program; United States citizenship or permanent resident status required.
$ Given: An unspecified number of fellowships awarded annually; fellowships and grants are renewable annually.
Application Information: Application forms required.
Deadline: January 15.
Contact: Special Programs Manager, GRPW.

Business and Professional Women's Clubs—New York State
Grace LeGendre Fellowships and Endowment Fund
239 Genesee Street
Mayro Building
Suite 212
Utica, NY 13501
(518) 585-7087

Description: Fellowships and grants for graduate students in all fields of study; tenable at accredited New York State institutions.
Restrictions: Limited to women applicants who are residents of New York State; United States citizenship or legal residency required.
$ Given: An unspecified number of $1,000 grants are awarded annually.
Application Information: Write for details.
Deadline: February 28.

**Business and Professional
Women's Foundation
BPW Career Advancement
Scholarships
2012 Massachusetts Avenue,
N.W.**
Washington, DC 20036
(202) 296-9118

Description: One-year scholarships for undergraduate and graduate study in all disciplines, with emphasis on computer science, education, science, and paralegal training; scholarships are awarded within 24 months of the applicant's completing and undergraduate or graduate program in the United States; recipients chosen on the basis of financial need; funding designed to improve recipients' chances for career advancement/success.
Restrictions: Limited to women only; applicants must be at least 30 years old; no funding for Ph.D. studies, study abroad, or correspondence courses; United States citizenship and affiliation with United States institution required.
$ Given: Approximately 150 scholarships of up to $1,000 each are awarded annually.
Application Information: Request application materials between October 1 and April 1.
Deadline: April 15.
Contact: Assistant Director, Education and Training.

**Business and Professional
Women's Foundation
BPW/Sears-Roebuck Loan
Fund for Women in Graduate
Business Studies**
2012 Massachusetts Avenue,
N.W.
Washington, DC 20036
(202) 296-9118

Description: Loans for master's degree candidates studying business administration at accredited institutions.
Restrictions: Limited to women only; BPW and Sears Foundation employees ineligible; United States citizenship required.
$ Given: An unspecified number of loans of up to $2,500 each are awarded annually.
Application Information: Request application materials between October 1 and April 1.
Deadline: May 1.
Contact: Education Department.

**Canadian Federation of
University Women
Georgette LeMoyne
Awardplain R55 Parkdale
Avenue
Ottawa, Ontario K1Y 1E5
Canada
(613) 722-8732**

Description: Award for graduate studies in any field; intended for women taking refresher studies at universities where instruction is in French.
Restrictions: Limited to women only; applicant must hold B.S./B.A. degree and have been accepted to proposed program of graduate study; Canadian citizenship or minimum landed immigrant status required.
$ Given: One award for $1,000 Canadian made annually.
Application Information: Write for details.
Deadline: November 30.
Contact: Chair, Fellowships Committee.

Canadian Federation of University Women CFUW Memorial Grant
55 Parkdale Avenue
Ottawa, Ontario K1Y 1E5
Canada
(613) 722-8732

Description: Grant for B.S./B.A. holders, to support graduate study in science and technology; recipients chosen on the basis of academic achievement, personal qualities, and potential.
Restrictions: Limited to women only; applicants must be accepted at intended places of study; Canadian citizenship or one-year landed immigrant status required.
$ Given: One grant of $1,000 Canadian awarded annually.
Application Information: Request application between July 1 and November 13.
Deadline: November 30.
Contact: Chair, Fellowships Committee.

Canadian Federation of University Women CFUW Polytechnique Commemorative Awards
55 Parkdale Avenue
Ottawa, Ontario K1Y 1E5
Canada
(613) 722-8732

Description: Awards for graduate studies in any field, with preference for studies related to women's issues.
Restrictions: Applicant must hold B.S./B.A. degree and have been accepted to proposed program of graduate study; Canadian citizenship or minimum one-year landed immigrant status required.
$ Given: One grant of $1,400 Canadian awarded annually.
Application Information: Write for details.
Deadline: November 30.
Contact: Fellowships Committee.

Canadian Federation of University Women Beverly Jackson Fellowship
55 Parkdale Avenue
Ottawa, Ontario K1Y 1E5
Canada
(613) 722-8732

Description: Fellowship for B.S./B.A. holders to pursue graduate work in any discipline; tenable at Ontario universities; recipients chosen on the basis of academic achievement, peronal qualities, and potential.
Restrictions: Limited to women only; minimum age 35; applicants must hold B.S./B.A. from recognized univerity and be accepted into proposed place of study; Canadian citizenship or minimum one-year landed immigrant status required.
$ Given: One fellowship for $3,500 Canadian is awarded annually.
Application Information: Application forms are available July 1 through November 13.
Deadline: November 30.
Contact: Chair, Fellowships Committee.

**Canadian Federation of
University Women
Margaret McWilliams
Predoctoral Fellowship**
55 Parkdale Avenue
Ottawa, Ontario K1Y 1E5
Canada
(613) 722-8732

Description: Fellowship for doctoral candidates in any discipline who hold master's degrees and are at least one year into doctoral program; recipients chosen on the basis of academic achievement, personal qualities, and potential.
Restrictions: Limited to women only; Canadian citizenship or minimum one-year landed immigrant status required.
$ Given: One fellowship of $8,000 Canadian is awarded annually.
Application Information: Application forms are available July 1 through November 13.
Deadline: November 30.
Contact: Chair, Fellowships Committee.

**Canadian Federation of
University Women
Margaret Dale Philip Award**
55 Parkdale Avenue
Ottawa, Ontario K1Y 1E5
Canada
(613) 722-8732

Description: Award to graduate students in the humanities and social sciences, with preference to applicants studying Canadian history; recipients chosen on the basis of academic achievement in college, personal qualities, and potential.
Restrictions: Limited to women only; applicants must hold B.S./B.A. degree and have been accepted to proposed program of graduate study; Canadian citizenship or minimum one-year landed immigrant status required.
$ Given: One grant of $1,000 Canadian is awarded annually.
Application Information: Write for details.
Deadline: November 30.
Contact: Fellowships Committee.

**Canadian Federation of
University Women
Professional Fellowship**
55 Parkdale Avenue
Ottawa, Ontario K1Y 1E5
Canada
(613) 722-8732

Description: Fellowship for graduate work below Ph.D. level; recipients chosen on the basis of academic, personal qualities, and potential.
Restrictions: Limited to women only; applicants must hold B.S./B.A. degree and have been accepted to proposed program of graduate study; Canadian citizenship or minimum one-year landed immigrant status required.
$ Given: Two fellowships for $5,000 Canadian each are awarded annually.
Application Information: Application forms available July 1 through November 13.
Deadline: November 30.
Contact: Chair, Fellowships Committee.

Canadian Federation of University Women
Alice E. Wilson Grants
55 Parkdale Avenue
Ottawa, Ontario K1Y 1E5
Canada
(613) 722-8732

Description: Grants for women pursuing graduate refresher work in any field; recipients chosen on the basis of academic achievement, personal qualities, and potential; special consideration given to applicants returning to academic study after several years.
Restrictions: Limited to women only; applicants must hold B.S./B.A. degree and have been accepted to proposed program of graduate study; Canadian citizenship or minimum one-year landed immigrant status required.
$ Given: At least five grants for $1,000 Canadian each are awarded annually.
Application Information: Application forms available July 1 through November 13.
Deadline: November 30.
Contact: Chair, Fellowships Committee.

Electrical Women's Round Table, Inc.
Julia Kiene Fellowship/Lyle Mamer Fellowship
P.O. Box 292793
Nashville, TN 37229-2793
(615) 890-1272

Description: One-year research fellowship for graduate students in communications, education, research, advertising, home economics, electrical and power engineering, and business administration; recipients chosen on the basis of academic achievement, financial need, and quality of proposed research.
Restrictions: Limited to women only; United States citizenship or legal residency required.
$ Given: One Julia Kiene Fellowship for $2,000 and one Lyle Mamer Fellowship for $1,000 are awarded annually; renewable.
Application Information: Write for details.
Deadline: March 1.
Contact: Fellowships Administrator.

Institute of International Education
Fulbright Internships in India
U.S. Student Programs Division
809 United Nations Plaza
New York, NY 10017-3580
(212) 984-5330

Description: Internships for master's candidates in child care, crafts, marketing, special education for the handicapped, sports education, and women's issues; for up to nine months of study in India for academic credit (June/July–March/April).
Restrictions: Knowledge of Indian language (esp. Hindi) useful but not required; applicants must be unmarried and at least 24 years old; United States citizenship required.
$ Given: An unspecified number of grants awarded annually; partial scholarship.
Application Information: Write for details.
Deadline: N/A.

Landscape Architecture Foundation
Edith H. Henderson Scholarshipplain R4401 Connecticut Avenue, N.W.
5th Floor
Washington, DC 20008
(202) 686-0068

Description: Scholarship for undergraduate seniors and graduate students in landscape architecture; recipients chosen on the basis of academic achievement and commitment to developing practical client communication skills.
Restrictions: Limited to women applicants enrolled at the University of Georgia.
$ Given: One scholarship of $1,000 awarded annually.
Application Information: Personal essay addressing the importance of communication skills required for application.
Deadline: May 4.
Contact: David Bohardt, Acting Executive Director.

Landscape Architecture Foundation
Harriet Barnhart Wimmer Scholarship
4401 Connecticut Avenue, N.W.
5th Floor
Washington, DC 20008
(202) 686-0068

Description: Scholarship to support final year of undergraduate or graduate studies in landscape architecture; recipients chosen on the basis of design excellence and environmental sensitivity of work submitted for consideration.
Restrictions: Limited to women applicants; group projects ineligible.
$ Given: One scholarship of $500 awarded annually.
Application Information: Write for details; assembled materials should be sent to Harriet Barnhart Wimmer Scholarship, c/o Wimmer, Yamada & Associates, 516 Fifth Avenue, San Diego, CA 92101, (619) 232-4004.
Deadline: May 4.
Contact: David Bohardt, Acting Executive Director.

National Women's Studies Association
NAIAD-NWSA Graduate Scholarships in Lesbian Studies
7100 Baltimore Avenue
Suite 304
College Park, MD 20742
(301) 403-0525

Description: Scholarships for master's and doctoral candidates in lesbian studies; recipients chosen on the basis of financial need and thesis/dissertation topic.
Restrictions: Membership in NWSA preferred.
$ Given: One scholarship for $1,000 awarded annually.
Application Information: Write for details.
Deadline: February 15.
Contact: Loretta Younger, Office Manager.

National Women's Studies Association
NWSA Scholarship in Jewish Women's Studies
7100 Baltimore Avenue
Suite 301
College Park, MD 20742
(301) 403-0525

Description: Scholarship for graduate students in Jewish women's studies; recipients chosen on the basis of financial need and academic achievement.
Restrictions: N/A.
$ Given: One scholarship awarded annually.
Application Information: Write for details.
Deadline: February 15.
Contact: Loretta Younger, Office Manager.

National Women's Studies Association Pergamon-NWSA Graduate Scholarships in Women's Studies
7100 Baltimore Avenue
Suite 301
College Park, MD 20742
(301) 403-0525

Description: Scholarship for master's and doctoral candidates in women's studies; recipients chosen on the basis of financial need and proposed research; preference for research project on women of color, Third World women, or women and class.
Restrictions: Membership in NWSA preferred.
$ Given: Two scholarships awarded annually; one for $1,000, one for $500.
Application Information: Write for details.
Deadline: February 15.
Contact: Loretta Younger, Office Manager.

Newberry Library Frances C. Allen Fellowships Committee on Awards
60 West Walton Street
Chicago, IL 60610-3380
(312) 943-9090

Description: One-month to one-year research fellowships for master's and doctoral candidates in the humanities and social sciences; tenable primarily at the D'Arcy McNickle Center for the History of the American Indian.
Restrictions: Limited to female Native American applicants.
$ Given: An unspecified number of fellowships awarded annually; each with stipend for living and travel expenses.
Application Information: Write for details.
Deadlines: February 1, August 1.

Phi Beta Kappa Society Mary Isabel Sibley Fellowship
1811 Q Street, N.W.
Washington, DC 20009
(202) 265-3808

Description: One-year fellowship for postdoctoral scholars and doctoral candidates at dissertation level for research on French language and literature or Greek language, literature, history and archaeology; recipients chosen on the basis of academic achievement and quality of proposed research.
Restrictions: Limited to unmarried women ages 25-35 only; recipients must devote full-time efforts to research.
$ Given: One fellowship for $10,000 is awarded annually; non-renewable.
Application Information: French fellowship awarded in even-numbered years; Greek fellowship awarded in odd-numbered years.
Deadline: January 15.
Contact: Linda D Surles, Program Officer.

Radcliffe College Jeanne Humphrey Block Dissertation Awards
Henry A. Murray
Research Center
10 Garden Street
Cambridge, MA 02138
(617) 495-8140
FAX (617) 495-8422

Description: Grants to doctoral candidates at dissertation level for research on the psychological development of girls and women; recipients chosen on the basis of proposed research; preference for proposals emphasizing use of Murray Center resources.
Restrictions: Limited to women applicants.
$ Given: An unspecified number of grants of $2,500 each are awarded annually.
Application Information: Write for details.
Deadline: April 1.

Radcliffe College
Life Patterns/Life Choices
Dissertation Awards
Henry A. Murray Research
Center
10 Garden Street
Cambridge, MA 02138
(617) 495-8140
FAX (617) 495-8422

Discription: Grants to doctoral candidates at dissertation level for research addressing the life choices and patterns of women; recipients chosen on the basis of proposed research; preference for proposals emphasizing use of Murray Center resources.
Restrictions: Limited to women applicants.
$ Given: An unspecified number of grants of $2,000 each are awarded annually.
Application Information: Write for details.
Deadline: April 1.

Sigma Delta Epsilon/
Graduate Women in Science
Eloise Gerry Fellowships
P.O. Box 19947
San Diego, CA 92159

Description: One-year research fellowships for graduate students and postdoctoral scholars in the biological and chemical sciences; recipients chosen on the basis of academic achievement, financial need, and proposed research.
Restrictions: Limited to women applicants only; funding may not be used for tuition; applicants may not apply simultaneously for other SDE fellowships.
$ Given: Three to six fellowships awarded annually; each for $1,500–$4,000.
Application Information: Write for details.
Deadline: December 1.
Contact: Helen D. Haller, Secretary.

Swedish Women's
Educational Association
International Swedish
Women's Educational
Association International
Scholarships
P.O. Box 2585
La Jolla, CA 92038-2585
(619) 587-0807

Description: Scholarships for graduate students in Swedish literature and language; tenable for graduate-level study at Scandinavian institutions.
Restrictions: Limited to women only; all nationalities may apply.
$ Given: An unspecified number of scholarships for $5,000 each are awarded annually.
Application Information: Write for details.
Deadline: April 1.
Contact: Boel Alkdal, Administrator.

Wellesley College
Anne Louise Barett
Fellowship
Office of Financial Aid
106 Central Street
Wellesley, MA 02181
(617) 235-0320

Description: Fellowship for B.S./B.A. holders and graduating college seniors in the fields of music theory, composition and history; tenable for full-time graduate study in the United States or abroad at institutions other than Wellesley; recipients chosen on the basis of merit and financial need.
Restrictions: Limited to women graduates of Wellesley.
$ Given: One fellowship of up to $3,000 is awarded annually.
Application Information: Request application form before November 25.
Deadline: December 11.
Contact: Secretary to the Committee on Graduate Fellowships.

Wellesley College
Ruth Ingersoll Goldmark
Fellowship
Office of Financial Aid
106 Central Street
Wellesley, MA 02181
(617) 235-0320

Description: Fellowship for B.S./B.A. holders and graduating college seniors in the fields of English literature, composition, and the classics; tenable for full-time graduate study in the United States or abroad at institutions other than Wellesley; recipients chosen on the basis of merit and financial need.
Restrictions: Limited to women graduates of Wellesley .
$ Given: One fellowship of up to $1,000 is awarded annually.
Application Information: Request application form before November 25.
Deadline: December 11.
Contact: Secretary to the Committee on Graduate Fellowships.

Wellesley College
Edna V. Moffett Fellowship
Office of Financial Aid
106 Central Street
Wellesley, MA 02181
(617) 235-0320

Description: Fellowship for B.S./B.A. holders and graduating college seniors in the field of history; tenable for full-time graduate study in the United States or abroad at institutions other than Wellesley; preference for individuals entering their first year of graduate study; recipients chosen on the basis of merit and financial need.
Restrictions: Limited to women graduates of Wellesley .
$ Given: One fellowship of up to $2,500 is awarded annually.
Application Information: Request application form before November 25.
Deadline: December 11.
Contact: Secretary to the Committee on Graduate Fellowships.

Wellesley College
Mary McEwin Schimke
Scholarships
Office of Financial Aid
Box GR
106 Central Street
Wellesley, MA 02181
(617) 235-0320

Description: Scholarships for B.S./B.A. in the fields of literature, history, and American studies; recipients chosen on the basis of merit and financial need; tenable for graduate study at institutions other than Wellesley; intended to afford relief from costs of household and child care during graduate study.
Restrictions: Limited to women applicants; minimum age 30; applicants must have received their bachelor's degrees from United States institutions.
$ Given: An unspecified number of scholarships of up to $1,000 each are awarded annually.
Application Information: Request application form before November 25.
Deadline: December 11.
Contact: Secretary to the Committee on Graduate Fellowships.

Wellesley College
Vida Dutton Scudder
Fellowship
Office of Financial Aid
106 Central Street
Wellesley, MA 02181
(617) 235-0320

Description: Fellowship for B.S./B.A. holders and graduating college seniors in the fields of literature, political science, and the social sciences; tenable for full-time graduate study in the United States or abroad at institutions other than Wellesley; recipients chosen on the basis of merit and financial need.
Restrictions: Limited to women graduates of Wellesley.
$ Given: One fellowship of up to $2,000 is awarded annually.
Application Information: Request application form before November 25.
Deadline: December 11.
Contact: Secretary to the Committee on Graduate Fellowships.

Wellesley College
M.A. Carland Shackford
Medical Fellowship
Office of Financial Aid
106 Central Street
Wellesley, MA 02181
(617) 235-0320

Description: Fellowship for medical students pursuing general medical practice (not psychiatry); recipients chosen on the basis of academic achievement and financial need.
Restrictions: Limited to women only; applicants may be graduates of any United States undergraduate academic institution.
$ Given: One fellowship for up to $3,500 awarded annually.
Application Information: Application forms available after November 20.
Deadline: Mid-December.
Contact: Secretary to the Committee on Graduate Fellowships.

Wellesley College
Harriet A. Shaw Fellowship
Office of Financial Aid
106 Central Street
Wellesley, MA 02181
(617) 235-0320

Description: Fellowship for B.S./B.A. in the fields of music and allied arts; tenable for full-time graduate study in the United States or abroad; recipients chosen on the basis of academic achievement and financial need.
Restrictions: Limited to women graduates of Wellesley.
$ Given: One fellowship of up to $3,000 is awarded annually.
Application Information: Request application form before November 25.
Deadline: December 11.
Contact: Secretary to the Committee on Graduate Fellowships.

**Woodrow Wilson National
Fellowship Foundation
Women's Studies Doctoral
Research Grants**
CN 5281
Princeton, NJ 08543
(609) 452-7007

Description: Research grants for doctoral candidates at
dissertation level in women's studies; recipients chosen on
the basis of proposed dissertation research.
Restrictions: Applicants should have completed all Ph.D.
requirements except dissertation at United States graduate
schools .
$ Given: Fifteen research grants for $1200 each are
awarded annually.
Application Information: Write for details.
Deadline: November 5.
Contact: Carolyn Q. Wilson, Director, Women's Studies
Program.

**State Historical Society of
Wisconsin
Alice E. Smith Fellowship**
816 State Street
Madison, WI 53706
(608) 264-6464

Description: Research fellowships for master's and doctoral candidates studying American history, especially that
of Wisconsin or the Midwest; recipients chosen on the basis
of proposed research.
Restrictions: Limited to women only.
$ Given: One fellowship for $2,000 is awarded annually.
Application Information: Write for details.
Deadline: July 15.
Contact: Michael E. Stevens, State Historian.

**Women's Research and
Education Institute
Congressional Fellowships on
Women and Public Policy**
1700 Eighteenth Street, N.W.
Suite 400
Washington, DC 20009
(202) 328-7070

Description: Congressional fellowship program designed
to train women as potential public policy leaders; fellowship runs September through April and involves 30 hrs/wk
work in a United States Congress office as a legislative aide
on policy issues affecting women; open to master's and doctoral candidates at United States institutions; relevant
disciplines include humanities, social sciences, biology and
biomedical sciences, engineering and applied sciences,
biomedical engineering, technology management and policy, business administration and management, health
services management and hospital administration, education, allied health professionals, medicine, nursing, public
and community health, and law; recipients chosen on the
basis of political/civic activity and interest in women's issues.
Restrictions: Limited to women applicants; nine hours
previous graduate coursework preferred; United States citizenship preferred.
$ Given: Eight to fifteen fellowships awarded annually;
each with $9,500 stipend plus $500 for health insurance and
up to $1,500 toward six hours tuition at home institution.
Application Information: Request application after
November 1.
Deadline: February 14.
Contact: Alison Dineen, Fellowship Director.

Ethnic Only, Ethnic Preferred, Foreign Nationals

American Association of University Women Educational Foundation AAUW International Fellowships
P.O. Box 4030
Iowa City, IA 52243-4030
(319) 337-1716

Description: Fellowships for one year of graduate study/research at an approved institution in the United States; recipients chosen on the basis of professional potential and importance of project to home country.
Restriction: Limited to women applicants; applicants must be citizens of countries other than the United States; applicants must hold B.A./B.S. or equivalent; proficiency in English required; recipients must return to home countries to work after fellowships are completed.
$ Given: An unspecified number of fellowships awarded annually; each for $15,065.
Application Information: Write for details.
Deadline: December 1.
Contact: International Fellowship Program.

American Association of University Women Educational Foundation AAUW Selected Professions Fellowships
P.O. Box 4030
Iowa City, IA 52243-4030
(319) 337-1716

Description: Fellowships for graduate students entering their final year of study in fields with traditionally low female representation, including architecture, business administration, computer science, dentistry, engineering, law, mathematics/statistics, medicine, and veterinary medicine; recipients chosen on the basis of academic achievement; tenable for full-time study at accredited United States institutions.
Restrictions: Limited to women who are members of minority groups; United States citizenship or permanent resident status required.
$ Given: An unspecified number of fellowships of $5,000–$9,500 each are awarded annually.
Application Information: Application forms available August 1 through November 1.
Deadline: December 15, February 1 for M.B.A.

American Home Economics Association Foundation Carley-Canoyer-Cutler Fellowships
1555 King Street
Alexandria, VA 22314
(703) 704-4600

Description: Fellowships for graduate students in consumer studies.
Restrictions: Minority group members or non-United States citizens only.
$ Given: One $3,000 fellowship awarded annually.

Application Information: $15 application fee for AHEA members; $30 for non-members.
Deadline: January 15.
Contact: Fellowships and Awards Committee.

American Home Economics Association Foundation Frieda A. DeKnight Memorial Fellowship
1555 King Street
Alexandria, VA 22314
(703) 704-4600

Description: Fellowship for master's and doctoral candidates in home economics, communication, and cooperative extension; recipients chosen on the basis of academic achievement.
Restrictions: African-American applicants only; United States citizenship or legal residency required.
$ Given: One fellowship of $3,000 awarded annually.
Application Information: $15 application fee for AHEA members, $30 for non-members.
Deadline: January 15.
Contact: Fellowships and Awards Committee

American Home Economics Association Foundation Marion K. Piper International Fellowship
1555 King Street
Alexandria, VA 22314
(703) 704-4600

Description: Fellowship for foreign graduate students to study home economics in the United States; recipients chosen on the basis of academic achievements, quality of proposed research/study.
Restrictions: Limited to non-United States citizens/legal residents.
$ Given: One fellowship of $3,000 awarded annually.
Application Information: $15 application fee for AHEA members, $30 for non-members.
Deadline: January 15.
Contact: Fellowships and Awards Committee.

American Home Economics Association Foundation Flemmie P. Kittrell Minorities Fellowship in Home Economics
1555 King Street
Alexandria, VA 22314
(703) 704-4600

Description: Fellowship for graduate students in home economics; recipients chosen on the basis of academic achievement and quality of proposed research/study; tenable at United States institutions.
Restrictions: Limited to members of United States minority groups and citizens of developing countries.
$ Given: One fellowship of $3,000 awarded annually.
Application Information: $15 application fee for AHEA members, $30 for non-members.
Deadline: January 15.
Contact: Fellowships and Awards Committee.

American Home Economics Association Foundation Ethel L. Parker Fellowship
1555 King Street
Alexandria, VA 22314
(703) 704-4600

Description: Fellowship for foreign graduate students in home economics; recipients chosen on the basis of academic achievement, quality of proposed research/study, and home countries' needs.
Restrictions: Eligibility limited to non-United States citizens/legal residents.
$ Given: One fellowship of $3,000 awarded annually.

Application Information: Write for details.
Deadline: January 15.
Contact: Fellowships and Awards Committee.

American Home Economics Association Foundation
D. Elizabeth Williams Fellowship
1555 King Street
Alexandria, VA 22314
(703) 704-4600

Description: Fellowship for graduate students in home economics; recipients chosen on the basis of academic achievement and quality of proposed research/study; tenable at United States institutions.
Restrictions: Open to non-United States citizens only.
$ Given: One fellowship of $3,000 awarded annually.
Application Information: Write for details.
Deadline: January 15.
Contact: Fellowships and Awards Committee.

American Institute of Certified Public Accountants Minority Accounting Scholarships
1211 Avenue of the Americas
New York, NY 10036-8775
(212) 596-6200

Description: Scholarships for undergraduate and graduate students majoring in accounting; recipients chosen on the basis of academic achievement.
Restrictions: Limited to minority group members only; United States citizenship or permanent resident status required.
$ Given: An unspecified number of scholarships awarded annually; varying amounts up to $5,000.
Application Information: Request application forms from the Institute.
Deadlines: July 1, December 1.

American Library Association
Louise Giles Minority Scholarship
50 East Huron Street
Chicago, IL 60611-2795
(312) 944-6780

Description: Scholarships for master's candidates in library sciences; recipients chosen on the basis of academic achievement, leadership characteristics, and commitment to library career.
Restrictions: Limited to African-American, Alaskan Native, Native American, Asian-American, and Pacific Islander applicants; United States or Canadian citizenship required; tenable only for graduate program accredited by ALA.
$ Given: One grant of $3,000 awarded annually; paid in two installments.
Application Information: Write for details.
Deadline: January 5.
Contact: Margaret Myers, Staff Liaison.

American Psychological Association
APA Minority Fellowship Program in Neuroscience
1200 Seventeenth Street, N.W.
Washington, DC 20036
(202) 955-7761

Description: Ten-month fellowships for doctoral candidates in neuroscience; recipients chosen on the basis of academic achievement, financial need, and commitment to future career in neuroscience research.
Restrictions: African-American, Hispanic, Native American, Alaskan Native, Asian-American, and Pacific Islander applicants preferred; applicants must be plan-

ning careers in neuroscience; United States or Canadian citizenship or permanent resident status required.
$ Given: An unspecified number of fellowships awarded annually; each for $7,084 plus cost-sharing arrangement for full tuition scholarship; renewable for up to three years if recipient maintains good academic standing.
Application Information: Write for details.
Deadline: January 15.
Contact: Dr. James M. Jones, Director; or Ernesto Guerra, Minority Fellowship Program.

American Psychological Association
APA Minority Fellowship Program in Psychology
1200 Seventeenth St, N.W.
Washington, DC 20036
(202) 955-7761

Description: Fellowship for doctoral candidates in psychology; one program to support the training of clinicians, another program to support the training of researchers; recipients chosen on the basis of academic achievement and financial need.
Restrictions: African-American, Hispanic, Native American, Alaskan Native, Asian-American, and Pacific Islander applicants preferred; United States citizenship or legal residency required; applicants must be planning careers in psychology.
$ Given: An unspecified number of fellowships awarded annually; $7,084 for ten months; renewable for up to three years.
Application Information: Write for details.
Deadline: January 15.
Contact: Dr. James M. Jones, Director; or Ernesto Guerra, Minority Fellowship Program.

American Society for Engineering Education
Helen Carr Minority Fellowships
1818 North Street, N.W.
Suite 600
Washington, DC 20036
(202) 331-3525

Description: One-year fellowships for doctoral candidates in engineering at the following schools: Hampton University, Morgan State University, Howard University, North Carolina A&T State University, Prairie View A&M University, Tennessee State University, Tuskegee University, and Southern University; recipients chosen on the basis of financial need.
Restrictions: Limited to African-American applicants only; applicants must intend to return to one of the historically black engineering colleges to teach; United States citizenship required.
$ Given: An unspecified number of fellowships awarded annually; each for up to $10,000/year; renewable.
Application Information: Write for details.
Deadlines: January 5, May 5.

Armenian General Benevolent Union Excellence Grant
585 Saddle River Road
Saddle Brook, NJ 07662
(201) 797-7600

Description: Grant for graduate students in Armenian studies, international affairs, education, public administration, and journalism; recipients chosen on the basis of outstanding academic achievement and competence in subject area.
Restrictions: Limited to individuals of Armenian descent who are enrolled at Columbia University, Harvard University, University of Michigan, or UCLA.
$ Given: One grant of $5,000 is awarded annually.
Application Information: Write for details.
Deadline: April 30.

Armenian General Benevolent Union Graduate Scholarship Program
585 Saddle River Road
Saddle Brook, NJ 07662
(201) 797-7600

Description: Scholarships for graduate students in law, medicine, international relations, and Armenian studies; recipients chosen on the basis of academic achievement, financial need, and involvement in the Armenian community.
Restrictions: Limited to individuals of Armenian descent who are enrolled in accredited United States institutions.
$ Given: Seventy grants of $1,000 are awarded annually; renewable.
Application Information: Write for details.
Deadline: April 30.

Armenian Students' Association of America Armenian Students' Association Scholarship
395 Concord Avenue
Belmont, MA 02178
(617) 484-9584

Description: Scholarships for undergraduate (sophomore, junior, senior) and graduate students in all disciplines; recipients chosen on the basis of financial need, academic achievement, self-help, and extracurricular involvement.
Restrictions: Limited to individuals of Armenian descent.
$ Given: Fifty-five scholarships awarded annually; each for $500–$1,500.
Application Information: Write for details.
Deadlines: January 15, March 15.
Contact: Christine Williamson, Scholarship Administrator.

Asian Cultural Council Asian Cultural Council Fellowship Grants
1290 Avenue of the Americas
Suite 3450
New York, NY 10104
(212) 373-4300

Description: Grants for doctoral candidates and postdoctoral scholars in the visual and performing arts, archaeology, printmaking, architecture, art history, conservation, crafts, dance, design, film, musicology, music, painting, photography, sculpture, and theater; funding primarily for Asian scholars to visit the United States (and some support for United States citizens to visit Asia) for 3- to 12-month fellowship periods.
Restrictions: N/A.

$ Given: An unspecified number of grants are awarded annually; each grant covers airfare, per diem, maintenance stipend, health insurance, and expenses.
Application Information: Write for details.
Deadline: February 1.

AT&T Bell Laboratories Cooperative Research Fellowships for Minorities
600 Mountain Avenue
Murray Hill, NJ 07974
(201) 582-4822

Description: Fellowships for graduate study toward Ph.D. degree, for graduating college seniors with the potential to become professional research scientists or engineers; relevant disciplines include chemistry, communications science, computer science, engineering, information science, materials science, mathematics, operations research, physics, and statistics; fellowship tenure includes one summer of work at AT&T; recipients chosen on the basis of academic achievement and proposed research.
Restrictions: Limited to African-American, Hispanic, and Native American applicants only; GRE exam scores required; United States citizenship or permanent resident status required.
$ Given: An unspecified number of fellowships awarded annually; each for $13,200/year plus tuition and fees and expenses.
Application Information: Write for details.
Deadline: January 15.
Contact: Special Programs Manager, CRFP.

Canadian Association of University Teachers
J.H. Stewart Reid Memorial Fellowship for Doctoral Studies
2675 Queensview Drive
Ottawa, Ontario ON K2B 8K2
Canada
(613) 820-2270

Description: Fellowship for doctoral candidates in all fields; tenable at Canadian institutions; recipients chosen on the basis of outstanding academic achievement.
Restrictions: Canadian citizenship or minimum one-year landed immigrant status required.
$ Given: One fellowship for $5,000 Canadian is awarded annually.
Application Information: Write for details.
Deadline: April 30.
Contact: Awards Officer.

Canadian Federation of University Women
Georgette LeMoyne Award
55 Parkdale Avenue
Ottawa, Ontario K1Y 1E5
Canada
(613) 722-8732

Description: Award for graduate studies in any field; intended for women taking refresher studies at universities where instruction is in French.
Restrictions: Limited to women only; applicant must hold B.S./B.A. degree and have been accepted to proposed program of graduate study; Canadian citizenship or minimum landed immigrant status required.
$ Given: One award for $1,000 Canadian made annually.

Application Information: Write for details.
Deadline: November 30.
Contact: Chair, Fellowships Committee.

Canadian Federation of University Women CFUW Memorial Grant
55 Parkdale Avenue
Ottawa, Ontario K1Y 1E5
Canada
(613) 722-8732

Description: Grant for B.S./B.A. holders, to support graduate study in science and technology; recipients chosen on the basis of academic achievement, personal qualities, and potential.
Restrictions: Limited to women only; applicants must be accepted at intended places of study; Canadian citizenship or one-year landed immigrant status required.
$ Given: One grant of $1,000 Canadian awarded annually.
Application Information: Request application between July 1 and November 13.
Deadline: November 30.
Contact: Chair, Fellowships Committee.

Canadian Federation of University Women CFUW Polytechnique Commemorative Awards
55 Parkdale Avenue
Ottawa, Ontario K1Y 1E5
Canada
(613) 722-8732

Description: Awards for graduate studies in any field, with preference for studies related to women's issues.
Restrictions: Applicant must hold B.S./B.A. degree and have been accepted to proposed program of graduate study; Canadian citizenship or minimum one-year landed immigrant status required.
$ Given: One grant of $1,400 Canadian awarded annually.
Application Information: Write for details.
Deadline: November 30.
Contact: Fellowships Committee.

Canadian Federation of University Women Beverly Jackson Fellowship
55 Parkdale Avenue
Ottawa, Ontario K1Y 1E5
Canada
(613) 722-8732

Description: Fellowship for B.S./B.A. holders to pursue graduate work in any discipline; tenable at Ontario universities; recipients chosen on the basis of academic achievement, personal qualities, and potential.
Restrictions: Limited to women only; minimum age 35; applicants must hold B.S./B.A. from recognized univerity and be accepted into proposed place of study; Canadian citizenship or minimum one-year landed immigrant status required.
$ Given: One fellowship for $3,500 Canadian is awarded annually.
Application Information: Application forms are available July 1 through November 13.
Deadline: November 30.
Contact: Chair, Fellowships Committee.

Canadian Federation of University Women Margaret McWilliams Predoctoral Fellowship
55 Parkdale Avenue
Ottawa, Ontario K1Y 1E5
Canada
(613) 722-8732

Description: Fellowship for doctoral candidates in any discipline who hold master's degree and are at least one year into doctoral program; recipients chosen on the basis of academic achievement, personal qualities, and potential.
Restrictions: Limited to women only; Canadian citizenship or minimum one-year landed immigrant status required.
$ Given: One fellowship of $8,000 Canadian is awarded annually.
Application Information: Application forms are available July 1 through November 13.
Deadline: November 30.
Contact: Chair, Fellowships Committee.

Canadian Federation of University Women Margaret Dale PhilipAward
55 Parkdale Avenue
Ottawa, Ontario K1Y 1E5
Canada
(613) 722-8732

Description: Award to graduate students in the humanities and social sciences, with preference to applicants studying Canadian history; recipients chosen on the basis of academic achievement in college, personal qualities, and potential.
Restrictions: Limited to women only; applicants must hold B.S./B.A. degree and have been accepted to proposed program of graduate study; Canadian citizenship or minimum one-year landed immigrant status required.
$ Given: One grant of $1,000 Canadian is awarded annually.
Application Information: Write for details.
Deadline: November 30.
Contact: Fellowships Committee.

Canadian Federation of University Women Professional Fellowship
55 Parkdale Avenue
Ottawa, Ontario K1Y 1E5
Canada
(613) 722-8732

Description: Fellowship for graduate work below Ph.D. level; recipients chosen on the basis of academic, personal qualities, and potential.
Restrictions: Limited to women only; applicants must hold B.S./B.A. degree and have been accepted to proposed program of graduate study; Canadian citizenship or minimum one-year landed immigrant status required.
$ Given: Two fellowships for $5,000 Canadian each are awarded annually.
Application Information: Application forms available July 1 through November 13.
Deadline: November 30.
Contact: Chair, Fellowships Committee.

**Canadian Federation of
University Women
Alice E. Wilson Grants**
55 Parkdale Avenue
Ottawa, Ontario K1Y 1E5
Canada
(613) 722-8732

Description: Grants for women pursuing graduate refresher work in any field; recipients chosen on the basis of academic achievement, personal qualities, and potential; special consideration given to applicants returning to academic study after several years.
Restrictions: Limited to women only; applicants must hold B.S./B.A. degree and have been accepted to proposed program of graduate study; Canadian citizenship or minimum one-year landed immigrant status required.
$ Given: At least five grants for $1,000 Canadian each are awarded annually.
Application Information: Application forms available July 1 through November 13.
Deadline: November 30.
Contact: Chair, Fellowships Committee.

**Committee of
Vice-Chancellors and
Principals
Overseas Research Student
Awards**
29 Tavistock Square
London WC1H 9EZ
United Kingdom
(71) 387 9231

Description: Grants to full-time graduate students/researchers in all fields attending colleges and universities in the United Kingdom; recipients chosen on the basis of academic achievement and proposed research.
Restrictions: For overseas students only; applicants may not be citizens of the European Union.
$ Given: An unspecified number of grants awarded annually; each for partial remission of tuition fees.
Application Information: Application form available from UK university registrars in December.
Deadline: April 28.

**Council on Social Work
Education
CSWE Doctoral Fellowships
in Social Work**
Minority Fellowship Program
1600 Duke Street
Alexandria, VA 22314
(703) 683-8080

Description: One-year fellowships for doctoral candidates to conduct mental health research relevant to ethnic minorities; recipients chosen on the basis of academic achievement, financial need, and quality of proposed research; preference for applicants planning careers in social work specializing in ethnic minority issues of mental health.
Restrictions: Preference for African-American, Hispanic, Native American, and Asian-American applicants, as well as applicants of other ethnic minority groups; M.S.W. degree required; applicants must be full-time doctoral students; United States citizenship or permanent resident status required.
$ Given: An unspecified number of one-year fellowships are awarded annually; each carries a $708/month stipend plus tuition support, as negotiated with recipient's university; renewable.
Application Information: Write for details.
Deadline: February 28.
Contact: Dr. E. Aracelis Francis, Director.

Dartmouth College Thurgood Marshall Dissertation Fellowships for African-American Scholars
6062 Wentworth Hall, Room 305
Hanover, NH 03755

Description: One-year residential fellowships for doctoral candidates at dissertation level in any discipline taught in the Dartmouth undergraduate curriculum; intended to allow completion of dissertation during fellowship tenure; participation includes ten-week undergraduate course instruction.
Restrictions: Limited to African-American scholars only; applicants must have completed all Ph.D. requirements except dissertation.
$ Given: An unspecified number of fellowships awarded annually; each with $20,000 stipend plus office space, library privileges, housing allowance, and $2,500 research assistance fund.
Application Information: Write for details.
Deadline: January 10.
Contact: Dorothea French, Assistant Dean.

East-West Center East-West Center Scholarship and Fellowship Program
1777 East-West Road
Honolulu, HI 96848
(808) 944-7735

Description: Funding for graduate students for program work at the University of Hawaii; for students taking a multidisciplinary approach to problems of international concern in areas of population, resource systems, environment, culture, and communication; recipients chosen on the basis of academic achievement and proposed course of study.
Restrictions: United States, Asian country, or Pacific Island citizenship required.
$ Given: An unspecified number of grants awarded annually; each grant covers stipend, housing, medical insurance, travel, and university fees; supports up to 24 months of M.A. study, up to 48 months of Ph.D. study.
Application Information: Write for details.
Deadline: Varies.
Contact: Award Services Officer.

Five Colleges, Inc. Five Colleges Fellowships Program for Minority Scholars
97 Spring Street
Amherst, MA 01002
(413) 256-8316

Description: Residential fellowships for doctoral candidates at dissertation level in all disciplines, to allow completion of dissertation and contact with faculty and students on host campus; tenable at Amherst, Hampshire, Mount Holyoke, Smith College, or University of Massachusetts.
Restrictions: Limited to minority group members only; applicants must have completed all Ph.D. requirements except dissertation.
$ Given: An unspecified number of fellowships awarded annually; each for $25,000 plus housing or housing assistance, office space, library privileges, and departmental affiliation at host college.

Application Information: Write for details.
Deadline: January 15.
Contact: Carol Angus, Fellowship Program Committee.

**Florida Education Fund
McKnight Doctoral
Fellowships**
201 East Kennedy Boulevard
Suite 1525
Tampa, FL 33602
(813) 272-2772

Description: Fellowships for graduate study at one of eleven participating doctoral-degree-granting universities in Florida in the fields of business, engineering, agriculture, biology, computer science, mathematics, physical science, and psychology; recipients chosen on the basis of academic achievement.
Restrictions: Limited to African-American applicants only; B.A./B.S. degree required; United States citizenship required.
$ Given: Twenty-five fellowships awarded annually; each for a maximum of five years of study, with an annual $11,000 stipend plus up to $5,000 in tuition and fees.
Application Information: Write for details.
Deadline: January 15.
Contact: Dr. Israel Tribble, Jr.

**Japanese American Citizens
League National Scholarship
and Student Aid Program**
1765 Sutter Street
San Francisco, CA 94115
(415) 921-5225

Description: Scholarships for undergraduate and graduate students, as well as for individuals involved in performing and creative arts projects reflecting the Japanese American experience and culture.
Restrictions: Applicants must be of Japanese descent; membership in Japanese American Citizens League (or having parent who is member) preferred; United States citizenship required.
$ Given: An unspecified number of scholarships awarded annually; varying amounts.
Application Information: Application forms are available from local JACL chapters in September; write national office for list of local and regional chapters.
Deadline: April 1.

**Kosciuszko Foundation Year
Abroad at the University of
Cracow Program**
15 East 65th Street
New York, NY 10021-6595
(212) 628-4552
FAX (212) 628-4552

Description: Grants to support participation in one-year program of academic study at the University of Cracow (Jagiellonian University) in Poland; funding made available to undergraduate upperclassmen and graduate students in the fields of Polish language, literature, history, and culture.
Restrictions: Applicants must have Polish background; United States or Canadian citizenship required.
$ Given: An unspecified number of grants awarded annually; each for tuition, housing, and monthly food/expense allowance; round-trip travel not covered.
Application Information: Write for details.
Deadline: November 15.
Contact: Grants Office.

**L.S.B. Leakey Foundation
Franklin Mosher Baldwin
Memorial Fellowships**
77 Jack London Square
Suite M
Oakland, CA 94607-3750
(510) 834-3636
FAX (510) 834-3640

Description: Fellowship for master's candidates in anthropology; tenable at any qualified institution in the world.
Restrictions: Limited to citizens of African nations.
$ Given: One fellowship of up to $8,500 awarded annually for nontuition expenses.
Application Information: Write for details.
Deadline: January 2.
Contact: D. Karla Savage, Ph.D., Program and Grants Officer.

**Medical Library Association
MLA Graduate Scholarships
for Minority Students**
6 North Michigan Avenue
Suite 300
Chicago, IL 60602
(312) 419-9094

Description: Scholarships for master's candidates in health sciences librarianship; recipients chosen on the basis of academic achievement and professional potential.
Restrictions: Limited to minority group applicants only; applicants must be entering an ALA-accredited school or have at least one-half the academic requirements yet to complete during the scholarship year; United States or Canadian citizenship required.
$ Given: One scholarship for $2,000 is awarded annually.
Application Information: Write for details.
Deadline: February 1.
Contact: Assistant to the Director of Professional Development.

**Mexican American Legal
Defense and Educational
Fund
Law School Scholarships for
Hispanics**
634 South Spring Street
11th Floor
Los Angeles, CA 90014
(213) 629-2512

Description: One-year scholarships tenable at any accredited law school; recipients chosen on the basis of academic achievement and financial need.
Restrictions: Limited to Hispanic-American applicants only; applicants must be enrolled full-time in law school; United States citizenship required.
$ Given: Twenty scholarships awarded annually; 19 for $1,000 each, one for $2,000; nonrenewable but re-application is allowed.
Application Information: Application form required.
Deadline: May 30.

**National Consortium for
Graduate Degrees for
Minorities in Engineering and
Science, Inc.
Graduate Engineering for
Minorities (GEM)
Fellowships**
P.O. Box 537
Notre Dame, IN 46556
(219) 287-1097

Description: Fellowships for master's candidates in engineering, physical and life sciences; recipients chosen on the basis of academic achievement.
Restrictions: Limited to African-American, Native American, Mexican American, and Puerto Rican applicants only; United States citizenship required.
$ Given: Two hundred and twenty-five Masters, 30 Ph.D. (English) and 30 Ph.D. (Science) fellowships awarded annually; each for tuition and fees at member institution plus $6,000/year living stipend and summer employment.

Application Information: Write for details.
Deadline: December 1.
Contact: Betty Jean Valdez.

National Italian American Foundation Scholarship Program
Silvio Conte Internship
1860 19th Street, N.W.
Washington, DC 20009
(202) 638-2137
FAX (202) 683-0002

Description: Internship for undergraduate and graduate students to work for one semester in Congressman Conte's Washington, DC office.
Restrictions: Applicants must be of Italian descent; recipient must write paper about the internship experience and its expected benefit to recipient's future career.
$ Given: One internship paying $1,000 is awarded annually.
Application Information: Send SASE for details.
Deadline: May 31.
Contact: Dr. Maria Lombardo, Education Director.

National Italian American Foundation Scholarship Program
Oresto A. and Maddalena Giargiari Endowment Medical Scholarships
1860 19th Street, N.W.
Washington, DC 20009
(202) 638-2137
FAX (202) 683-0002

Description: Scholarships for second-, third-, and fourth-year medical students at approved United States medical schools; recipients chosen on the basis of academic achievement and financial need.
Restrictions: Applicants must be of Italian descent.
$ Given: An unspecified number of scholarships for $5,000 each are awarded annually.
Application Information: Application materials must be submitted in triplicate.
Deadline: May 31.
Contact: Dr. Maria Lombardo, Education Director.

National Italian American Foundation Scholarship Program
Italian American Regional Scholarships
1860 19th Street, N.W.
Washington, DC 20009
(202) 638-2137
FAX (202) 683-0002

Description: Scholarships for high school, undergraduate, and graduate students in all fields; regions are East Coast, Midwest, Southwest, and Mid-Atlantic; recipients chosen on the basis of academic achievement and financial need.
Restrictions: Applicants must be of Italian descent.
$ Given: Fifteen scholarships awarded annually; each for $500–$2,500.
Application Information: Send SASE for details.
Deadline: May 31.
Contact: Dr. Maria Lombardo, Education Director.

National Italian American Foundation Scholarship Program
Michael and Francesca Marinelli Scholarships
1860 19th Street, N.W.
Washington, DC 20009
(202) 638-2137
FAX (202) 638-0002

Description: Scholarships for graduate students in the DC area and for undergraduates at Nova University in Florida; relevant disciplines limited to science and business; recipients chosen on the basis of academic achievement and financial need.
Restrictions: Applicants must be of Italian descent.
$ Given: Two scholarships for $2,000 each are awarded annually.

Application Information: Essay required.
Deadline: May 31.
Contact: Dr. Maria Lombardo, Education Director.

National Italian American Foundation Scholarship Program Matching Law Fellowships
1860 19th Street, N.W.
Washington, DC 20009
(202) 638-2137
FAX (202) 638-0002

Description: Fellowships for graduate law students; recipients chosen on the basis of 750-word essay describing the contributions of Italian-Americans to the American judicial system.
Restrictions: N/A.
$ Given: Five fellowships for $1,000 each are awarded annually.
Application Information: Send SASE for details.
Deadline: May 31.
Contact: Dr. Maria Lombardo, Education Director.

National Italian American Foundation Scholarship Program Stella Business Scholarship
1860 19th Street, N.W.
Washington, DC 20009
(202) 638-2137
FAX (202) 638-0002

Description: Scholarship for undergraduate and graduate students in business; recipients chosen on the basis of academic achievement and financial need.
Restrictions: Applicants must be of Italian descent.
$ Given: One scholarship for $1,000 is awarded annually.
Application Information: Send SASE for details.
Deadline: May 31.
Contact: Dr. Maria Lombardo, Education Director.

National Italian American Foundation Scholarship Program Vincent Visceglia General Graduate Scholarships
1860 19th Street, N.W.
Washington, DC 20009
(202) 638-2137
FAX (202) 638-0002

Description: Scholarships for master's and doctoral candidates in Italian studies; recipients chosen on the basis of academic achievement and financial need.
Restrictions: Applicants must be of Italian descent or be working on M.A. or Ph.D. in Italian studies.
$ Given: An unspecified number of scholarships for $1,000 each are awarded annually.
Application Information: Application must be filled in triplicate; write for details.
Deadline: May 31.
Contact: Dr. Maria Lombardo, Education Director.

National Medical Fellowships, Inc. William and Charlotte Cadbury Award
110 West 32nd Street
8th Floor
New York, NY 10001
(212) 714-1007

Description: Award for senior medical student; recipients chosen on the basis of academic achievement, leadership, and community service.
Restrictions: Limited to minority group members only; applicants must attend United States medical schools.
$ Given: One award made annually; for $2,000 plus certificate of merit.

Application Information: Applicants must be nominated by medical school deans; medical schools must provide letters of recommendation and transcripts for nominees.
Deadline: June 30 for nomination.
Contact: Programs Department.

National Medical Fellowships, Inc.
The Commonwealth Fund Medical Fellowships for Minorities
110 West 32nd Street
8th Floor
New York, NY 10001
(212) 714-1007

Description: Eight- to twelve-week fellowships for second- and third-year medical students to work in major research laboratories under the supervision/tutelage of prominent biomedical scientists; recipients chosen on the basis of academic achievement.
Restrictions: Limited to minority group members only; applicants must attend accredited United States medical schools and must be interested in careers in research/academic medicine.
$ Given: Thirty-five fellowships awarded annually; each for $6,000.
Application Information: Applicants must be nominated by medical school deans.
Deadline: September for nomination; application deadline follows.
Contact: Programs Department.

National Medical Fellowships, Inc.
Irving Graef Memorial Scholarship
110 West 32nd Street
8th Floor
New York, NY 10001
(212) 714-1007

Description: Two-year scholarship for rising third-year medical students; recipients chosen on the basis of academic achievement, leadership, and community service.
Restrictions: Limited to minority group members only; applicants must have received NMF assistance during second year of medical school.
$ Given: One scholarship for $2,000 is awarded annually.
Application Information: Applicants must be nominated by medical school deans.
Deadline: July for nomination; August 25 for application.
Contact: Programs Department.

National Medical Fellowships, Inc.
Henry G. Halladay Awards
110 West 32nd Street
8th Floor
New York, NY 10001
(212) 714-1007

Description: Supplemental scholarships for individuals accepted into the first year of medical school despite significant obstacles; recipients chosen on the basis of recommendations, personal statement, and financial need.
Restrictions: Limited to black male applicants only; applicants must be accepted at accredited United States medical schools.
$ Given: Five scholarships for $760 each are awarded annually.

Application Information: Recipients chosen from General Scholarship applicants.
Deadline: August 31.
Contact: Programs Department.

National Medical Fellowships, Inc.
George Hill Memorial Scholarship
110 West 32nd Street
8th Floor
New York, NY 10001
(212) 714-1007

Description: Scholarship for incoming first-year medical students; recipients chosen on the basis of financial need, academic achievement, leadership, and community service.
Restrictions: Limited to African-American applicants only; applicants must be residents of Westchester County, New York and must be accepted at accredited United States medical schools.
$ Given: One scholarship for $4,000/year is awarded annually; renewable annually.
Application Information: Application forms included with General Scholarship application forms.
Deadline: N/A.
Contact: Programs Department.

National Medical Fellowships, Inc.
Franklin C. McLean Award
110 West 32nd Street
8th Floor
New York, NY 10001
(212) 714-1007

Description: Award for senior medical students; recipients chosen on the basis of academic achievement, leadership, and community service.
Restrictions: Limited to minority group members only; applicants must be enrolled in accredited United States medical schools.
$ Given: One award for $3,000 is made annually.
Application Information: Applicants must be nominated by medical school deans; medical schools must provide letters of recommendation and transcripts for nominees.
Deadline: June 30 for nomination.
Contact: Programs Department.

National Medical Fellowships, Inc.
Metropolitan Life Foundation Awards Program for Academic Excellence in Medicine
110 West 32nd Street
8th Floor
New York, NY 10001
(212) 714-1007

Description: Awards for second- and third-year medical students; recipients chosen on the basis of academic achievement, leadership, financial need, and potential for contribution to the field of medicine.
Restrictions: Limited to minority group members only; applicants must attend medical schools in or be residents of the following areas: San Francisco, CA; Tampa, FL; Atlanta, GA; Aurora, IL; Wichita, KS; New York, NY; Tulsa, OK; Pittsburgh, PA; Scranton, PA; Warwick, RI; Greenville, SC; and San Antonio, TX.
$ Given: Up to ten awards made annually; each for $2,500.

Application Information: Applicants must be nominated by medical school deans.
Deadline: August for nomination.
Contact: Programs Department.

National Medical Fellowships, Inc.
National General Medical Scholarships for Minorities
110 West 32nd Street
8th Floor
New York, NY 10001
(212) 714-1007

Description: Scholarships for second- and third-year medical students in M.D. programs at accredited United States medical schools.
Restrictions: Limited to minority group members only.
$ Given: 760 scholarships awarded annually; each for $500–$4,000.
Application Information: Write for details.
Deadline: May 31.
Contact: Scholarships Department.

National Medical Fellowships, Inc.
National Medical Association Special Awards Program
110 West 32nd Street
8th Floor
New York, NY 10001
(212) 714-1007

Description: Need-based awards for medical students; recipients chosen on the basis of academic achievement, leadership, and potential for contribution to the field of medicine, as well as financial need; NMA Merit Scholarship (four per year), Slack Award for Medical Journalism (one per year), Beecham/NMA Scholarship (one per year), and Ford/NMA Scholarship (one per year).
Restrictions: Limited to African-American applicants only; applicants must attend accredited M.D. or D.O. degree-granting United States medical schools.
$ Given: Seven awards made annually; each for $1,350–$2,500.
Application Information: Applicants must be nominated by medical school deans.
Deadline: May for nomination.
Contact: NMA Special Awards Program.

National Medical Fellowships, Inc.
NMF–Gerber Pediatrics Fellowship
110 West 32nd Street
8th Floor
New York, NY 10001
(212) 714-1007

Description: Fellowship for senior-year medical students who plan careers in pediatric medicine; recipients chosen on the basis of academic achievement, leadership, and financial need.
Restrictions: Limited to minority group members only; applicants must match for pediatric residencies; applicants must attend the following schools: University of Michigan Medical School, Michigan State University School of Human Medicine, or Wayne State University School of Medicine.
$ Given: One fellowship awarded annually; $2,000 stipend plus certificate of merit.

Application Information: Applicants must be nominated by medical school deans and chairs of departments of pediatrics.
Deadline: January for nomination.
Contact: Pediatrics Fellowship Administrator.

National Medical Fellowships, Inc.
James H. Robinson Memorial Prizes in Surgery
110 West 32nd Street
8th Floor
New York, NY 10001
(212) 714-1007

Description: Prizes to senior medical students for outstanding performance in surgery.
Restrictions: Limited to minority group members only; applicants must attend accredited United States medical schools; good academic standing required.
$ Given: Two prizes of $500 each are awarded annually.
Application Information: Applicants must be nominated by medical school deans and chairs of departments of surgery.
Deadline: December for nomination; January 12 for application.
Contact: Programs Department.

National Medical Fellowships, Inc.
Aura E. Severinghaus Award
110 West 32nd Street
8th Floor
New York, NY 10001
(212) 714-1007

Description: Award to senior medical students for outstanding academic achievement, leadership, and community service.
Restrictions: Limited to minority group members only; applicants must attend Columbia University's College of Physicians and Surgeons.
$ Given: One award for $2,000 is made annually.
Application Information: Recipients chosen by committee of faculty and administrators at Columbia.
Deadline: N/A.
Contact: Programs Department.

National Research Council
NRC/Ford Predoctoral and Dissertation Fellowships for Minorities
Fellowships Office
2101 Constitution Avenue, N.W.
Washington, DC 20418
(202) 334-2872

Description: Fellowships for graduate students in the humanities, social sciences, biological and agricultural sciences, physical sciences and mathematics, and engineering and applied sciences; recipients chosen on the basis of academic achievement and proposed research.
Restrictions: Limited to members of minority groups; United States citizenship or legal residency required.
$ Given: Fifty-five fellowships awarded; $11,500 for fellow, $6,000 for institution; 20 dissertation fellowships available for $18,000.
Application Information: Write for details.
Deadline: November 5.

Natural Sciences and Engineering Research Council of Canada NSERC Postgraduate Scholarships in Science Librarianship and Documentation
200 Kent Street
Ottawa, Ontario K1A 1H5
Canada
(613) 992-8203

Description: One-year scholarships for first- and second-year study toward M.L.S. degree in library science; recipients chosen on the basis of academic achievement, commitment to field, and relevant experience.
Restrictions: Applicants must have B.S. degree in science or engineering; Canadian citizenship or permanent resident status required.
$ Given: A few scholarships awarded annually; each for $13,500 Canadian plus travel allowance.
Application Information: Write for details.
Deadline: December 1.
Contact: Nadine Bohan; Information Officer.

New York University AEJMC Summer Internship for Minorities in Journalism
269 Mercer Street
Suite 601
New York, NY 10003
(212) 998-2130

Description: Summer internships for college upperclassmen and graduate students; participation includes actual work, journalism courses, workshops, and onsite visits; media worksites include TV Guide, New York Times, radio stations, public relations companies, advertising firms, and broadcasting companies.
Restrictions: Limited to minority group members only, especially African-American, Hispanic, Native American, Eskimo, and Asian-American applicants.
$ Given: An unspecified number of internships awarded annually; each pays at least $200/week.
Application Information: Request application form by December 3.
Deadline: December 11.
Contact: Glenda Noel-Doyle, AEJMC Internship Coordinator, Institute of Afro-American Affairs.

Newberry Library Frances C. Allen Fellowships
Committee on Awards
60 West Walton Street
Chicago, IL 60610-3380
(312) 943-9090

Description: One-month to one-year research fellowships for master's and doctoral candidates in the humanities and social sciences; tenable primarily at the D'Arcy McNickle Center for the History of the American Indian.
Restrictions: Limited to female Native American applicants.
$ Given: An unspecified number of fellowships awarded annually; each with stipend for living and travel expenses.
Application Information: Write for details.
Deadlines: February 1, August 1.

Oak Ridge Institute for Science and Education Nuclear Engineering and Health Physics Fellowships
P.O. Box 117
Oak Ridge, TN 37831-0117
(615) 576-3428

Description: One-year fellowship for graduate students studying nuclear science and engineering or health physics at participating Oak Ridge Associated Universities with practicum at various DOE facilities; recipients chosen on the basis of academic achievement, career goals, and interests.
Restrictions: N/A.
$ Given: An unspecified number of fellowships awarded annually; each with $14,400 stipend, plus $300/month during practicum, and travel, tuition and fees; renewable for up to four years.
Application Information: Write for details.
Deadline: January 25.

Organization of American States OAS Regular Training Program Fellowships Department of Fellowships and Training
17th Street and Constitution Avenue, N.W.
Washington, DC 20006
(202) 458-3000

Description: Three-month to two-year fellowships for graduate students in all fields except medicine to pursue advanced study or research in other countries; tenable at OAS member countries; fellowships intended to contribute to host country on economic, social, technical, and cultural levels; recipients chosen on the basis of academic achievement and financial need.
Restrictions: Applicants must be citizens of OAS member countries; applicants must hold B.S./B.A. or equivalent and must be accepted at university or research facility for proposed work; language proficiency required.
$ Given: An unspecified number of fellowships awarded annually; each to cover expenses, tuition, and stipend, varying by country.
Application Information: Write for details.
Deadline: March 31.

Philip Morris Fellowships for Artists of Color
Maryland Institute College of Art
1300 West Mount Royal Avenue
Baltimore, MD 21217
(410) 225-2255

Description: Two-year fellowships for master's degree candidates in the fine arts; to support work toward M.F.A. degree in painting, printmaking, sculpture, graphic design, or photography at the following participating schools: California Institute of the Arts, Cranbrook Academy of Art, Maryland Institute College of Art, School of Art Institute of Chicago, and Yale School of Art; recipients chosen on the basis of financial need.
Restrictions: Limited to African-American, Hispanic, Asian-American, and Native American applicants, as well as other applicants of color.
$ Given: Four fellowships awarded at each school annually; each for $10,000/year (for two years), supplementing financial aid offered by art schools.

Application Information: Write for details.
Deadline: March 1 (may vary).
Contact: Dr. Leslie King-Hammond, Program Director.

Population Council
Population Council
Fellowships in the Social
Sciences
1 Dag Hammarskjold Plaza
New York, NY 10017
(212) 339-0667

Description: Fellowships for doctoral candidates at dissertation level and mid-career professionals seeking master's degrees; for study/research combining population studies and such other social science disciplines as anthropology, sociology, economics, geography, public health, and public administration; recipients chosen on the basis of academic achievement and proposed research.
Restrictions: Research/study must be carried out at institution with strong program in population studies; preference to applicants with employment experience in population studies or family planning; strong preference for nationals of developing countries who are committed to returning to their home countries in population-related careers.
$ Given: An unspecified number of fellowships awarded annually; monthly stipend based on place of study and other factors.
Application Information: Women encouraged to apply.
Deadline: November 15.
Contact: Manager, Fellowships Program.

REFORMA, The National
Association to Promote
Library Services to the
Spanish Speaking
REFORMA Scholarships in
Library and Information
Science
Auroria Library
Lawrence at 11th Street
Denver, CO 80204-2096
(303) 556-3526

Description: Scholarships for individuals studying library and information science; recipients chosen on the basis of academic achievement and financial need.
Restrictions: Applicants must speak Spanish and must demonstrate a desire to serve the Spanish-speaking community.
$ Given: An unspecified number of $1,000 scholarships are awarded annually.
Application Information: Write for details.
Deadline: May 15.
Contact: Orlando Archibeque, Scholarship Committee Chair.

School of American Research
Katrin H. Lamon Resident
Scholar Program for Native
Americans
P.O. Box 2188
Santa Fe, NM 87504
(505) 982-2919

Description: Nine-month residential fellowship for postdoctoral scholars and doctoral candidates at dissertation level in anthropology and related social sciences; intended to provide recipients with intellectual stimulation of campus life plus time to write up results of compiled field work/research.
Restrictions: Limited to Native American applicants.
$ Given: One fellowship awarded annually; maximum $29,000 stipend plus housing and office; nonrenewable.

Application Information: Write for details.
Deadline: December 1.
Contact: Resident Scholar Coordinator.

**Smithsonian Institution
Minority Students Internships**
Office of Fellowships and
Grants
955 L'Enfant Plaza
Suite 7300
Washington, DC 20560
(202) 287-3271

Description: Nine- to twelve-week internships for undergraduate upperclassmen and graduate students in the humanities, social sciences, natural sciences, and physical sciences; internship program includes participation in ongoing research or activities at the Museum plus supervised independent research in any bureau; recipients chosen on the basis of academic achievement and proposed research.
Restrictions: Limited to minority group applicants.
$ Given: An unspecified number of internship positions are awarded annually; $250/week undergraduate stipend, $300/week graduate stipend.
Application Information: Write for details.
Deadlines: February 15, June 15, and October 15.

**Social Sciences and
Humanities Research Council
of Canada
Jules and Gabrielle Leger
Fellowships**
Fellowships Division
350 Albert Street
Box 1610
Ottawa, Ontario K1P 6G4
Canada
(613) 992-0525

Description: One-year fellowships for university-affiliated and private scholars at graduate level in the humanities and social sciences, to support research and writing on the historical/contemporary contribution of the Crown and its representatives; tenable at recognized university/institution for at least eight months of full-time work; recipients chosen on the basis of academic achievement.
Restrictions: Canadian citizenship required.
$ Given: An unspecified number of fellowships awarded in alternate years; each for $40,000 Canadian plus $10,000 Canadian for research/travel expenses.
Application Information: Fellowships offered in odd-numbered years.
Deadline: October 1.
Contact: Helene Regnier, Fellowships Division.

**Social Sciences and
Humanities Research Council
of Canada
SSHRC Doctoral Fellowships**
Fellowships Division
350 Albert Street
Box 1610
Ottawa, Ontario K1P 6G4
Canada
(613) 992-3145

Description: Two-year renewable fellowships for doctoral candidates in the humanities, and social sciences; tenable in Canada or abroad; recipients chosen on the basis of academic achievement and proposed research.
Restrictions: Applicants must have completed one year of doctoral study; Canadian citizenship or permanent resident status required.
$ Given: Six hundred fellowships awarded annually, plus 600 annual renewables; each for up to $14,436 Canadian per year plus relocation costs.
Application Information: Write for details.
Deadline: October 15.

**Social Sciences and
Humanities Research Council
of Canada
SSHRC Queen's Fellowships**
Fellowships Division
350 Albert Street
Box 1610
Ottawa, Ontario K1P 6G4
Canada
(613) 992-3145

Description: One-year fellowships for graduate students in social sciences and humanities, to support study toward Ph.D. in Canadian studies at Canadian institutions.
Restrictions: Canadian citizenship required; must have completed one year of graduate study.
$ Given: One to two fellowships awarded annually; each for up to $14,436 Canadian plus tuition and travel allowance; nonrenewable.
Application Information: Applicants automatically eligible if currently studying Canadian studies at Canadian University; no application.
Deadline: October 15.
Contact: Heather Steele, Director, Fellowships Division.

**Southern Illinois University at
Carbondale
Minority Doctoral
Fellowships in Science and
Engineering**
Graduate School
Woody Hall, B-114
Carbondale, IL 62901
(618) 536-7791

Description: Three-year fellowships for doctoral candidates in the life sciences, physical sciences, and engineering; recipients chosen on the basis of GRE or other national standardized test scores.
Restrictions: Limited to minority group applicants; applicants of Mexican or Puerto Rican descent preferred; United States citizenship required.
$ Given: Ten to twenty fellowships awarded annually; each for $15,000/year plus full tuition and fees (for three years).
Application Information: Write for details.
Deadline: February 2.
Contact: Dr. Harry Daniels, Associate Dean.

**Special Libraries Association
Affirmative Action
Scholarship**
1700 Eighteenth Street, N.W.
Washington, DC 20009
(202) 234-4700

Description: Scholarship for master's candidates and graduating college; tenable at United States or Canadian institution of library and information science; preference to students with interest in special librarianship; recipients chosen on the basis of academic achievement and financial need.
Restrictions: Limited to minority group applicants only; United States or Canadian citizenship required.
$ Given: One scholarship for $6,000 each is awarded annually.
Application Information: Write for details.
Deadline: October 31.
Contact: Laura Devlin.

University of Oslo
International Summer School
University of Oslo
International Summer School
(ISS) Scholarships
c/o Saint Olaf College
1520 Saint Olaf College
Northfield, MN 55057
(507) 663-3269

Description: Scholarship for undergraduate upperclassmen and master's degree candidates studying Norwegian medical care/health services, and Norwegian literature, peace research, and energy/environment issues; to attend six-week summer school (June–August) in Oslo; recipients chosen on the basis of academic achievement and financial need.
Restrictions: N/A.
$ Given: A large number of scholarships; normally cover room, board, incidental expenses; no tuition fee.
Application Information: Application forms available from Norwegian Embassy or the North American Admissions Office.
Deadline: March 1.
Contact: JoAnn Kleber, Administrator, North American Admissions Office.

Wenner-Gren Foundation for
Anthropological Research
Developing Countries
Training Fellowships
220 Fifth Avenue
16th Floor
New York, NY 10001
(212) 683-5000

Description: Six-month to three-year training fellowships for doctoral candidates and nondegree scholars in anthropology.
Restrictions: Applicants must be residents of developing countries, and must be able to demonstrate unavailability of adequate training programs in home countries; applicants from the following places are not eligible: Abu-Dhabi, Australia, Bahrain, Brunei, Canada, Hong Kong, Israel, Japan, Kuwait, Libya, New Caledonia, New Zealand, Puerto Rico, Qatar, Saudi Arabia, United Arab Emirates, United States, Commonwealth of Independent States, and Western European countries; recipients must plan to return and work in home countries.
$ Given: An unspecified number of fellowships awarded annually; each for up to $12,500 per year.
Application Information: Applicants must be sponsored by home institution and host country institution.
Deadline: Nine months prior to anticipated start of training program.
Contact: Dr. Sydel Silverman, President.

Williams College
Gaius Charles Bolin
Fellowships for Minority
Graduate Students
Hopkins Hall
Williamstown, MA 01267
(413) 597-4352

Description: One-year residential fellowships at Williams College for doctoral candidates at dissertation level in the humanities, natural sciences, social sciences, or behavioral sciences; fellowships tenure includes teaching responsibilities for only one semester course; recipients chosen on the basis of academic achievement and promise as college teachers.

Restrictions: Limited to minority group applicants.

$ Given: Two fellowships awarded annually; each for $25,000 plus up to $2,500 for research expenses.

Application Information: Write for details.

Deadline: January 15.

Contact: Michael McPherson, Dean of the Faculty.

Study/Research Abroad

American Academy in Rome
Samuel H. Kress
Foundation
Predoctoral Fellowships
7 East 60th Street
New York, NY 10022-1001
(212) 751-7200

Description: Two 2-year fellowships for independent study and research; one fellowship in classical art history, one fellowship in Italian art history; tenable at the American Academy in Rome; awarded to doctoral candidates who have completed coursework and are beginning the second year of dissertation work; recipients chosen on the basis of proposed research.
Restrictions: United States citizenship required.
$ Given: Two fellowships awarded annually; amount varies; travel allowance included.
Application Information: Write for details.
Deadline: November 15.
Contact: Fellowship Coordinator.

American Academy
in Rome
National Endowment for the
Arts/AAR Advanced
Fellowships in Design Arts
7 East 60th Street
New York, NY 10022-1001
(212) 751-7200

Description: Three 6-month fellowships in architecture, design arts and landscape architecture; tenable at the American Academy in Rome.
Restrictions: Applicants must be B.A./B.S. holders with at least seven years professional experience in the relevant fields; United States citizenship required.
$ Given: Three fellowships awarded annually; $5,000 stipend plus $800 travel allowance each.
Application Information: Write for details.
Deadline: November 15.
Contact: Fellowship Coordinator.

American Academy in Rome
National Gallery of Art
Predoctoral Fellowship in Art
History
7 East 60th Street
New York, NY 10022-1001
(212) 751-7200

Description: One-year fellowship for doctoral candidates in art history to conduct independent study/research at the American Academy in Rome; award made by National Gallery of Art jury with Academy representation.
Restrictions: Applicants must be sponsored by their schools; United States citizenship required.
$ Given: One fellowship awarded annually; cash award for travel, expenses, study, room and board.
Application Information: Application must be submitted by chairperson of graduate art history department at United States university; for details, contact Professor Henry Millon, National Gallery of Art, 6th and Constitution Avenues, N.W., Washington, DC 20565.
Deadline: November 15.
Contact: Fellowship Coordinator.

American Academy in Rome
Rome Prize Creative
Disciplines Fellowships
7 East 60th Street
New York, NY 10022-1001
(212) 751-7200

Description: Six to twelve-month fellowships for independent creative work or researching architecture, landscape design, musical composition, fine arts, classical studies, archaeology, and art history; tenable at the American Academy in Rome.
Restrictions: Applicants must hold bachelor's or master's degree; United States citizenship required.
$ Given: Thirty fellowships awarded annually; each with stipend of $7,500–$17,000 plus housing and studio.
Application Information: Write for details.
Deadline: November 15.
Contact: Fellowship Coordinator.

American Academy in Rome
Rome Prize Fellowships
School of Classical Studies
7 East 60th Street
New York, NY 10022-1001
(212) 751-7200

Description: One-year residential fellowships for doctoral candidates in classical studies, archaeology, classical art, history of art, postclassical humanistic studies, and medieval and Renaissance studies; tenable at the American Academy in Rome.
Restrictions: Applicants must have completed all doctoral coursework and one year of dissertation work; recipients may not hold job or travel extensively during fellowship year.
$ Given: An unspecified number of fellowships awarded annually; each with $7,500 stipend plus $800 travel allowance.
Application Information: Write for details.
Deadline: November 15.
Contact: Fellowships Coordinator.

American Academy
in Rome
Rome Prize Fellowships
School of Fine Arts
7 East 60th Street
New York, NY 10022-1001
(212) 751-7200

Description: Several one-year fellowships in architecture, landscape architecture, design art, painting, sculpture, visual arts, and musical compositions; tenable at the American Academy in Rome.
Restrictions: Painting, sculpture, and visual arts candidates need not hold a degree but must have three years professional commitment, clear ability, and current studio work; architecture and landscape architecture candidates need appropriate degree; other applicants need B.A. degree; recipients may not hold job or travel extensively during fellowship year.
$ Given: Ten fellowships awarded annually; each with $7,500 stipend plus $800 travel allowance and $600 allowance for supplies for painters, sculptors, and visual artists.
Application Information: Write for details.
Deadline: November 15.
Contact: Fellowships Coordinator.

American Council of Learned Societies
Eastern European Advanced Graduate Training Fellowships
Office of Fellowships
and Grants
228 East 45th Street
New York, NY 10017-3398
(212) 697-1505

Description: Fellowships for graduate students to study the humanities and social sciences as related to Eastern Europe (Albania, Bulgaria, Czech Republic, Germany, Hungary, Poland, Romania, Slovakia, and (former) Yugoslavia); recipients chosen on the basis of academic achievement, financial need, and quality of proposed research.
Restrictions: United States citizenship or legal residency required; must have completed two years of graduate study by June 30 following deadline.
$ Given: An unspecified number of fellowships awarded annually; the predoctoral fellowship has a maximum of $12,000.
Application Information: Write for details.
Deadline: December 1.

American Council of Learned Societies
Eastern European Dissertation Fellowships
Office of Fellowships
and Grants
228 East 45th Street
New York, NY 10017-3398
(212) 697-1505

Description: Fellowships for doctoral dissertation research related to Eastern Europe (Albania, Bulgaria, Czech Republic, Germany, Hungary, Poland, Romania, Slovakia, and (former) Yugoslavia); for research-related study at a university abroad, but not within Eastern Europe; for doctoral candidates in the humanities and social sciences; recipients chosen on the basis of academic achievement, financial need, and quality of proposed research.
Restrictions: United States citizenship or legal residency required.
$ Given: An unspecified number of fellowships awarded annually; each carries an annual stipend of up to $15,000; renewable for second year.
Application Information: Write for details.
Deadline: December 1.

American Council of Learned Societies
Fellowships for Dissertation Research Abroad Related to China
Office of Fellowships
and Grants
228 East 45th Street
New York, NY 10017-3398
(212) 697-1505

Description: Fellowships for doctoral dissertation research related to China; for research-related travel abroad, but not within the People's Republic of China or within the United States; for doctoral candidates in the humanities and social sciences; recipients chosen on the basis of academic achievement, financial need, and quality of proposed research.
Restrictions: Foreign national applicants must be enrolled as full-time Ph.D. candidates at United States universities.
$ Given: An unspecified number of fellowships awarded annually; each carries an annual stipend of up to $15,000.
Application Information: Write for details.
Deadline: December 1.

American Home Economics Association Foundation Ethel L. Parker Fellowship
1555 King Street
Alexandria, VA 22314
(703) 704-4600

Description: Fellowship for foreign graduate students in home economics; recipients chosen on the basis of academic achievement, quality of proposed research/study, and home countries' needs.
Restrictions: Eligibility limited to non-United States citizens/legal residents.
$ Given: One fellowship of $3,000 awarded annually.
Application Information: Write for details.
Deadline: January 15.
Contact: Fellowships and Awards Committee.

American Institute of Pakistan Studies American Institute of Pakistan Studies Fellowships
P.O. Box 7568
Wake Forest University
Winston-Salem, NC 27109
(919) 759-5453

Description: Fellowships for doctoral candidates, postdoctoral scholars, and professional researchers to undertake study/research in Pakistan; for students of humanities and social sciences, especially rural development, agriculture, local government, economics, demography, history, and culture; recipients chosen on the basis of proposed research.
Restrictions: Doctoral candidates must have completed all preliminary Ph.D. requirements; United States citizenship required.
$ Given: An unspecified number of fellowships awarded annually; each to cover air travel, maintenance, rental allowance, research allowance, internal travel, and excess baggage allowance.
Application Information: Write for details.
Deadline: January 1.
Contact: Dr. Charles H. Kennedy, Director.

American Research Center in Egypt Fellowships for Research in Egypt
New York University
50 Washington Square South
NYU Kevorkian Center
New York, NY 10012
(212) 998-8890

Description: Fellowships for doctoral candidates and postdoctoral scholars in archaeology, art, humanities, and social sciences in Egypt; recipients chosen on the basis of quality of proposed research; intended as maintenance support for research conducted in Egypt for 3- to 12-month period.
Restrictions: Proficiency in Arabic required; recipients may not hold outside employment during fellowship period; United States and Egyptian citizens only.
$ Given: Up to 20 fellowships awarded annually; each with stipend of $1,000/month plus round-trip airfare and dependents' stipends, if needed.
Application Information: Write for details.
Deadline: November 1.
Contact: Dr. Terence Walz, United States Director.

**American Research Institute
in Turkey
ARIT Fellowships**
University Museum
33rd and Spruce Streets
Philadelphia, PA 19104
(215) 898-3474

Description: Fellowships for doctoral candidates to conduct research concerning Turkey in ancient, medieval, and modern times in any field of the humanities or social sciences; recipients chosen on the basis of quality of proposed research; intended as maintenance support for dissertation research in Turkey over 1- to 12-month fellowship period.
Restrictions: Applicants must have satisfied all doctoral requirements except dissertation; recipients must obtain research permission from the Turkish government; applicants must be affiliated with United States or Canadian institutions.
$ Given: Six to ten fellowships for $1,000–$4,000 per year are awarded annually.
Application Information: Write for details.
Deadline: November 15.
Contact: Nancy Leinwand.

**American Research Institute
in Turkey
Bosphorus University
Summer Turkish Language
Program**
University Museum
33rd and Spruce Streets
Philadelphia, PA 19104
(215) 898-3474

Description: Fellowships for college graduates through doctoral candidates; for the study of Turkish language in an 8-week summer program at Bosphorus University in Istanbul; recipients chosen on the basis of academic achievement (minimum 3.0 GPA).
Restrictions: Preference for individuals planning career in Turkish studies; two years of college-level Turkish language courses or equivalent required (written and oral exam required); United States citizenship or permanent resident status required.
$ Given: Ten to fifteen grants are awarded annually; grant covers tuition, maintenance stipend, and round-trip travel; non-renewable.
Application Information: Write for details.
Deadline: February 15.
Contact: Nancy Leinwand.

**American School of Classical
Studies at Athens Fellowships**
993 Lenox Drive, Suite 101
Lawrenceville, NJ 08648
(609) 844-7577

Description: Fellowships for graduate students to engage in study/research in Greece for one academic year; intended for students of archaeology, classical studies, classical art history, and ancient Greece; named fellowships include Thomas Day Seymour Fellowship, John Williams White Fellowship, Samuel H. Kress Fellowship, and James Rignall Wheeler Fellowship.
Restrictions: Applicants must be affiliated with United States or Canadian institution; United States or Canadian citizenship required; B.A. major in classics or classical archaeology required.
$ Given: Four fellowships awarded annually; each for $5,650 plus fees, room and partial board.

Application Information: Write for details.
Deadline: January 5.
Contact: Committee on Admissions and Fellowships.

American School of Classical Studies at Athens
Gennadeion Fellowship
993 Lenox Drive, Suite 101
Lawrenceville, NJ 08648
(609) 844-7577

Description: Fellowship for doctoral candidates at dissertation level to engage in study/research at the Gennadius Library in Athens for one academic year; intended for students of Byzantine and Greek studies; recipients chosen on the basis of academic achievement and quality of proposed research.
Restrictions: Applicants must be affiliated with a United States or Canadian institution; United States or Canadian citizenship required.
$ Given: One fellowship awarded annually for $5,650 plus, fees, room, and partial board.
Application Information: Write for details.
Deadline: January 31.
Contact: Committee on Admissions and Fellowships.

American School of Classical Studies at Athens
Jacob Hirsch Fellowship
993 Lenox Drive, Suite 101
Lawrenceville, NJ 08648
(609) 844-7577

Description: Fellowship for doctoral candidates at dissertation level to engage in study/research in Greece; intended for students of archaeology; recipients chosen on the basis of academic achievement and quality of proposed research.
Restrictions: United States or Israeli citizenship required.
$ Given: One fellowship awarded annually for $5,650 plus room and partial board; non-renewable.
Application Information: Write for details.
Deadline: January 31.
Contact: Committee on Admissions and Fellowships.

American School of Classical Studies at Athens
Summer Study in Archaeology
993 Lenox Drive, Suite 101
Lawrenceville, NJ 08648
(609) 844-7577

Description: Scholarships for graduate students to support summer study in archaeology with and emphasis on topography and antiquities of Greece; tenable in Greece at the School in Athens.
Restrictions: Applicants must be affiliated with a United States institution; United States or Canadian citizenship required.
$ Given: Five scholarships to cover tuition, room and partial board.
Application Information: Write for details.
Deadline: February 1.
Contacts Committee on Admissions and Fellowships.

American Schools of Oriental Research
George A. Barton Fellowship at the Albright Institute for Archaeological Research, Jerusalem
3301 North Charles Street
Baltimore, MD 21218
(401) 516-3498

Description: Residential fellowships for doctoral study in humanistic disciplines of the Middle East; for one to five months of study/research at the Albright Institute in Jerusalem; recipients chosen on the basis of proposed research.
Restrictions: Fellowship may not be used for summer study.
$ Given: An unspecified number of fellowships are awarded annually; each with a $2,000 stipend plus room and half-board.
Application Information: Write for details.
Deadlines: September 15, October 15.
Contact: Dr. Rudolph H. Dornemann, Administrative Director.

American Schools of Oriental Research Endowment for Biblical Research Summer Research Grants & Travel Scholarships
3301 North Charles Street
Baltimore, MD 21218
(401) 516-3498

Description: Grants and scholarships for graduate and seminary students; for study of archaeology, linguistics, natural sciences, and anthropology in the Holy Land; recipients chosen on the basis of proposed study/research.
Restrictions: Membership in ASOR required; citizenship in any country outside the Middle East required.
$ Given: Two one to three-month research grants of $1,500 each are awarded annually; 16 summer travel scholarships of $1,000 each are awarded annually.
Application Information: Write for details.
Deadline: February 1.
Contact: Dr. Rudolph H. Dornemann, Administrative Director.

American Schools of Oriental Research
Samuel H. Kress Foundation Fellowship at the Albright Institute for Archaeological Research, Jerusalem
3301 North Charles Street
Baltimore, MD 21218
(401) 516-3498

Description: Residential fellowships for doctoral candidates at dissertation level in art history, archaeology, and architecture; for 9–10 months of dissertation research at the Albright Institute in Jerusalem; recipients chosen on the basis of proposed research.
Restrictions: N/A.
$ Given: An unspecified number of fellowships awarded annually; each with $4,500 stipend plus room and half-board.
Application Information: Write for details.
Deadline: October 15.
Contact: Dr. Rudolph H. Dornemann, Administrative Director.

Archaeological Institute of America
Anna C. and Oliver C. Colburn Fellowship
675 Commonwealth Avenue
Boston, MA 02215
(617) 353-9361

Description: One-year fellowship for doctoral candidates and postdoctoral scholars, for study/research in classical studies; tenable at the American School of Classical Studies in Athens.
Restrictions: United States or Canadian citizenship or legal residency required.
$ Given: One fellowship of $5,500–$6,000 is awarded annually.
Application Information: Write for details.
Deadline: February 1.
Contact: Colburn Fellowship.

Archaeological Institute of America
Olivia James Traveling Fellowships
675 Commonwealth Avenue
Boston, MA 02215
(617) 353-9361

Description: Fellowships for doctoral candidates at dissertation level in architecture; for travel to Greece, the Aegean islands, Sicily, southern Italy, Asia Minor, and/or Mesopotamia; recipients chosen on the basis of proposed research/study.
Restrictions: Preference to project of at least 6 months duration; no funding for field excavation; United States citizenship or legal residency required.
$ Given: One fellowship of up to $15,000 is awarded annually.
Application Information: Write for details.
Deadline: November 15.
Contact: Olivia James Traveling Fellowship.

Archaeological Institute of America
Harriet Pomerance Fellowship
675 Commonwealth Avenue
Boston, MA 02215
(617) 353-9361

Description: Fellowship for doctoral candidates studying Aegean Bronze Age archaeology; for travel to the Mediterranean; recipients chosen on the basis of proposed research/study.
Restrictions: United States or Canadian citizenship required.
$ Given: One fellowship of $3,000 is awarded annually; non-renewable.
Application Information: Write for details.
Deadline: November 15.
Contact: Harriet Pomerance Fellowship.

Asian Cultural Council
Fellowship Grants
1290 Avenue of the Americas
Suite 3450
New York, NY 10104
(212) 373-4300

Description: Grants for doctoral candidates and postdoctoral scholars in the visual and performing arts, archaeology, printmaking, architecture, art history, conservation, crafts, dance, design, film, musicology, music, painting, photography, sculpture, and theater; funding primarily for Asian scholars to visit the United States (and some support for United States citizens to visit Asia) for 3- to 12-month fellowship periods.
Restrictions: N/A.

$ **Given:** An unspecified number of grants are awarded annually; each grant covers airfare, per diem, maintenance stipend, health insurance, and expenses.
Application Information: Write for details.
Deadline: February 1.

Association of College and Research Libraries Martinus Nijhoff International West European Specialist Study Grant
50 East Huron Street
Chicago, IL 60611
(312) 280-2510
(800) 545-2433

Description: Grant for scholars in library science to travel for 10 days to study West European professional librarianship; recipients chosen on the basis of proposed research.
Restrictions: Personal membership in ALA required.
$ **Given:** An unspecified number of grants are awarded annually; award covers air travel, surface travel, expenses, room, and board.
Application Information: Write for details.
Deadline: December 1.
Contact: Mary Taylor.

Atlantic Salmon Federation Bensinger-Liddle Salmon Fellowship
P.O. Box 429
Saint Andrews, New Brunswick
EOG 2X0
Canada
(506) 529-4581

Description: Fellowship to support individual research overseas on Atlantic salmon conservation and management; recipients chosen on the basis of research capability and benefit of proposed research.
Restrictions: United States or Canadian citizenship required in even-numbered years; United Kingdom citizenship required in odd-numbered years.
$ **Given:** One fellowship for $10,000 Canadian awarded annually.
Application Information: For application form, contact the United States office, Atlantic Salmon Federation, P.O. Box 807, Calais, ME 04619.
Deadline: March 1.
Contact: Cheryl Carter.

Beta Phi Mu International Library and Information Science Honor Society Harold Lancour Scholarship for Foreign Study
School of Library and Information Science
University of Pittsburgh
Pittsburgh, PA 15260
(412) 624-9435

Description: Scholarship for professional librarians and graduate students in library science (in ALA-accredited graduate programs), for foreign study and research; recipients chosen on the basis of proposed research.
Restrictions: N/A.
$ **Given:** An unspecified number of scholarships of $1,000 are awarded annually.
Application Information: Write for details.
Deadline: March 1.
Contact: Executive Secretary.

Canadian Embassy
Canadian Studies Graduate
Student Fellowships
501 Pennsylvania Avenue,
N.W.
Washington, DC 20001
(202) 682-1740

Description: Fellowships for doctoral candidates in the humanities, social sciences, fine arts, business, law, or environmental studies who are working on dissertation topics related in substantial part to Canada; funding for dissertation research in Canada over a three to nine-month fellowship period.
Restrictions: Applicants must be doctoral students at accredited institutions in Canada or the United States; applicants must have completed all degree requirements other than the dissertation; United States citizenship or permanent resident status required.
$ Given: An unspecified number of fellowships with $850/month stipends are awarded annually; non-renewable.
Application Information: Write for details.
Deadline: October 30.
Contact: Dr. Norman T. London, Academic Relations Officer.

CDS International
Robert Bosch
Foundation Fellowships
330 Seventh Avenue
19th Floor
New York, NY 10001
(212) 760-1400
FAX (212) 268-1288

Description: Nine-month internships at German government and business institutions (September–May) for master's degree holders and professionals in communications, journalism, economics, political science, public affairs, business administration, law, and German studies; German internships provided in a framework of government and commerce; recipients chosen on the basis of academic achievement, evidence of leadership, and community participation.
Restrictions: Recipients must be proficient in German by the start of the internship (fees for language courses reimbursed); United States citizenship required.
$ Given: Fifteen fellowships awarded annually; each with DM3,500/month stipend plus travel expenses and possible spouse stipend.
Application Information: Write for details.
Deadline: October 15.
Contact: Rick Blanckmeister, Program Officer.

Committee of
Vice-Chancellors and
Principals
Overseas Research Student
Awards
29 Tavistock Square
London WC1H 9EZ
United Kingdom
(71) 387 9231

Description: Grants to full-time graduate students/researchers in all fields attending colleges and universities in the United Kingdom; recipients chosen on the basis of academic achievement and proposed research.
Restrictions: For overseas students only; applicants may not be citizens of the European Union.
$ Given: An unspecified number of grants awarded annually; each for partial remission of tuition fees.
Application Information: Application form available from UK university registrars in December.
Deadline: April 28.

Committee on Scholarly Communication with the People's Republic of China National Program for Advanced Study and Research in China—Graduate Program
1055 Thomas Jefferson Street, N.W.
Suite 2013
Washington, DC 20007
(202) 337-1250

Description: Funding for one academic year of advanced study/research in China; for master's and doctoral candidates in the humanities and social sciences; recipients chosen on the basis of academic achievement and proposed research; tenable at university or research institute in China.
Restrictions: Three years of Chinese language training; United States citizenship required.
$ Given: N/A.
Application Information: Write for details.
Deadline: October 16.
Contact: Program Officer.

Council for European Studies Pre-Dissertation Fellowship Program
Box 44
Schermerhorn Hall
Columbia University
New York, NY 10027
(212) 854-4172

Description: Two- to three-month research fellowships in European Union countries for doctoral candidates in European history, sociology, political science, anthropology, and economics.
Restrictions: Applicants must have completed at least two years of graduate study; language proficiency required; United States citizenship or permanent resident status required.
$ Given: Three grants of $3,000 each are awarded annually.
Application Information: Write for details.
Deadline: February 1.

Friedrich Ebert Foundation Doctoral Research Fellowships
950 Third Avenue
27th Floor
New York, NY 10022-2705
(212) 688-8770
or (212) 688-8775

Description: Five- to twelve-month residential study/research fellowships in Germany for doctoral candidates at dissertation level in political science, sociology, history, or economics as related to German/European affairs or German-American relations.
Restrictions: Applicants must have completed all degree requirements except dissertation; affiliation with American university required; knowledge of German adequate for research required; United States citizenship required.
$ Given: An unspecified number of fellowships awarded annually; each with DM1,150/month stipend plus airfare, domestic travel allowance, tuition and fees, luggage/books allowance, and dependents' allowance (if needed).
Application Information: Write for details.
Deadline: February 28.
Additional Addresses: 806 Fifteenth Street, N.W., Suite 230, Washington, DC 20005, (202) 347-5570; and Godesberger Allee 149, Bonn 2, D-5300, Germany.

**Friedrich Ebert Foundation
Pre-Dissertation/Advanced
Graduate Fellowships**
950 Third Avenue
27th Floor
New York, NY 10022-2705
(212) 688-8770
or (212) 688-8775

Description: Five- to twelve-month independent study/research fellowships in Germany for doctoral candidates in political science, sociology, history, or economics as related to German/European affairs or German-American relations.
Restrictions: Applicants must have completed as least two years of graduate study at an American university; knowledge of German adequate for research required; United States citizenship required.
$ Given: An unspecified number of fellowships awarded annually; each with DM1,010/month stipend plus airfare, domestic travel allowance, tuition and fees, luggage/books allowance, and dependents' allowance (if needed).
Application Information: Write for details.
Deadline: February 28
Additional Addresses: 806 Fifteenth Street, N.W., Suite 230, Washington, DC 20005, (202) 347-5570; and Godesberger Allee 149, Bonn 2, D-5300, Germany.

**Eta Sigma Phi National
Classics Honor Society
Eta Sigma Phi Summer
Scholarships**
University of South Dakota
Box 171
Vermillion, SD 57069
(605) 677-5468

Description: Summer scholarships for study at the American Academy in Rome or the American School of Classical Studies in Athens; for recent college graduates who majored in Latin, Greek, or the classics; recipients can earn six semester hours of graduate-level credit during summer session.
Restrictions: Preference for students planning to teach classics; membership in Eta Sigma Phi required; Ph.D. candidates ineligible; applicants must have graduated college within the past five years.
$ Given: Two scholarships awarded annually; $2,400 to attend the American Academy in Rome, $2,600 to attend the American School of Classical Studies in Athens.
Application Information: Request application forms from Professor Thomas Sienkewicz, Department of Classics, Monmouth College, Monmouth, IL 61462.
Deadline: December 5.
Contact: Brent M. Froberg, Executive Secretary, Department of Classics.

Foundation for European Language and Educational Centers
Intensive European Language Courses Scholarships
Scholarship Department
Eurocentres
Seestrasse 247
Zurich CH-8038
Switzerland
(01) 485-5251

Description: Partial scholarships for three-month foreign language courses in English, French, German, Italian, and Spanish; each course held in country where language is spoken; recipients chosen on the basis of financial need and prior knowledge of language to be studied.
Restrictions: Applicants must be ages 18-30 and must have at least two years of professional experience in any field.
$ Given: An unspecified number of scholarships are awarded annually; each for between $250 and $750, which covers only part of the course tuition.
Application Information: Write for details.
Deadlines: January 15, March 31, June 15, and October 15.
Contact: Eric Steenbergen, Students' Assistance Department.

French Embassy
Scientific Services
Chateaubriand Research Scholarships for the Exact Sciences,
Engineering, and Medicine
Department of Science
and Technology
4101 Reservoir Road, N.W.
Washington, DC 20007
(202) 944-6241

Description: Six- to twelve-month research scholarship for doctoral candidates at dissertation level, as well as postdoctoral scholars, to conduct research in France at French universities, engineering schools, and private laboratories; language training sessions provided; relevant disciplines include biological and agricultural sciences, physical sciences and mathematics, engineering and applied sciences, medicine, nutrition, optometry and vision sciences, pharmacy and pharmaceuticals sciences, and veterinary medicine and sciences; recipients chosen on the basis of proposed research.
Restrictions: Each applicant must be registered at United States university and already in contact with French host institution; United States citizenship required.
$ Given: Twenty to thirty scholarships awarded annually; each for 9,000 francs per month plus airfare and health insurance.
Application Information: Application forms must be submitted with faculty recommendation.
Deadline: January 31.

**German Academic Exchange Service
German Studies Summer Seminar Grants for Graduate Students and Ph.D. Candidates**
950 Third Avenue
19th Floor
New York, NY 10022
(212) 758-3223
FAX (212) 755-5780

Description: Six-week interdisciplinary seminars at the University of California, Berkeley, for advanced graduate students and doctoral candidates in the humanities and social sciences, including students of German intellectual and social history; for the study of Germany after World War II; recipients chosen on the basis of academic achievement; participants eligible for academic credit.
Restrictions: Working knowledge of German required; United States citizenship required.
$ Given: An unspecified number of grants are awarded annually; each with a $1,500 stipend, to be applied toward the $450 course fee and living expenses.
Application Information: Write for details.
Deadline: March 15.
Contact: Barbara Motyka.

**German Academic Exchange Service
Short Term Visits to Germany Research Grants for Ph.D. Candidates and Recent Ph.D.s**
950 Third Avenue
19th Floor
New York, NY 10022
(212) 758-3223
FAX (212) 755-5780

Description: Two to six months of grant funding for doctoral candidates and recent Ph.D.s to conduct research/study in Germany; for work in all fields; recipients chosen on the basis of academic achievement.
Restrictions: Maximum eligible age range of 32–35; working knowledge of German required; United States citizenship required; affiliation with United States university required.
$ Given: An unspecified number of grants are awarded annually; each with monthly stipend, travel allowance, and health insurance.
Application Information: Write for details.
Deadline: November 1.
Contact: Barbara Motyka.

**German Academic Exchange Service
Summer Language Study Grants at Goethe Institutes for Undergraduate and Graduate Students**
950 Third Avenue
19th Floor
New York, NY 10022
(212) 758-3223
FAX (212) 755-5780

Description: Grants for two-month intensive German language course at the Goethe Institutes in Germany for undergraduate upperclassmen and graduate students; recipients chosen on the basis of academic achievement.
Restrictions: Basic knowledge of German required, three semesters of college-level German preferred; applicants must be between the ages of 18 and 32; United States citizenship required; full-time enrollment in United States university required; individuals with previous study experience in Germany ineligible; previous language scholarship recipients ineligible; majors in modern languages and literatures ineligible.
$ Given: An unspecified number of grants are awarded annually; each for tuition and fees, plus room and partial board; no travel allowance.

Application Information: Write for details.
Deadline: January 31.
Contact: Barbara Motyka.

Institute for European History Research Fellowships
Alte Universitaetsstrasse 19
Mainz 1
D-6500
Germany
(061) 31 39 93 60

Description: Residential fellowships at the Institute for doctoral candidates and postdoctoral scholars studying the history of Europe and European religion from the 16th to the 20th century; recipients chosen on the basis of academic achievement and proposed research.
Restrictions: Open to all nationalities; applicants must have thorough command of German.
$ Given: Twenty fellowships of DM13,080–DM17,280 each are awarded annually.
Application Information: Write for details.
Deadline: February, June, October.
Contact: For European History program, contact Professor Dr. Karl Otmar Freiherr von Aretin, (06131) 226143; for History of European Religion program, contact Professor Dr. Peter Manns, (06131) 224870.

Institute of International Education
Colombian Government Study and Research Grants
U.S. Student Programs Division
809 United Nations Plaza
New York, NY 10017-3580
(212) 984-5330

Description: Grants for B.S./B.A. holders to pursue up to two years of study/research at Colombian universities; relevant disciplines include agriculture, biology, business administration, economics, chemistry, engineering, education, health services administration, economics, chemistry, engineering, education, health services administration, geography, history, Latin American literature, law, linguistics, political science, physics, regulatory development, public health, and remote sensing interpretation.
Restrictions: United States citizenship required.
$ Given: An unspecified number of grants awarded annually; each for a modest monthly stipend, plus tuition and fees, health insurance, book/materials allowance, and one-way return airfare upon completion of study.
Application Information: Write for details.
Deadline: October 31.

Institute of International Education
Fulbright Fixed Sum–Bulgarian Government Grants
U.S. Student Programs Division
809 United Nations Plaza
New York, NY 10017-3580
(212) 984-5330

Description: Grants for B.A./B.S. holders in the humanities, physical sciences, and social sciences; for a six- to nine-month residency/exchange in Bulgaria (September–June).
Restrictions: Knowledge of Bulgarian language required; United States citizenship required; applicants must meet all Fulbright eligibility requirements.
$ Given: An unspecified number of grants awarded annually; Bulgarian government funds stipend, housing, and health/accident insurance; Fulbright provides fixed

sum for round-trip transportation plus additional monthly stipend.
Application Information: Write for details.
Deadline: October 31.
Contact: United States Student Program Division.

Institute of International Education
Fulbright Fixed Sum–Syrian Government Grants
U.S. Student Programs Division
809 United Nations Plaza
New York, NY 10017-3580
(212) 984-5330

Description: Grants for B.A./B.S. holders in Arabic language and culture, history, and geography; for study at the University of Damascus.
Restrictions: Applicants studying modern social sciences not eligible; minimum two years of Arabic language study or demonstrated proficiency required; United States citizenship required; applicants must meet all Fulbright funding.
$ Given: An unspecified number of grants awarded annually; monthly stipend, tuition, and health insurance, supplemented by Fulbright funding.
Application Information: Write for details.
Deadline: October 31.
Contact: Campus Fulbright program advisor.

Institute of International Education
Fulbright–Spanish Government Grants
U.S. Student Programs Division
809 United Nations Plaza
New York, NY 10017-3580
(212) 984-5330

Description: Grants for B.A./B.S. holders studying anthropology, archaeology, art history, ceramics, philology, economics, Hispano-American studies, history, law, Mediterranean Studies, musicology, philosophy, political science, sociology, and Spanish language and literature; for study at a Spanish university.
Restrictions: Fluency in Spanish (written and spoken) required; United States citizenship required; applicants must meet all Fulbright eligibility requirements.
$ Given: An unspecified number of grants awarded annually; Spanish government funds tuition and stipend; Fulbright funds round-trip transportation, and expense allowance.
Application Information: Write for details.
Deadline: October 31.

Institute of International Education
Fulbright Travel–Iceland Government Grants
U.S. Student Programs Division
809 United Nations Plaza
New York, NY 10017-3580
(212) 984-5330

Description: Grants for B.A./B.S. holders studying Icelandic language, literature, and history; for eight months of advanced study at the University of Iceland in Reykjavik.
Restrictions: Knowledge of Icelandic, Old Norse, or other Scandinavian language required for language/literature study; United States citizenship required; applicants must meet all Fulbright eligibility requirements.

$ **Given:** An unspecified number of grants awarded annually; cash stipend plus tuition.
Application Information: Write for details.
Deadline: October 31.

**Institute of
International Education
Germanistic Society of
America Fellowships**
U.S. Student Programs
Division
809 United Nations Plaza
New York, NY 10017-3580
(212) 984-5330

Description: Fellowships for master's degree holders
and some B.A./B.S. holders studying German language
and literature, art history, history, economics, philosophy, international law, political science, and public
affairs; for one academic year of study in Germany.
Restrictions: United States citizenship required;
applicants must meet all Fulbright eligibility requirements.
$ **Given:** Up to eight fellowships awarded annually;
each for $10,000 plus consideration for a Fulbright
Travel Grant.
Application Information: Write for details.
Deadline: October 31.

**Institute of International
Education
Study and Research Grants
for U.S. Citizens**
U.S. Student Programs
Division
809 United Nations Plaza
New York, NY 10017-3580
(212) 984-5330

Description: Grants to support study and research in all
fields, as well as professional training in the creative and
performing arts; tenable at institutions of higher learning
outside of the United States for one year; list of participating countries in any given year may be obtained from
IIE.
Restrictions: Open to United States citizens with B.A.
or equivalent; acceptable plan of study and proficiency
in host country's language required.
$ **Given:** A variable number of grants awarded
annually; covers international transportation, language
or orientation course (where appropriate), tuition, book
and maintenance allowances, and health and accident insurance.
Application Information: If currently enrolled in a college or university, apply to the campus Fulbright
Program Advisor; applications also available from IIE.
Deadline: October 31.

**Institute of International
Education
Lusk Memorial Fellowships**
U.S. Student Programs
Division
809 United Nations Plaza
New York, NY 10017-3580
(212) 984-5330

Description: Grants for individuals in the creative and
performing arts; for one academic year of study in the
United Kingdom and Italy.
Restrictions: Written and spoken proficiency in Italian
required for study in Italy; applicants must have completed at least four years of professional study; United
States citizenship required.

$ Given: An unspecified number of grants awarded annually; maintenance allowance, health/accident insurance, and round-trip travel allowance.
Application Information: Write for details.
Deadline: October 31.

International Research and Exchanges Board
IREX Research Exchange Program with Mongolia
1616 H Street, N.W.
Washington, DC 20006
(202) 628-8188

Description: Two- to ten-month exchange program for doctoral candidates to study in Mongolia; relevant disciplines include the humanities, social sciences, and natural sciences; recipients chosen on the basis of proposed research.
Restrictions: Command of host country's language required; United States citizenship required.
$ Given: An unspecified number of fellowships awarded annually; varying amounts.
Application Information: Write for details.
Deadline: October 15.
Contact: Cynthia Graves, Program Officer.

International Research and Exchanges Board
IREX United States–Republics of the Former USSR Summer Exchange of Language Teachers
1616 H Street, N.W.
Washington, DC 20006
(202) 628-8188

Description: Seven-week exchange program for language teachers and exceptional graduate students to study the Russian language at Moscow State University in Russia; recipients chosen on the basis of language ability.
Restrictions: Applicants must be employed as teachers of Russian at college level, and must have completed at least four years of college-level Russian courses and have at least two years of teaching experience; United States citizenship required.
$ Given: Twenty to twenty-five grants awarded annually; each for tuition, housing, stipend, travel, and other expenses.
Application Information: Write for details.
Deadline: December 15.
Contact: Myra Lee, Program Officer.

Japan Foundation Dissertation Fellowships
142 West 57th Street
6th Floor
New York, NY 10019
(212) 949-6360

Description: Fellowships for two to 14 months of dissertation research in Japan; funding made available to doctoral candidates at dissertation level in the humanities and social sciences, with emphasis on political science, law, economics, business, and journalism—as related to Japan; recipients chosen on the basis of academic achievement and quality of proposed research.
Restrictions: Applicants must be proficient in Japanese; no funding for Japanese language study; recipients may not hold other fellowships concurrently.

$ Given: Thirteen fellowships awarded annually; each for ¥310,000 plus further allowances including one round-trip air ticket.
Application Information: Write for details.
Deadline: November 1.

Japan Ministry of Education, Science, and Culture Japanese Government (Monbusho) Scholarship Program
2-2 Kasumigaseki, 3-chome
Chiyoda-ku
Tokyo 100
Japan
03-581-4211

Description: Eighteen-month to two-year scholarships for non-Japanese graduate students to study at Japanese universities and research institutes; Research Students Program is specifically designed for graduate students (undergraduate program also available) in the humanities, social sciences, music, fine arts, and natural sciences; open to citizens of countries with educational exchange agreements with Japan.
Restrictions: Language proficiency required (12- to 18-month language training program required if language skills deemed insufficient); applicants must be under age 35.
$ Given: An unspecified number of scholarships awarded annually; each to cover monthly stipend, airfare, tuition, and expense allowance.
Application Information: For further information, contact Japanese Embassy or Consulate.
Deadline: June 15, September 30.
Contact: Student Exchange Division.

Kosciuszko Foundation Graduate Studies and Research in Poland Program
15 East 65th Street
New York, NY 10021-6595
(212) 628-4552
FAX (212) 628-4552

Description: Grants to allow Americans to pursue graduate and postgraduate studies in Poland in any subject.
Restrictions: Applicants must have strong command of Polish language; United States citizenship required; Polish studies background required.
$ Given: An unspecified number of grants awarded annually; each for tuition, room, board, and monthly stipend for living expenses.
Application Information: Write for details.
Deadline: January 15.
Contact: Grants Office.

Kosciuszko Foundation Year Abroad at the University of Cracow Program
15 East 65th Street
New York, NY 10021-6595
(212) 628-4552
FAX (212) 628-4552

Description: Grants to support participation in one-year program of academic study at the University of Cracow (Jagiellonian University) in Poland; funding made available to undergraduate upperclassmen and graduate students in the fields of Polish language, literature, history, and culture.
Restrictions: Applicants must have Polish background; United States or Canadian citizenship required.

$ Given: An unspecified number of grants awarded annually; each for tuition, housing, and monthly food/expense allowance; round-trip travel not covered.
Application Information: Write for details.
Deadline: November 15.
Contact: Grants Office.

**Samuel H. Kress Foundation
Art History Travel Fellowships**
174 East 80th Street
New York, NY 10021
(212) 861-4993

Description: Fellowships for doctoral candidates at dissertation level in art history to travel for the purpose of viewing original materials/works; recipients chosen on the basis of academic achievement, financial need, and necessity of travel.
Restrictions: United States citizenship or enrollment in United States university required.
$ Given: Fifteen to twenty fellowships awarded annually; varying amounts.
Application Information: Applicants must be nominated by their art history departments.
Deadline: November 30.
Contact: Lisa Ackerman, Chief Administrative Officer.

**L.S.B. Leakey Foundation
Franklin Mosher Baldwin
Memorial Fellowships**
77 Jack London Square
Suite M
Oakland, CA 94607-3750
(510) 834-3636
FAX (510) 834-3640

Description: Fellowship for master's candidates in anthropology; tenable at any qualified institution in the world.
Restrictions: Limited to citizens of African nations.
$ Given: One fellowship of up to $8,500 awarded annually for nontuition expenses.
Application Information: Write for details.
Deadline: January 2.
Contact: D. Karla Savage, Ph.D., Program and Grants Officer.

**L.S.B. Leakey Foundation
Foraging Peoples Study
Fellowships**
77 Jack London Square
Suite M
Oakland, CA 94607-3750
(510) 834-3636
FAX (510) 834-3640

Description: Fellowship for doctoral candidates studying contemporary foraging peoples; recipients chosen on the basis of proposed research; preference for urgent research projects that might not ordinarily be funded by other agencies.
Restrictions: N/A.
$ Given: One occasional fellowship of up to $20,000 awarded for one to two years of field expenses.
Application Information: Write for details.
Deadlines: Preapplication and curriculum vitae due October 15; formal application due January 2.
Contact: D. Karla Savage, Ph.D., Program and Grants Officer.

Metropolitan Museum of Art
Theodore Rousseau Scholarships
Office of Academic Programs
Fifth Avenue and 82nd Street
New York, NY 10028
(212) 570-3710

Description: Fellowships for master's and doctoral candidates in art history, for study in Europe; intended to allow recipients first-hand examination of painting in major European collections.
Restrictions: Applicants must have completed at least one year of graduate training; applicants should be planning careers as museum curators of painting.
$ Given: An unspecified number of fellowships awarded annually; $25,000 for senior fellow; $15,000 for predoctoral fellow, plus $2,500 travel allowance.
Application Information: Write for details.
Deadline: November 12.
Contact: Pia Quintano, Fellowships Coordinator.

Norwegian Information Service in the United States
Norwegian Emigration Fund of 1975 Scholarships and Grants for Americans
825 Third Avenue
17th Floor
New York, NY 10022
(212) 421-7333

Description: Grants for American master's and doctoral candidates to visit Norway to study history and relations between the United States and Norway.
Restrictions: United States citizenship or permanent resident status required.
$ Given: An unspecified number of grants of NKr5,000–NKr40,000 each are awarded annually.
Application Information: Write for details.
Deadline: July 1.
Contact: Grants and Scholarships Section.

Norwegian Information Service in the United States
Norwegian Marshall Fund Grants
825 Third Avenue
17th Floor
New York, NY 10022
(212) 421-7333

Description: Grants for American master's and doctoral candidates in science and the humanities to conduct research abroad.
Restrictions: United States citizenship required.
$ Given: An unspecified number of grants of up to $5,000 each are awarded annually.
Application Information: Request application forms from Norway-American Association, Drammensveien 20 C, Oslo 2, 0255, Norway, (02) 44.76.83.
Deadline: March 15.
Contact: Grants and Scholarships Section.

Norwegian Information Service in the United States
SASS Travel Grants
825 Third Avenue
17th Floor
New York, NY 10022
(212) 421-7333

Description: Grants for master's and doctoral candidates who have passed preliminary exams, as well as for Norwegian language/culture teachers, for study/research in Norway.
Restrictions: United States citizenship or permanent resident status required; membership in SASS (Society for the Advancement of Scandinavian Study) required.
$ Given: An unspecified number of grants of $750–$1,500 each are awarded annually.
Application Information: Write for details.
Deadline: April 15.
Contact: Grants and Scholarships Section.

Organization of American States
OAS Regular Training Program Fellowships
Department of Fellowships and Training
17th Street and Constitution Avenue, N.W.
Washington, DC 20006
(202) 458-3000

Description: Three-month to two-year fellowships for graduate students in all fields except medicine to pursue advanced study or research in other countries; tenable at OAS member countries; fellowships intended to contribute to host country on economic, social, technical, and cultural levels; recipients chosen on the basis of academic achievement and financial need.
Restrictions: Applicants must be citizens of OAS member countries; applicants must hold B.S./B.A. or equivalent and must be accepted at university or research facility for proposed work; language proficiency required.
$ Given: An unspecified number of fellowships awarded annually; each to cover expenses, tuition, and stipend, varying by country.
Application Information: Write for details.
Deadline: March 31.

Pacific Cultural Foundation
Grants for Chinese Studies
Palace Office Building
Suite 807
Taipei, Taiwan 10567
Republic of China
(02) 752-7424 through -7429
(six phone lines)

Description: Grants for master's degree holders for research in Chinese studies; four types of studies grants: research, writing, publication, and seminar; recipients chosen on the basis of proposed work/research.
Restrictions: Applicants must be residents of the free world.
$ Given: Approximately 80 grants of $2,000–$5,000 each are awarded annually.
Application Information: Separate application for travel grant available.
Deadlines: March 1, September 1.

Pitt Rivers Museum
James A. Swan Fund
Oxford University
South Parks Road
Oxford, England OX1 3PP
0865-270927

Description: Grants for individuals to travel to Africa to pursue study/research on the hunter-gatherer peoples of Africa; recipients chosen on the basis of proposed research.
Restrictions: N/A.
$ Given: Ten grants of 1,000 pounds–2,000 pounds each are awarded annually; renewable.
Application Information: No application form; submit research proposal and proposed budget.
Deadline: Applications accepted continuously.
Contact: Dr. Schuyler Jones, Curator.

Rotary Foundation of Rotary International
Rotary Foundation Ambassadorial Scholarships
1560 Sherman Avenue
Evanston, IL 60201
(708) 866-3000

Description: Scholarships for graduate students with B.A./B.S. degree in any discipline; for one academic year in another country with Rotary club.
Restrictions: Applicants must be ages 18–30; members of Rotary clubs, as well as spouses and lineal descendants of members and employees of Rotary clubs, are ineligible; language proficiency test required in host

country's language; open to citizens of all countries with Rotary clubs.
$ Given: An unspecified number of scholarships are awarded annually; each to cover transportation, academic fees, educational supplies, room and board, and additional expenses.
Application Information: By nomination from local Rotary club, each of which designs its own selection criteria.
Deadline: July 15.
Contact: Local Rotary club.

Social Science Research Council
Advanced German and European Studies Doctoral Dissertation Fellowships
605 Third Avenue
New York, NY 10158
(212) 661-0280

Description: Nine- to 24-month residential fellowships for doctoral candidates at dissertation level to study at the Free University of Berlin; for dissertation work addressing the economic, political, and social aspects of modern and contemporary German and European affairs; recipients chosen on the basis of academic achievement and proposed research.
Restrictions: Good command of German required; United States citizenship or permanent resident status required.
$ Given: An unspecified number of fellowships awarded annually; each covers monthly stipend and travel expenses.
Application Information: Write for details.
Deadline: January 1.

Social Science Research Council
Africa Doctoral Dissertation Research Fellowships
605 Third Avenue
New York, NY 10158
(212) 661-0280

Description: Nine- to 18-month fellowships for doctoral candidates at dissertation level to conduct field work on humanities/social sciences topic as related to sub-Saharan Africa; recipients chosen on the basis of academic achievement, proposed research, and fluency in project-relevant African/European languages.
Restrictions: Good command of project-relevant languages required; no funding for coursework; United States citizenship or enrollment in United States university required.
$ Given: An unspecified number of fellowships awarded annually; each for up to $25,000.
Application Information: Write for details.
Deadline: November 1.

**Social Science Research
Council
Africa Predissertation
Research Fellowships**
605 Third Avenue
New York, NY 10158
(212) 661-0280

Description: Fellowships for doctoral candidates to take
short-term field trips to Africa for preliminary dissertation research; for dissertation work in the humanities
and social sciences; Africanist and non-Africanist students encouraged to apply in such underrepresented
disciplines as economics, psychology, sociology, and the
humanities; recipients chosen on the basis of academic
achievement and proposed research.
Restrictions: Applicants must have completed one year
of graduate study and been accepted into full-time Ph.D.
program; United States citizenship or full-time enrollment in United States university required.
$ Given: An unspecified number of fellowships
awarded annually; each for up to $25,000.
Application Information: Write for details.
Deadline: November 1.

**Social Science Research
Council
Africa Training and
Dissertation Research
Fellowships on Agricultural
and Health**
605 Third Avenue
New York, NY 10158
(212) 661-0280

Description: Fellowships to support doctoral candidates
for up to 12 months of natural/technical science training
and 9-18 months of field research and Write-Up in Africa; for dissertation work in the social sciences as
related to African agriculture and health; recipients chosen on the basis of academic achievement and proposed
research.
Restrictions: United States citizenship or full-time
enrollment in United States university required.
$ Given: An unspecified number of fellowships
awarded annually; maximum award $45,000.
Application Information: Proposal should state dissertation topic, proposed research site, and preliminary plans
for training.
Deadline: November 1.
Contact: Africa Program.

**Social Science Research
Council
International Predissertation
Research Fellowships**
605 Third Avenue
New York, NY 10158
(212) 661-0280

Description: Fellowships for doctoral candidates in the
early stages of Ph.D. programs in the social sciences, to
promote internationalization of graduate training and to
focus research on the developing world; relevant disciplines include political science, economics, and
sociology; tenable for 12 months of support over two-
year period, for domestic and overseas study.
Restrictions: Applicants must be full-time students in
Ph.D. degree-granting programs at the following
schools: University of California at Berkeley, UCLA,
University of California at San Diego, University of Chicago, Columbia, Cornell, Duke, Harvard, Indiana
University at Bloomington, University of Michigan, University of Minnesota at Twin Cities, Northwestern,
University of Pennsylvania, Princeton, Stanford, Univer-

sity of Texas at Austin, University of Washington, University of Wisconsin at Madison, and Yale; no funding for dissertation research.
$ Given: An unspecified number of fellowships awarded annually; each for $1,500 for domestic study plus allowance for overseas expenses.
Application Information: Write for details.
Deadline: N/A.
Contact: Dr. Ellen Perecman, Program Director.

Social Science Research Council
Korea Doctoral Dissertation Fellowships
605 Third Avenue
New York, NY 10158
(212) 661-0280

Description: Nine- to 18-month fellowships for doctoral candidates at dissertation level in the humanities and social sciences to pursue research in Korea and/or other country justified by research; recipients chosen on the basis of academic achievement, proposed research, and proficiency in Korean.
Restrictions: Good command of Korean required; United States citizenship or full-time enrollment in United States university required.
$ Given: An unspecified number of fellowships awarded annually; each for $9,000–$10,000.
Application Information: Write for details.
Deadline: January 1.

Social Science Research Council
Latin America and the Caribbean Doctoral Dissertation Research Fellowships
605 Third Avenue
New York, NY 10158
(212) 661-0280

Description: Nine- to 18-month fellowships for doctoral candidates at dissertation level to conduct field research on humanities/social sciences topics as related to Latin America or the Caribbean; recipients chosen on the basis of academic achievement and proposed research.
Restrictions: Open to all nationalities; full-time enrollment in United States university graduate program required.
$ Given: An unspecified number of fellowships awarded annually; varying amounts.
Application Information: Write for details.
Deadline: November 1.
Contact: Eric Hershberg.

Social Science Research Council
MacArthur Foundation Fellowships on International Peace and Security in a Changing World
605 Third Avenue
New York, NY 10158
(212) 661-0280

Description: Fellowship support for up to two years of research in the setting and nation of the recipient's choice; funding made available to doctoral candidates at dissertation level, postdoctoral scholars, and professionals studying international peace and security (in disciplines of humanities, social sciences, physical sciences, and natural sciences); recipients chosen on the basis of proposed research.
Restrictions: Open to all nationalities.

$ **Given:** Approximately eight fellowships awarded annually; $12,500–$17,500 per year predoctoral fellow; $25,000–$30,000 per year postdoctoral fellow.
Application Information: Write for details.
Deadline: December 1.
Contact: Felicia Sullivan.

Social Science Research Council
South Asia Doctoral Dissertation and Advanced Research Fellowships
605 Third Avenue
New York, NY 10158
(212) 661-0280

Description: Nine- to 18-month fellowships for doctoral candidates to conduct dissertation-related or advanced field research in Bangladesh, Nepal, and Sri Lanka, Pakistan, Bhutan, Maldives for dissertation work in the humanities and social sciences, business administration, and management; recipients chosen on the basis of academic achievement, proposed research, and proficiency in a major South Asian language.
Restrictions: United States citizenship or full-time enrollment in United States university required.
$ **Given:** Up to 15 fellowships awarded annually; varying amounts.
Application Information: Write for details.
Deadline: November 1.

Social Science Research Council
Southeast Asia Doctoral Dissertation and Advanced Research Fellowships
605 Third Avenue
New York, NY 10158
(212) 661-0280

Description: Nine- to 18-month fellowships for doctoral candidates to conduct dissertation-related or advanced field research in Brunei, Burma, Indonesia, Laos, Kampuchea, Malaysia, Thailand, Singapore, the Philippines, or Vietnam; for dissertation work in the humanities and social sciences, including law, public health, and public planning; recipients chosen on the basis of academic achievement, proposed research, and proficiency in a major Southeast Asian language.
Restrictions: United States citizenship or full-time enrollment in United States university required.
$ **Given:** An unspecified number of fellowships awarded annually; varying amounts.
Application Information: Write for details.
Deadline: November 1.

Social Science Research Council
Western Europe Doctoral Dissertation Research Fellowships
605 Third Avenue
New York, NY 10158
(212) 661-0280

Description: Nine- to 18-month fellowships for doctoral candidates to conduct dissertation field research in Western Europe; for dissertation work in the humanities and social sciences as related to Western Europe; recipients chosen on the basis of academic achievement and proposed research.
Restrictions: United States citizenship or full-time enrollment in United States university required.

$ Given: Twelve to fifteen fellowships awarded annually; varying amounts.
Application Information: Write for details.
Deadline: November 1.

**Social Sciences and
Humanities Research Council
of Canada
SSHRC Doctoral Fellowships**
Fellowships Division
350 Albert Street
Box 1610
Ottawa, Ontario K1P 6G4
Canada
(613) 992-3145

Description: Two-year renewable fellowships for doctoral candidates in the humanities, and social sciences; tenable in Canada or abroad; recipients chosen on the basis of academic achievement and proposed research.
Restrictions: Applicants must have completed one year of doctoral study; Canadian citizenship or permanent resident status required.
$ Given: Six hundred fellowships awarded annually, plus 600 annual renewables; each for up to $14,436 Canadian per year plus relocation costs.
Application Information: Write for details.
Deadline: October 15.

**Swedish Institute
International Summer
Courses Scholarships**
P.O. Box 7434
Stockholm S-103 91
Sweden
46-8-789 20 00

Description: Scholarship for four-week summer courses (July–August) at Swedish folk high schools throughout Sweden, for study in Swedish language, culture, and literature; instruction in Swedish; classes six hours/day, five days/week.
Restrictions: Minimum age 18; language proficiency requirement, dependent on level of study.
$ Given: A few scholarships awarded annually; varying amounts.
Application Information: Write for details.
Deadline: March 31.
Contact: Brita Holm, Course Director; or Pernilla Eldblom, Course Secretary.

**Swedish Women's
Educational Association
International Swedish
Women's Educational
Association International
Scholarships**
P.O. Box 2585
La Jolla, CA 92038-2585
(619) 587-0807

Description: Scholarships for graduate students in Swedish literature and language; tenable for graduate-level study at Scandinavian institutions.
Restrictions: Limited to women only; all nationalities may apply.
$ Given: An unspecified number of scholarships for $5,000 each are awarded annually.
Application Information: Write for details.
Deadline: April 1.
Contact: Boel Alkdal, Administrator.

University of North Carolina at Chapel Hill
Gilbert Chinard French History and Literature Research Grants
Romance Languages
Department
CB3170
Chapel Hill, NC 27599

Description: Grants for doctoral candidates at dissertation level and recent Ph.D.s (within past six years) for two months' study of French history and literature in France; recipients chosen on the basis of academic achievement and proposed work.
Restrictions: Applicants must be affiliated with United States universities; United States citizenship or permanent resident status required.
$ Given: Two to three grants for $750 each are awarded annually.
Application Information: Write for details.
Deadline: January 15.
Contact: Catherine Maley, President, Institut Français de Washington.

University of Oslo
International Summer School
University of Oslo
International Summer School
(ISS) Scholarships
c/o Saint Olaf College
1520 Saint Olaf College
Northfield, MN 55057
(507) 663-3269

Description: Scholarship for undergraduate upperclassmen and master's degree candidates studying Norwegian medical care/health services, and Norwegian literature, peace research, and energy/environment issues; to attend six-week summer school (June–August) in Oslo; recipients chosen on the basis of academic achievement and financial need.
Restrictions: N/A.
$ Given: A large number of scholarships; normally cover room, board, incidental expenses; no tuition fee.
Application Information: Application forms available from Norwegian Embassy or the North American Admissions Office.
Deadline: March 1.
Contact: JoAnn Kleber, Administrator, North American Admissions Office.

Wellesley College
Anne Louise Barett Fellowship
Office of Financial Aid
106 Central Street
Wellesley, MA 02181
(617) 235-0320

Description: Fellowship for B.S./B.A. holders and graduating college seniors in the fields of music theory, composition and history; tenable for full-time graduate study in the United States or abroad at institutions other than Wellesley; recipients chosen on the basis of merit and financial need.
Restrictions: Limited to Wellesley graduates.
$ Given: One fellowship of up to $3,000 is awarded annually.
Application Information: Request application form before November 25.
Deadline: December 11.
Contact: Secretary to the Committee on Graduate Fellowships.

Wellesley College
Ruth Ingersoll Goldmark
Fellowship
Office of Financial Aid
106 Central Street
Wellesley, MA 02181
(617) 235-0320

Description: Fellowship for B.S./B.A. holders and graduating college seniors in the fields of English literature, composition, and the classics; tenable for full-time graduate study in the United States or abroad at institutions other than Wellesley; recipients chosen on the basis of merit and financial need.
Restrictions: Limited to women graduates of Wellesley.
$ Given: One fellowship of up to $1,000 is awarded annually.
Application Information: Request application form before November 25.
Deadline: December 11.
Contact: Secretary to the Committee on Graduate Fellowships.

Wellesley College
Edna V. Moffett Fellowship
Office of Financial Aid
106 Central Street
Wellesley, MA 02181
(617) 235-0320

Description: Fellowship for B.S./B.A. holders and graduating college seniors in the field of history; tenable for full-time graduate study in the United States or abroad at institutions other than Wellesley; preference for individuals entering their first year of graduate study; recipients chosen on the basis of merit and financial need.
Restrictions: Limited to women graduates of Wellesley.
$ Given: One fellowship of up to $2,500 is awarded annually.
Application Information: Request application form before November 25.
Deadline: December 11.
Contact: Secretary to the Committee on Graduate Fellowships.

Wellesley College
Mary McEwin Schimke
Scholarships
Office of Financial Aid
Box GR
106 Central Street
Wellesley, MA 02181
(617) 235-0320

Description: Scholarships for B.S./B.A. holders in the fields of literature, history, and American studies; recipients chosen on the basis of merit and financial need; tenable for graduate study at institutions other than Wellesley; intended to afford relief from costs of household and child care during graduate study.
Restrictions: Limited to women applicants; minimum age 30; applicants must have received their bachelor's degrees from United States institutions.
$ Given: An unspecified number of scholarships of up to $1,000 each are awarded annually.
Application Information: Request application form before November 25.
Deadline: December 11.
Contact: Secretary to the Committee on Graduate Fellowships.

Wellesley College
Vida Dutton Scudder
Fellowship
Office of Financial Aid
106 Central Street
Wellesley, MA 02181
(617) 235-0320

Description: Fellowship for B.S./B.A. holders and graduating college seniors in the fields of literature, political science, and the social sciences; tenable for full-time graduate study in the United States or abroad at institutions other than Wellesley; recipients chosen on the basis of merit and financial need.
Restrictions: Limited to Wellesley graduates.
$ Given: One fellowship of up to $2,000 is awarded annually.
Application Information: Request application form before November 25.
Deadline: December 11.
Contact: Secretary to the Committee on Graduate Fellowships.

World Health Organization
WHO Fellowships
525 23rd Street, N.W.
Washington, DC 20037
(202) 861-3200

Description: One-year or shorter fellowships for individual or group health training/study in another country; intended for training/study not available in recipient's own country; relevant disciplines include public health administration, environmental health, medical social work, maternal and child health, communicable diseases, laboratory services, clinical medicine, basic medical sciences, and medical/allied education; recipients chosen on the basis of academic achievement and proposed study/training.
Restrictions: Applicants must be planning careers in public health; language proficiency required, as appropriate.
$ Given: An unspecified number of fellowships awarded annually; each to cover monthly stipend, tuition, and books.
Application Information: Contact WHO for detailed information booklet; application forms are available from national health administrations.
Deadline: At least six months prior to study.

All Areas of Study

American Association of University Women Educational Foundation AAUW American Fellowships
P.O. Box 4030
Iowa City, IA 52243-4030
(319) 337-1716

Description: Fellowships for full-time doctoral students and postdoctoral scholars, for research in all disciplines; recipients chosen on the basis of academic achievement and commitment to women's issues in professional career
Restriction: Limited to women applicants; United States citizenship or permanent resident status required.
$ Given: Eight fellowships awarded annually, one for a senior fellow and seven for less experienced researchers; each for $20,000–$25,000.
Application Information: Write for details.
Deadline: November 1.
Contact: American Fellowship Program.

American Association of University Women Educational Foundation AAUW Dissertation Fellowships
P.O. Box 4030
Iowa City, IA 52243-4030
(319) 337-1716

Description: Fellowships to support doctoral candidates in full-time dissertation work for at least twelve months in any field.
Restrictions: Limited to women applicants; applicants must have completed all coursework and exams for Ph.D. by November; United States citizenship required.
$ Given: An unspecified number of fellowships awarded annually; each for $13,500 which may not be used for tuition or loan repayment.
Application Information: Application forms must be requested in writing.
Deadline: November 15.
Contact: Dissertation Fellowship Program.

American Association of University Women Educational Foundation AAUW International Fellowships
P.O. Box 4030
Iowa City, IA 52243-4030
(319) 337-1716

Description: Fellowships for one year of graduate study/research at an approved institution in the United States; recipients chosen on the basis of professional potential and importance of project to home country
Restriction: Limited to women applicants; applicants must be citizens of countries other than the United States; applicants must hold B.A./B.S. or equivalent; proficiency in English required; recipients must return to home countries to work after fellowships are completed.
$ Given: An unspecified number of fellowships awarded annually; each for $15,065.
Application Information: Write for details.
Deadline: December 1.
Contact: International Fellowship Program.

**American Foundation
for the Blind
Karen D. Carsel
Memorial Scholarship**
15 West 16th Street
New York, NY 10011
(212) 620-2064

Description: Funding to support full-time graduate studies; recipients chosen on the basis of financial need.
Restrictions: Limited to legally blind applicants only; United States citizenship required.
$ Given: One grant for $500 is awarded annually.
Application Information: Applications must include proof of legal blindness, proof of graduate school acceptance, evidence of financial need, personal statement, and letters of recommendation.
Deadline: April 1.
Contact: Leslye S. Piqueras, National Consultant in Low Vision.

**Armenian Students'
Association of America
Armenian Students'
Association Scholarship**
395 Concord Avenue
Belmont, MA 02178

Description: Scholarships for undergraduate (sophomore, junior, senior) and graduate students in all disciplines; recipients chosen on the basis of financial need, academic achievement, self-help, and extracurricular involvement.
Restrictions: Limited to individuals of Armenian descent.
$ Given: 55 scholarships awarded annually; each for $500–$1,500.
Application Information: Write for details.
Deadlines: January 15, March 15.
Contact: Christine Williamson, Scholarship Administrator.

**Business and Professional
Women's Clubs—
New York State
Grace LeGendre Fellowships
and Endowment Fund**
239 Genesee Street
Mayro Building
Suite 212
Utica, NY 13501
(518) 585-7087

Description: Fellowships and grants for graduate students in all fields of study; tenable at accredited New York State institutions.
Restrictions: Limited to women applicants who are residents of New York State; United States citizenship or legal residency required.
$ Given: An unspecified number of $1,000 grants are awarded annually.
Application Information: Write for details.
Deadline: February 28.

**Business and
Professional Women's
Foundation
BPW Career Advancement
Scholarships**
2012 Massachusetts Avenue,
N.W.
Washington, DC 20036
(202) 296-9118

Description: One-year scholarships for undergraduate and graduate study in all disciplines, with emphasis on computer science, education, science, and paralegal training; scholarships are awarded within 24 months of the applicant's completing an undergraduate or graduate program in the United States; recipients chosen on the basis of financial need; funding designed to improve recipients' chances for career advancement/success.
Restrictions: Limited to women only; applicants must be at least 30 years old; no funding for Ph.D. studies, study

abroad, or correspondence courses; United States citizenship and affiliation with United States institution required.
$ Given: Approximately 150 scholarships of up to $1,000 each are awarded annually.
Application Information: Request application materials between October 1 and April 1.
Deadline: April 15.
Contact: Assistant Director, Education and Training.

Canadian Association of University Teachers J.H. Stewart Reid Memorial Fellowship for Doctoral Studies
2675 Queensview Drive
Ottawa, Ontario K2B 8K2
Canada
(613) 820-2270

Description: Fellowship for doctoral candidates in all fields; tenable at Canadian institutions; recipients chosen on the basis of outstanding academic achievement.
Restrictions: Canadian citizenship or minimum one-year landed immigrant status required.
$ Given: One fellowship for $5,000 Canadian is awarded annually.
Application Information: Write for details.
Deadline: April 30.
Contact: Awards Officer.

Canadian Federation of University Women Georgette LeMoyne Award
55 Parkdale Avenue
Ottawa, Ontario K1Y 1E5
Canada
(613) 722-8732

Description: Award for graduate studies in any field; intended for women taking refresher studies at universities where instruction is in French.
Restrictions: Limited to women only; applicant must hold B.S./B.A. degree and have been accepted to proposed program of graduate study; Canadian citizenship or minimum landed immigrant status required.
$ Given: One award for $1,000 Canadian made annually.
Application Information: Write for details.
Deadline: November 30.
Contact: Chair, Fellowships Committee.

Canadian Federation of University Women CFUW Polytechnique Commemorative Awards
55 Parkdale Avenue
Ottawa, Ontario K1Y 1E5
Canada
(613) 722-8732

Description: Awards for graduate studies in any field, with preference for studies related to women's issues.
Restrictions: Applicant must hold B.S./B.A. degree and have been accepted to proposed program of graduate study; Canadian citizenship or minimum one-year landed immigrant status required.
$ Given: One grant of $1,400 Canadian awarded annually.
Application Information: Write for details.
Deadline: November 30.
Contact: Fellowships Committee.

**Canadian Federation of
University Women
Beverly Jackson Fellowship**
55 Parkdale Avenue
Ottawa, Ontario K1Y 1E5
Canada
(613) 722-8732

Description: Fellowship for B.S./B.A. holders to pursue
graduate work in any discipline; tenable at Ontario universities; recipients chosen on the basis of academic
achievement, peronal qualities, and potential.
Restrictions: Limited to women only; minimum age 35;
applicants must hold B.S./B.A. from recognized univerity and be accepted into proposed place of study;
Canadian citizenship or minimum one-year landed immigrant status required.
$ Given: One fellowship for $3,500 Canadian is awarded
annually.
Application Information: Application forms are
available July 1 through November 13.
Deadline: November 30.
Contact: Chair, Fellowships Committee.

**Canadian Federation of
University Women
Margaret McWilliams
Predoctoral Fellowship**
55 Parkdale Avenue
Ottawa, Ontario K1Y 1E5
Canada
(613) 722-8732

Description: Fellowship for doctoral candidates in any
discipline who hold master's degree and are at least one
year into doctoral program; recipients chosen on the basis of academic achievement, personal qualities, and
potential.
Restrictions: Limited to women only; Canadian
citizenship or minimum one-year landed immigrant
status required.
$ Given: One fellowship of $8,000 Canadian is awarded
annually.
Application Information: Application forms are
available July 1 through November 13.
Deadline: November 30.
Contact: Chair, Fellowships Committee.

**Canadian Federation of
University Women
Professional Fellowship**
55 Parkdale Avenue
Ottawa, Ontario K1Y 1E5
Canada
(613) 722-8732

Description: Fellowship for graduate work below Ph.D.
level; recipients chosen on the basis of academic, personal qualities, and potential.
Restrictions: Limited to women only; applicants must
hold B.S./B.A. degree and have been accepted to proposed program of graduate study; Canadian citizenship
or minimum one-year landed immigrant status required.
$ Given: Two fellowships for $5,000 Canadian each are
awarded annually.
Application Information: Application forms available
July 1 through November 13.
Deadline: November 30.
Contact: Chair, Fellowships Committee.

Canadian Federation of University Women Alice E. Wilson Grants
55 Parkdale Avenue
Ottawa, Ontario K1Y 1E5
Canada
(613) 722-8732

Description: Grants for women pursuing graduate refresher work in any field; recipients chosen on the basis of academic achievement, personal qualities, and potential; special consideration given to applicants returning to academic study after several years.
Restrictions: Limited to women only; applicants must hold B.S./B.A. degree and have been accepted to proposed program of graduate study; Canadian citizenship or minimum one-year landed immigrant status required.
$ Given: At least five grants for $1,000 Canadian each are awarded annually.
Application Information: Application forms available July 1 through November 13.
Deadline: November 30.
Contact: Chair, Fellowships Committee.

Committee of Vice-Chancellors and Principals Overseas Research Student Awards
29 Tavistock Square
London WC1H 9EZ
United Kingdom
(71) 387 9231

Description: Grants to full-time graduate students/researchers in all fields attending colleges and universities in the United Kingdom; recipients chosen on the basis of academic achievement and proposed research.
Restrictions: For overseas students only; applicants may not be citizens of the European Union.
$ Given: An unspecified number of grants awarded annually; each for partial remission of tuition fees.
Application Information: Application form available from UK university registrars in December.
Deadline: April 28.

Dartmouth College Thurgood Marshall Dissertation Fellowships for African-American Scholars
6062 Wentworth Hall, Room 305
Hanover, NH 03755

Description: One-year residential fellowships for doctoral candidates at dissertation level in any discipline taught in the Dartmouth undergraduate curriculum; intended to allow completion of dissertation during fellowship tenure; participation includes ten-week undergraduate course instruction.
Restrictions: Limited to African-American scholars only; applicants must have completed all Ph.D. requirements except dissertation.
$ Given: An unspecified number of fellowships awarded annually; each with $20,000 stipend plus office space, library privileges, housing allowance, and $2,500 research assistance fund.
Application Information: Write for details.
Deadline: January 10.
Contact: Dorothea French, Assistant Dean.

Five Colleges, Inc.
Five Colleges Fellowships
Program for Minority Scholars
97 Spring Street
Amherst, MA 01002
(413) 256-8316

Description: Residential fellowships for doctoral candidates at dissertation level in all disciplines, to allow completion of dissertation and contact with faculty and students on host campus; tenable at Amherst, Hampshire, Mount Holyoke, Smith College, or University of Massachusetts.
Restrictions: Limited to minority group members only; applicants must have completed all Ph.D. requirements except dissertation .
$ Given: An unspecified number of fellowships awarded annually; each for $25,000 plus housing or housing assistance, office space, library privileges, and departmental affiliation at host college.
Application Information: Write for details.
Deadline: January 15.
Contact: Carol Angus, Fellowship Program Committee.

German Academic Exchange Service
Short Term Visits to Germany Research Grants for Ph.D. Candidates and Recent Ph.D.s
950 Third Avenue
19th Floor
New York, NY 10022
(212) 758-3223
FAX (212) 755-5780

Description: Two to six month of grant funding for doctoral candidates and recent Ph.D.s to conduct research/study in Germany; for work in all fields; recipients chosen on the basis of academic achievement.
Restrictions: Maximum eligible age range of 32-35; working knowledge of German required; United States citizenship required; affiliation with United States university required.
$ Given: An unspecified number of grants are awarded annually; each with monthly stipend, travel allowance, and health insurance.
Application Information: Write for details.
Deadline: November 1.
Contact: Barbara Motyka.

Institute of International Education
Colombian Government Study and Research Grants
US Student Program Division
809 United Nations Plaza
New York, NY 10017-3580
(212) 984-5330

Description: Grants for B.S./B.A. holders to pursue up to two years of study/research at Colombian Universities; relevant disciplines include agriculture, biology, business administration, economics, chemistry, engineering, education, health services administration, economics, chemistry, engineering, education, health services administration, geography, history, Latin American literature, law, linguistics, political science, physics, regulatory development, public health, and remote sensing interpretation.
Restrictions: United States citizenship required.
$ Given: An unspecified number of grants awarded annually; each for modest monthly stipend, plus tuition and fees, health insurance, book/materials allowance, and one-way return airfare upon completion of study.
Application Information: Write for details.
Deadline: October 31.

**Institute of International
Education
Fulbright Fixed
Sum-Bulgarian Government
Grants**
U.S. Student Program
Division
809 United Nations Plaza
New York, NY 10017-3580
(212) 984-5330

Description: Grants for B.A./B.S. holders in the humanities, physical sciences, and social sciences; for a six- to nine-month residency/exchange in Bulgaria (September–June).
Restrictions: Knowledge of Bulgarian language required; United States citizenship required; applicants must meet all Fulbright eligibility requirements.
$ Given: An unspecified number of grants awarded annually; Bulgarian government funds stipend, housing, and health/accident insurance; Fulbright provides fixed sum for round-trip transportation plus additional monthly stipend.
Application Information: Write for details.
Deadline: October 31.
Contact: United States Student Programs Division.

**Institute of International
Education
Fulbright - Spanish
Government Grants**
U.S. Student Program Division
809 United Nations Plaza
New York, NY 10017-3580
(212) 984-5330

Description: Grants for B.A./B.S. holders studying anthropology, archaeology, art history, ceramics, philology, economics, Hispano-American studies, history, law, Mediterranean Studies, musicology, philosophy, political science, sociology, and Spanish language and literature; for study at a Spanish university.
Restrictions: Fluency in Spanish (written and spoken) required; United States citizenship required; applicants must meet all Fulbright eligibility requirements.
$ Given: An unspecified number of grants awarded annually; Spanish government funds tuition and stipend; Fulbright funds round-trip transportation, and expense allowance.
Application Information: Write for details.
Deadline: October 31.

**Institute of International
Education
Germanistic Society of
America Fellowships**
U.S. Student Program Division
809 United Nations Plaza
New York, NY 10017
(212) 984-5330

Description: Fellowships for master's degree holders and some B.A./B.S. holders studying German language and literature, art history, history, economics, philosophy, international law, political science, and public affairs; for one academic year of study in Germany.
Restrictions: United States citizenship required; applicants must meet all Fulbright eligibility requirements.
$ Given: Up to eight fellowships awarded annually; each for $10,000 plus consideration for a Fulbright Travel Grant.
Application Information: Write for details.
Deadline: October 31.

Institute of International Education
Study and Research Grants for United States Citizens
U.S. Student Program Division
809 United Nations Plaza
New York, NY 10017-3580
(212) 984-5330

Description: Grants to support study and research in all fields, as well as professional training in the creative and performing arts; tenable at institutions of higher learning outside of the United States for one year; list of participating countries in any given year may be obtained from IIE.
Restrictions: Open to United States citizens with B.A. or equivalent; acceptable plan of study and proficiency in host country's language required.
$ Given: A variable number of grants awarded annually; covers international transportation, language or orientation course (where appropriate), tuition, book and maintenance allowances, and health and accident insurance.
Application Information: If currently enrolled in a college or university, apply to the campus Fulbright Program Advisor; applications also available from IIE.
Deadline: October 31.

Japan Ministry of Education, Science, and Culture
Japanese Government (Monbusho) Scholarship Program
2-2 Kasumigaseki, 3-chome
Chiyoda-ku
Tokyo 100
Japan
03-581-4211

Description: Eighteen-month to two-year scholarships for non-Japanese graduate students to study at Japanese universities and research institutes; Research Students Program is specifically designed for graduate students (undergraduate program also available) in the humanities, social sciences, music, fine arts, and natural sciences; open to citizens of countries with educational exchange agreements with Japan.
Restrictions: Language proficiency required (12- to 18-month language training program required if language skills deemed insufficient); applicants must be under age 35.
$ Given: An unspecified number of scholarships awarded annually; each to cover monthly stipend, airfare, tuition, and expense allowance.
Application Information: For further information, contact Japanese Embassy or Consulate.
Deadlines: June 15, September 30.
Contact: Student Exchange Division.

Japanese American Citizens League
National Scholarship and Student Aid Program
1765 Sutter Street
San Francisco, CA 94115
(415) 921-5225

Description: Scholarships for undergraduate and graduate students, as well as for individuals involved in performing and creative arts projects reflecting the Japanese American experience and culture.
Restrictions: Applicants must be of Japanese descent; membership in Japanese American Citizens League (or having parent who is member) preferred; United States citizenship required.
$ Given: An unspecified number of scholarships awarded annually; varying amounts.

Application Information: Application forms are available from local JACL chapters in September; write national office for list of local and regional chapters. **Deadline:** April 1.

National Collegiate Athletic Association
NCAA Postgraduate Scholarships
6201 College Boulevard
Overland Park, KS 66211
(913) 339-1906

Description: Scholarships for varsity college athletes in sports which NCAA conducts national championships; for full-time graduate study in any field; recipients chosen on the basis of academic achievement (minimum 3.0 GPA), athletic achievement, and capability for graduate study.
Restrictions: N/A.
$ Given: One hundred and twenty-five scholarships are awarded annually: 29 in football, 28 in basketball (14 to men, 14 to women), and 68 in other varsity sports (34 to men, 34 to women); varying amounts.
Application Information: Applicants must be nominated by college director of athletics during final season of NCAA eligibility; maximum two football, two basketball (one man, one woman), and four other sports (two men, two women) nominations per NCAA member school per year.
Deadlines: October 2 for football; March 4 for basketball; April 14 for other varsity sports.
Contact: Fannie B. Vaughan, Executive Assistant.

National Italian American Foundation Scholarship Program
Silvio Conte Internship
1860 19th Street, N.W.
Washington, DC 20009
(202) 638-2137
FAX (202) 683-0002

Description: Internship for undergraduate and graduate students to work for one semester in Congressman Conte's Washington, DC office.
Restrictions: Applicants must be of Italian descent; recipient must write paper about the internship experience and its expected benefit to recipient's future career.
$ Given: One internship paying $1,000 is awarded annually.
Application Information: Send SASE for details.
Deadline: May 31.
Contact: Dr. Maria Lombardo, Education Director.

National Italian American Foundation Scholarship Program
Italian American Regional Scholarships
1860 19th Street, N.W.
Washington, DC 20009
(202) 638-2137
FAX (202) 683-0002

Description: Scholarships for high school, undergraduate, and graduate students in all fields; regions are East Coast, Midwest, Southwest, and Mid-Atlantic; recipients chosen on the basis of academic achievement and financial need.
Restrictions: Applicants must be of Italian descent.
$ Given: Fifteen scholarships awarded annually; each for $500–$2,500.
Application Information: Send SASE for details.
Deadline: May 31.
Contact: Dr. Maria Lombardo, Education Director.

National Research Council NRC/Ford Predoctoral and Dissertation Fellowships for Minorities
Fellowships Office
2101 Constitution Avenue, N.W.
Washington, DC 20418
(202) 334-2872

Description: Fellowships for graduate students in the humanities, social sciences, biological and agricultural sciences, physical sciences and mathematics, and engineering and applied sciences; recipients chosen on the basis of academic achievement and proposed research.
Restrictions: Limited to members of minority groups; United States citizenship or legal residency required.
$ Given: **Fifty-five** fellowships awarded; $11,500 for fellow, $6,000 for Institution; 20 dissertation fellowships available for $18,000.
Application Information: Write for details.
Deadline: November 5.

New York State Senate Richard J. Roth Journalism Fellowships
State Capitol
Room 500A
Albany, NY 12247
(518) 445-2611
FAX (518) 432-5470

Description: One-year fellowships for master's and doctoral candidates in all disciplines to work full-time in the office of the press secretary of the New York State Senate; recipients chosen on the basis of academic achievement, strong commitment to public service, established skills, and outstanding ability and versatility.
Restrictions: New York state residency and full-time enrollment in accredited graduate program at a New York state university required; United States citizenship required.
$ Given: One fellowship position filled annually; $22,575 stipend.
Application Information: Write for details.
Deadline: May 10.
Contact: Senate Student Program Office.

Norwood University Alden B. Dow Creativity Center Summer Residency Program
Alden B. Dow Creativity Center
Midland, MI 48640-2398
(517) 837-4478

Description: Ten-week residency program (June-August), held at the Institute, for individuals to conduct independent research to develop innovative projects in all fields; projects should hold promise of impact on their respective fields; recipients chosen on the basis of proposed project.
Restrictions: Open to all nationalities; applicants must speak English.
$ Given: An unspecified number of grants are awarded annually; each to cover travel within the United States, room, board, stipend, and project costs.
Application Information: Write for details.
Deadline: December 31.
Contact: Carol B. Coppage, Executive Director.

Organization of American States
OAS Regular Training Program Fellowships
Department of Fellowships and Training
17th Street and Constitution Avenue, N.W.
Washington, DC 20006
(202) 458-3000

Description: Three-month to two-year fellowships for graduate students in all fields except medicine to pursue advanced study or research in other countries; tenable at OAS member countries; fellowships intended to contribute to host country on economic, social, technical, and cultural levels; recipients chosen on the basis of academic achievement and financial need.
Restrictions: Applicants must be citizens of OAS member countries; applicants must hold B.S./B.A. or equivalent and must be accepted at university or research facility for proposed work; language proficiency required.
$ Given: An unspecified number of fellowships awarded annually; each to cover expenses, tuition, and stipend, varying by country.
Application Information: Write for details.
Deadline: March 31.

Phi Eta Sigma
National Honor Society
Phi Eta Sigma Scholarships
228 Foy Union Building
Auburn University, AL 36849

Description: Scholarships for B.S./B.A. holders to support first year of graduate study in any field; recipients chosen on the basis of academic achievement.
Restrictions: Membership in Phi Eta Sigma required.
$ Given: Fifty fellowships are awarded annually (10 for graduate students, 40 for undergraduates); each for $1,000–$2,000.
Application Information: Write for details.
Deadline: March 1.
Contact: Local chapter advisor.

Phi Kappa F : Foundation
Phi Kappa Phi Graduate Fellowships
Louisiana State University
P.O. Box 16000
Baton Rouge, LA 70893

Description: Fellowships for B.S./B.A. holders to support the first year of graduate study; recipients chosen on the basis of academic achievement.
Restrictions: Active membership in Phi Kappa Phi required.
$ Given: 50 fellowships for $7,000 each are awarded annually; 30 honorable mentions for $500 each are also awarded annually.
Application Information: Applicants must be nominated by the university's chapter of Phi Kappa Phi.
Deadline: March 1.
Contact: Local chapter secretary.

President's Commission on White House Fellowships
White House Fellowships
712 Jackson Place, N.W.
Washington, DC 20503
(202) 395-4522

Description: Twelve-month appointments as special assistants to the Vice President, Cabinet members, and the Presidential staff; fellowships include participation in educational program; positions available for students in public affairs, education, the sciences, business, and the professions; recipients chosen on the basis of leadership qualities, commitment to community service, and career/academic achievement.

Restrictions: Limited to young adults, ages 30-39; civilian federal employees are ineligible; recipients may not hold official state or local office while serving as White House fellows; United States citizenship required.

$ Given: Eleven to nineteen wage-earning fellowships for up to a maximum of $65,000 are awarded annually.

Application Information: Write for details.

Deadline: December 15.

Contact: Phyllis A. Williams.

Rotary Foundation of Rotary International
Rotary Foundation Ambassadorial Scholarships
1560 Sherman Avenue
Evanston, IL 60201
(708) 866-3000

Description: Scholarships for graduate students with B.A./B.S. degree in any discipline; for one academic year in another country with Rotary club.

Restrictions: Applicants must be ages 18-30; members of Rotary clubs, as well as spouses and lineal descendants of members and employees of Rotary clubs, are ineligible; language proficiency test required in host country's language; open to citizens of all countries with Rotary clubs.

$ Given: An unspecified number of scholarships are awarded annually; each to cover transportation, academic fees, educational supplies, room and board, and additional expenses.

Application Information: By nomination from local Rotary club, each of which designs its own selection criteria.

Deadline: July 15.

Contact: Local Rotary club.

Social Science Research Council
MacArthur Foundation Fellowships on International Peace and Security in a Changing World
605 Third Avenue
New York, NY 10158
(212) 661-0280

Description: Fellowship support for up to two years of research in the setting and nation of the recipient's choice; funding made available to doctoral candidates at dissertation level, postdoctoral scholars, and professionals studying international peace and security (in disciplines of humanities, social sciences, physical sciences, and natural sciences); recipients chosen on the basis of proposed research.

Restrictions: Open to all nationalities.

$ Given: Approximately eight fellowships awarded annually; $12,500–$17,500 per year predoctoral fellow; $25,000–$30,000 per year postdoctoral fellow.

Application Information: Write for details.

Deadline: December 1.

Contact: Felicia Sullivan.

Winterthur Museum, Garden, and Library
Winterthur Museum Visiting Research Scholars
Office of Advanced Studies
Winterthur, DE 19735
(302) 888-4649

Description: One-month to one-year residential fellowships for doctoral candidates in all disciplines related to the Winterthur collections; intended for scholars who have been granted awards from other institutions but need a place to work/research; fellowship tenure features full access to museum resources and rental housing on Winterthur grounds; recipients chosen on the basis of proposed research.
Restrictions: N/A.
$ Given: An unspecified number of positions available; no stipend.
Application Information: Write for details.
Deadline: December 1.
Contact: Research Fellowship Program.

Women's Research and Education Institute
Congressional Fellowships on Women and Public Policy
1700 18th Street, N.W.
Suite 400
Washington, DC 20009
(202) 328-7070

Description: Congressional fellowship program designed to train women as potential public policy leaders; fellowship runs September through April and involves 30 hrs/wk work in a United States Congress office as a legislative aide on policy issues affecting women; open to master's and doctoral candidates at United States institutions; relevant disciplines include humanities, social sciences, biology and biomedical sciences, engineering and applied sciences, biomedical engineering, technology management and policy, business administration and management, health services management and hospital administration, education, allied health professionals, medicine, nursing, public and community health, and law; recipients chosen on the basis of political/civic activity and interest in women's issues.
Restrictions: Limited to women applicants; nine hours previous graduate coursework preferred; United States citizenship preferred.
$ Given: Eight to fifteen fellowships awarded annually; each with $9,500 stipend plus $500 for health insurance and up to $1,500 toward six hours tuition at home institution.
Application Information: Request application after November 1.
Deadline: February 14.
Contact: Alison Dineen, Fellowship Director.

Bibliography: Graduate, Postgraduate, and Research

The Directory of Research Grants. Phoenix: Oryx Press, 1996
Free Money for Graduate School. New York: Facts On File, 1996
The Graduate Scholarship Directory: The Complete Guide to Scholarships, Fellow-ships, Grants, and Loans for Graduate and Professional Study. Englewood Cliffs, NJ: Prentice-Hall, 1993
The Grants Register. New York: St. Martin's Press, 1995–1997

Index